LOOKING THE OTHER WAY . . .

As a manga, *Danganronpa Another Episode: Ultra Despair Girls* reads right-to-left, so this page is actually the back of the book. Sometimes, you've got to look the other way to keep moving forward. See, Toko's doing it. Take life lessons from a serial killer!

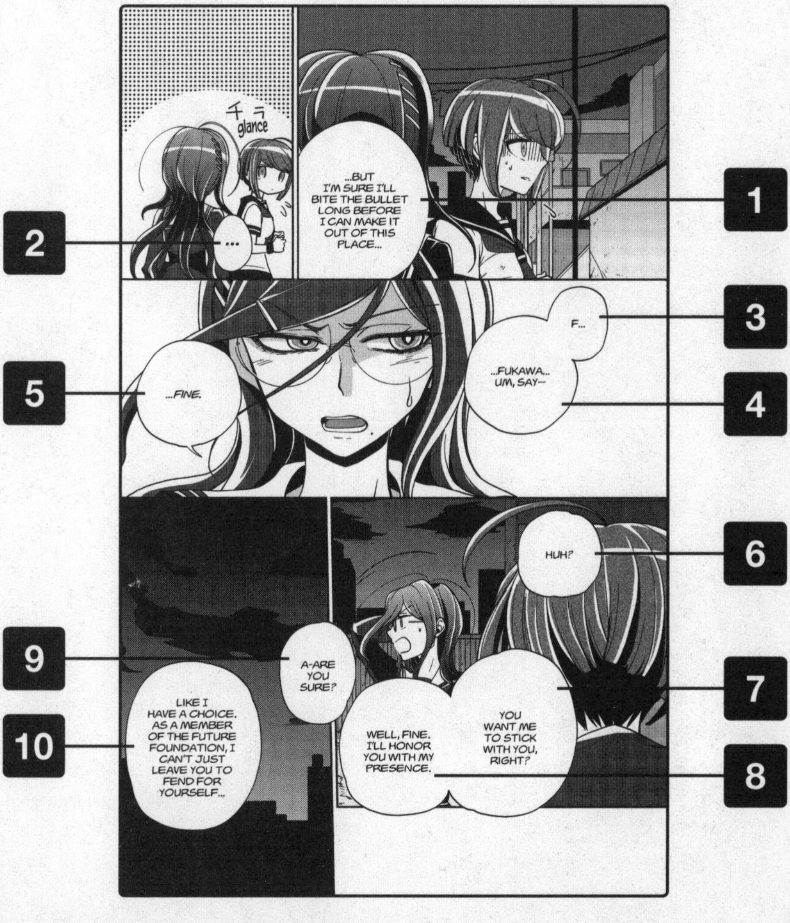
1 ...BUT I'M SURE I'LL BITE THE BULLET LONG BEFORE I CAN MAKE IT OUT OF THIS PLACE...
チラ glance
2 ...
3 F...
4 ...FUKAWA... UM, SAY--
5 ...FINE.
6 HUH?
7 YOU WANT ME TO STICK WITH YOU, RIGHT?
8 WELL, FINE. I'LL HONOR YOU WITH MY PRESENCE.
9 A-ARE YOU SURE?
10 LIKE I HAVE A CHOICE. AS A MEMBER OF THE FUTURE FOUNDATION, I CAN'T JUST LEAVE YOU TO FEND FOR YOURSELF...

REPENT, SINNERS! THEY'RE BACK!

Miss the anime?
Try the *Panty & Stocking with Garterbelt* manga! Nine ALL-NEW stories of your favorite filthy fallen angels, written and drawn by TAGRO, with a special afterword by *Kill La Kill* director Hiroyuki Imaishi!
978-1-61655-735-5 | $9.99

HATSUNE MIKU: ACUTE
Art and story by Shiori Asahina
Miku, Kaito, and Luka! Once they were all friends making songs—but while Kaito might make a duet with Miku or a duet with Luka, a love song all three of them sing together can only end in sorrow!

ISBN 978-1-50670-341-1 | $10.99

HATSUNE MIKU: RIN-CHAN NOW!
Story by Sezu, Art by Hiro Tamura
Miku's sassy blond friend takes center stage in this series that took inspiration from the music video "Rin-chan Now!" The video is now a manga of the same name—written, drawn, and edited by the video creators!

VOLUME 1
978-1-50670-313-8 | $10.99

VOLUME 2
978-1-50670-314-5 | $10.99

VOLUME 3
978-1-50670-315-2 | $10.99

VOLUME 4
978-1-50670-316-9 | $10.99

HATSUNE MIKU: MIKUBON
Art and story by Ontama
Hatsune Miku and her friends Rin, Len, and Luka enroll at the St. Diva Academy for Vocaloids! At St. Diva, a wonderland of friendship, determination, and even love unfolds! But can they stay out of trouble, especially when the mad professor of the Hachune Miku Research Lab is nearby . . . ?

ISBN 978-1-50670-231-5 | $10.99

UNOFFICIAL HATSUNE MIX
Art and story by KEI
Miku's original illustrator, KEI, produced a best-selling omnibus manga of the musical adventures (and misadventures!) of Miku and her fellow Vocaloids Rin, Len, Luka, and more—in both beautiful black-and-white and charming color!

ISBN 978-1-61655-412-5 | $19.99

HATSUNE MIKU: FUTURE DELIVERY
Story by Satoshi Oshio, Art by Hugin Miyama
In the distant future, Asumi—a girl who has no clue to her memories but a drawing of a green-haired, ponytailed person—finds her only friend in Asimov, a battered old delivery robot. The strange companions travel the stars together in search of the mysterious "Miku," only to learn the legendary idol has taken different forms on many different worlds!

VOLUME 1
ISBN 978-1-50670-361-9 | $10.99

VOLUME 2
ISBN 978-1-50670-362-6 | $10.99

WHO'S THAT GIRL WITH THE LONG GREEN PONYTAILS YOU'VE BEEN SEEING EVERYWHERE? IT'S HATSUNE MIKU, THE VOCALOID— THE SYNTHESIZER SUPERSTAR WHO'S SINGING YOUR SONG!

AVAILABLE AT YOUR LOCAL COMICS SHOP OR BOOKSTORE

DARK HORSE MANGA

DarkHorse.com

HATSUNE MIKU

TO FIND A COMICS SHOP IN YOUR AREA, VISIT COMICSHOPLOCATOR.COM. For more information or to order direct, visit DarkHorse.com

ACUTE © WhiteFlame, © SHIORI ASAHINA. MIKUBON © ONTAMA. RIN CHAN NOW © sezu/HIRO TAMURA. UNOFFICIAL HATSUNE MIX © Kei. © Crypton Future Media, Inc. Hatsune Miku: Mirai Diary: © Hugin MIYAMA 2014 © Satoshi Oshio © Crypton Future Media, Inc.

www.piapro.net ● ɪᴏᴘʀᴏ. Dark Horse Manga ™ is a trademark of Dark Horse Comics, LLC. The Dark Horse logo is a registered trademark of Dark Horse Comics LLC. All rights reserved. (BL 7009)

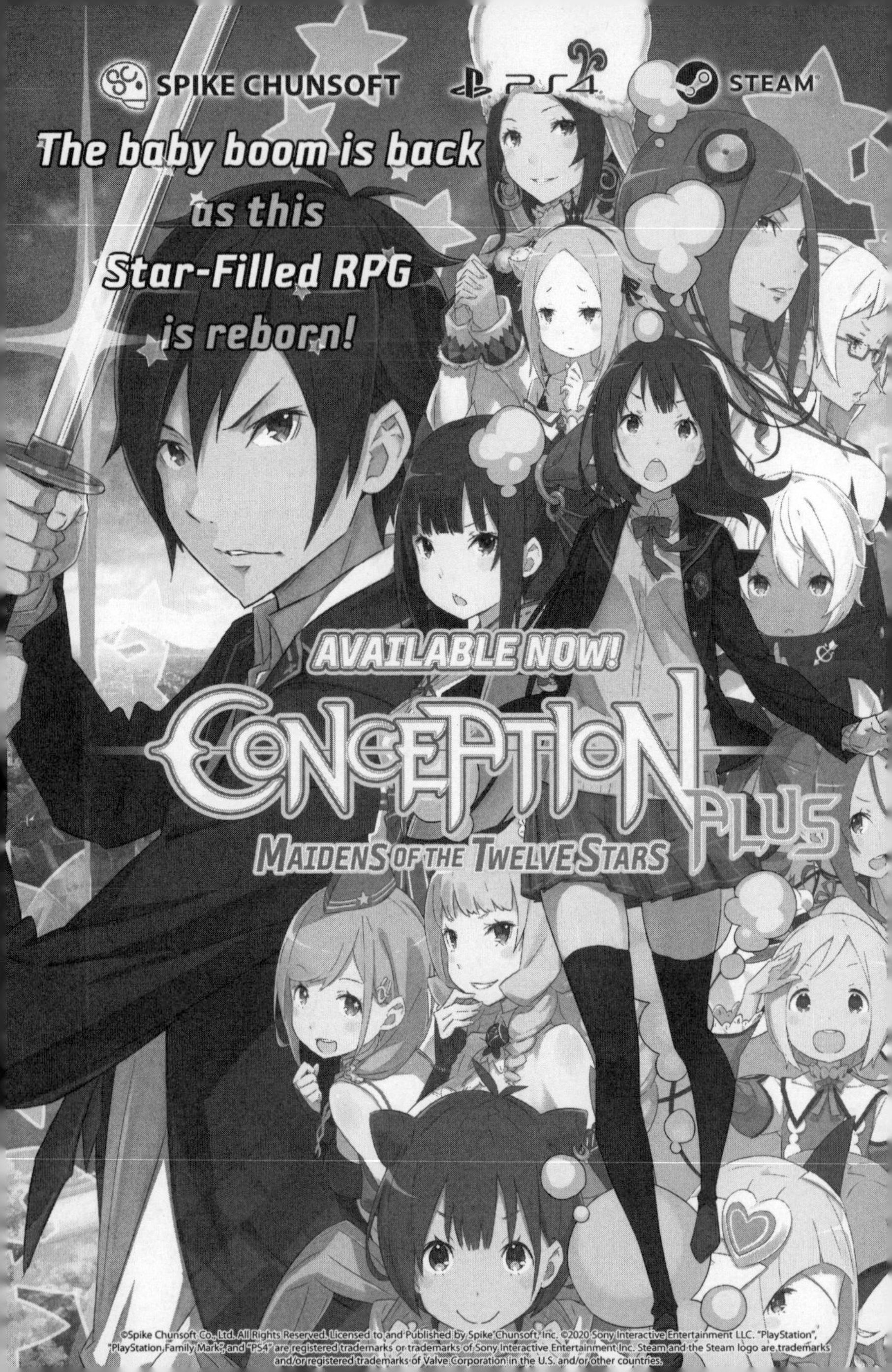

絶対絶望少女

2

Danganronpa Another Episode:
Ultra Despair Girls

Manga By
HAJIME TOUYA

Created By
SPIKE CHUNSOFT

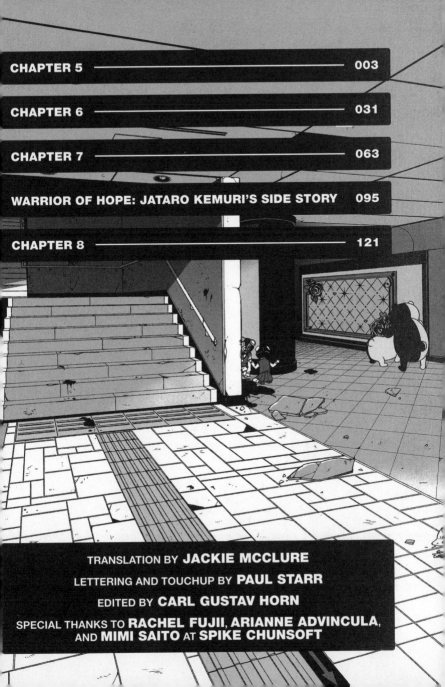

TRANSLATION BY **JACKIE MCCLURE**

LETTERING AND TOUCHUP BY **PAUL STARR**

EDITED BY **CARL GUSTAV HORN**

SPECIAL THANKS TO **RACHEL FUJII, ARIANNE ADVINCULA,**
AND **MIMI SAITO** AT SPIKE CHUNSOFT

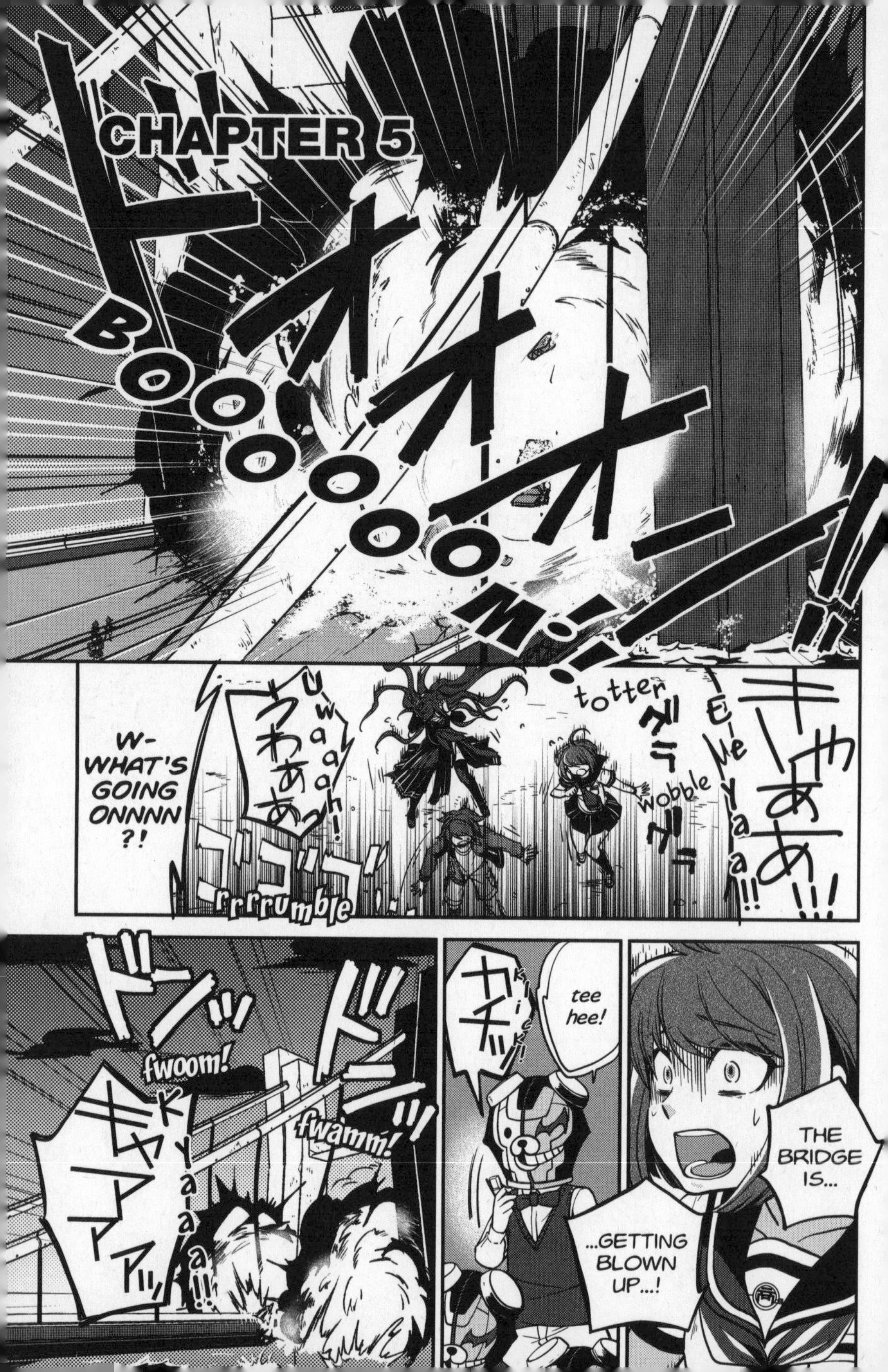

CHAPTER 5
BOOOOOOOM!!
キャあああ!!!
Eeeyaaa!!!
totter
wobble
W-WHAT'S GOING ONNNN?!
うわああっ
Uwaaah!
rrrrumble
THE BRIDGE IS...
...GETTING BLOWN UP...!
kick
tee hee!
fwoom!
fwamm!
Kyaaaa!!

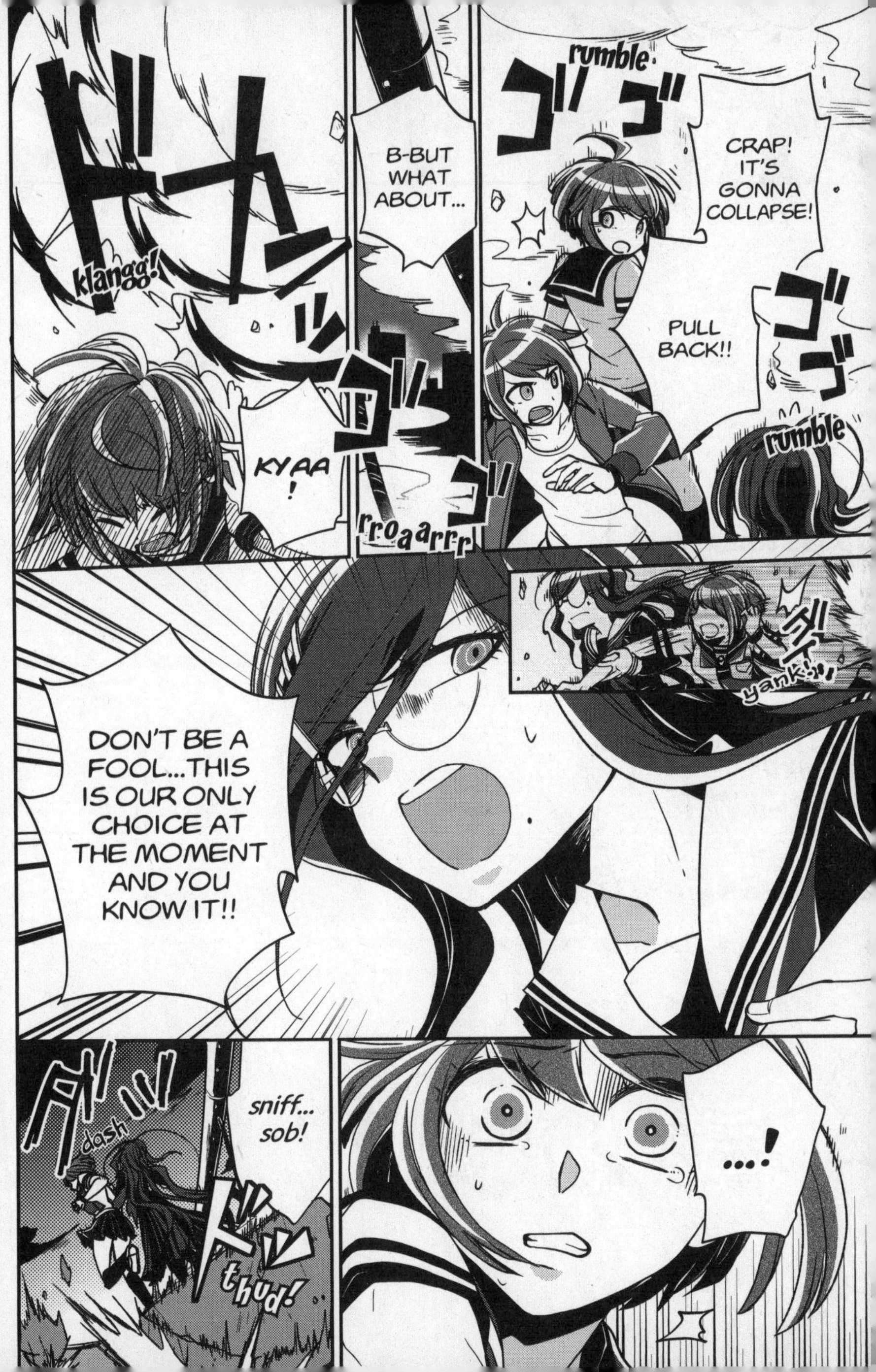

rumble
CRAP! IT'S GONNA COLLAPSE!
PULL BACK!!
rumble
B-BUT WHAT ABOUT...
rroaarrr
klangg!
KYAA!
yank!
DON'T BE A FOOL...THIS IS OUR ONLY CHOICE AT THE MOMENT AND YOU KNOW IT!!
...!
sniff... sob!
dash
thud!

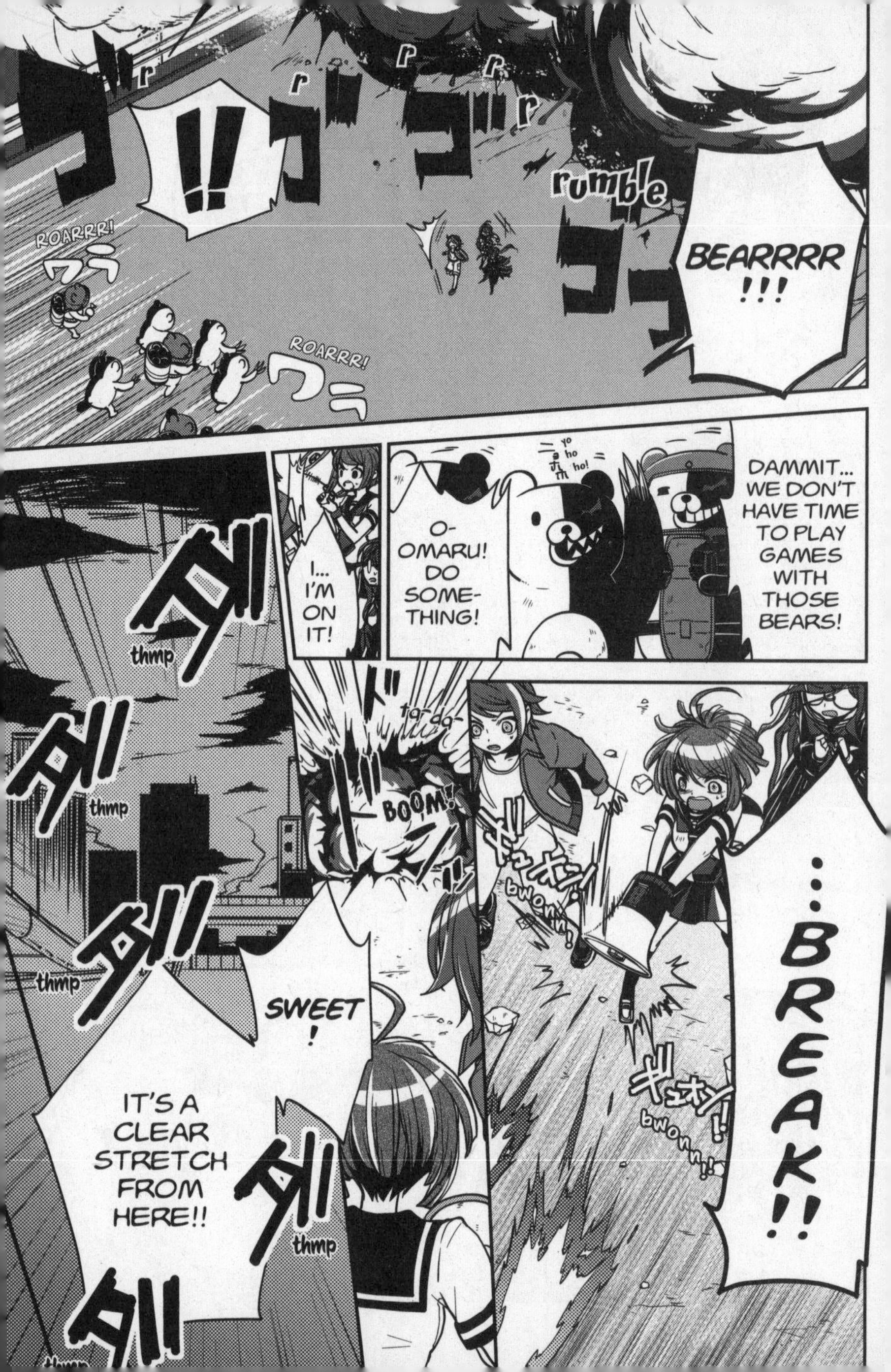

BEARRRR!!!
rumble
r r r r
ROARRR!
ワラ
ROARRR!
ワラ
DAMMIT... WE DON'T HAVE TIME TO PLAY GAMES WITH THOSE BEARS!
yo ho ho!
O-OMARU! DO SOMETHING!
I... I'M ON IT!
...BREAK!!
bwonn!
bwonn!!
BOOM!
ta-da-
thmp
thmp
thmp
SWEET!
IT'S A CLEAR STRETCH FROM HERE!!
thmp

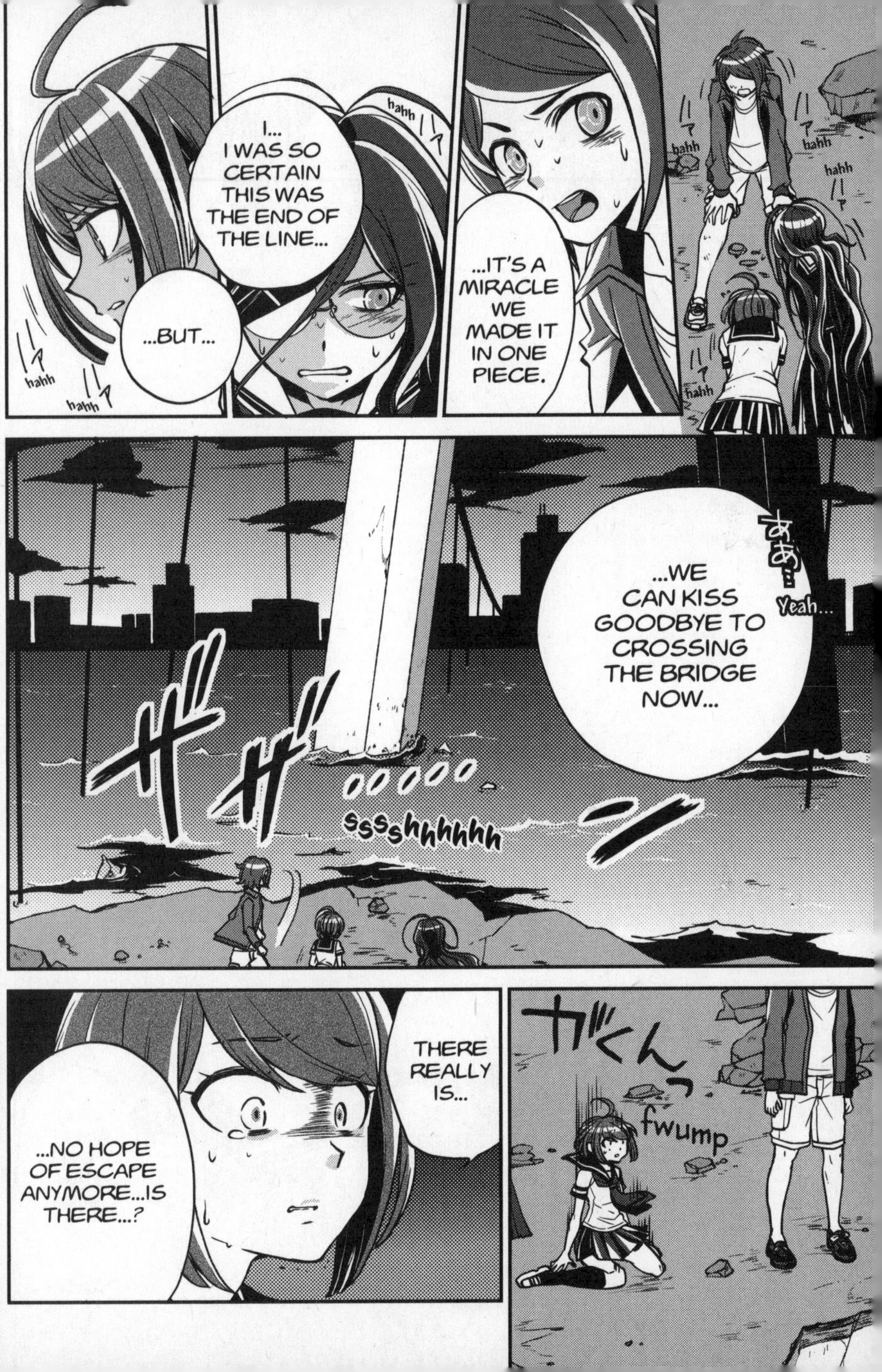
hahh
hahh
hahh
hahh
...IT'S A MIRACLE WE MADE IT IN ONE PIECE.
I... I WAS SO CERTAIN THIS WAS THE END OF THE LINE...
hahh
...BUT...
hahh
hahh
ああ…
Yeah...
...WE CAN KISS GOODBYE TO CROSSING THE BRIDGE NOW...
ssshhhhhhh
ガくん
fwump
THERE REALLY IS...
...NO HOPE OF ESCAPE ANYMORE...IS THERE...?

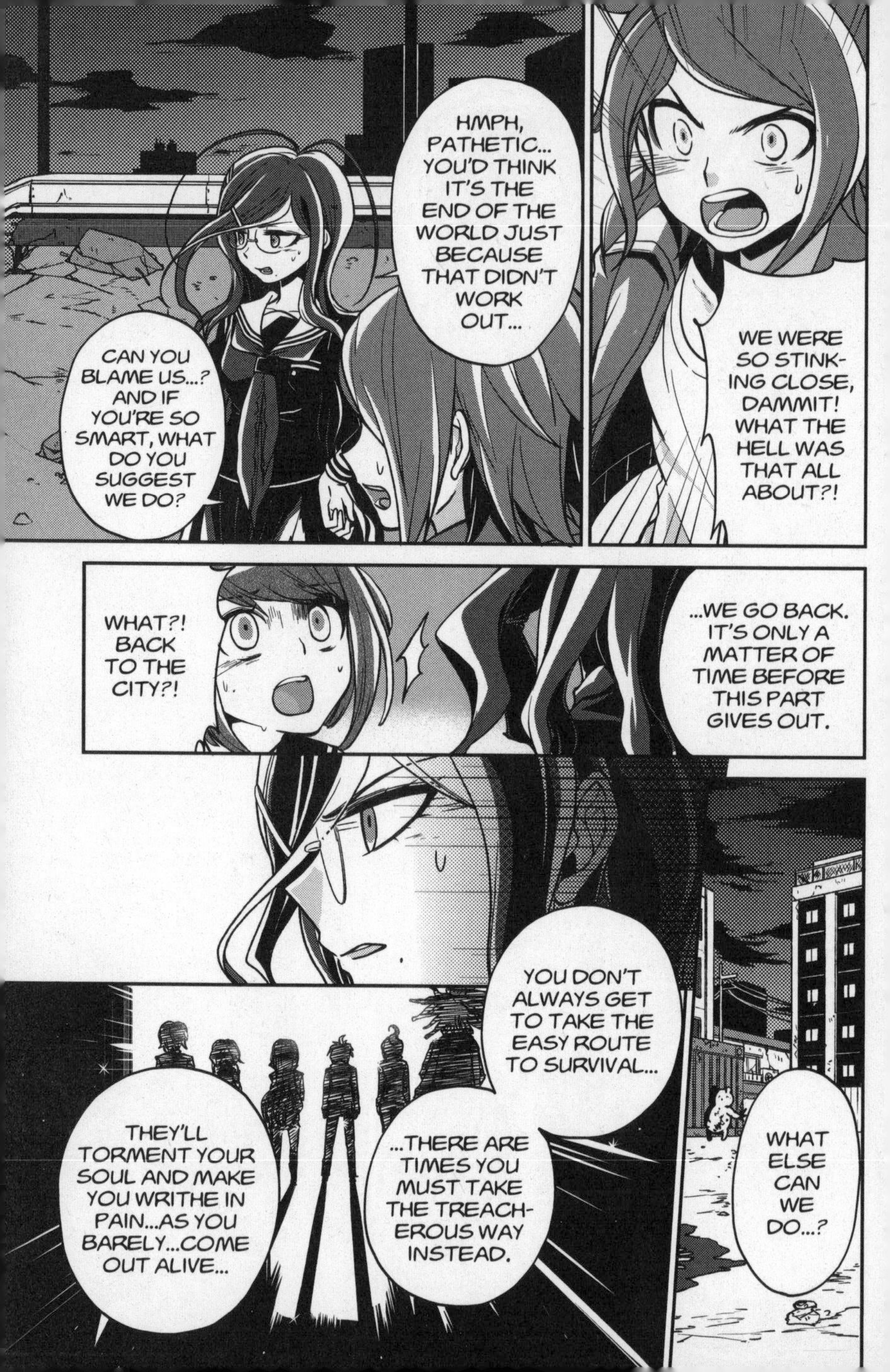
WE WERE SO STINK-ING CLOSE, DAMMIT! WHAT THE HELL WAS THAT ALL ABOUT?!
HMPH, PATHETIC... YOU'D THINK IT'S THE END OF THE WORLD JUST BECAUSE THAT DIDN'T WORK OUT...
CAN YOU BLAME US...? AND IF YOU'RE SO SMART, WHAT DO YOU SUGGEST WE DO?
...WE GO BACK. IT'S ONLY A MATTER OF TIME BEFORE THIS PART GIVES OUT.
WHAT?! BACK TO THE CITY?!
WHAT ELSE CAN WE DO...?
YOU DON'T ALWAYS GET TO TAKE THE EASY ROUTE TO SURVIVAL...
...THERE ARE TIMES YOU MUST TAKE THE TREACH-EROUS WAY INSTEAD.
THEY'LL TORMENT YOUR SOUL AND MAKE YOU WRITHE IN PAIN...AS YOU BARELY...COME OUT ALIVE...

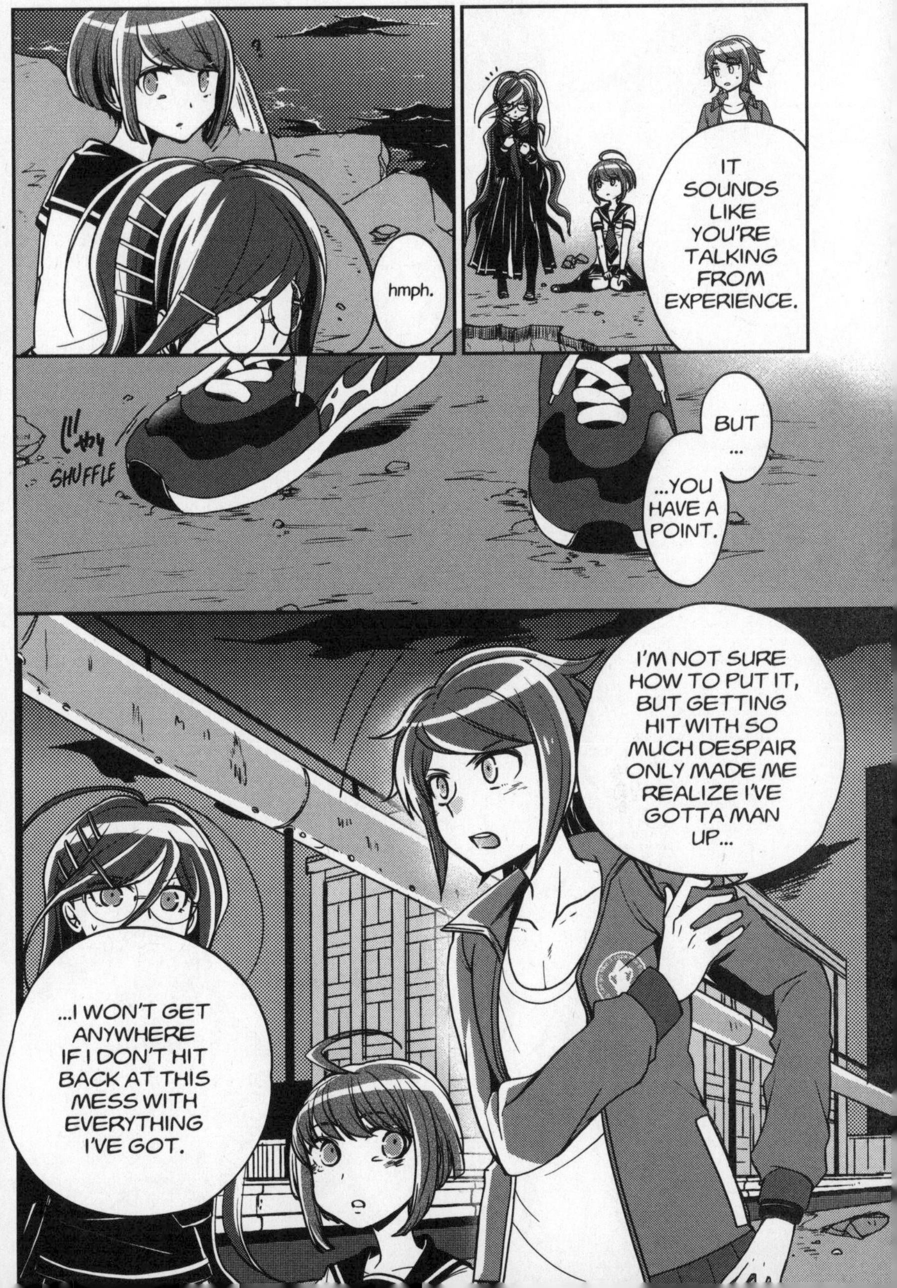
IT SOUNDS LIKE YOU'RE TALKING FROM EXPERIENCE.
hmph.
BUT ...
...YOU HAVE A POINT.
じゃり
SHUFFLE
I'M NOT SURE HOW TO PUT IT, BUT GETTING HIT WITH SO MUCH DESPAIR ONLY MADE ME REALIZE I'VE GOTTA MAN UP...
...I WON'T GET ANYWHERE IF I DON'T HIT BACK AT THIS MESS WITH EVERYTHING I'VE GOT.

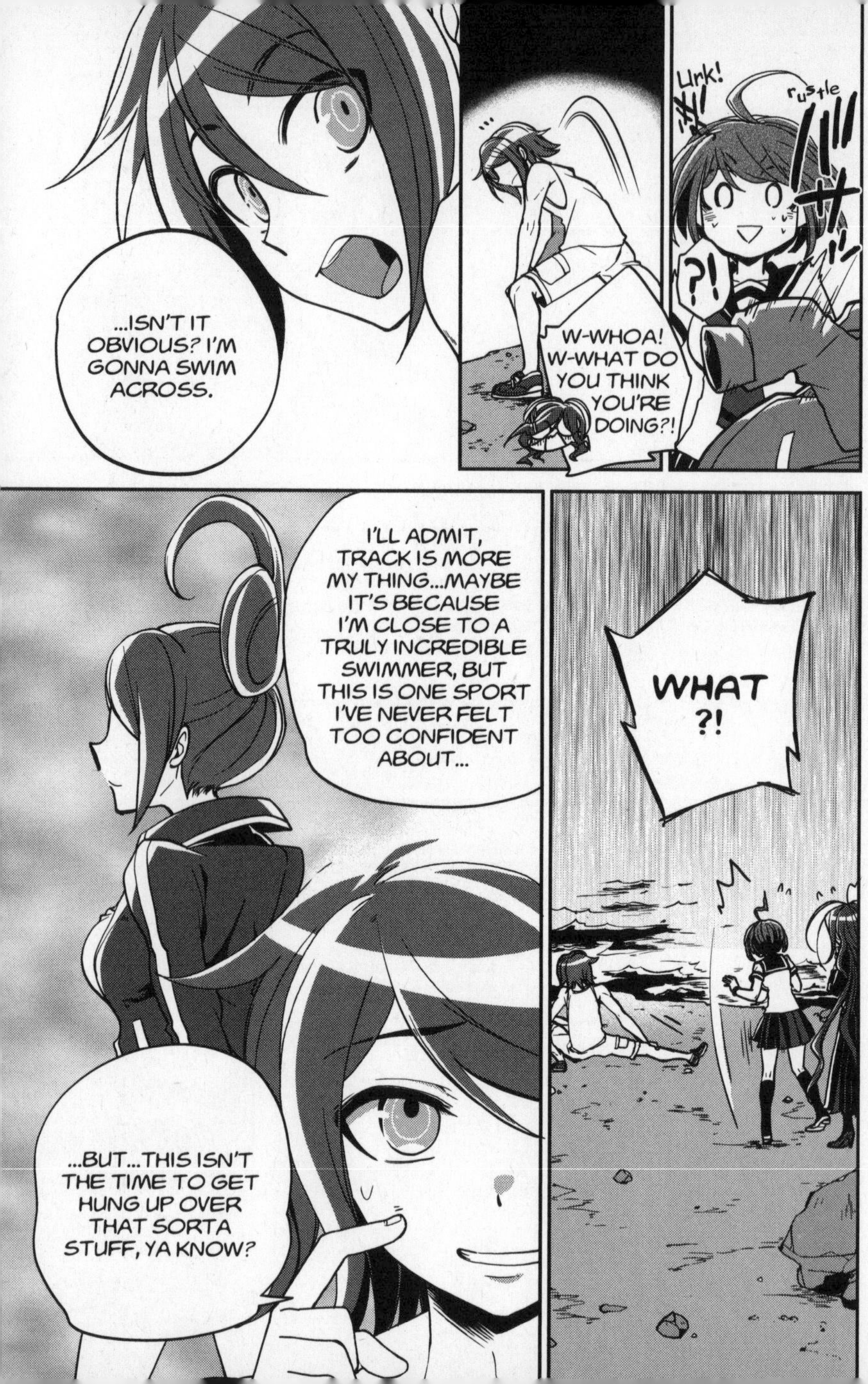
Urk!
rustle
?!
W-WHOA! W-WHAT DO YOU THINK YOU'RE DOING?!
...ISN'T IT OBVIOUS? I'M GONNA SWIM ACROSS.
WHAT?!
I'LL ADMIT, TRACK IS MORE MY THING...MAYBE IT'S BECAUSE I'M CLOSE TO A TRULY INCREDIBLE SWIMMER, BUT THIS IS ONE SPORT I'VE NEVER FELT TOO CONFIDENT ABOUT...
...BUT...THIS ISN'T THE TIME TO GET HUNG UP OVER THAT SORTA STUFF, YA KNOW?

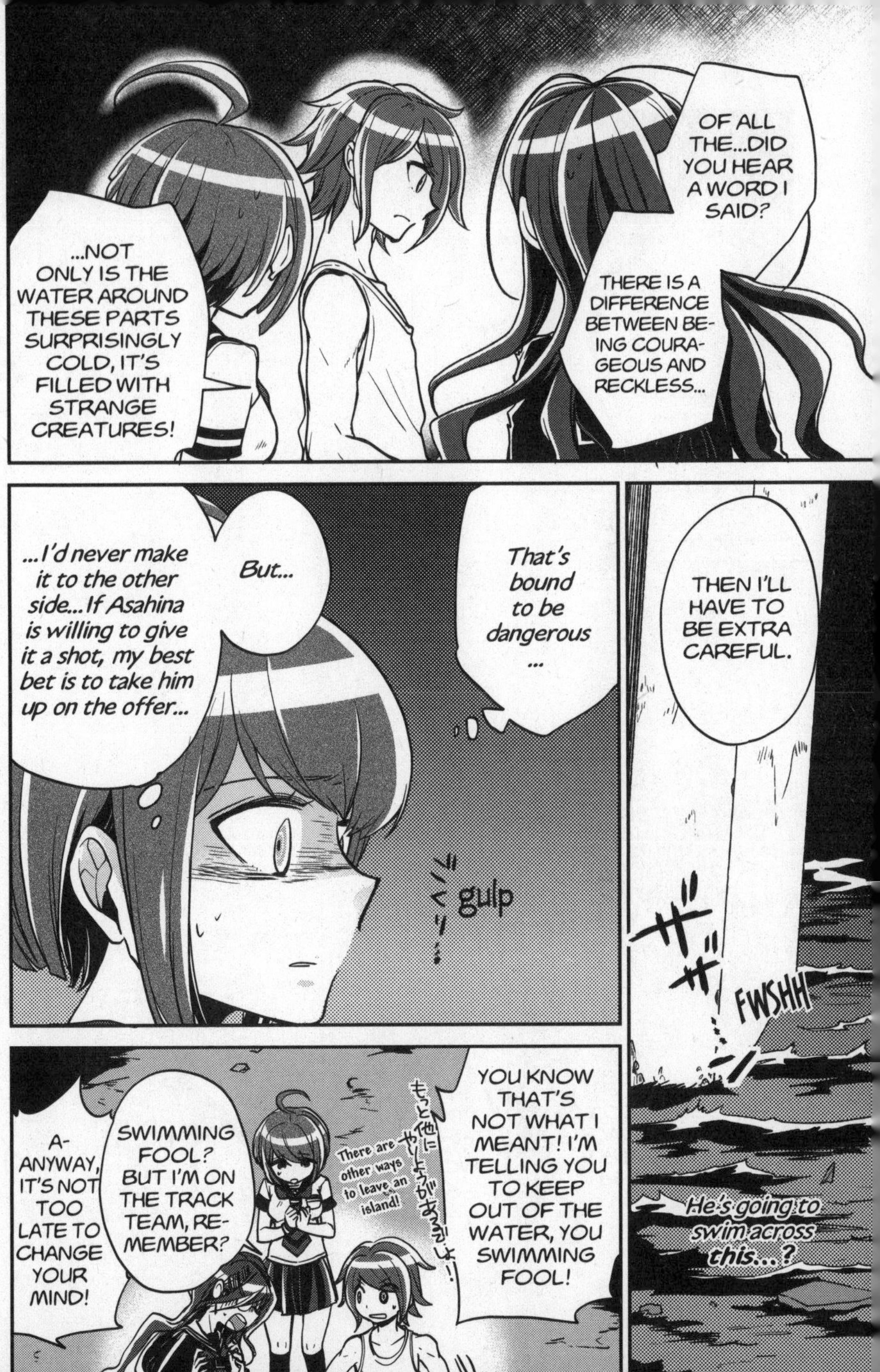
OF ALL THE...DID YOU HEAR A WORD I SAID?
THERE IS A DIFFERENCE BETWEEN BE-ING COURA-GEOUS AND RECKLESS...
...NOT ONLY IS THE WATER AROUND THESE PARTS SURPRISINGLY COLD, IT'S FILLED WITH STRANGE CREATURES!
THEN I'LL HAVE TO BE EXTRA CAREFUL.
FWSHH
He's going to swim across ***this...?***
That's bound to be dangerous ...
But...
...I'd never make it to the other side...If Asahina is willing to give it a shot, my best bet is to take him up on the offer...
gulp
YOU KNOW THAT'S NOT WHAT I MEANT! I'M TELLING YOU TO KEEP OUT OF THE WATER, YOU SWIMMING FOOL!
There are other ways to leave an island!
SWIMMING FOOL? BUT I'M ON THE TRACK TEAM, RE-MEMBER?
A- ANYWAY, IT'S NOT TOO LATE TO CHANGE YOUR MIND!

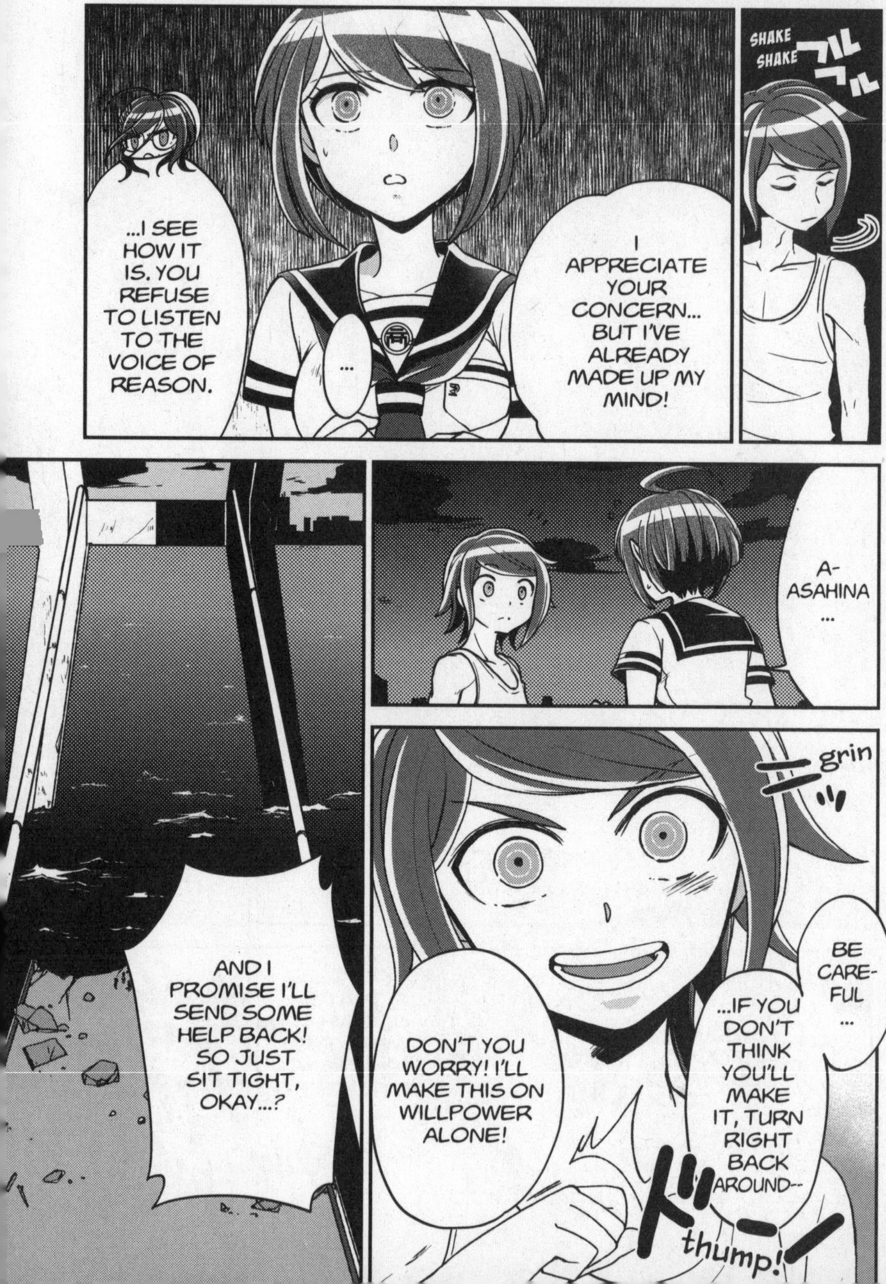
SHAKE SHAKE
フルフル
I APPRECIATE YOUR CONCERN... BUT I'VE ALREADY MADE UP MY MIND!
...
...I SEE HOW IT IS. YOU REFUSE TO LISTEN TO THE VOICE OF REASON.
A-ASAHINA...
ニッ
grin
BE CAREFUL...
...IF YOU DON'T THINK YOU'LL MAKE IT, TURN RIGHT BACK AROUND--
DON'T YOU WORRY! I'LL MAKE THIS ON WILLPOWER ALONE!
ドーン
thump!
AND I PROMISE I'LL SEND SOME HELP BACK! SO JUST SIT TIGHT, OKAY...?

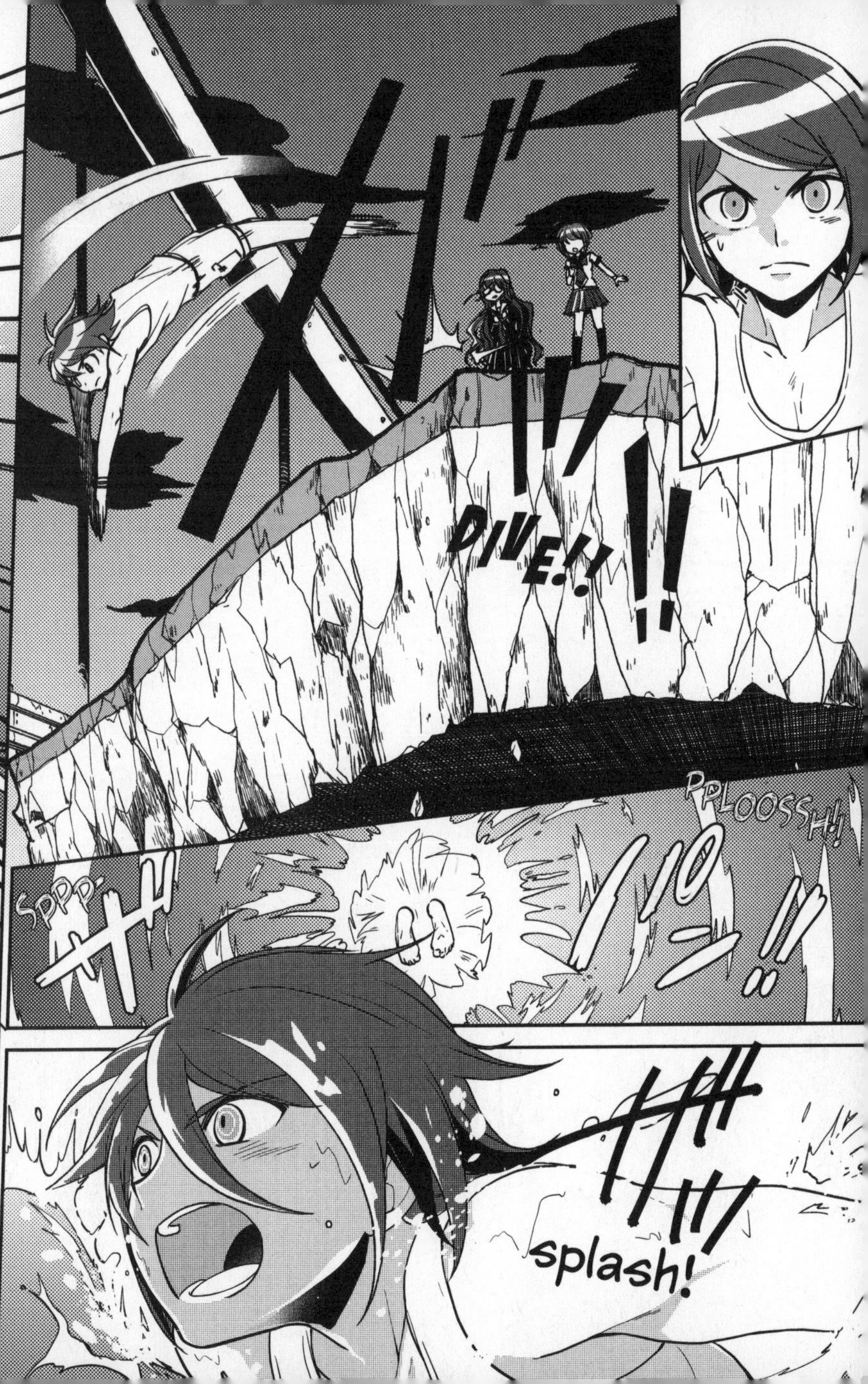
DIVE!!
PPLOOSSH!
SPPP-
splash!

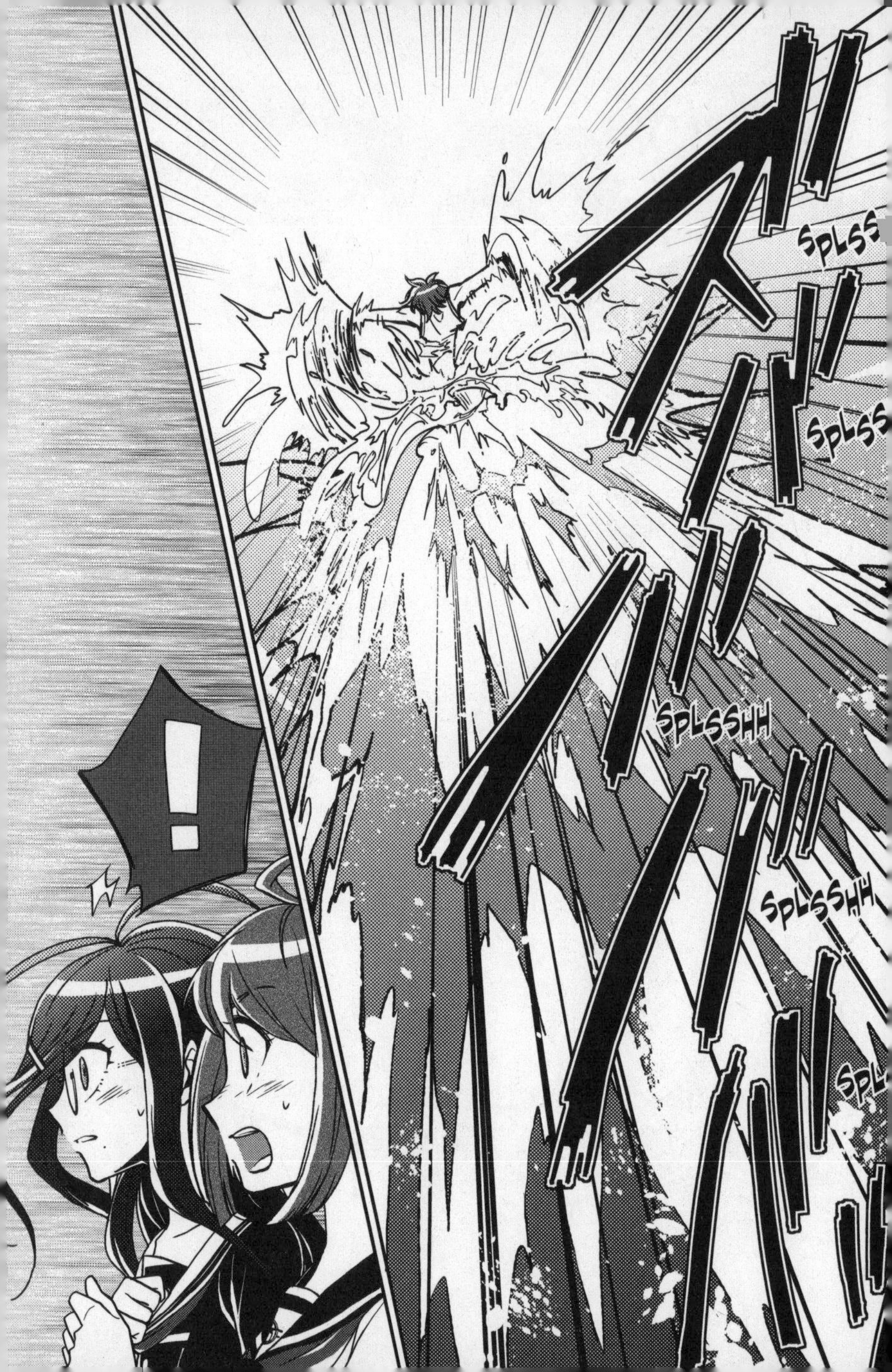
SPLSS
SPLSS
SPLSSHH
SPLSSHH
SPL
!

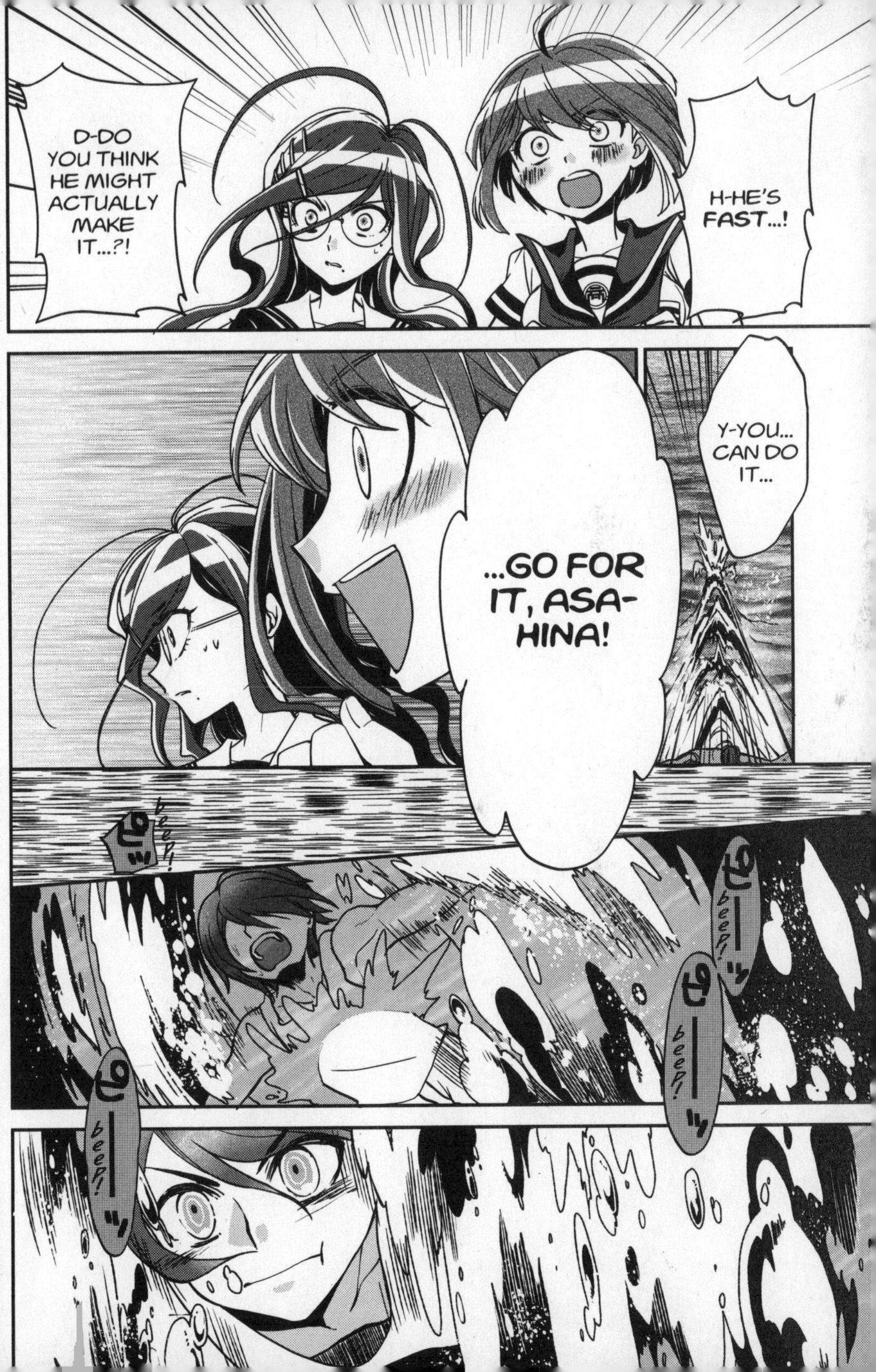
H-HE'S FAST...!
D-DO YOU THINK HE MIGHT ACTUALLY MAKE IT...?!
Y-YOU... CAN DO IT...
...GO FOR IT, ASA-HINA!
beep!
beep!
beep!
beep!

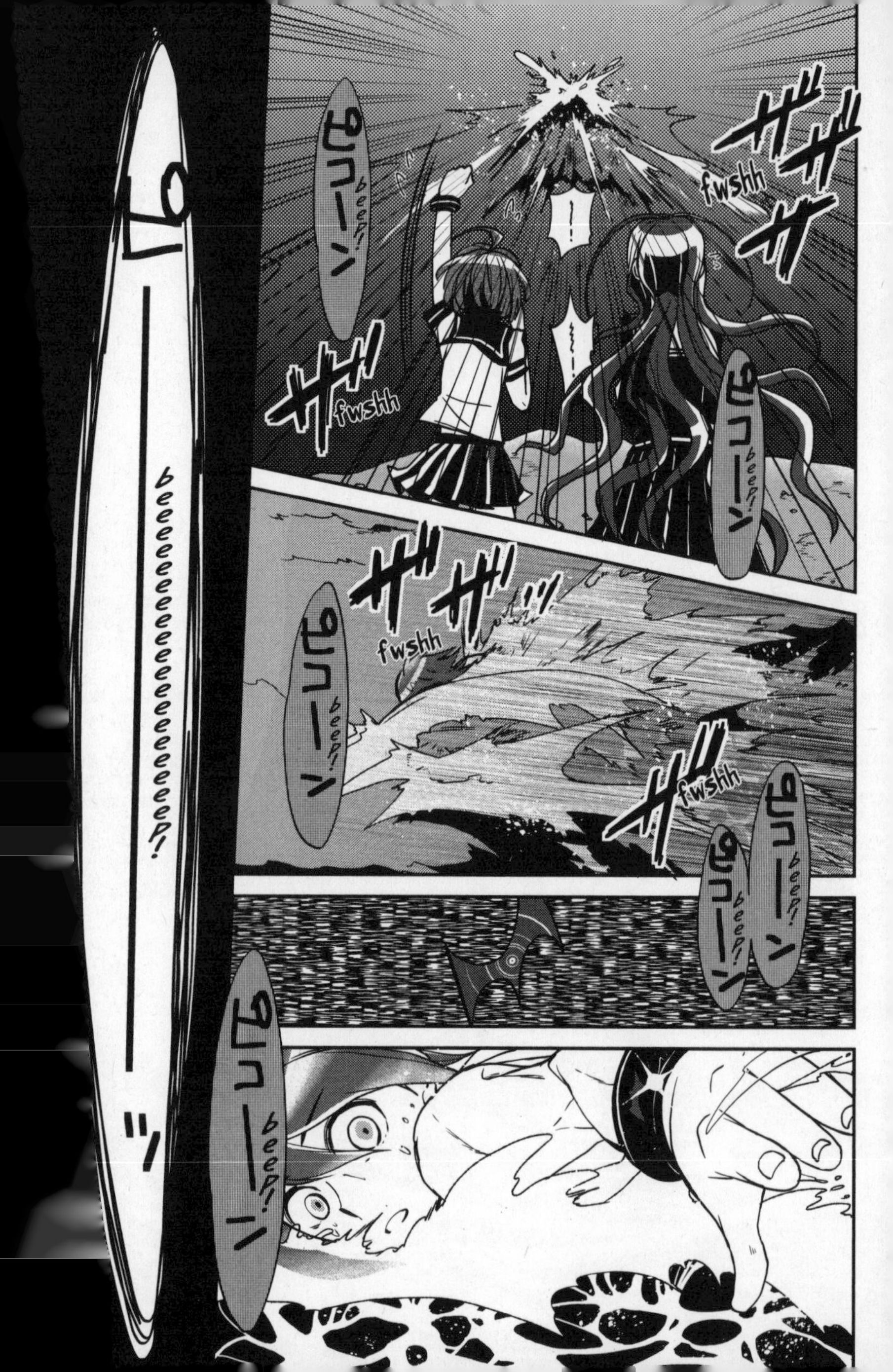
ザザザ
fwshh
ピコーン
beep!
ザザ
fwshh
ピコーン
beep!
ザザ
fwshh
ピコーン
beep!
ザザ
fwshh
ピコーン
beep!
ピコーン
beep!
ピコーン
beep!
ピコ―――ンッ
beeeeeeeeeeeeeeeeeeeeeeep!

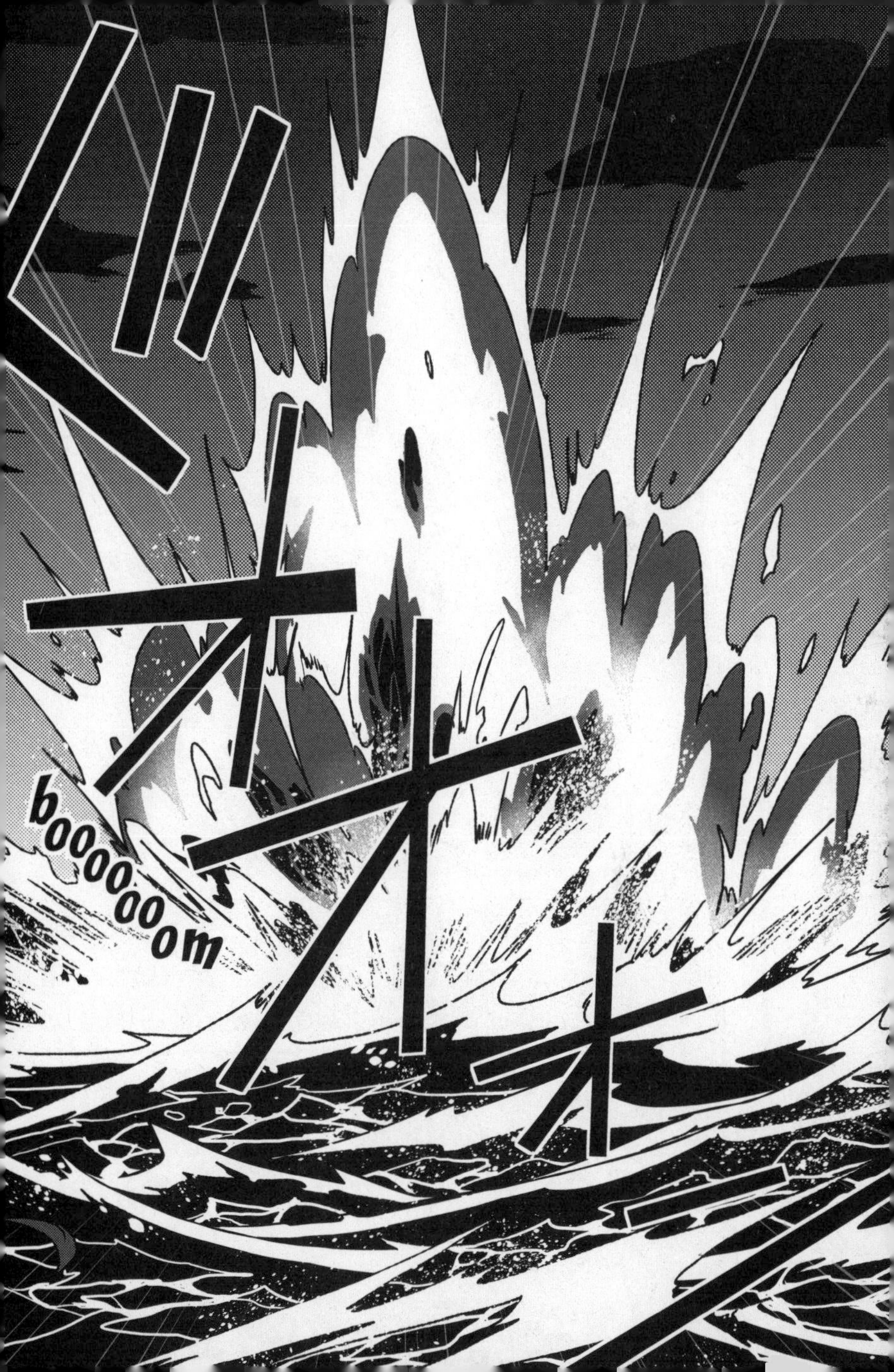
booooooom

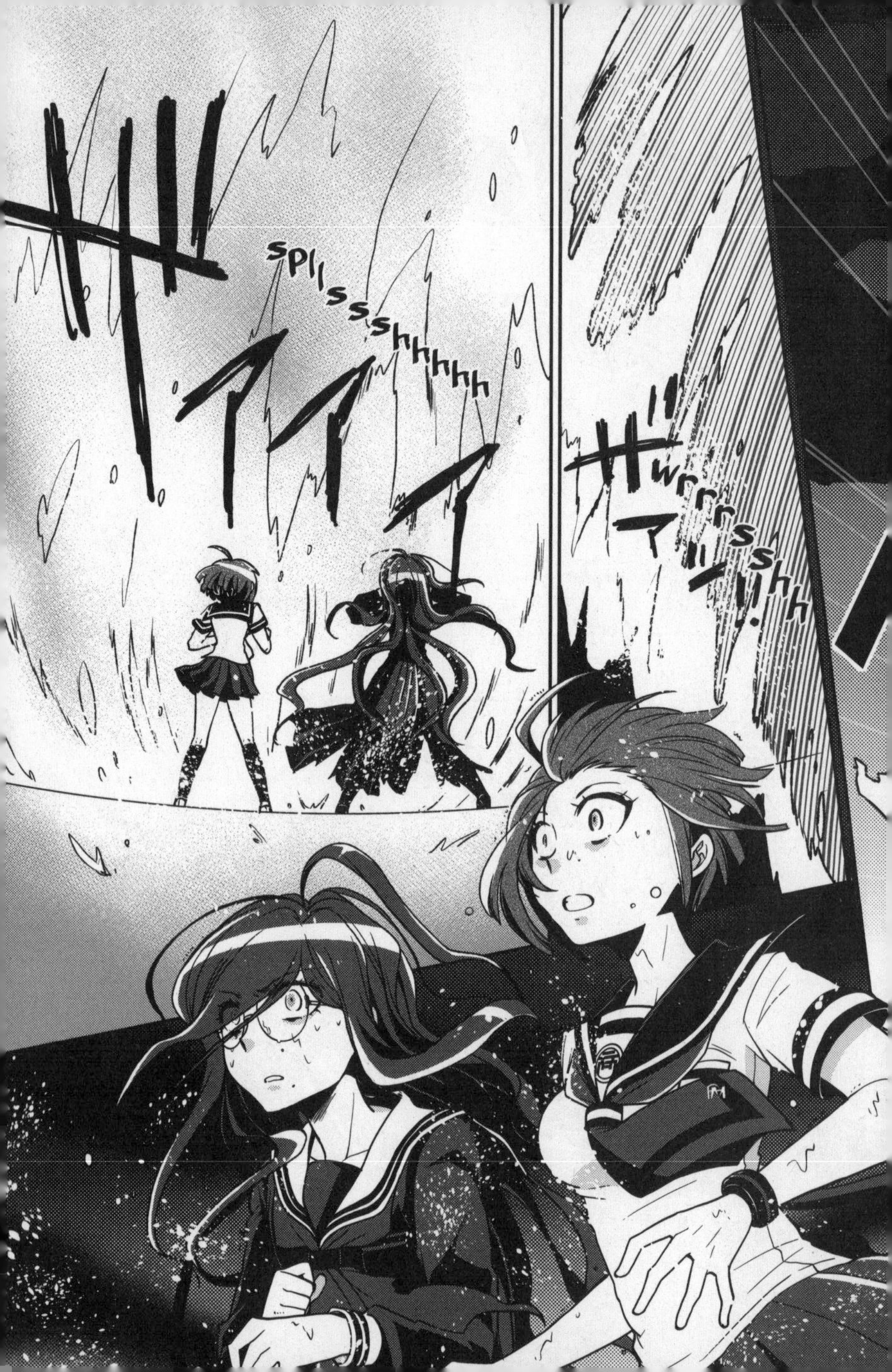
wrrrrsshh
spllssshhhhhh

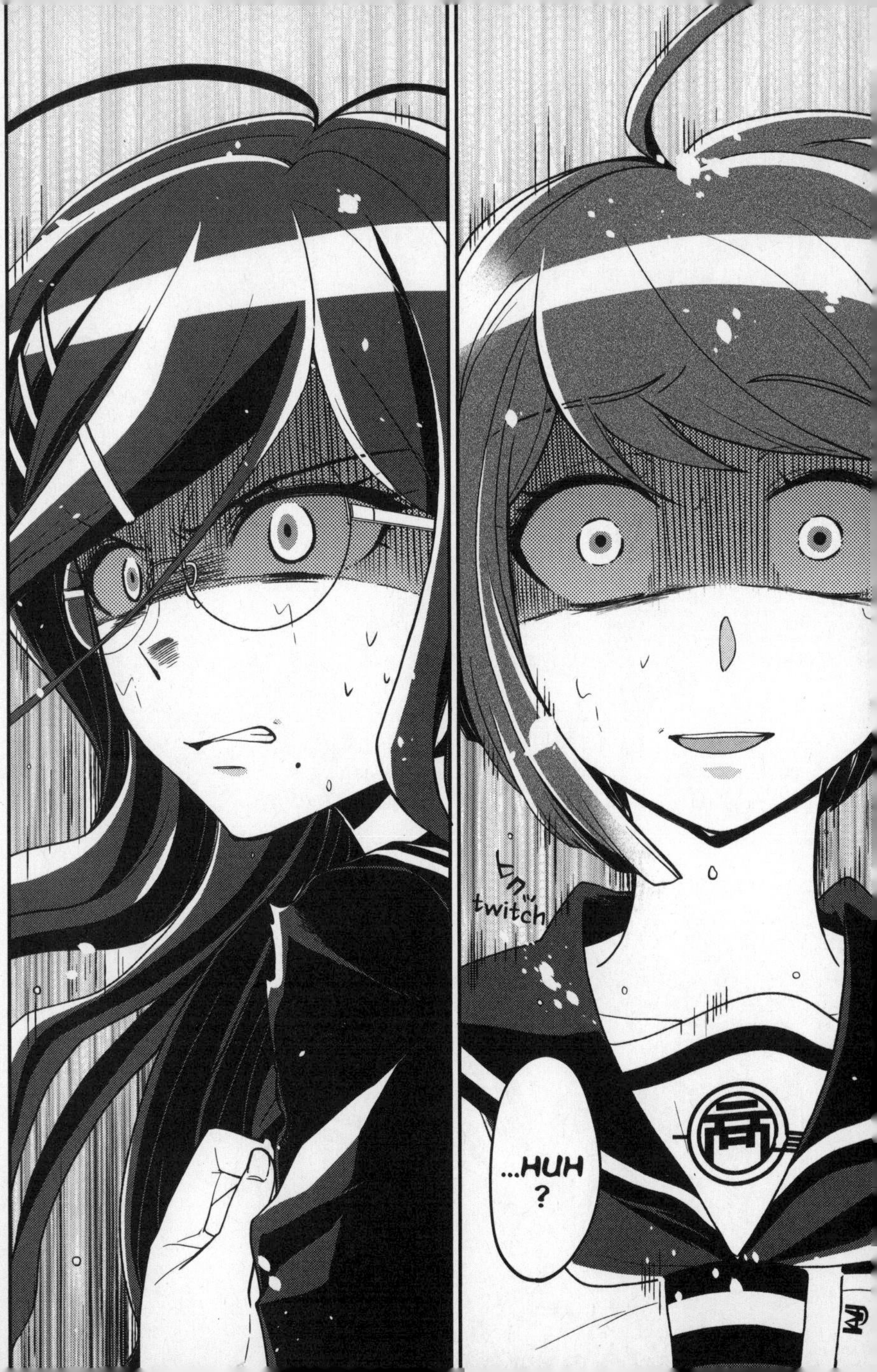
twitch
...HUH?

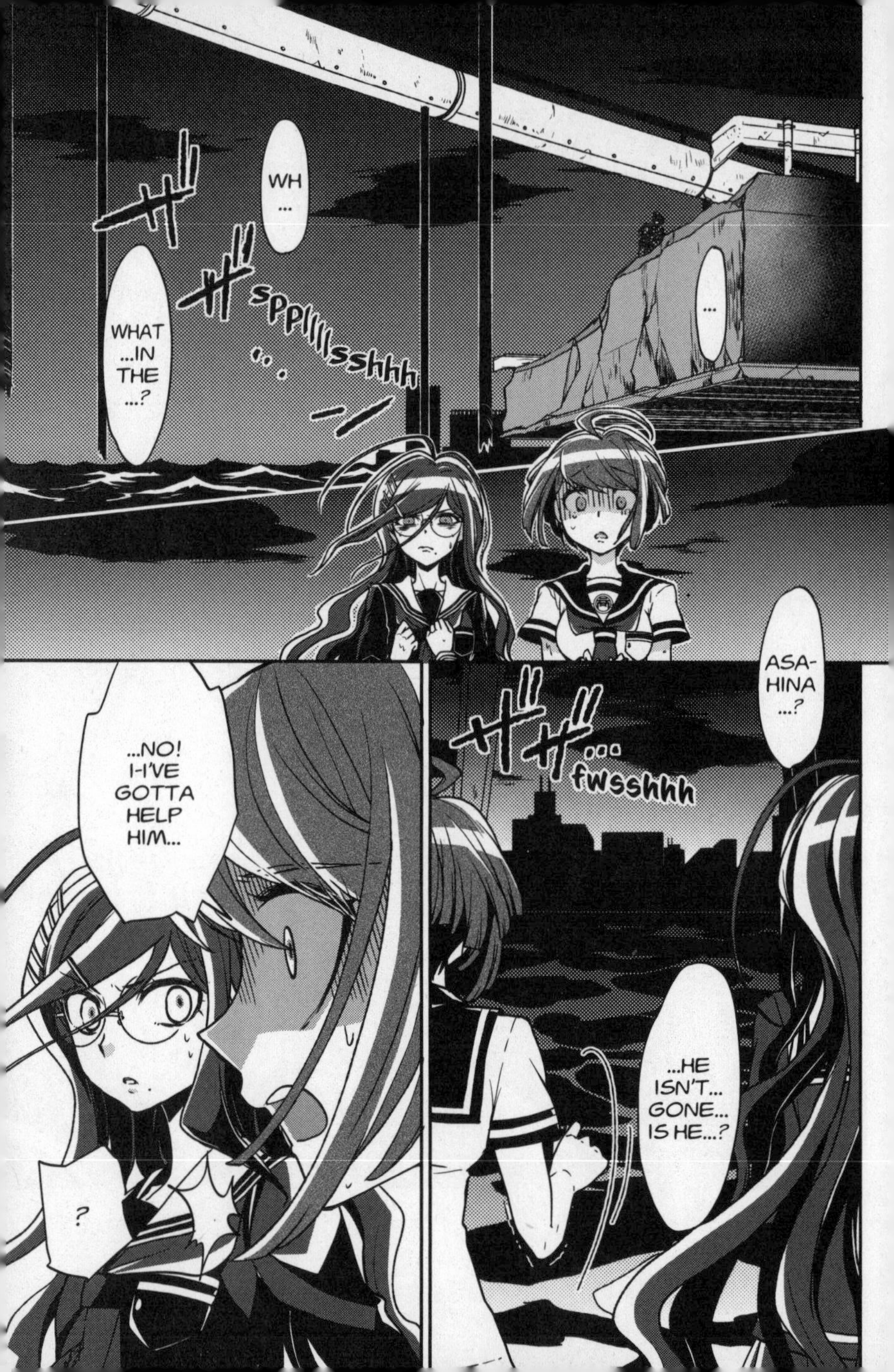
...
WH ...
spplllsshhh
WHAT ...IN THE ...?
ASA-HINA ...?
...fwsshhh
...HE ISN'T... GONE... IS HE...?
...NO! I-I'VE GOTTA HELP HIM...
?

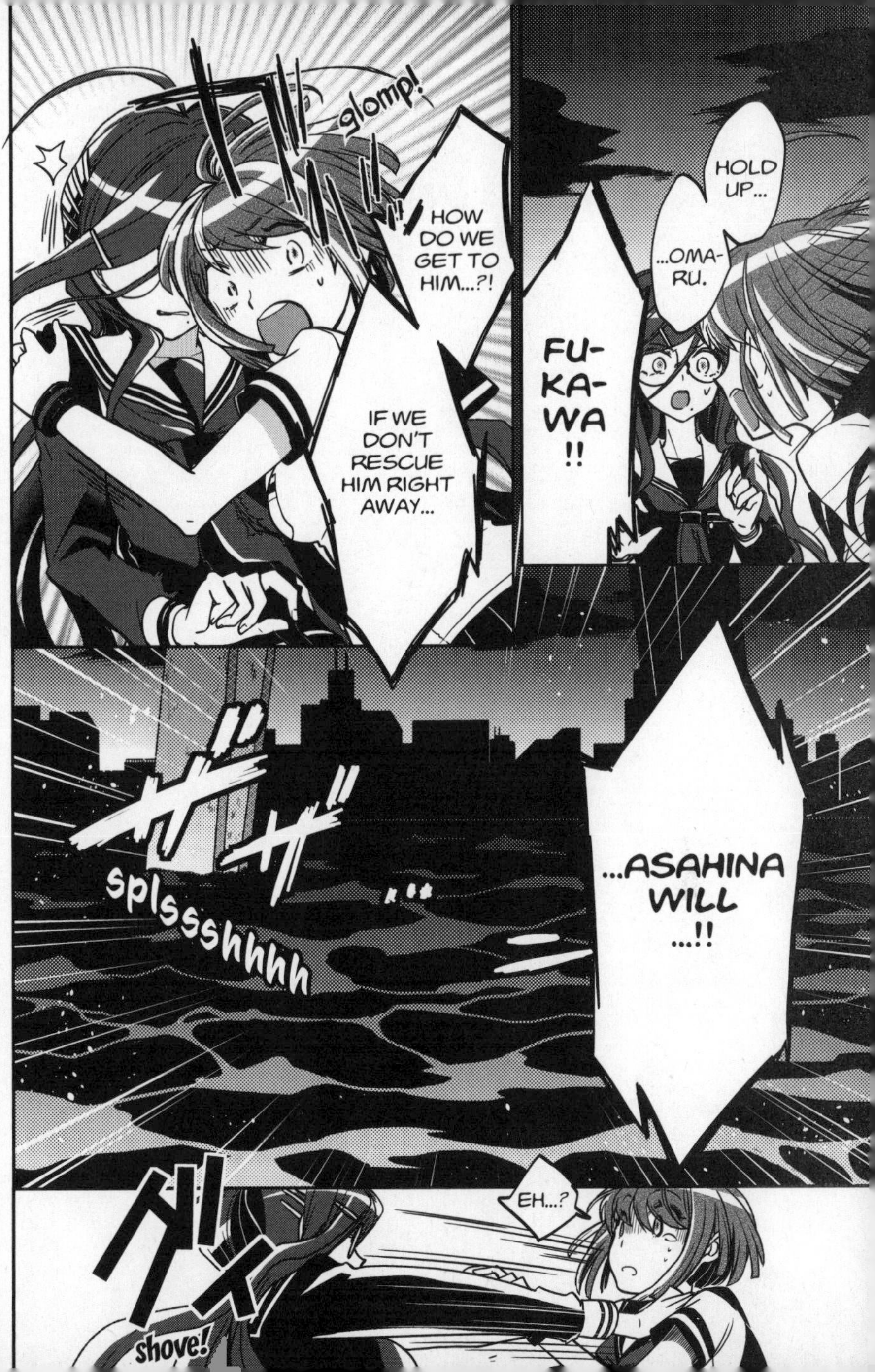
HOLD UP...
...OMA-RU.
FU-KA-WA !!
glomp!
HOW DO WE GET TO HIM...?!
IF WE DON'T RESCUE HIM RIGHT AWAY...
...ASAHINA WILL ...!!
splssshhhh
EH...?
shove!

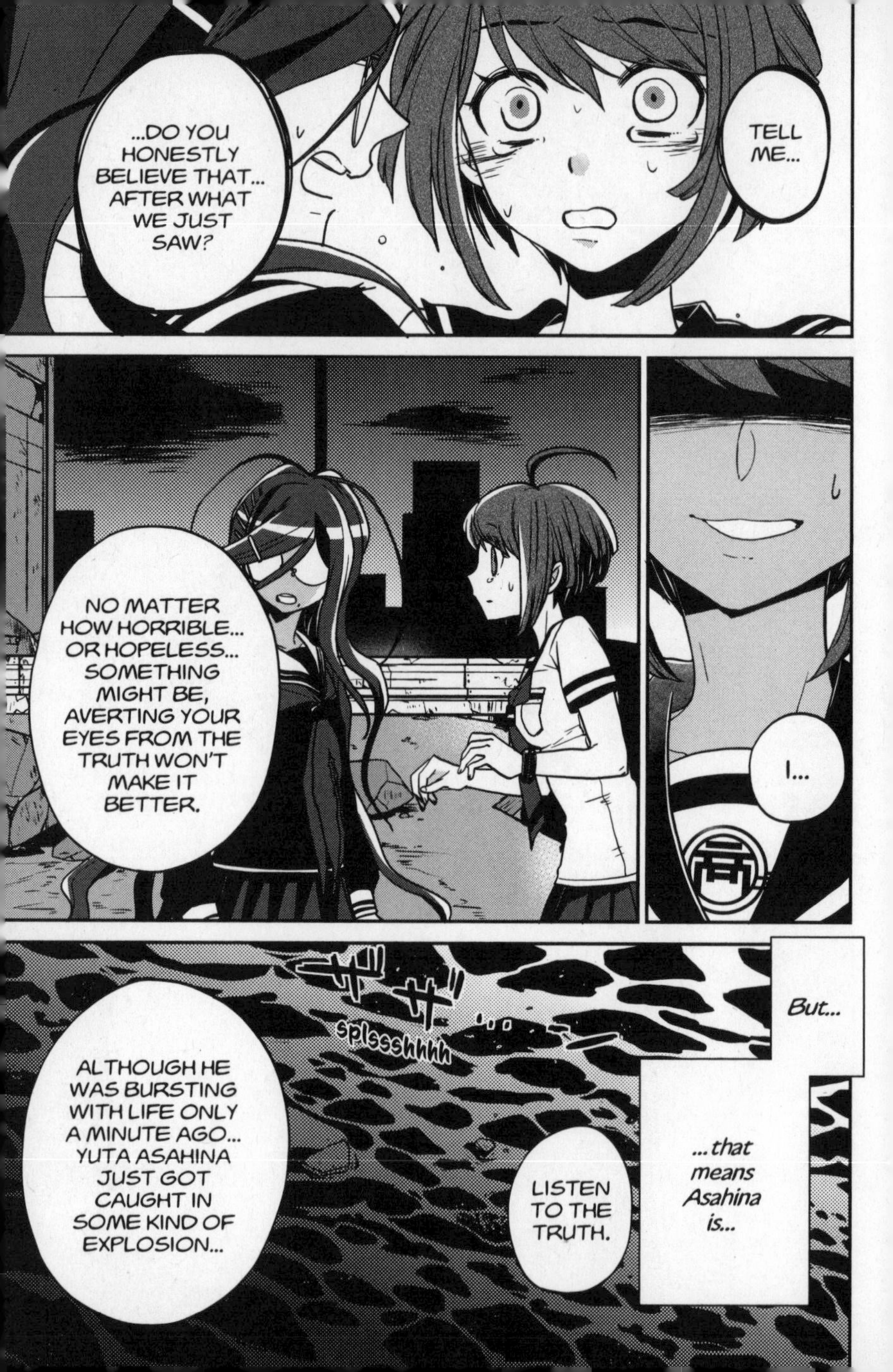
TELL ME...
...DO YOU HONESTLY BELIEVE THAT... AFTER WHAT WE JUST SAW?
I...
NO MATTER HOW HORRIBLE... OR HOPELESS... SOMETHING MIGHT BE, AVERTING YOUR EYES FROM THE TRUTH WON'T MAKE IT BETTER.
But...
splssshhhh
...that means Asahina is...
LISTEN TO THE TRUTH.
ALTHOUGH HE WAS BURSTING WITH LIFE ONLY A MINUTE AGO... YUTA ASAHINA JUST GOT CAUGHT IN SOME KIND OF EXPLOSION...

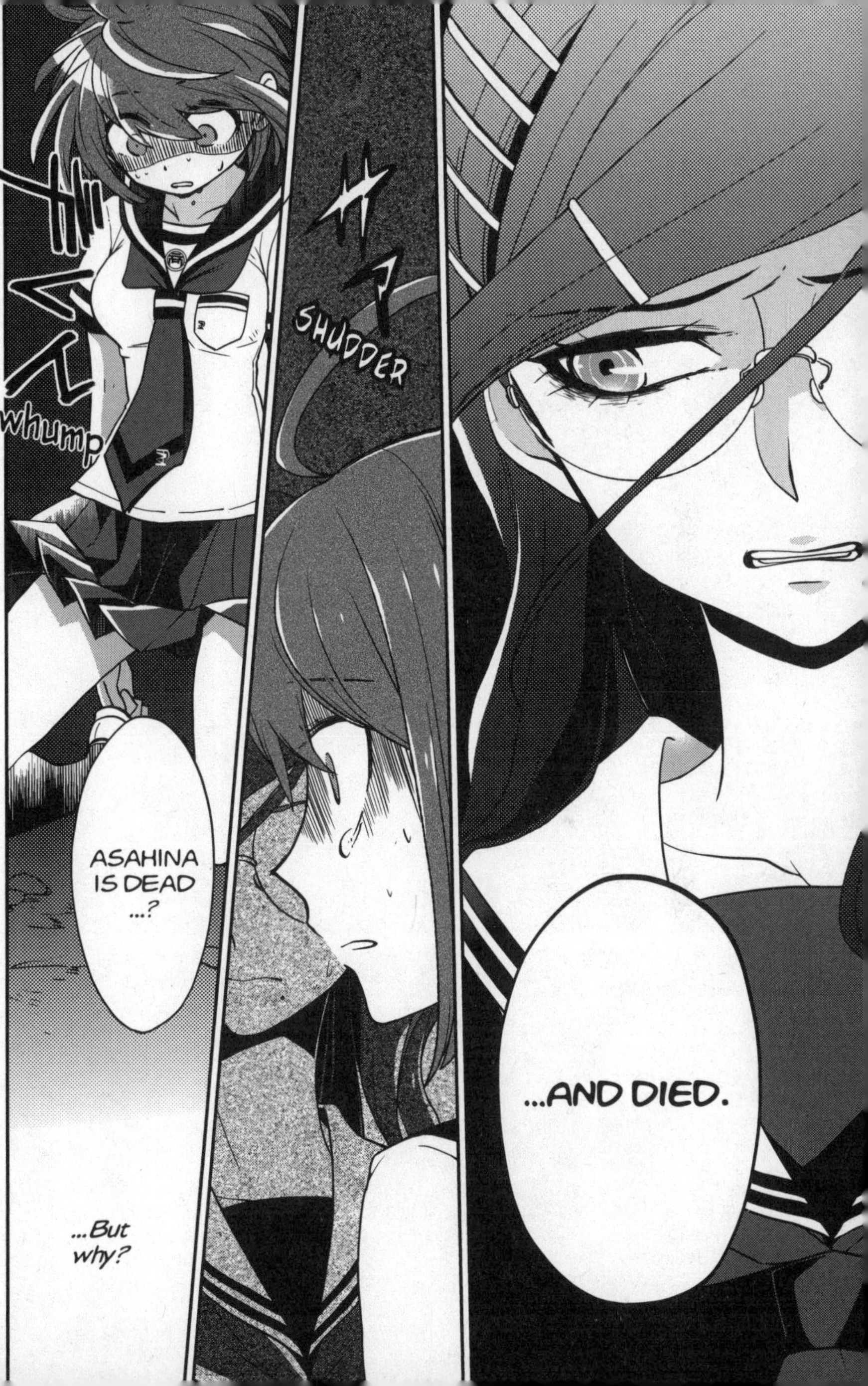
...AND DIED.
SHUDDER
whump
ASAHINA IS DEAD ...?
...But why?

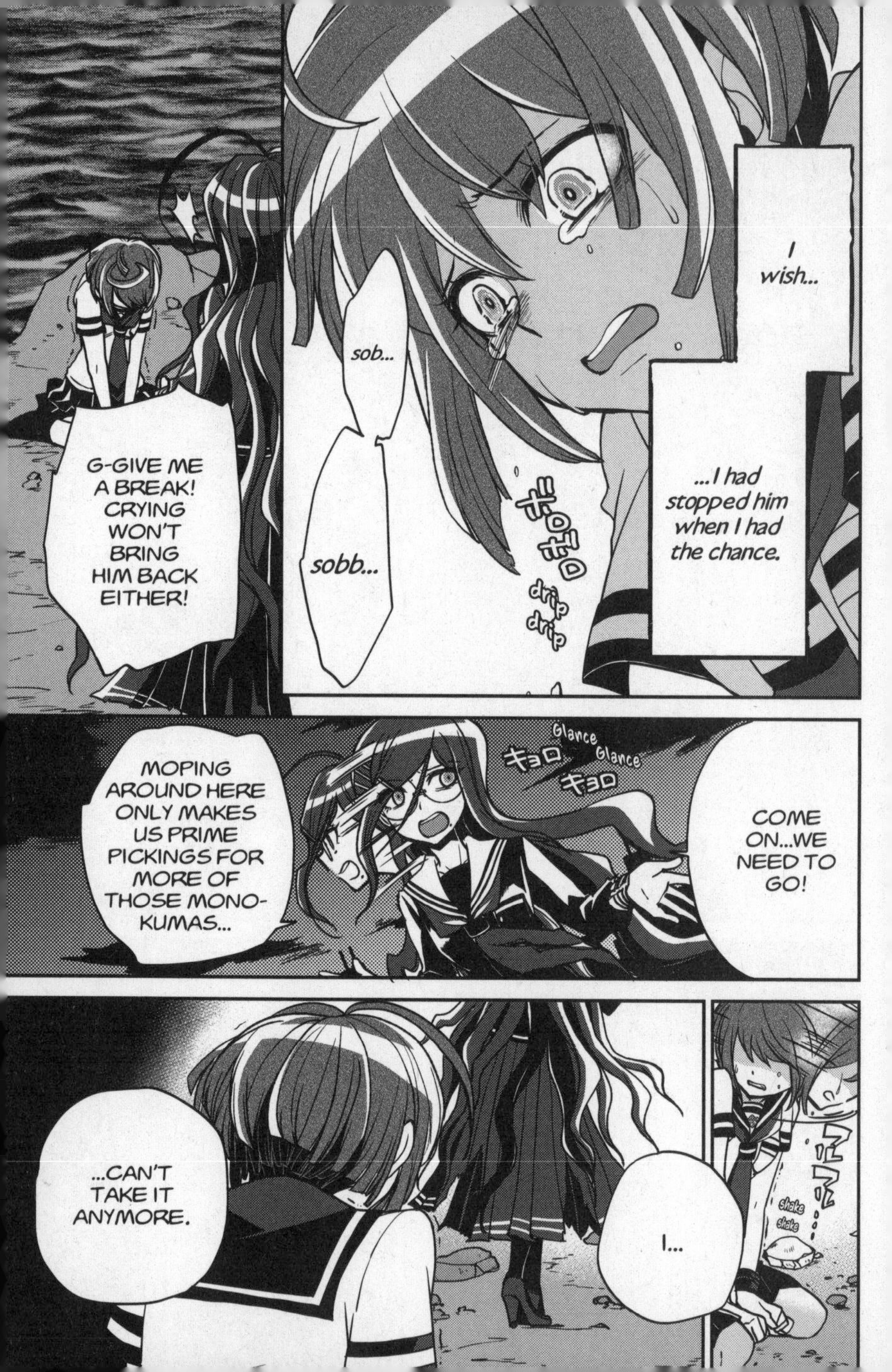
I wish...
...I had stopped him when I had the chance.
sob...
sobb...
ボロボロ
drip drip
G-GIVE ME A BREAK! CRYING WON'T BRING HIM BACK EITHER!
COME ON...WE NEED TO GO!
キョロ Glance
キョロ Glance
MOPING AROUND HERE ONLY MAKES US PRIME PICKINGS FOR MORE OF THOSE MONO-KUMAS...
shake shake
I...
...CAN'T TAKE IT ANYMORE.

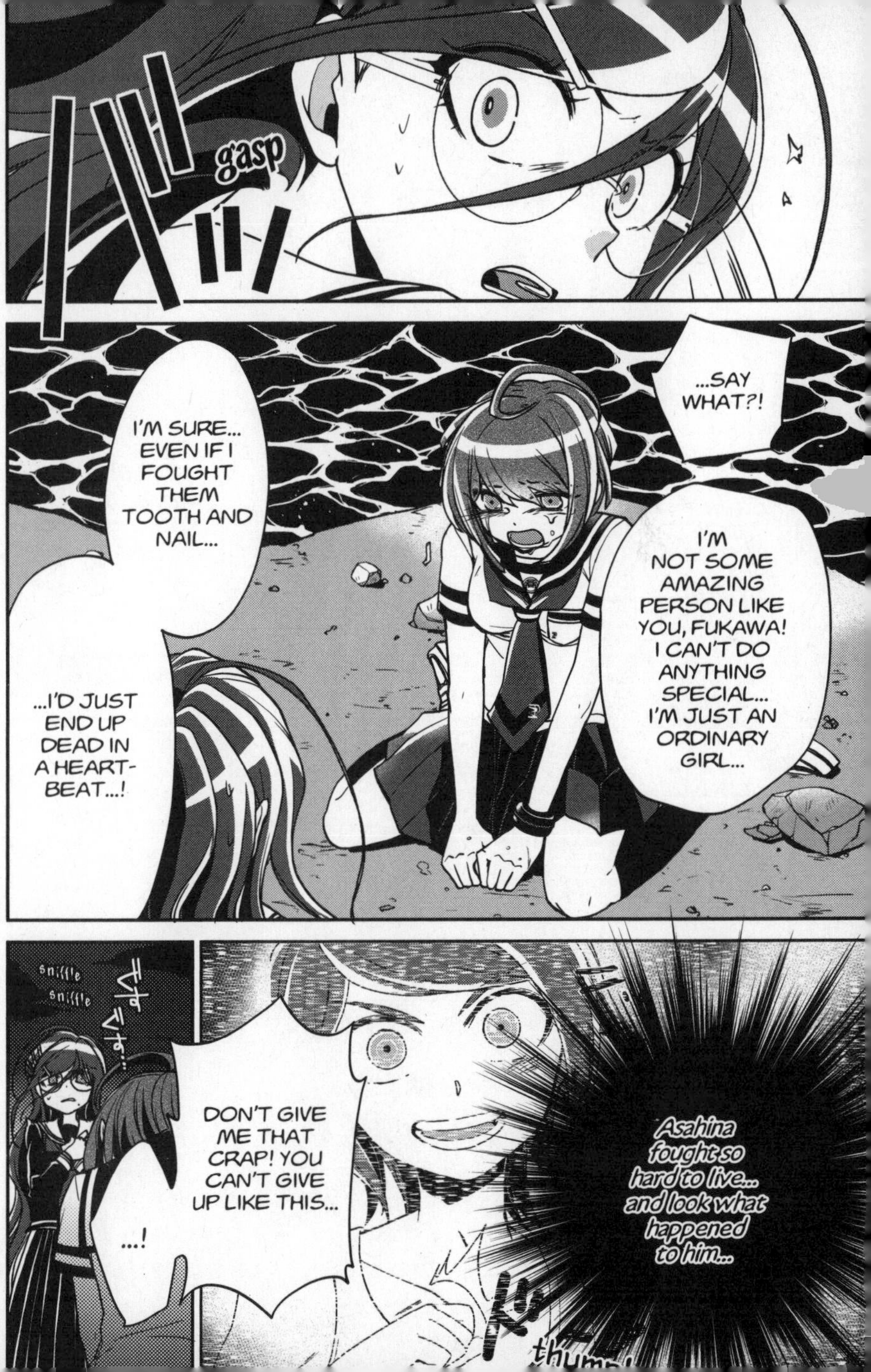
gasp
...SAY WHAT?!
I'M NOT SOME AMAZING PERSON LIKE YOU, FUKAWA! I CAN'T DO ANYTHING SPECIAL... I'M JUST AN ORDINARY GIRL...
I'M SURE... EVEN IF I FOUGHT THEM TOOTH AND NAIL...
...I'D JUST END UP DEAD IN A HEART-BEAT...!
Asahina fought so hard to live... and look what happened to him...
DON'T GIVE ME THAT CRAP! YOU CAN'T GIVE UP LIKE THIS...
sniffle
sniffle
...!

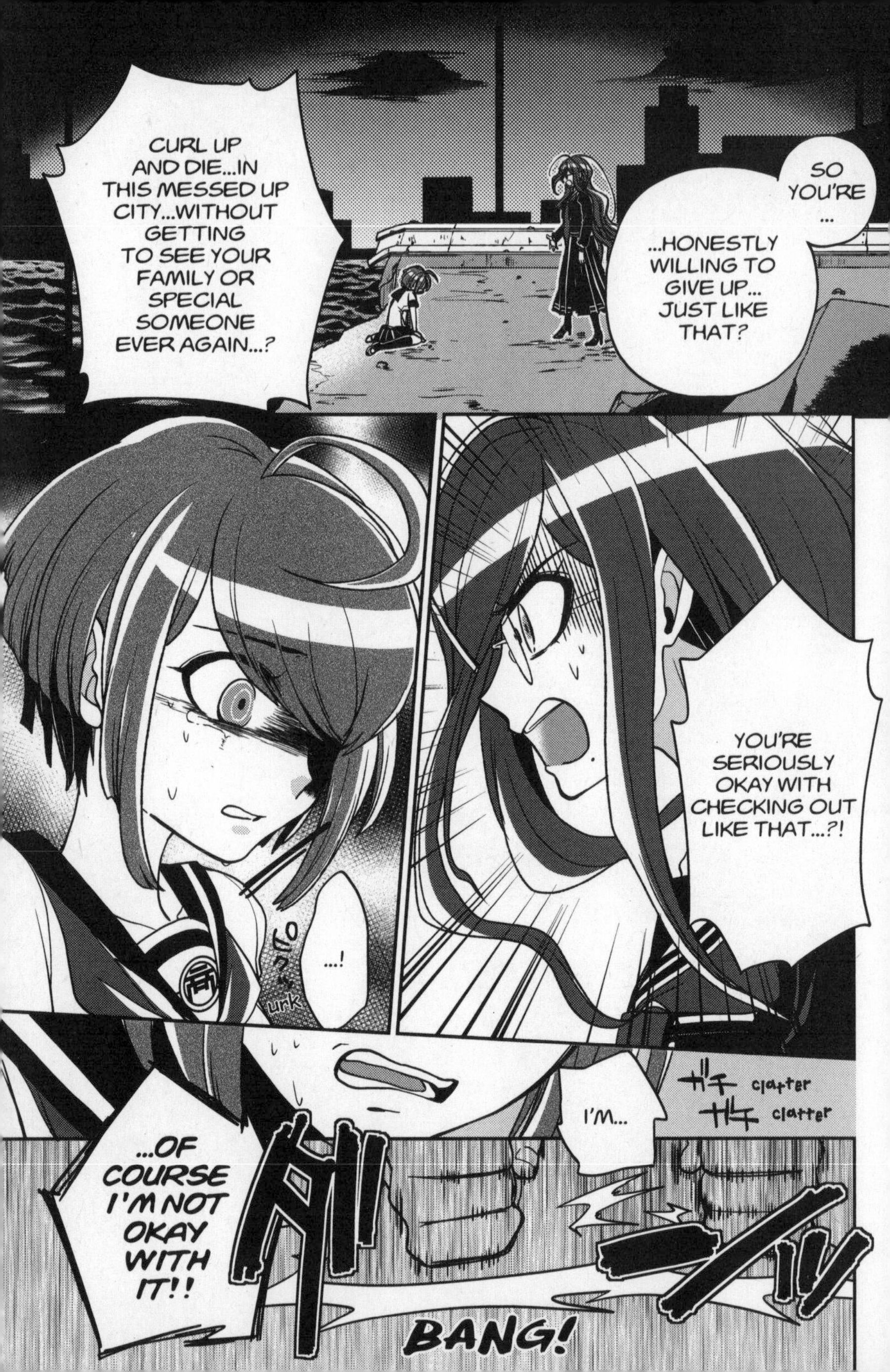
SO YOU'RE ...
...HONESTLY WILLING TO GIVE UP... JUST LIKE THAT?
CURL UP AND DIE...IN THIS MESSED UP CITY...WITHOUT GETTING TO SEE YOUR FAMILY OR SPECIAL SOMEONE EVER AGAIN...?
YOU'RE SERIOUSLY OKAY WITH CHECKING OUT LIKE THAT...?!
urk
...!
clatter
clatter
I'M...
...OF COURSE I'M NOT OKAY WITH IT!!
BANG!

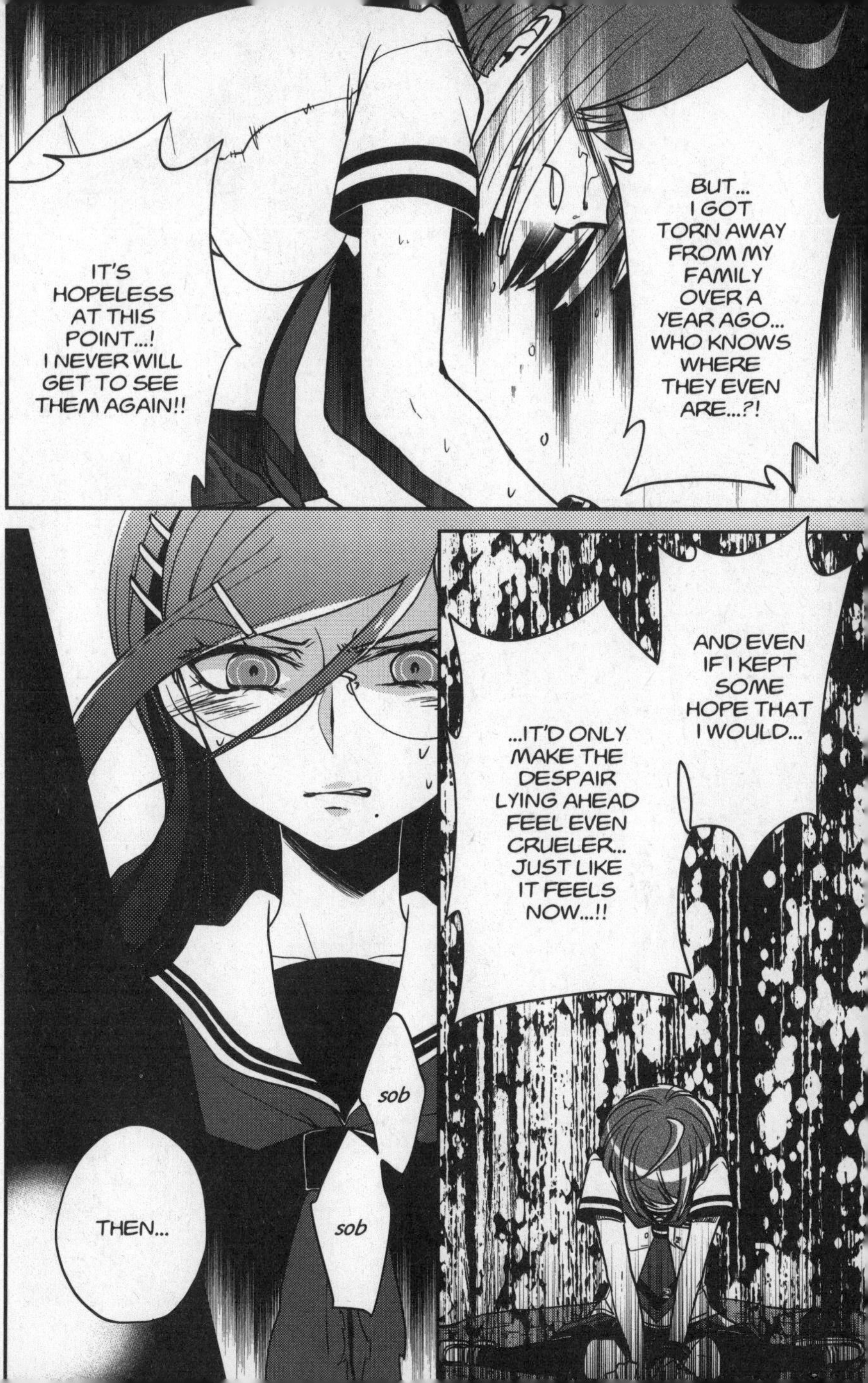
BUT... I GOT TORN AWAY FROM MY FAMILY OVER A YEAR AGO... WHO KNOWS WHERE THEY EVEN ARE...?!
IT'S HOPELESS AT THIS POINT...! I NEVER WILL GET TO SEE THEM AGAIN!!
AND EVEN IF I KEPT SOME HOPE THAT I WOULD...
...IT'D ONLY MAKE THE DESPAIR LYING AHEAD FEEL EVEN CRUELER... JUST LIKE IT FEELS NOW...!!
sob
sob
THEN...

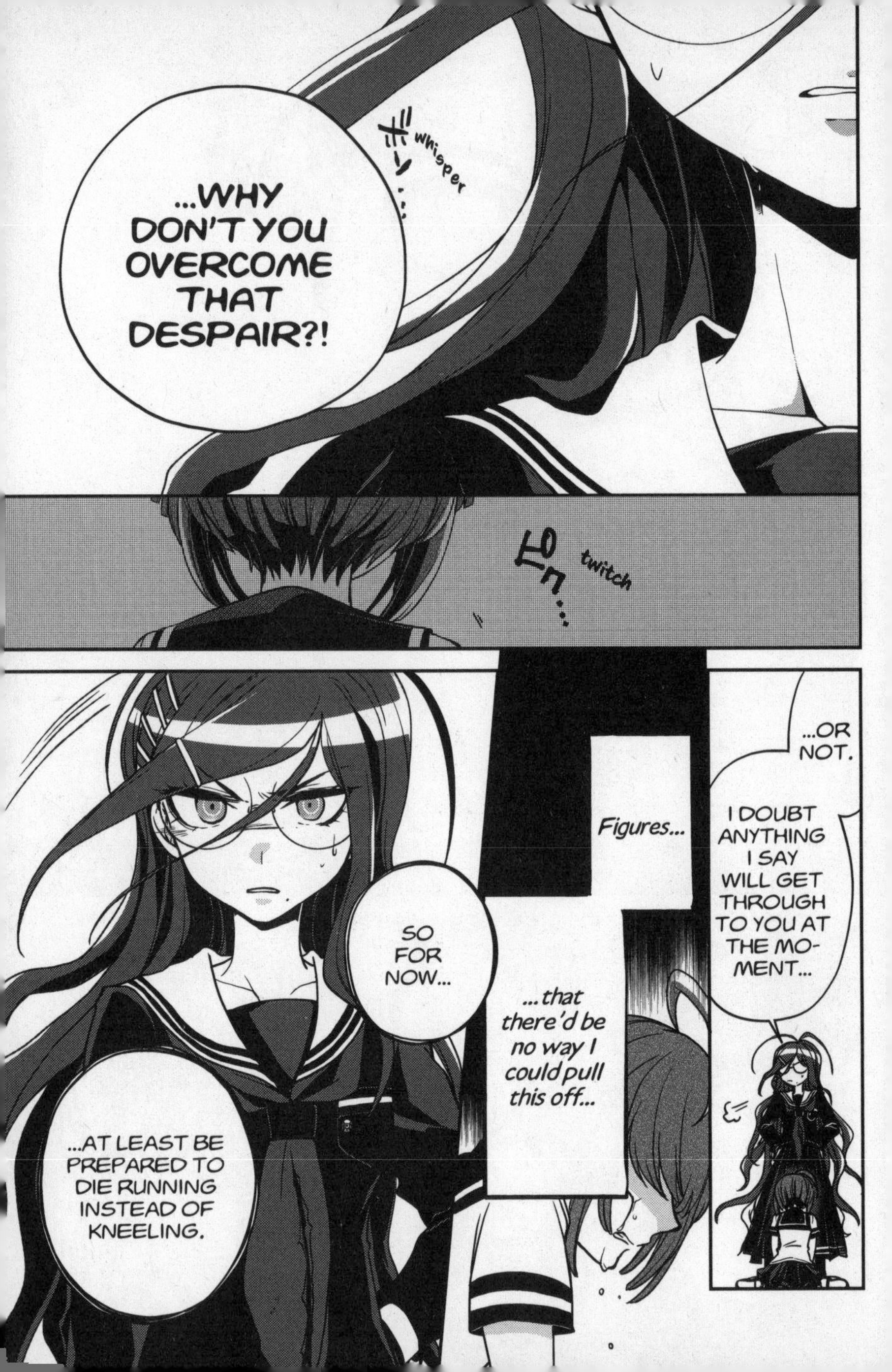
whisper
...WHY DON'T YOU OVERCOME THAT DESPAIR?!
twitch
...OR NOT.
I DOUBT ANYTHING I SAY WILL GET THROUGH TO YOU AT THE MO-MENT...
Figures...
...that there'd be no way I could pull this off...
SO FOR NOW...
...AT LEAST BE PREPARED TO DIE RUNNING INSTEAD OF KNEELING.

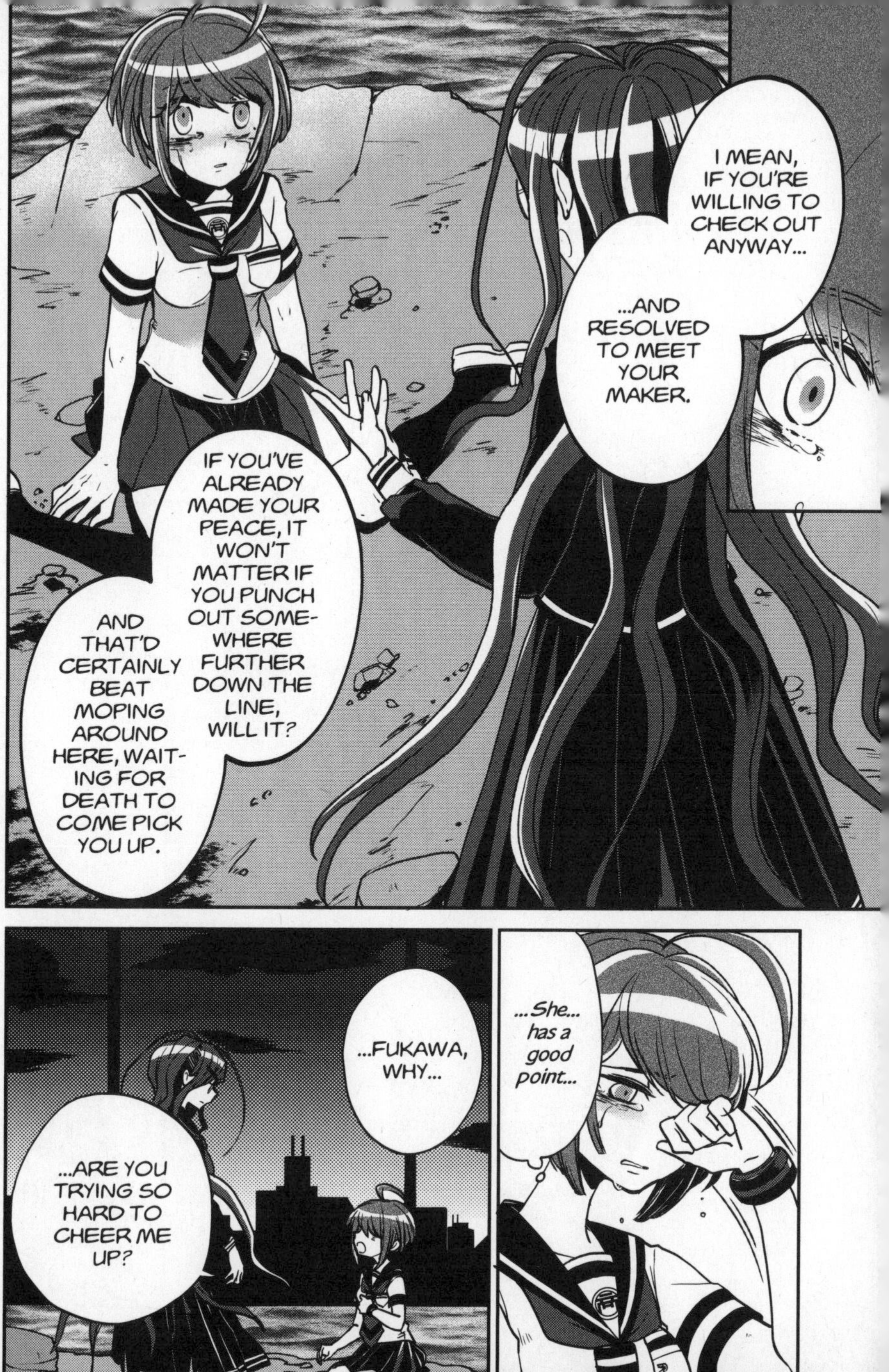
I MEAN, IF YOU'RE WILLING TO CHECK OUT ANYWAY...
...AND RESOLVED TO MEET YOUR MAKER.
IF YOU'VE ALREADY MADE YOUR PEACE, IT WON'T MATTER IF YOU PUNCH OUT SOME-WHERE FURTHER DOWN THE LINE, WILL IT?
AND THAT'D CERTAINLY BEAT MOPING AROUND HERE, WAIT-ING FOR DEATH TO COME PICK YOU UP.
...She... has a good point...
...FUKAWA, WHY...
...ARE YOU TRYING SO HARD TO CHEER ME UP?

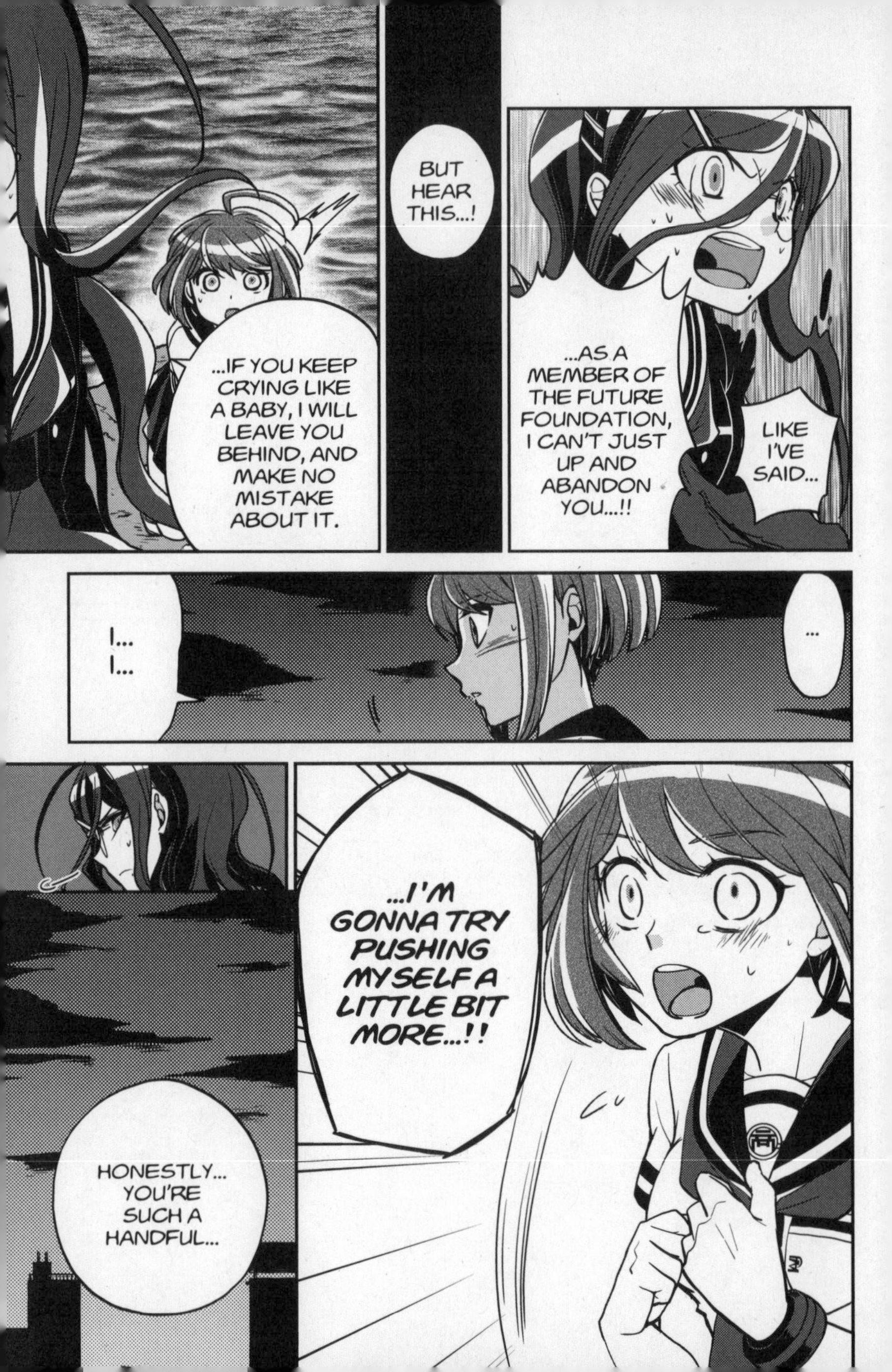
LIKE I'VE SAID...
...AS A MEMBER OF THE FUTURE FOUNDATION, I CAN'T JUST UP AND ABANDON YOU...!!
BUT HEAR THIS...!
...IF YOU KEEP CRYING LIKE A BABY, I WILL LEAVE YOU BEHIND, AND MAKE NO MISTAKE ABOUT IT.
...
I... I...
...I'M GONNA TRY PUSHING MYSELF A LITTLE BIT MORE...!!
HONESTLY... YOU'RE SUCH A HANDFUL...

Danganronpa Another Episode:
Ultra Despair Girls

CHAPTER 6

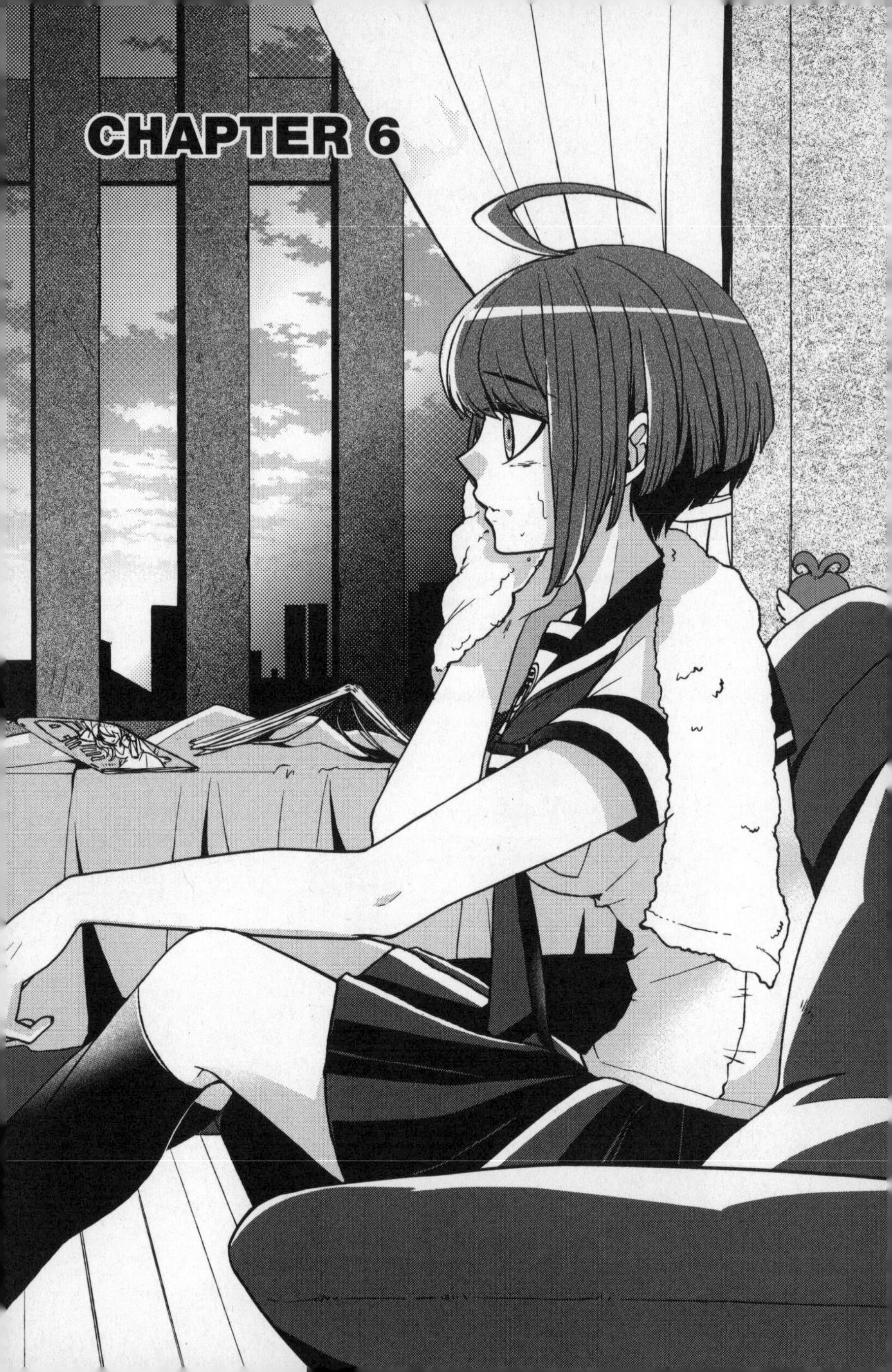

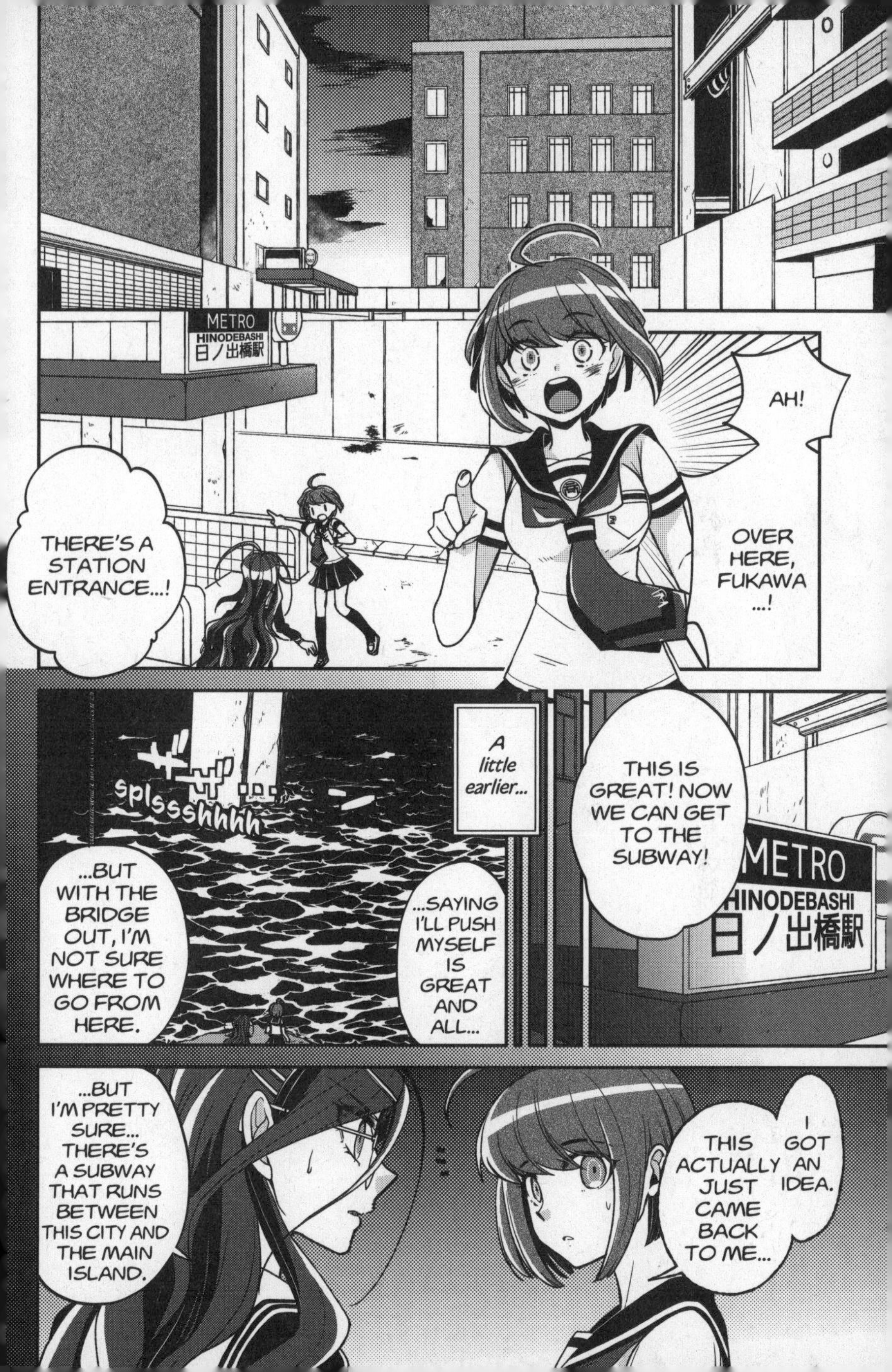
METRO
HINODEBASHI
日ノ出橋駅
AH!
OVER HERE, FUKAWA ...!
THERE'S A STATION ENTRANCE...!
METRO
HINODEBASHI
日ノ出橋駅
THIS IS GREAT! NOW WE CAN GET TO THE SUBWAY!
A little earlier...
...SAYING I'LL PUSH MYSELF IS GREAT AND ALL...
...BUT WITH THE BRIDGE OUT, I'M NOT SURE WHERE TO GO FROM HERE.
splssshhhh
I GOT AN IDEA.
THIS ACTUALLY JUST CAME BACK TO ME...
...BUT I'M PRETTY SURE... THERE'S A SUBWAY THAT RUNS BETWEEN THIS CITY AND THE MAIN ISLAND.

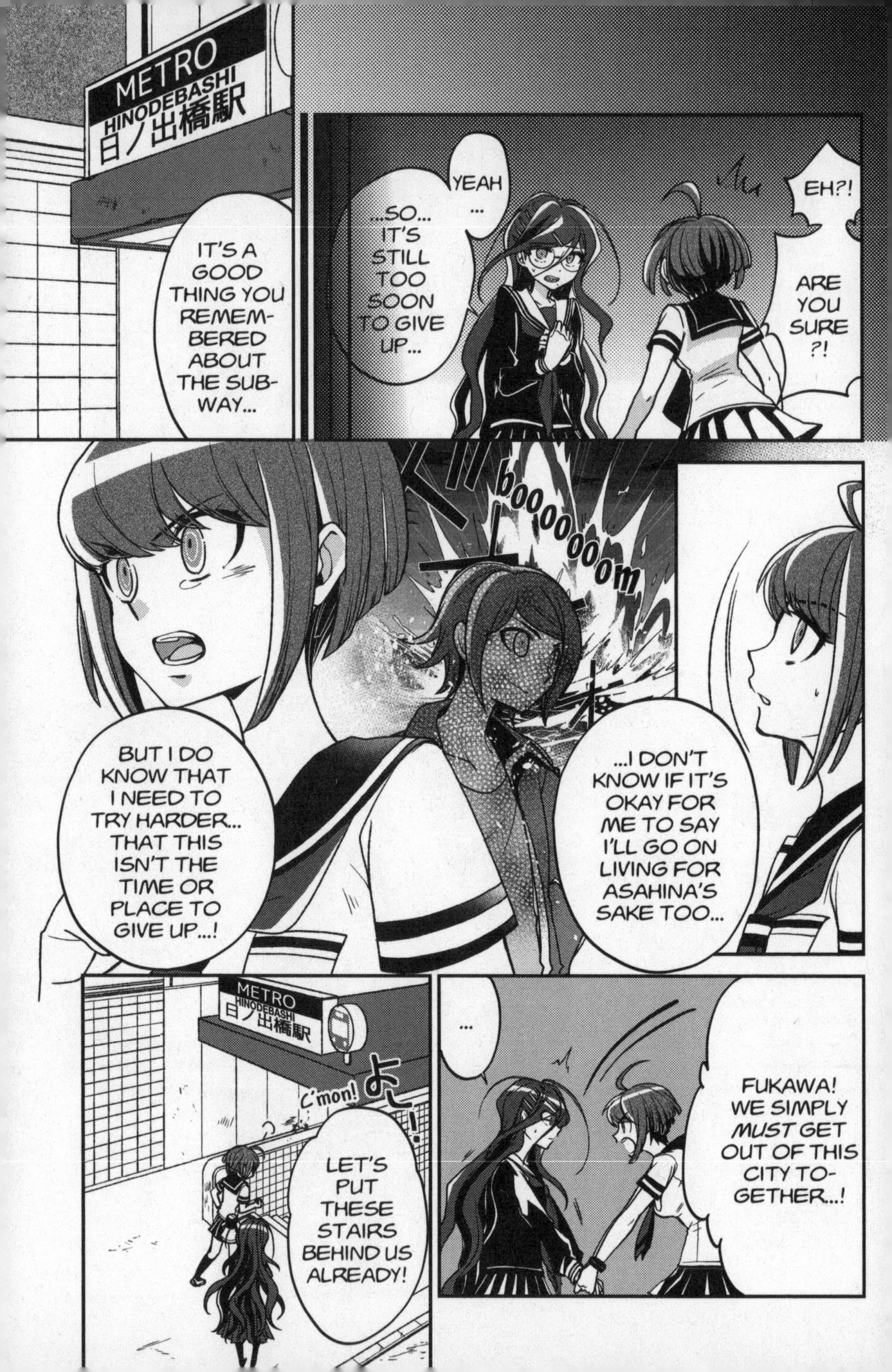
EH?!
ARE YOU SURE ?!
YEAH ...
...SO... IT'S STILL TOO SOON TO GIVE UP...
METRO
HINODEBASHI
日ノ出橋駅
IT'S A GOOD THING YOU REMEMBERED ABOUT THE SUBWAY...
boooooooom
...I DON'T KNOW IF IT'S OKAY FOR ME TO SAY I'LL GO ON LIVING FOR ASAHINA'S SAKE TOO...
BUT I DO KNOW THAT I NEED TO TRY HARDER... THAT THIS ISN'T THE TIME OR PLACE TO GIVE UP...!
FUKAWA! WE SIMPLY *MUST* GET OUT OF THIS CITY TOGETHER...!
...
METRO
HINODEBASHI
日ノ出橋駅
よし!
C'mon!
LET'S PUT THESE STAIRS BEHIND US ALREADY!

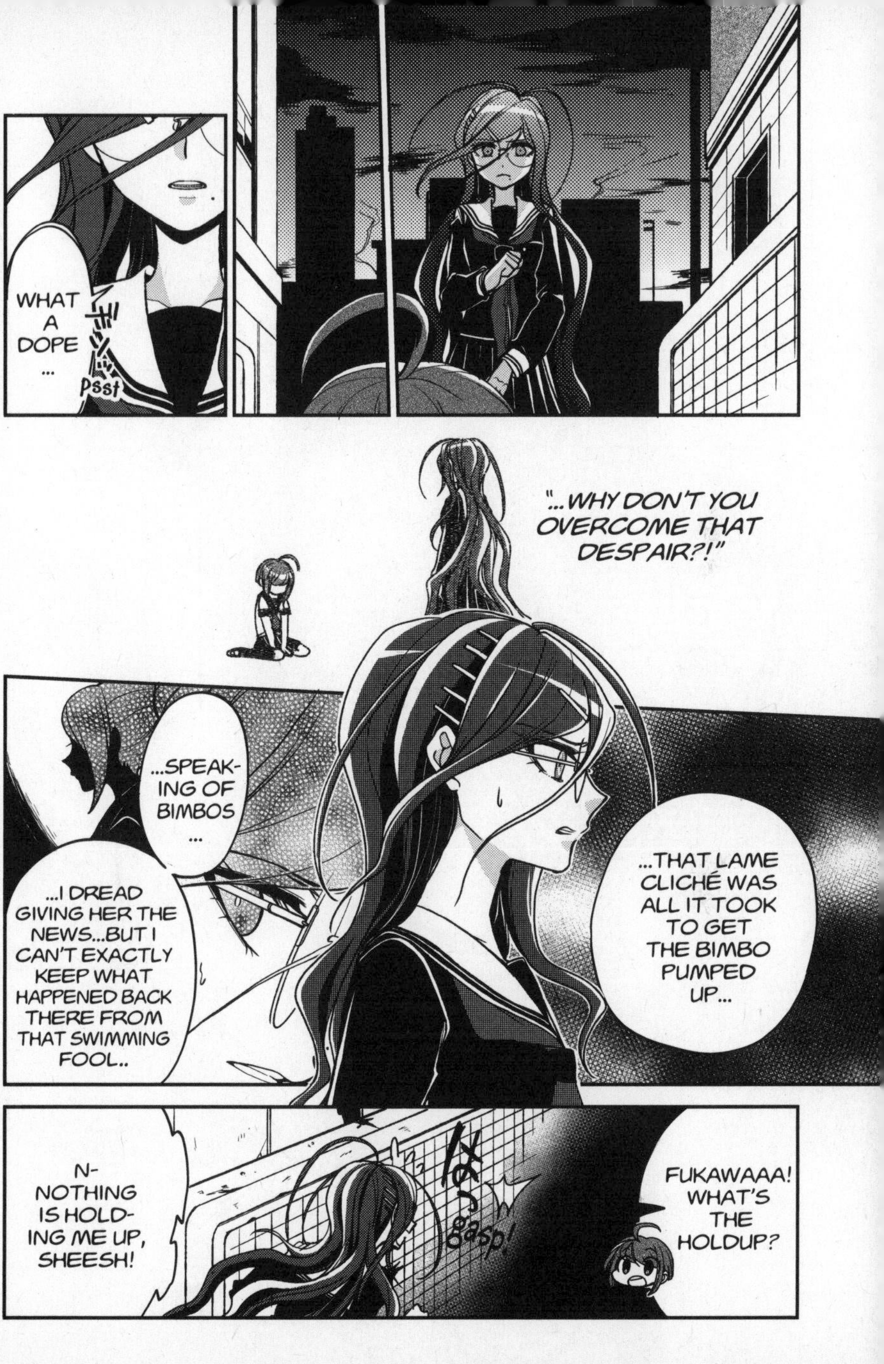
WHAT A DOPE ...
Psst
"...WHY DON'T YOU OVERCOME THAT DESPAIR?!"
...THAT LAME CLICHÉ WAS ALL IT TOOK TO GET THE BIMBO PUMPED UP...
...SPEAKING OF BIMBOS ...
...I DREAD GIVING HER THE NEWS...BUT I CAN'T EXACTLY KEEP WHAT HAPPENED BACK THERE FROM THAT SWIMMING FOOL..
FUKAWAAA! WHAT'S THE HOLDUP?
gasp!
N-NOTHING IS HOLDING ME UP, SHEESH!

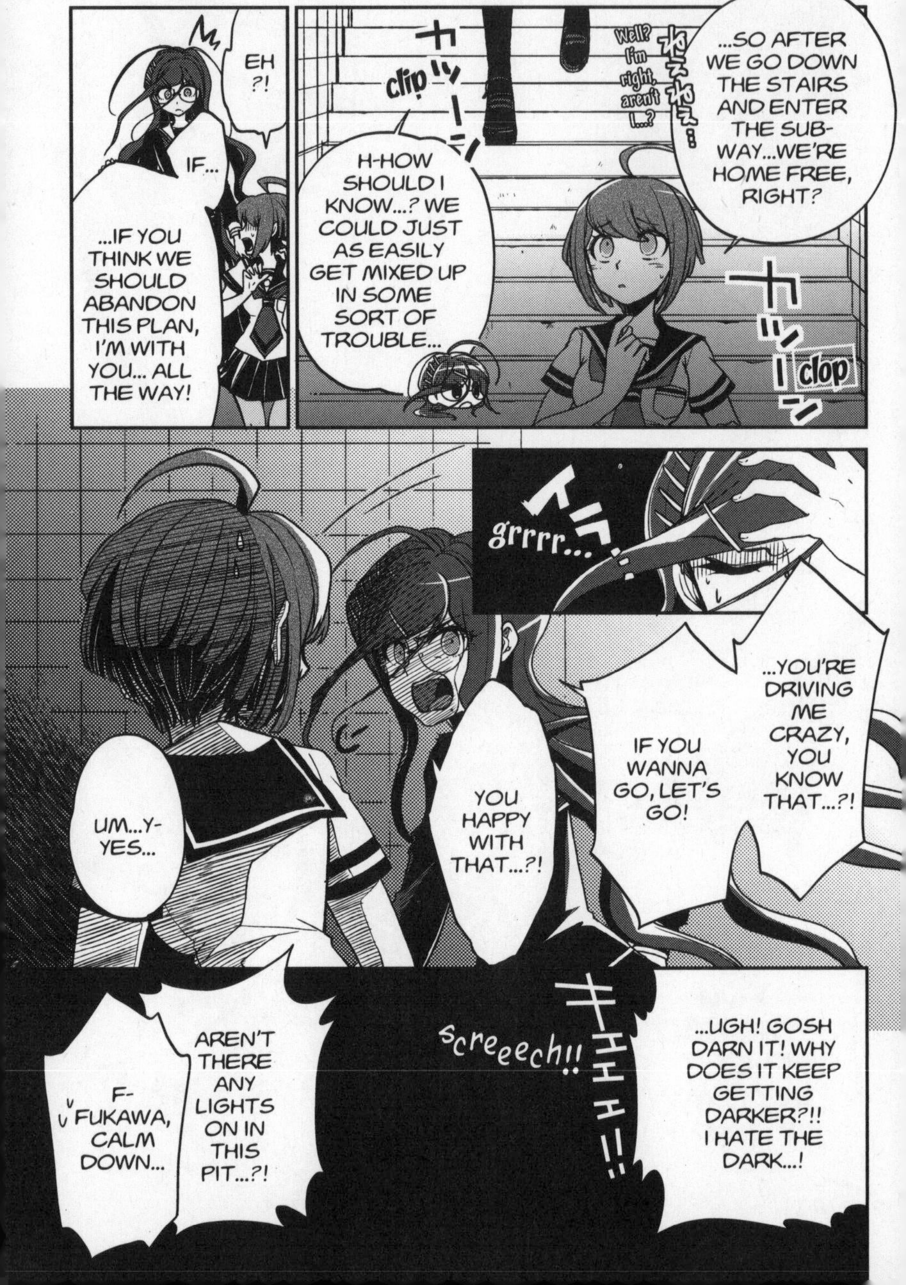
...SO AFTER WE GO DOWN THE STAIRS AND ENTER THE SUB-WAY...WE'RE HOME FREE, RIGHT?
Well? I'm right, aren't I...?
clip
H-HOW SHOULD I KNOW...? WE COULD JUST AS EASILY GET MIXED UP IN SOME SORT OF TROUBLE...
clop
EH?!
IF...
...IF YOU THINK WE SHOULD ABANDON THIS PLAN, I'M WITH YOU... ALL THE WAY!
grrrr...
...YOU'RE DRIVING ME CRAZY, YOU KNOW THAT...?!
IF YOU WANNA GO, LET'S GO!
YOU HAPPY WITH THAT...?!
UM...Y-YES...
...UGH! GOSH DARN IT! WHY DOES IT KEEP GETTING DARKER?!! I HATE THE DARK...!
screeech!!
AREN'T THERE ANY LIGHTS ON IN THIS PIT...?!
F-FUKAWA, CALM DOWN...

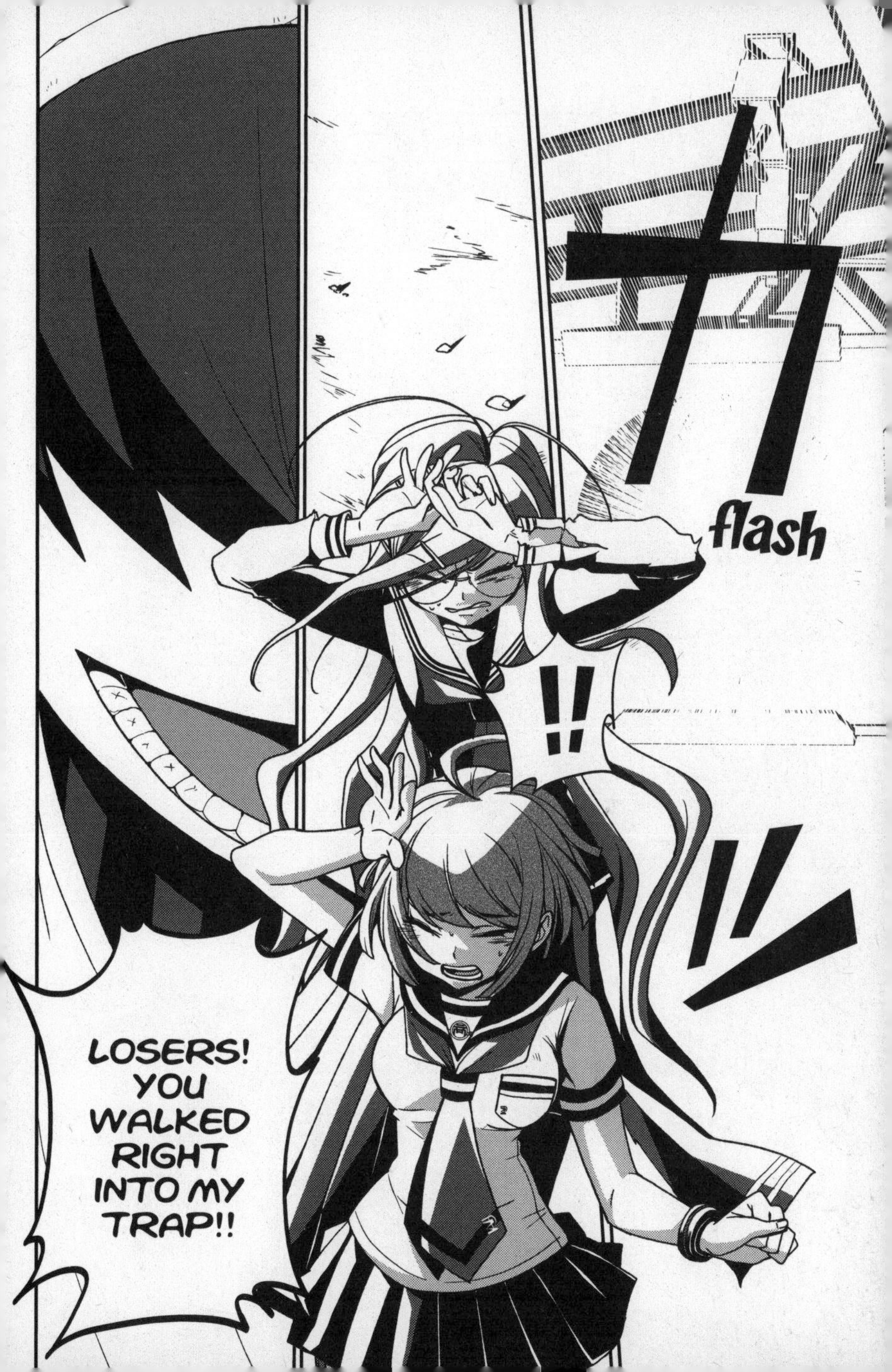

flash
!!
LOSERS! YOU WALKED RIGHT INTO MY TRAP!!

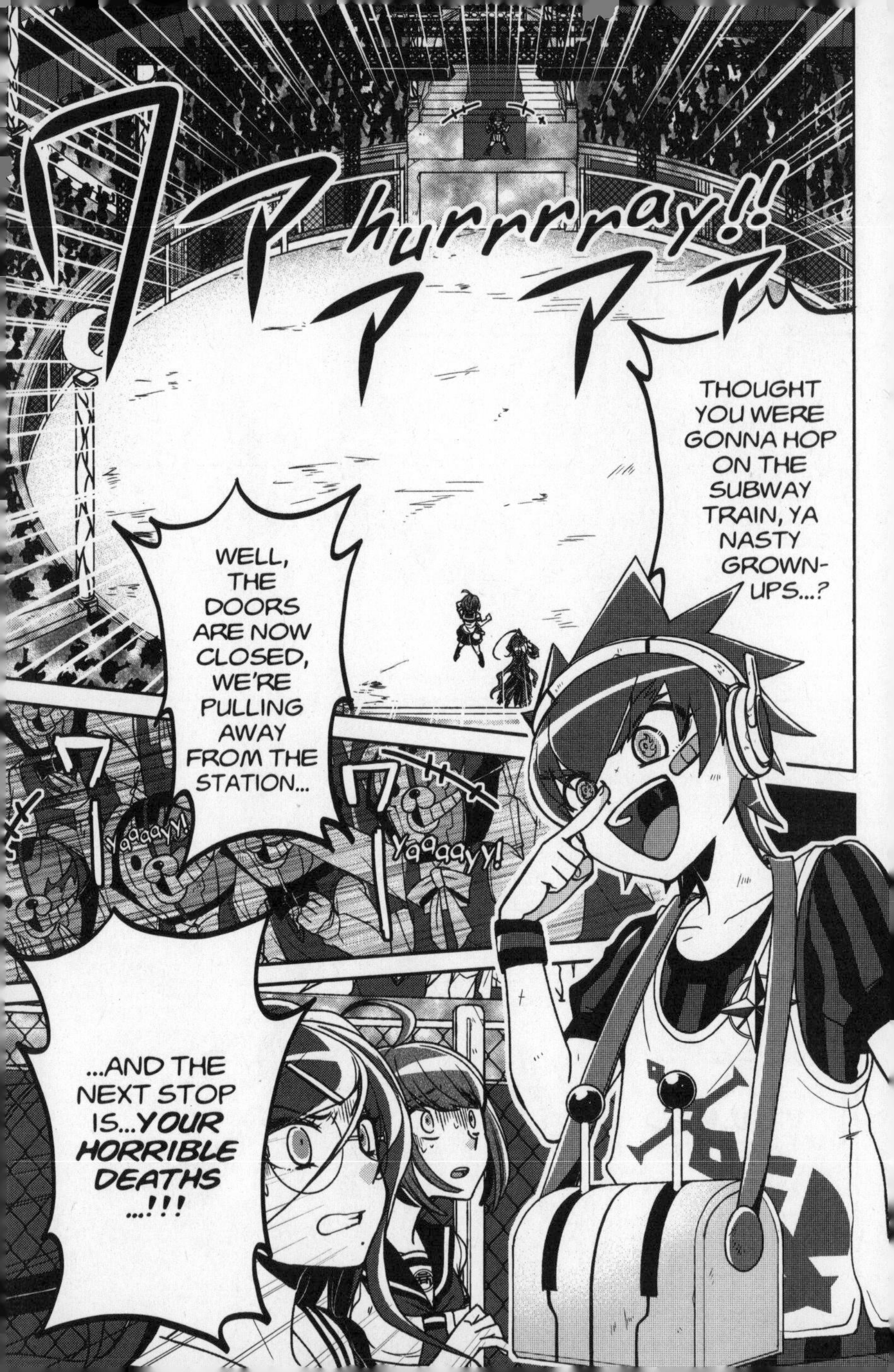
hurrrray!!
THOUGHT YOU WERE GONNA HOP ON THE SUBWAY TRAIN, YA NASTY GROWN-UPS...?
WELL, THE DOORS ARE NOW CLOSED, WE'RE PULLING AWAY FROM THE STATION...
Yaaaayy!
Yaaaayy!
...AND THE NEXT STOP IS... ***YOUR HORRIBLE DEATHS*** ...!!!

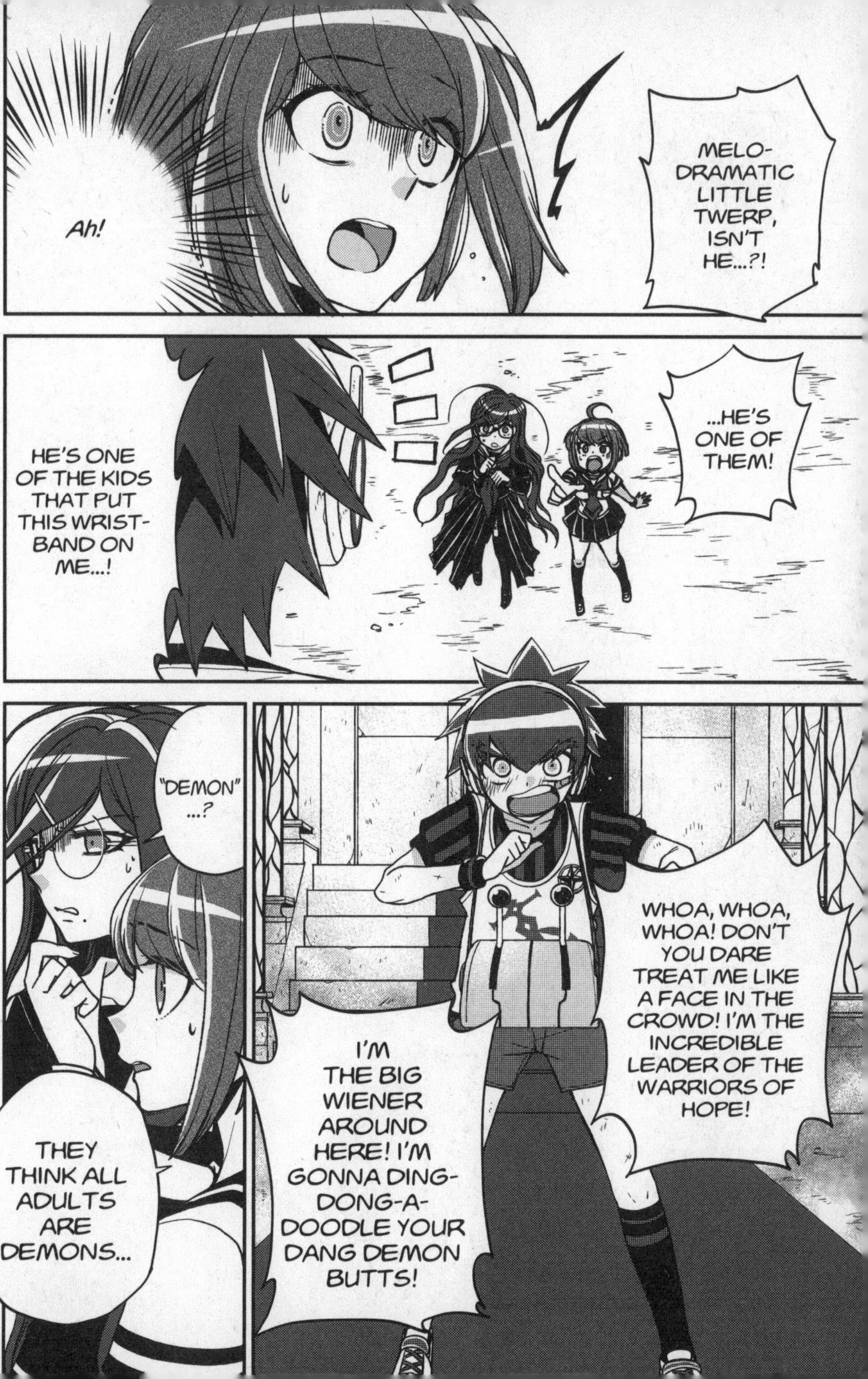

MELO-DRAMATIC LITTLE TWERP, ISN'T HE...?!
Ah!
...HE'S ONE OF THEM!
HE'S ONE OF THE KIDS THAT PUT THIS WRIST-BAND ON ME...!
WHOA, WHOA, WHOA! DON'T YOU DARE TREAT ME LIKE A FACE IN THE CROWD! I'M THE INCREDIBLE LEADER OF THE WARRIORS OF HOPE!
I'M THE BIG WIENER AROUND HERE! I'M GONNA DING-DONG-A-DOODLE YOUR DANG DEMON BUTTS!
"DEMON" ...?
THEY THINK ALL ADULTS ARE DEMONS...

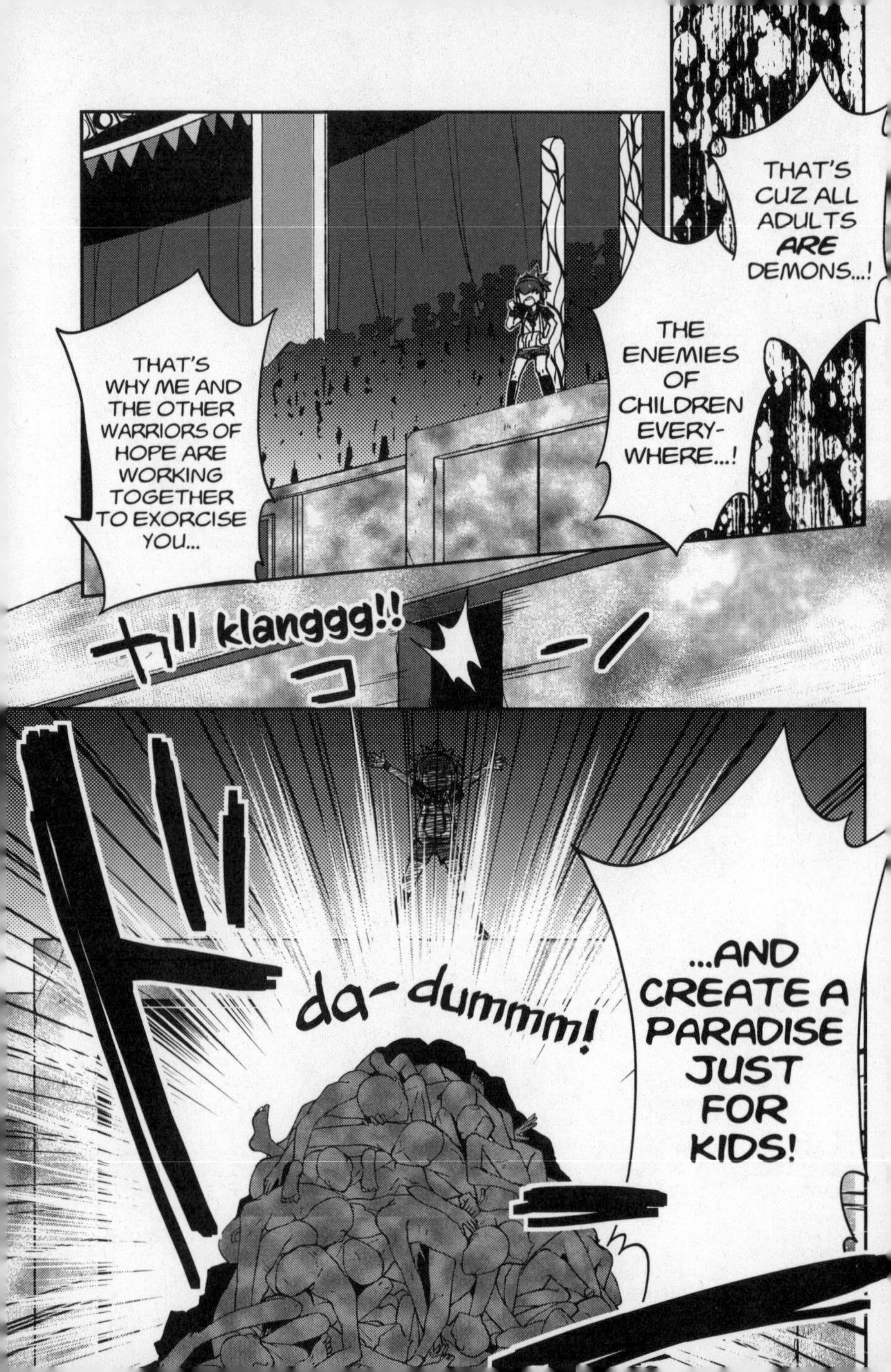
THAT'S CUZ ALL ADULTS ***ARE*** DEMONS...!
THE ENEMIES OF CHILDREN EVERY-WHERE...!
THAT'S WHY ME AND THE OTHER WARRIORS OF HOPE ARE WORKING TOGETHER TO EXORCISE YOU...
klanggg!!
...AND CREATE A PARADISE JUST FOR KIDS!
da-dummmm!

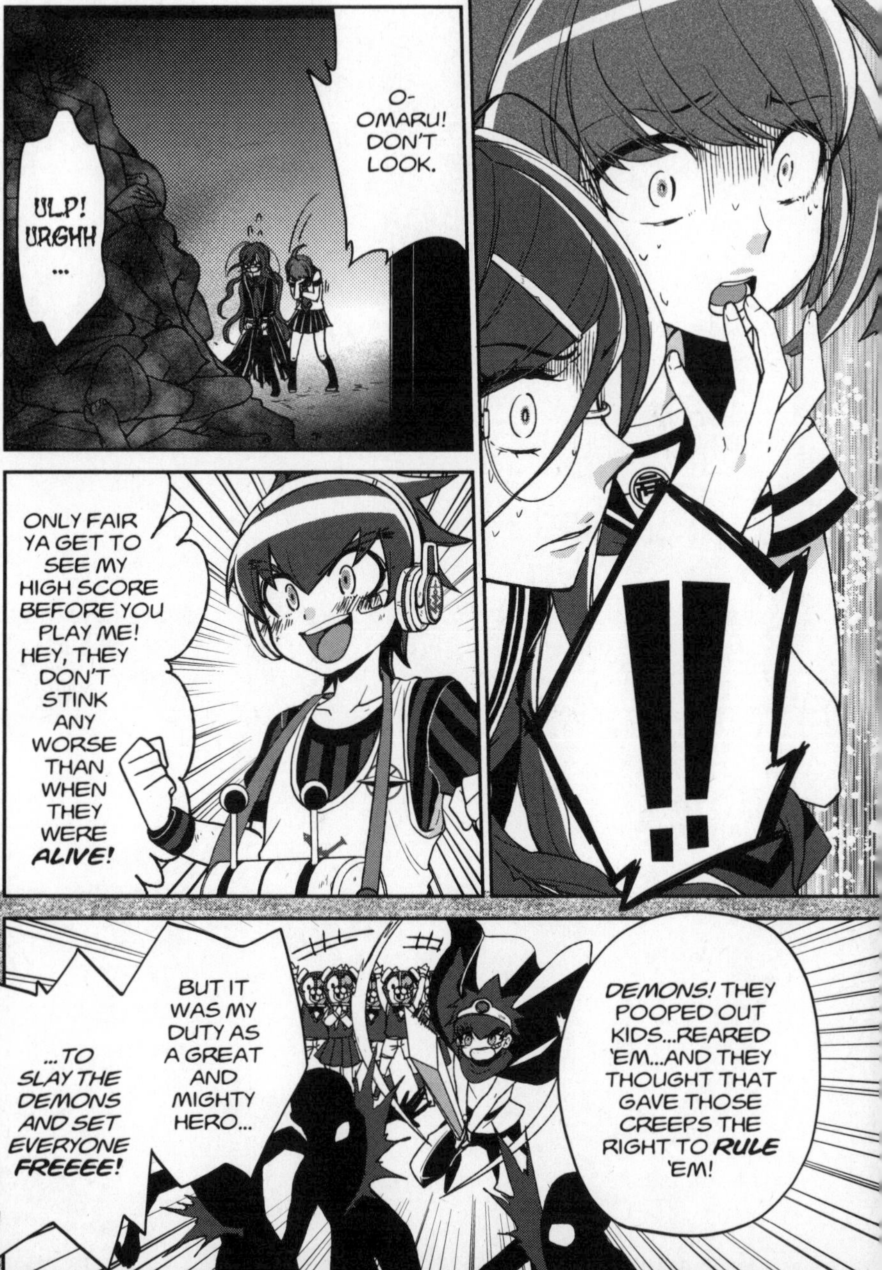
!!
O-OMARU! DON'T LOOK.
ULP! URGHH ...
ONLY FAIR YA GET TO SEE MY HIGH SCORE BEFORE YOU PLAY ME! HEY, THEY DON'T STINK ANY WORSE THAN WHEN THEY WERE ***ALIVE!***
DEMONS! THEY POOPED OUT KIDS...REARED 'EM...AND THEY THOUGHT THAT GAVE THOSE CREEPS THE RIGHT TO ***RULE*** 'EM!
BUT IT WAS MY DUTY AS A GREAT AND MIGHTY HERO...
...TO SLAY THE DEMONS AND SET EVERYONE ***FREEEE!***

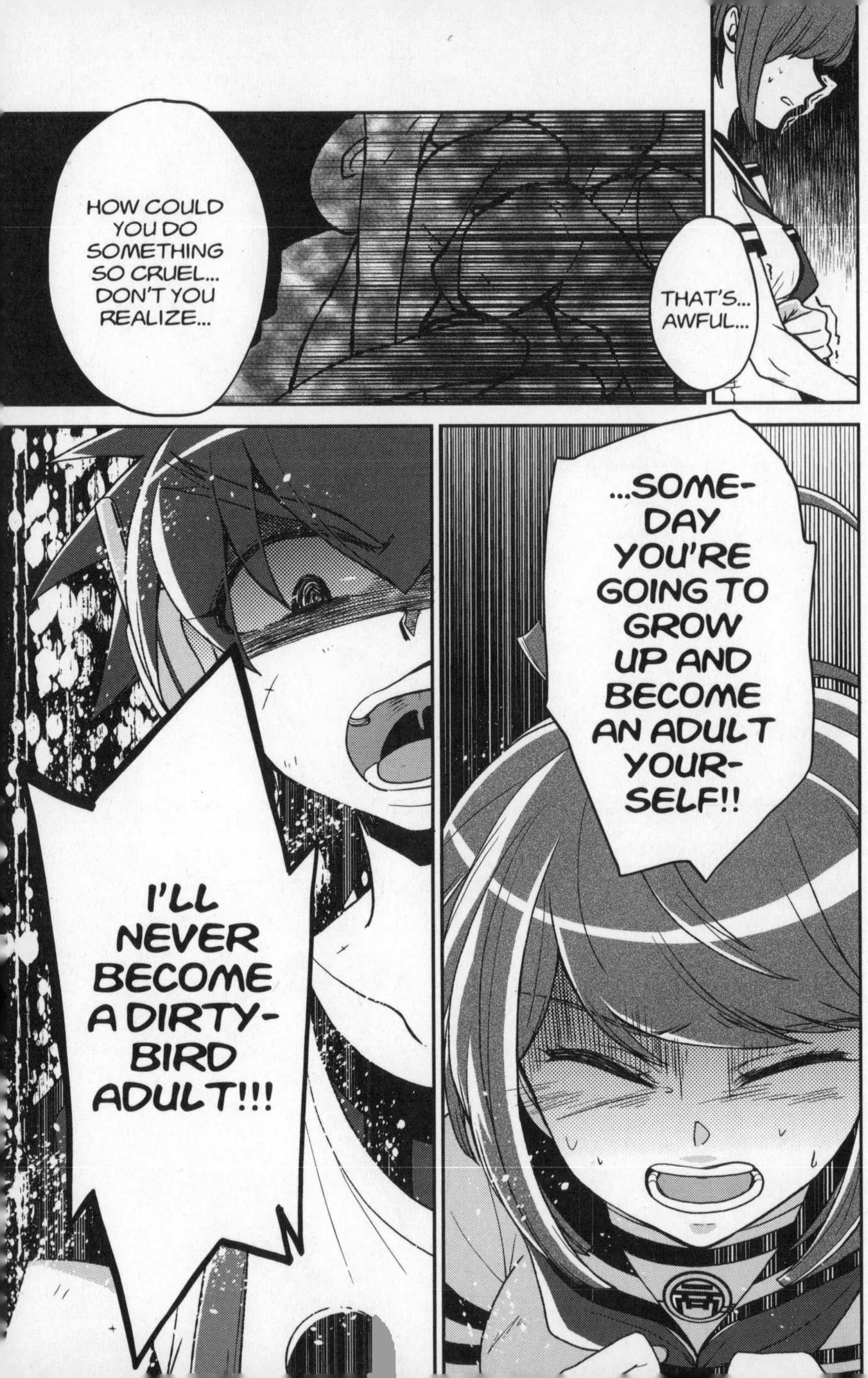
THAT'S... AWFUL...
HOW COULD YOU DO SOMETHING SO CRUEL... DON'T YOU REALIZE...
...SOME-DAY YOU'RE GOING TO GROW UP AND BECOME AN ADULT YOUR-SELF!!
I'LL NEVER BECOME A DIRTY-BIRD ADULT!!!

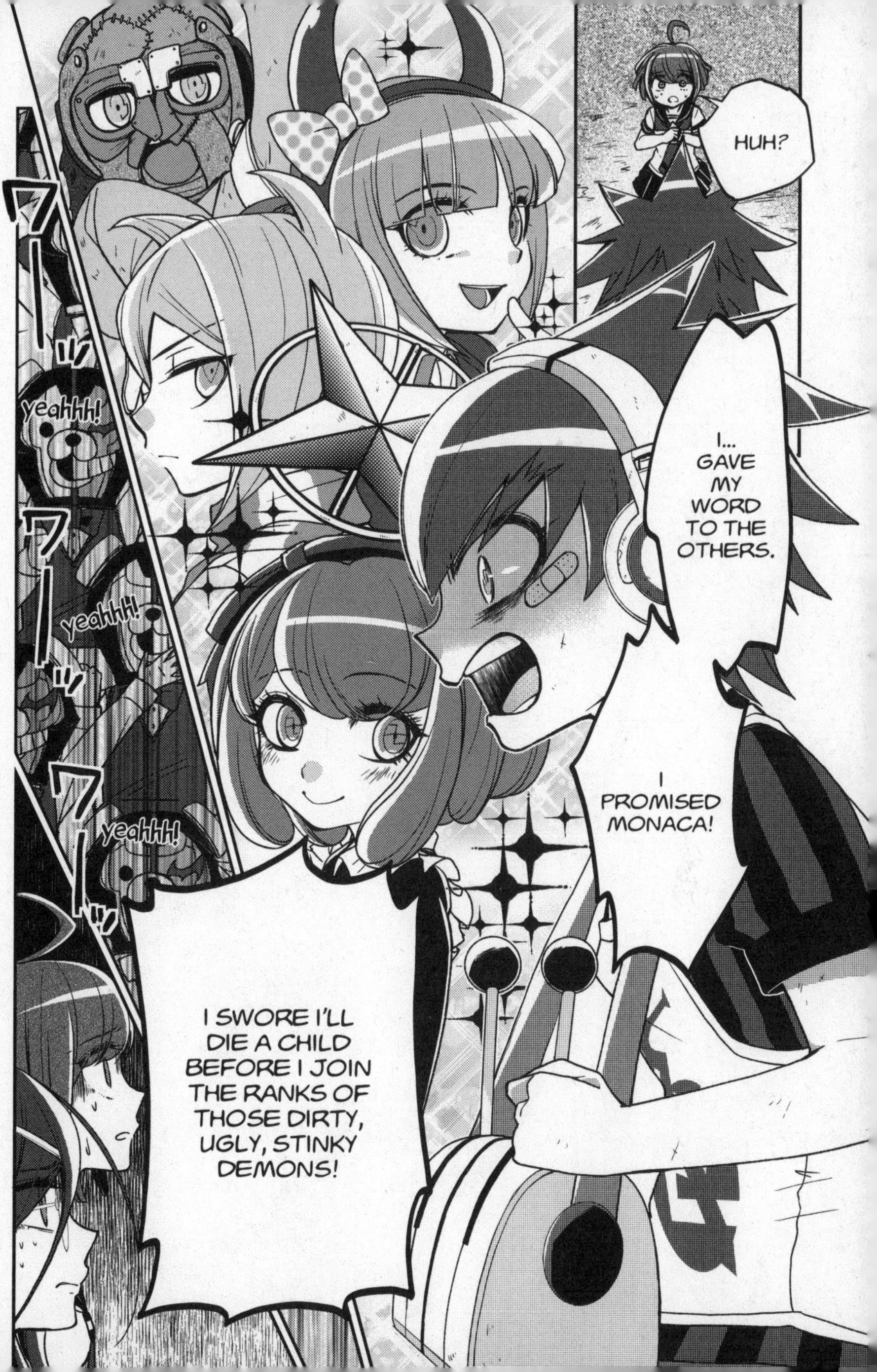
HUH?
I... GAVE MY WORD TO THE OTHERS.
I PROMISED MONACA!
yeahhh!
yeahhh!
yeahhh!
I SWORE I'LL DIE A CHILD BEFORE I JOIN THE RANKS OF THOSE DIRTY, UGLY, STINKY DEMONS!

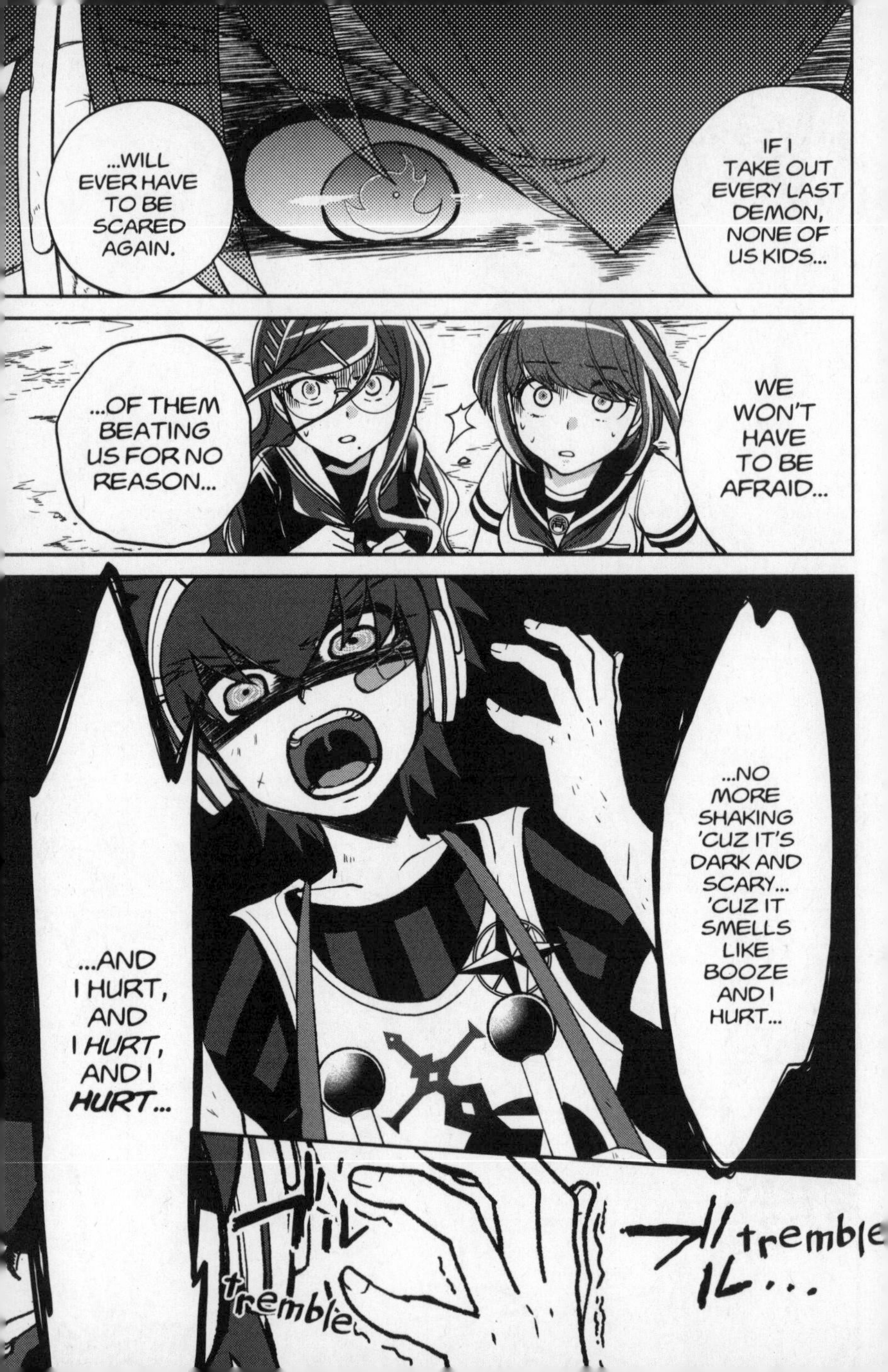
IF I TAKE OUT EVERY LAST DEMON, NONE OF US KIDS...
...WILL EVER HAVE TO BE SCARED AGAIN.
WE WON'T HAVE TO BE AFRAID...
...OF THEM BEATING US FOR NO REASON...
...NO MORE SHAKING 'CUZ IT'S DARK AND SCARY... 'CUZ IT SMELLS LIKE BOOZE AND I HURT...
...AND I HURT, AND I *HURT*, AND I ***HURT***...
tremble
tremble

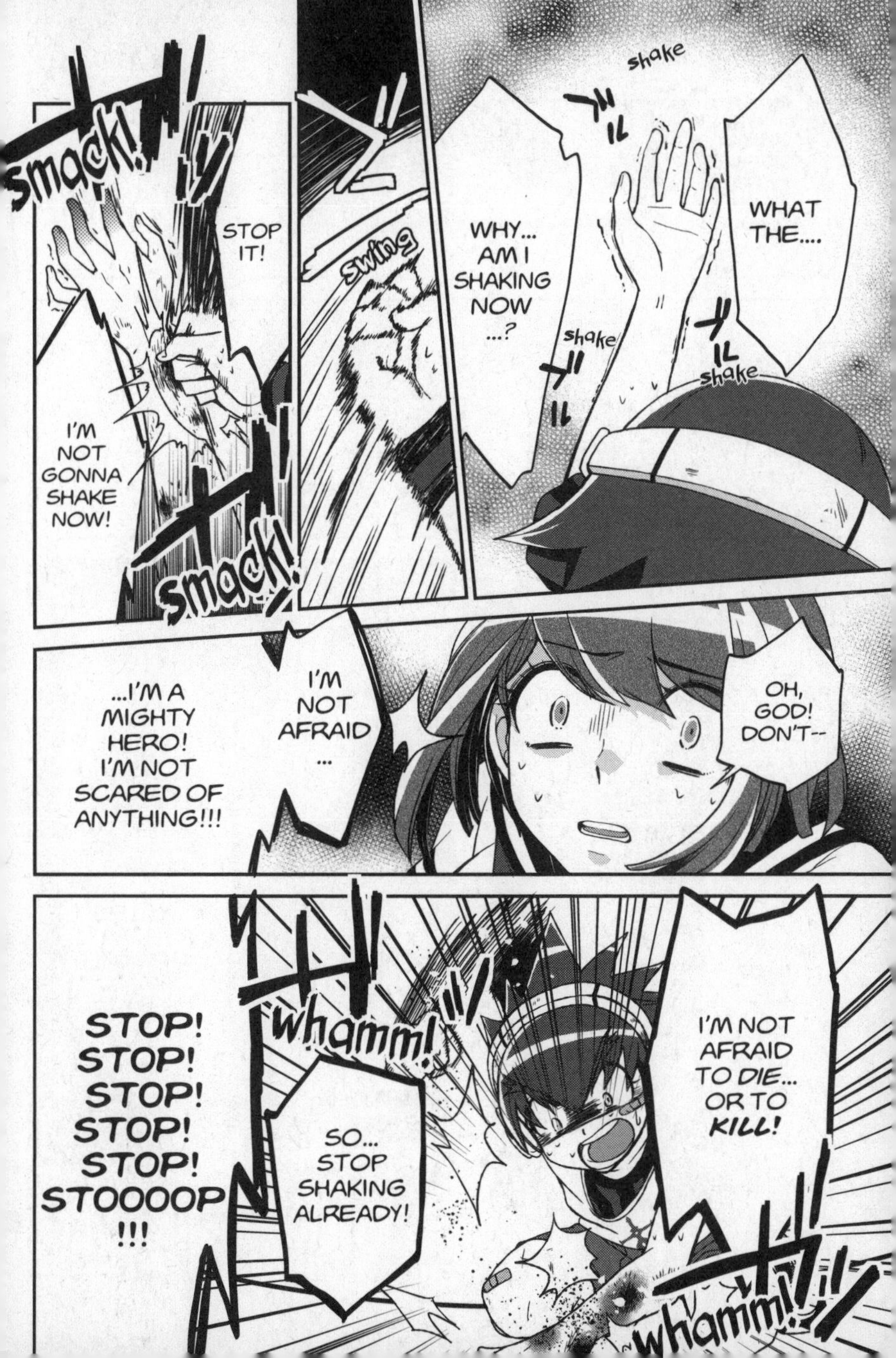
shake
WHAT THE....
WHY... AM I SHAKING NOW ...?
shake
shake
swing
smack!
STOP IT!
I'M NOT GONNA SHAKE NOW!
smack!
OH, GOD! DON'T--
I'M NOT AFRAID ...
...I'M A MIGHTY HERO! I'M NOT SCARED OF ANYTHING!!!
I'M NOT AFRAID TO DIE... OR TO KILL!
whamm!
SO... STOP SHAKING ALREADY!
whamm!
STOP! STOP! STOP! STOP! STOP! STOOOOP!!!

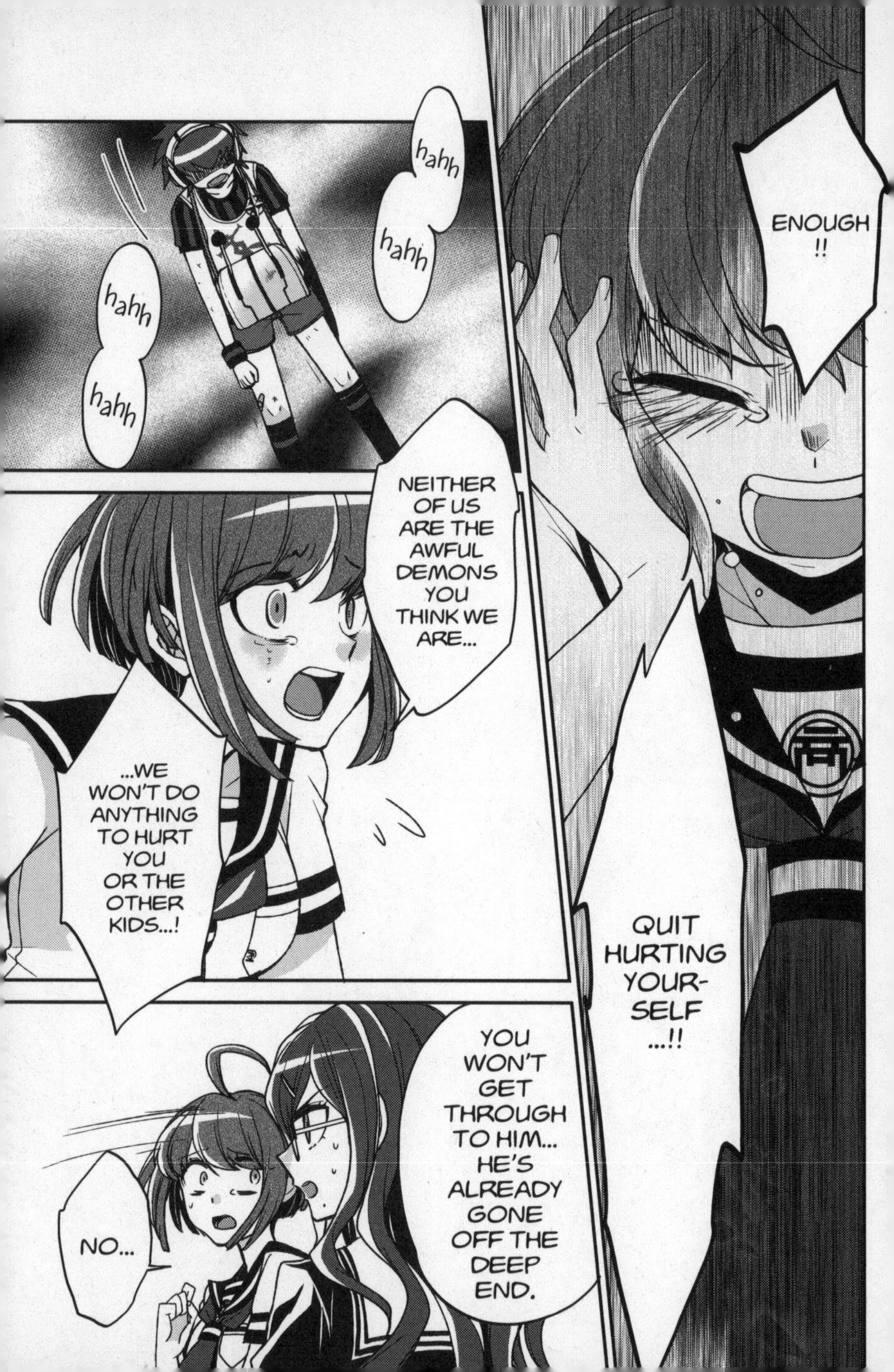
ENOUGH !!
QUIT HURTING YOUR-SELF ...!!
hahh
hahh
hahh
hahh
NEITHER OF US ARE THE AWFUL DEMONS YOU THINK WE ARE...
...WE WON'T DO ANYTHING TO HURT YOU OR THE OTHER KIDS...!
YOU WON'T GET THROUGH TO HIM... HE'S ALREADY GONE OFF THE DEEP END.
NO...

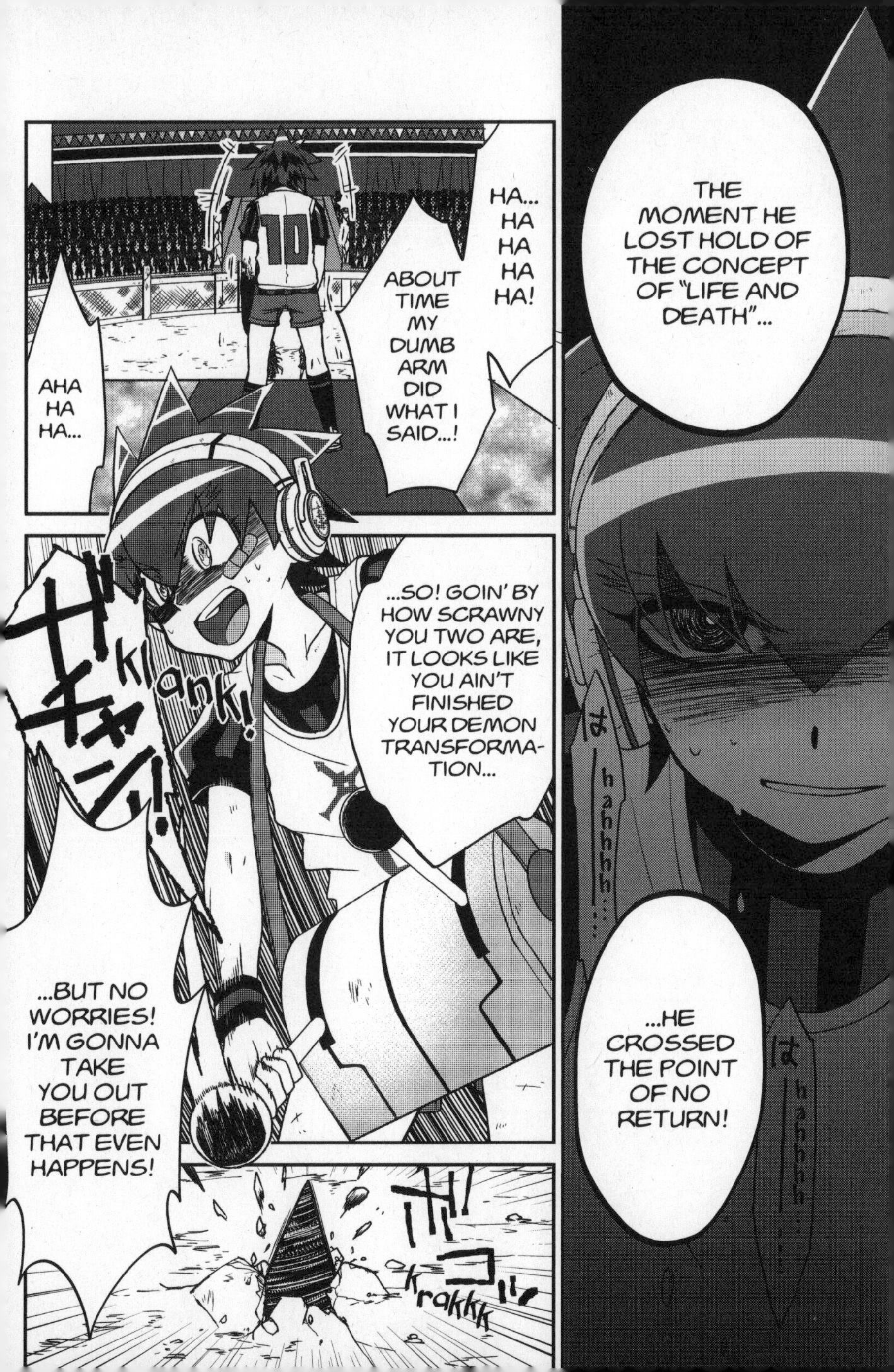
THE MOMENT HE LOST HOLD OF THE CONCEPT OF "LIFE AND DEATH"...
は— hahhhh...
...HE CROSSED THE POINT OF NO RETURN!
は— hahhhh...
HA... HA HA HA HA!
ABOUT TIME MY DUMB ARM DID WHAT I SAID...!
AHA HA HA...
...SO! GOIN' BY HOW SCRAWNY YOU TWO ARE, IT LOOKS LIKE YOU AIN'T FINISHED YOUR DEMON TRANSFORMATION...
klank!
...BUT NO WORRIES! I'M GONNA TAKE YOU OUT BEFORE THAT EVEN HAPPENS!
krakkk

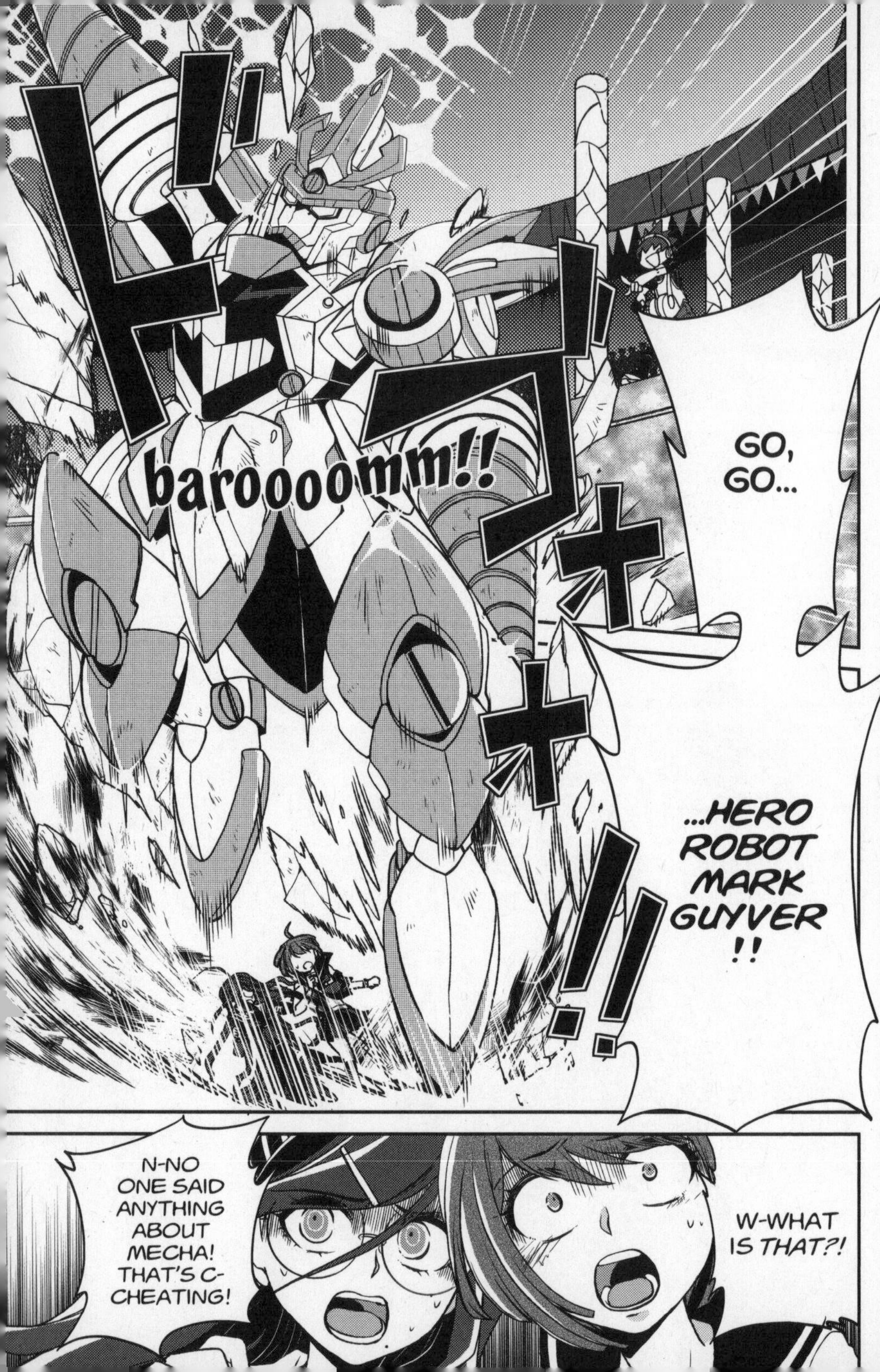
GO, GO...
...HERO ROBOT MARK GUYVER!!
baroooomm!!
W-WHAT IS THAT?!
N-NO ONE SAID ANYTHING ABOUT MECHA! THAT'S C-CHEATING!

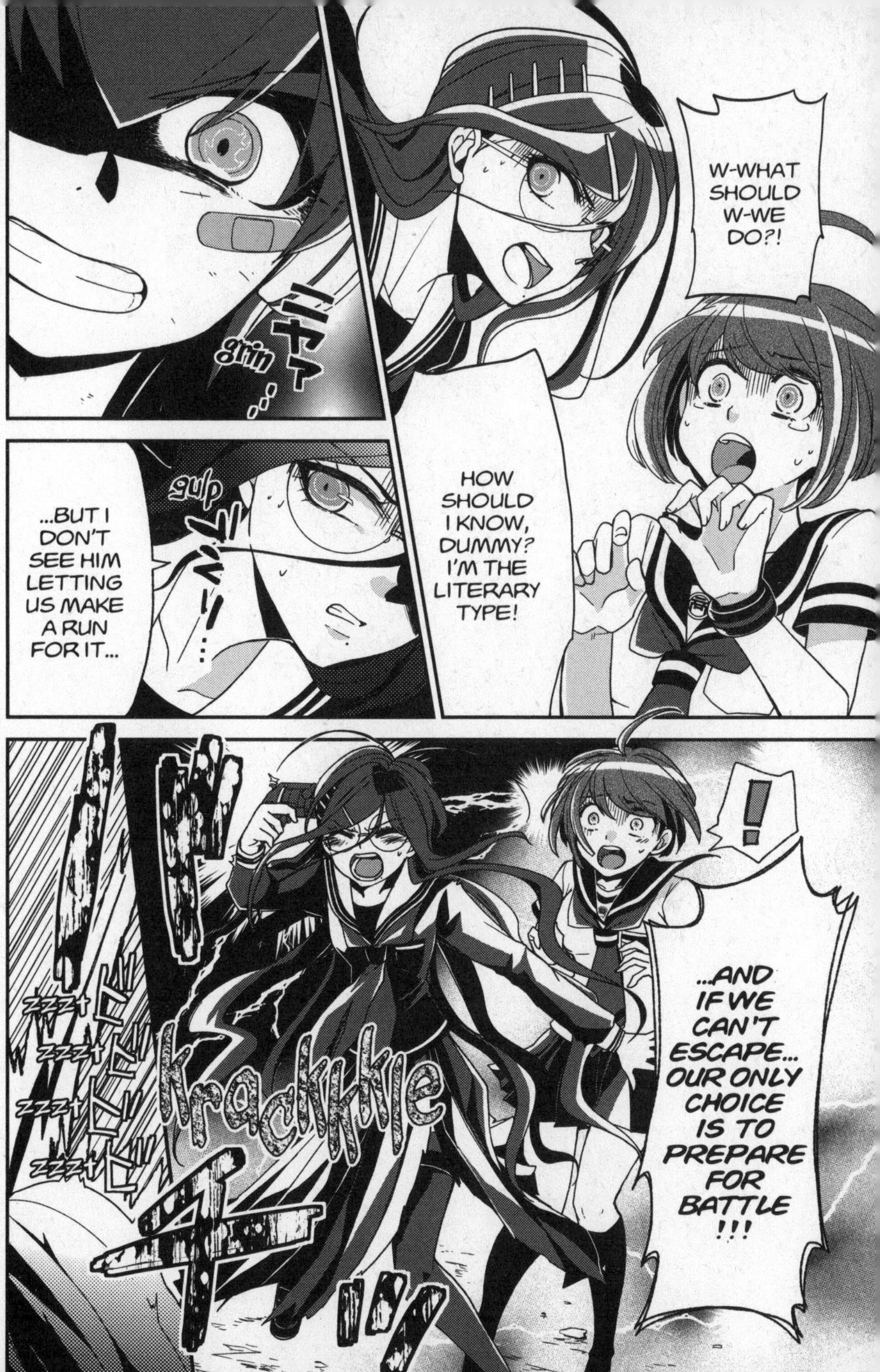
W-WHAT SHOULD W-WE DO?!
HOW SHOULD I KNOW, DUMMY? I'M THE LITERARY TYPE!
grin
...BUT I DON'T SEE HIM LETTING US MAKE A RUN FOR IT...
gulp
!
...AND IF WE CAN'T ESCAPE... OUR ONLY CHOICE IS TO PREPARE FOR BATTLE!!!
krackkle

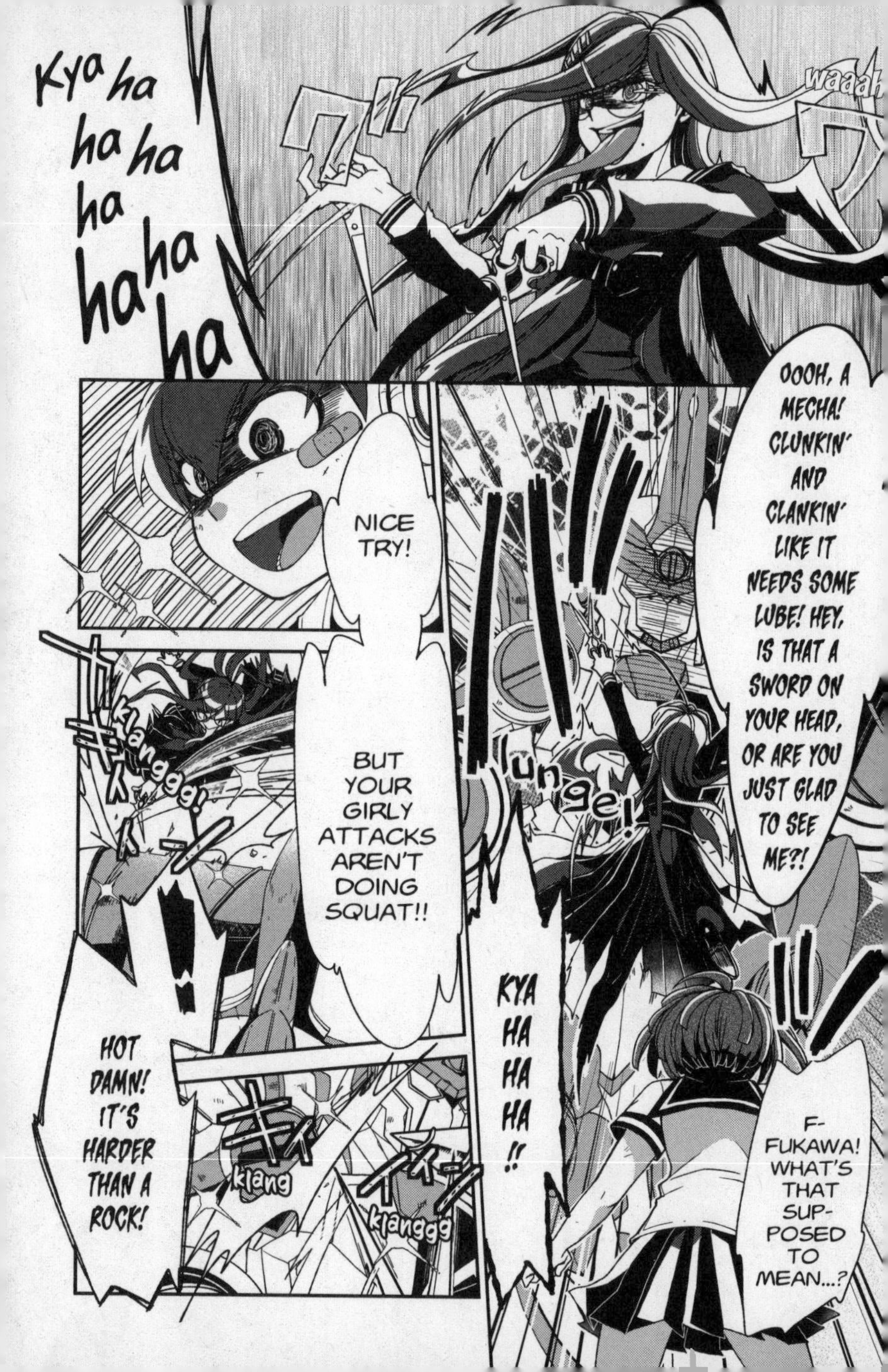
Kya ha ha ha ha ha hahaha ha
waaah
OOOH, A MECHA! CLUNKIN' AND CLANKIN' LIKE IT NEEDS SOME LUBE! HEY, IS THAT A SWORD ON YOUR HEAD, OR ARE YOU JUST GLAD TO SEE ME?!
lunge!
KYA HA HA HA HA !!
F-FUKAWA! WHAT'S THAT SUP-POSED TO MEAN...?
NICE TRY!
BUT YOUR GIRLY ATTACKS AREN'T DOING SQUAT!!
klanggg!
HOT DAMN! IT'S HARDER THAN A ROCK!
klang
klanggg

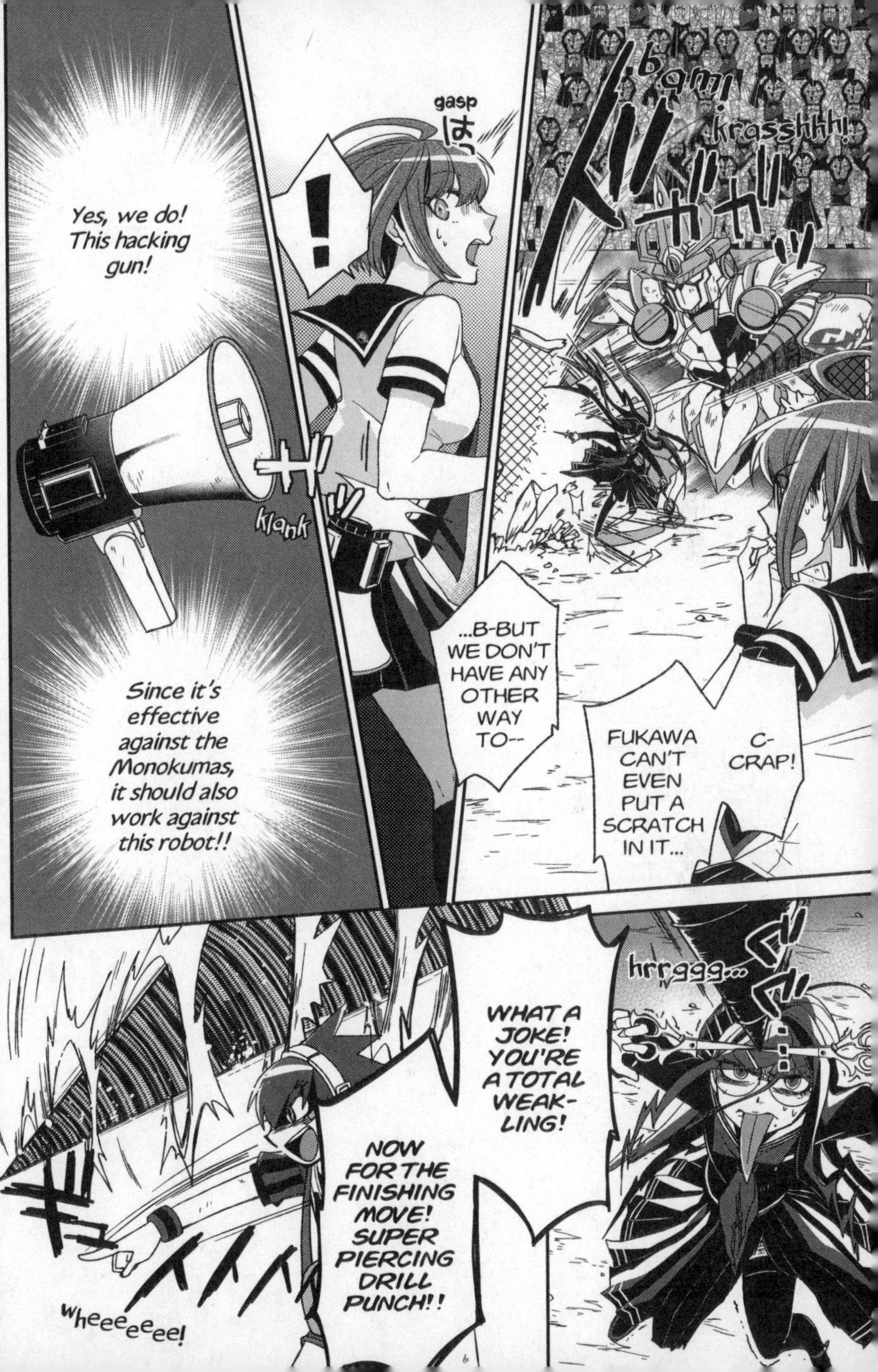
bam!
krasshhh!
C-CRAP!
FUKAWA CAN'T EVEN PUT A SCRATCH IN IT...
...B-BUT WE DON'T HAVE ANY OTHER WAY TO--
gasp
はっ
!
Yes, we do! This hacking gun!
klank
Since it's effective against the Monokumas, it should also work against this robot!!
hrrggg...
WHAT A JOKE! YOU'RE A TOTAL WEAK-LING!
NOW FOR THE FINISHING MOVE! SUPER PIERCING DRILL PUNCH!!
wheeeeeee!

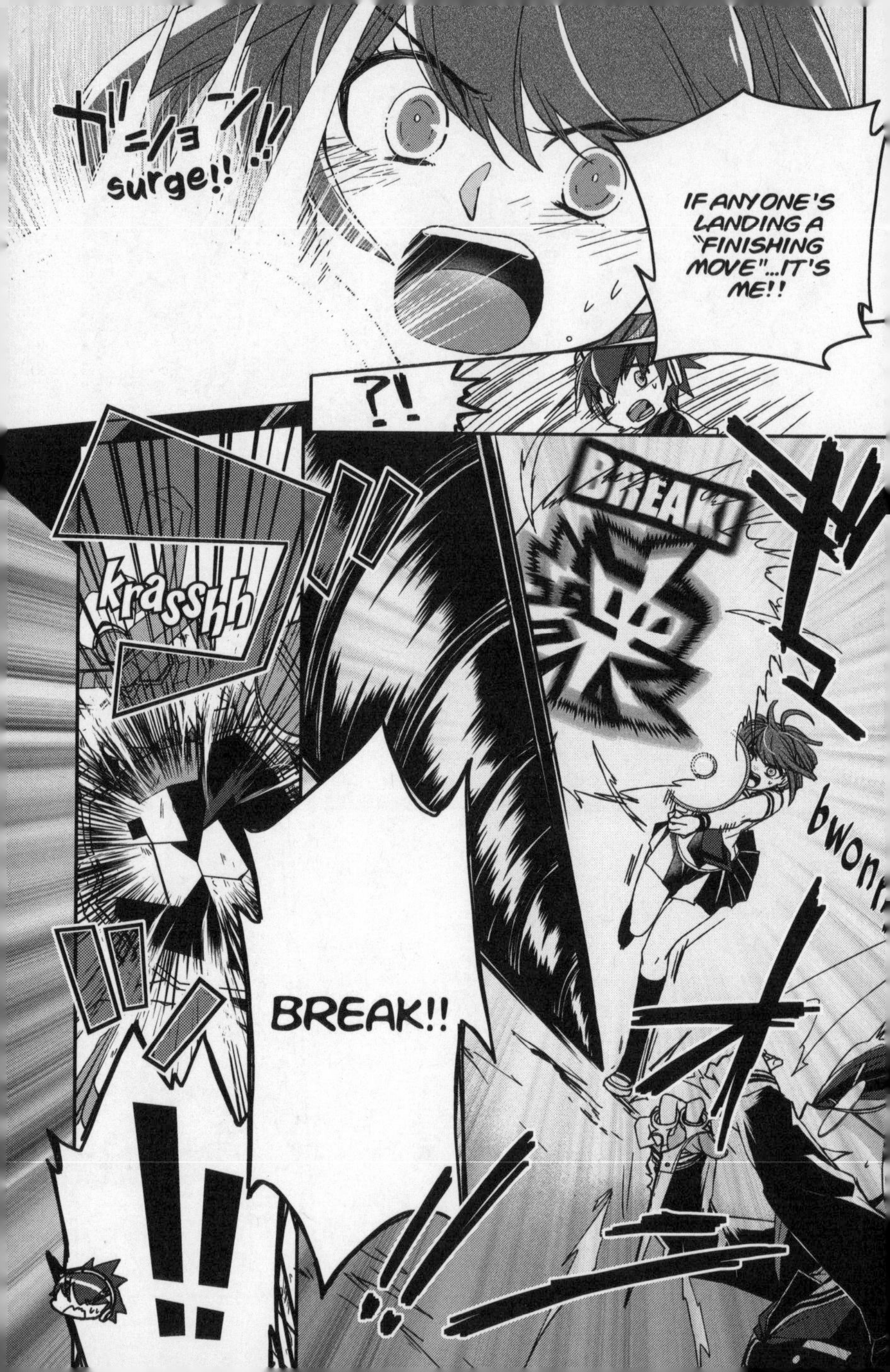
IF ANYONE'S LANDING A "FINISHING MOVE"...IT'S ME!!
surge!!
?!
BREAK!
bwonn
krasshh
BREAK!!

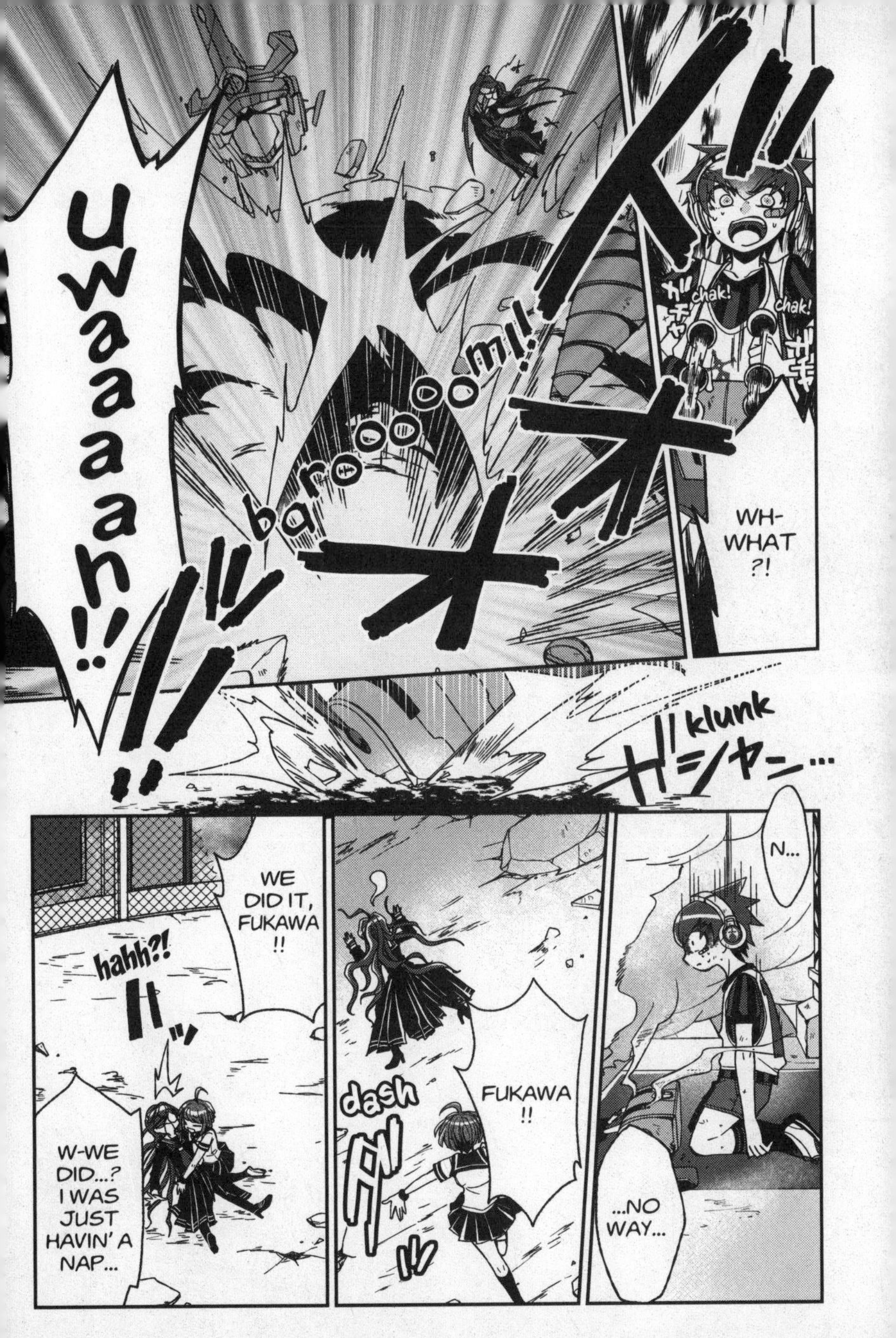
chak!
chak!
WH-WHAT?!
baroooom!!
Uwaaaaah!!
klunk
N...
...NO WAY...
dash
FUKAWA!!
WE DID IT, FUKAWA!!
hahh?!
W-WE DID...? I WAS JUST HAVIN' A NAP...

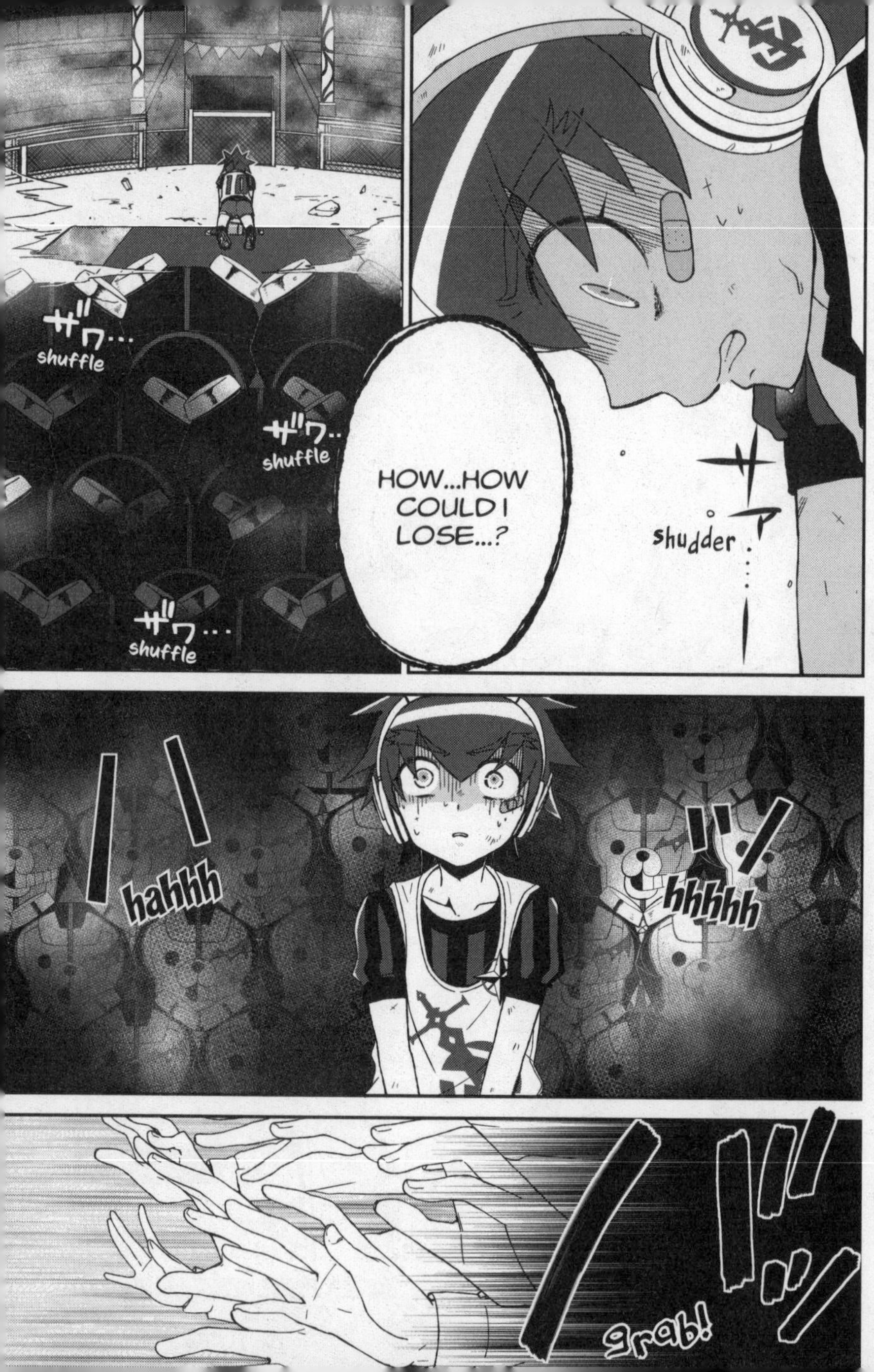
shudder
HOW...HOW COULD I LOSE...?
ザワ… shuffle
ザワ… shuffle
ザワ… shuffle
hahhh
hhhhh
grab!

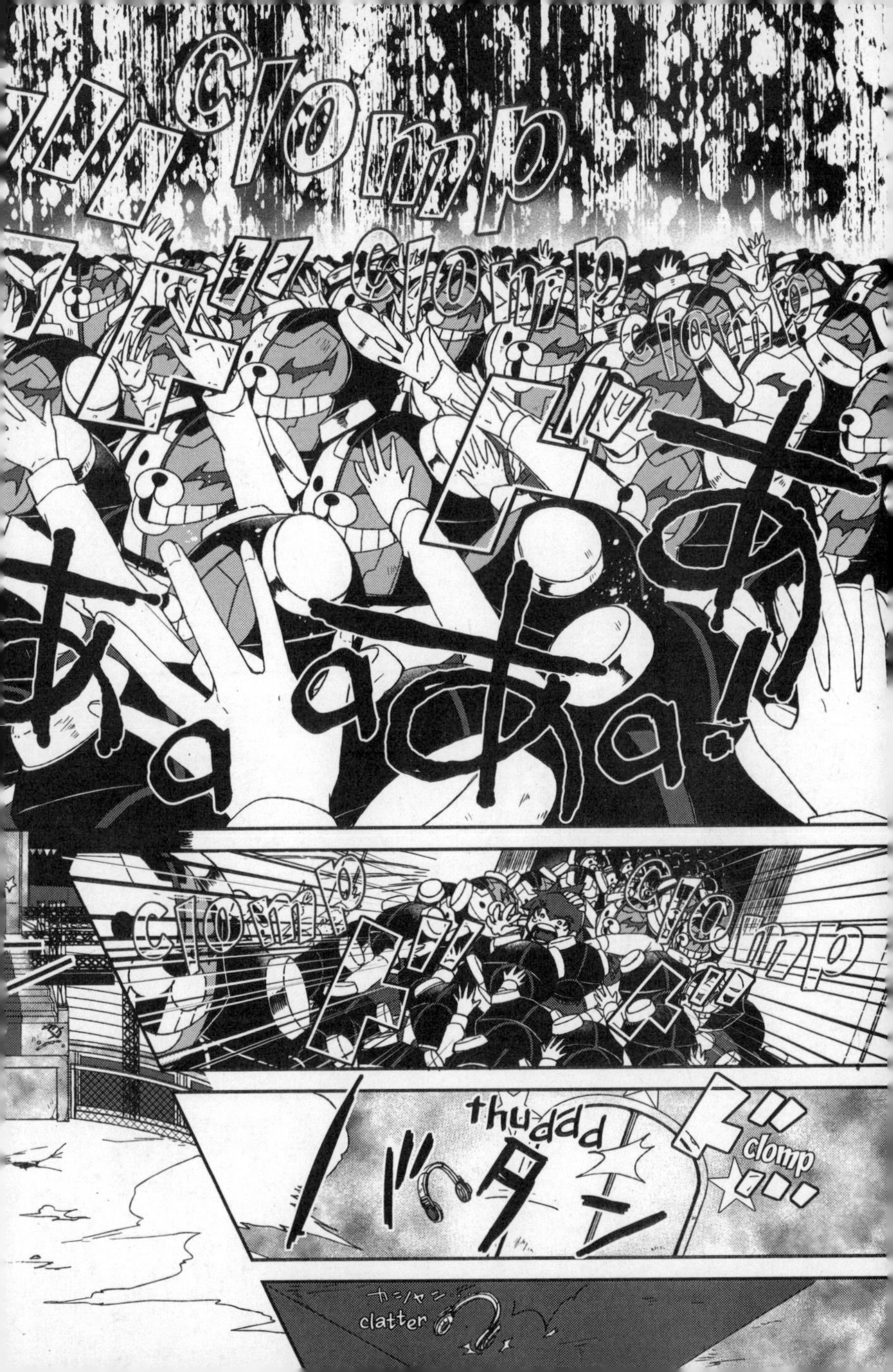
clomp
clomp
clomp
aaaa!
clomp
clomp
thuddd
clomp
clatter

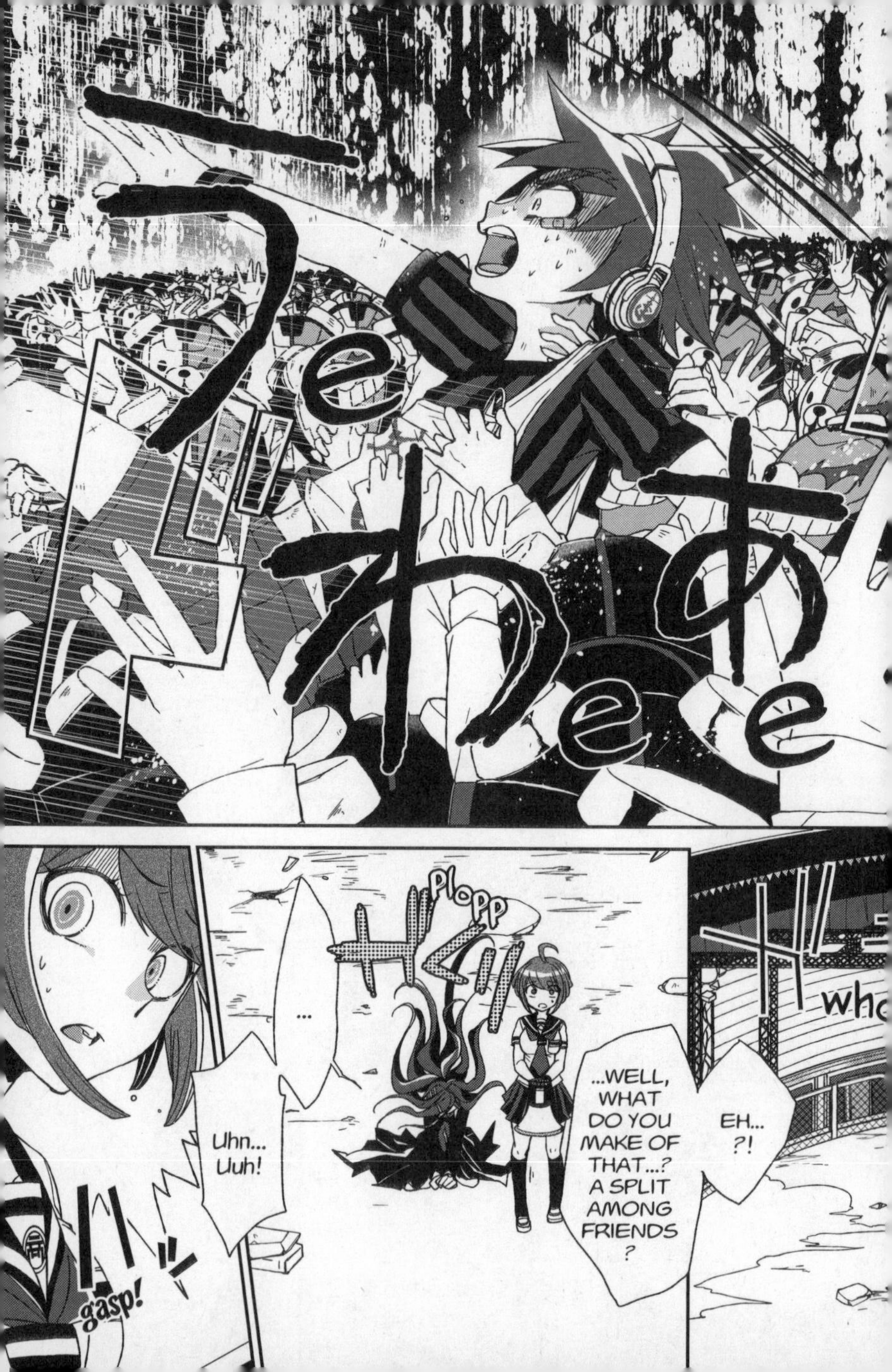
who
EH... ?!
...WELL, WHAT DO YOU MAKE OF THAT...? A SPLIT AMONG FRIENDS ?
Plopp
...
Uhn... Uuh!
gasp!

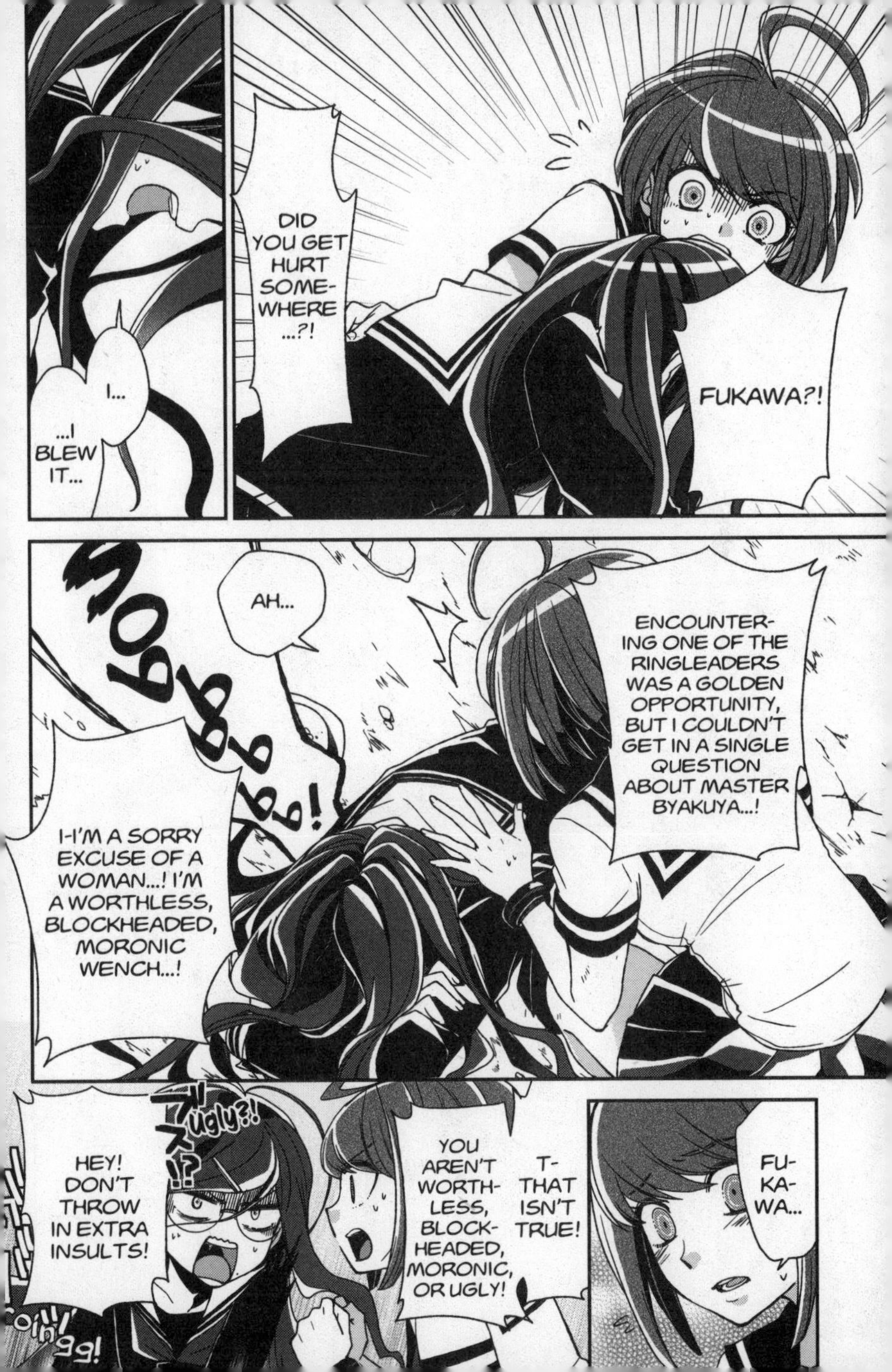
FUKAWA?!
DID YOU GET HURT SOME-WHERE ...?!
I...
...I BLEW IT...
ENCOUNTER-ING ONE OF THE RINGLEADERS WAS A GOLDEN OPPORTUNITY, BUT I COULDN'T GET IN A SINGLE QUESTION ABOUT MASTER BYAKUYA...!
AH...
I-I'M A SORRY EXCUSE OF A WOMAN...! I'M A WORTHLESS, BLOCKHEADED, MORONIC WENCH...!
FU-KA-WA...
T-THAT ISN'T TRUE!
YOU AREN'T WORTH-LESS, BLOCK-HEADED, MORONIC, OR UGLY!
ブス!?
ugly?!
HEY! DON'T THROW IN EXTRA INSULTS!

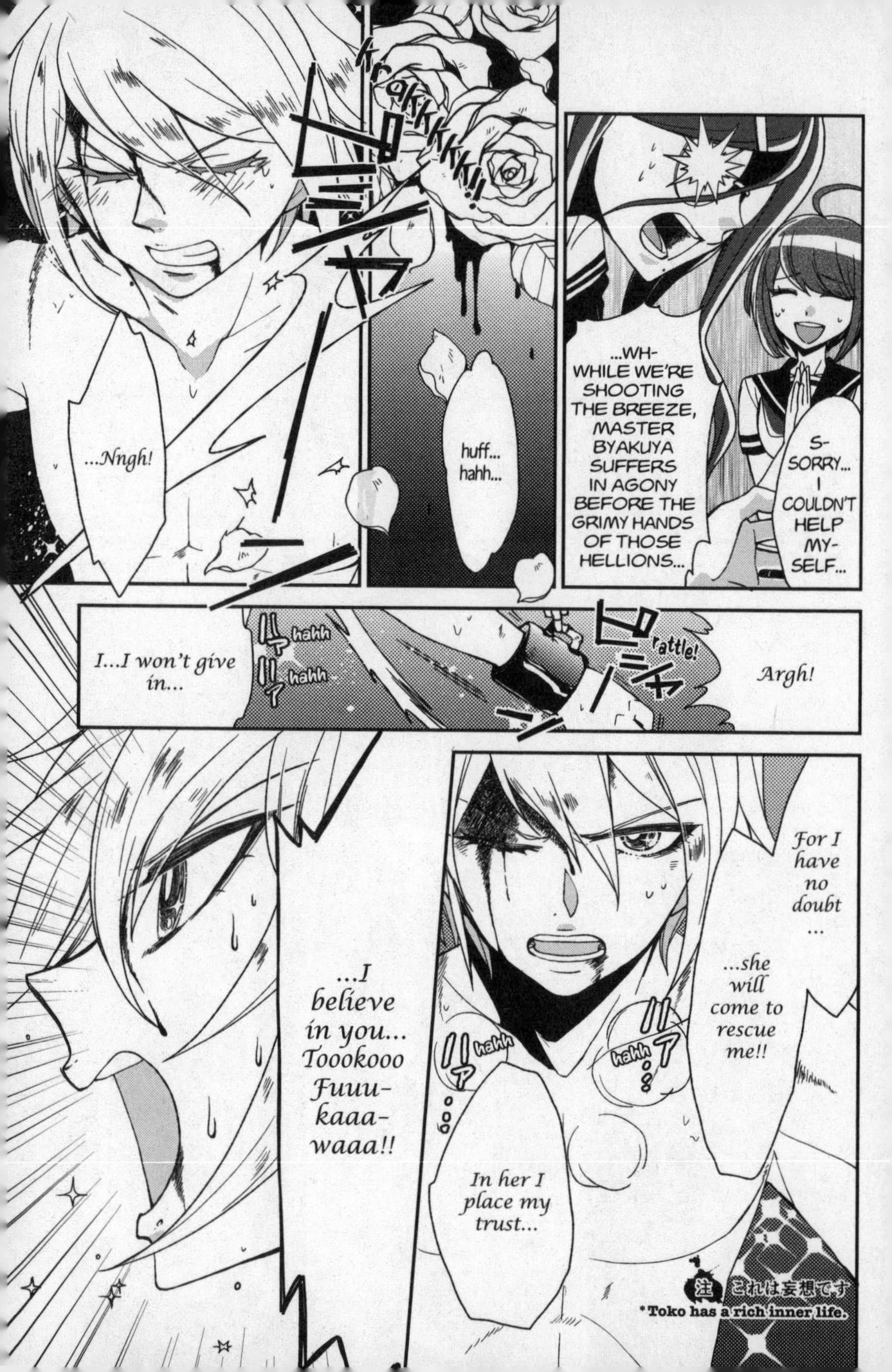
...WH- WHILE WE'RE SHOOTING THE BREEZE, MASTER BYAKUYA SUFFERS IN AGONY BEFORE THE GRIMY HANDS OF THOSE HELLIONS...
S- SORRY... I COULDN'T HELP MY- SELF...
krakkkkkk!!
huff... hahh...
...Nngh!
Argh!
rattle!
hahh
hahh
I...I won't give in...
For I have no doubt...
...she will come to rescue me!!
hahh
hahh
In her I place my trust...
...I believe in you... Toookooo Fuuu- kaaa- waaa!!
注 これは妄想です
*Toko has a rich inner life.

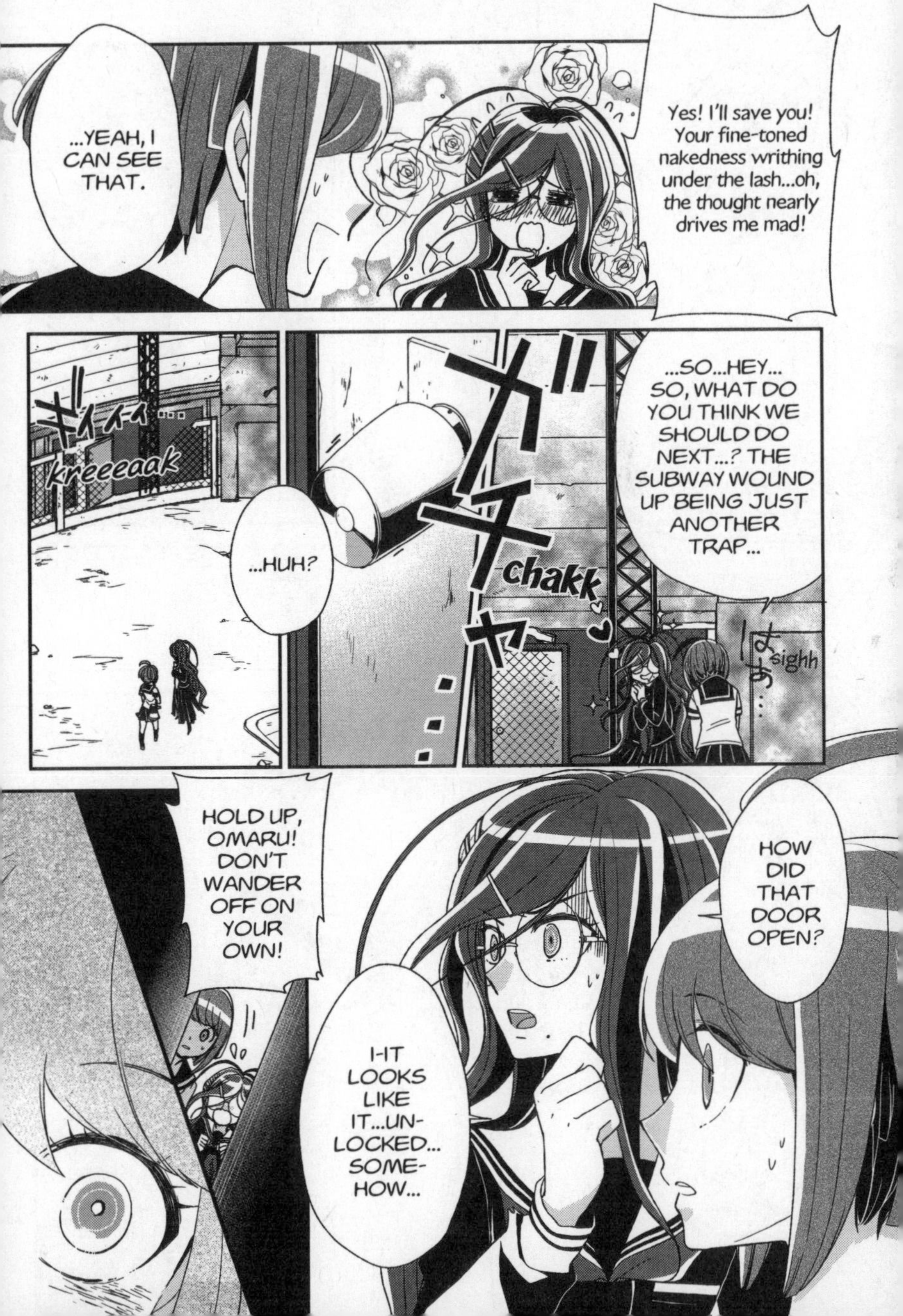
Yes! I'll save you! Your fine-toned nakedness writhing under the lash...oh, the thought nearly drives me mad!
...YEAH, I CAN SEE THAT.
...SO...HEY... SO, WHAT DO YOU THINK WE SHOULD DO NEXT...? THE SUBWAY WOUND UP BEING JUST ANOTHER TRAP...
はあ
sighh
ガチャ
chakk
...HUH?
ギィイイ
kreeeaak
HOW DID THAT DOOR OPEN?
I-IT LOOKS LIKE IT...UN-LOCKED... SOME-HOW...
HOLD UP, OMARU! DON'T WANDER OFF ON YOUR OWN!

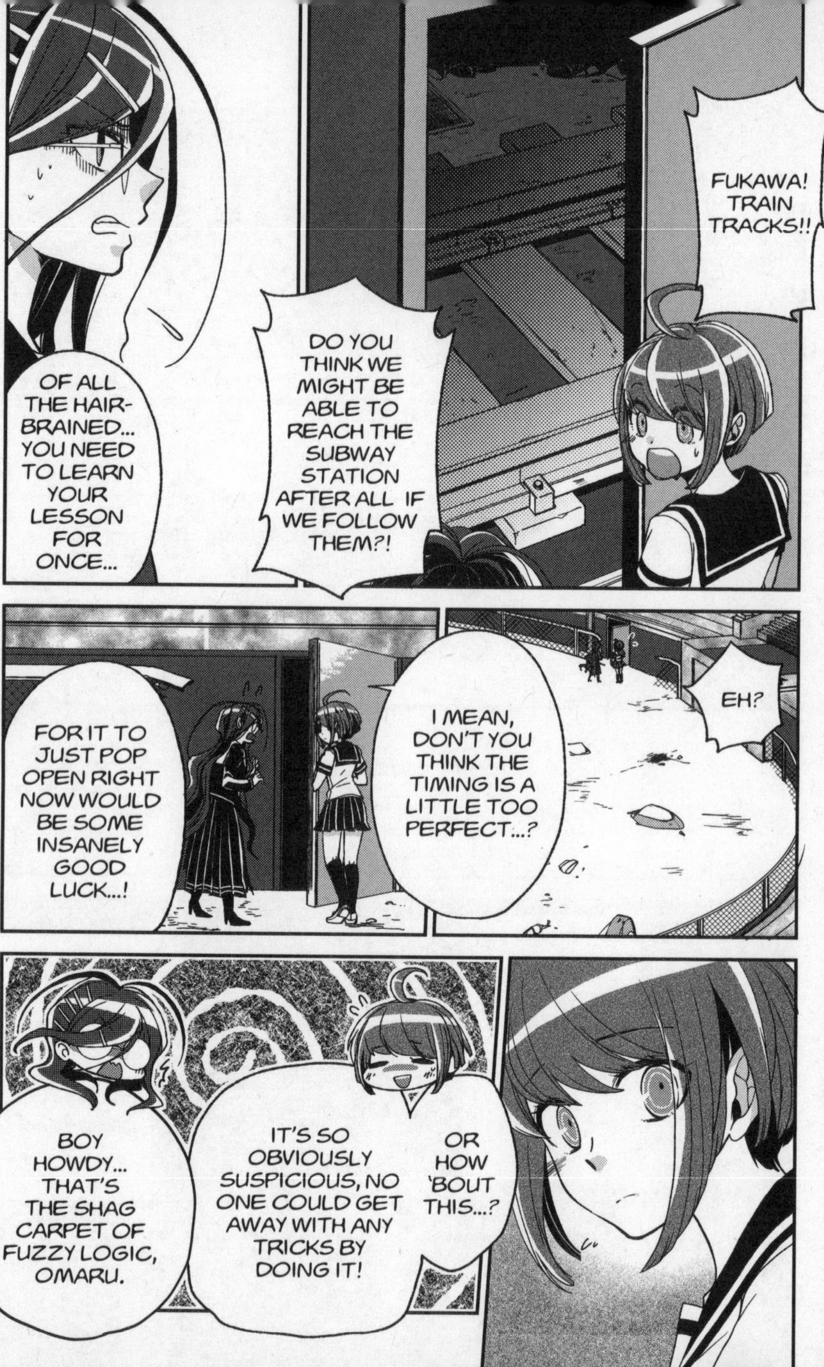
FUKAWA! TRAIN TRACKS!!
DO YOU THINK WE MIGHT BE ABLE TO REACH THE SUBWAY STATION AFTER ALL IF WE FOLLOW THEM?!
OF ALL THE HAIR-BRAINED... YOU NEED TO LEARN YOUR LESSON FOR ONCE...
EH?
I MEAN, DON'T YOU THINK THE TIMING IS A LITTLE TOO PERFECT...?
FOR IT TO JUST POP OPEN RIGHT NOW WOULD BE SOME INSANELY GOOD LUCK...!
OR HOW 'BOUT THIS...?
IT'S SO OBVIOUSLY SUSPICIOUS, NO ONE COULD GET AWAY WITH ANY TRICKS BY DOING IT!
BOY HOWDY... THAT'S THE SHAG CARPET OF FUZZY LOGIC, OMARU.

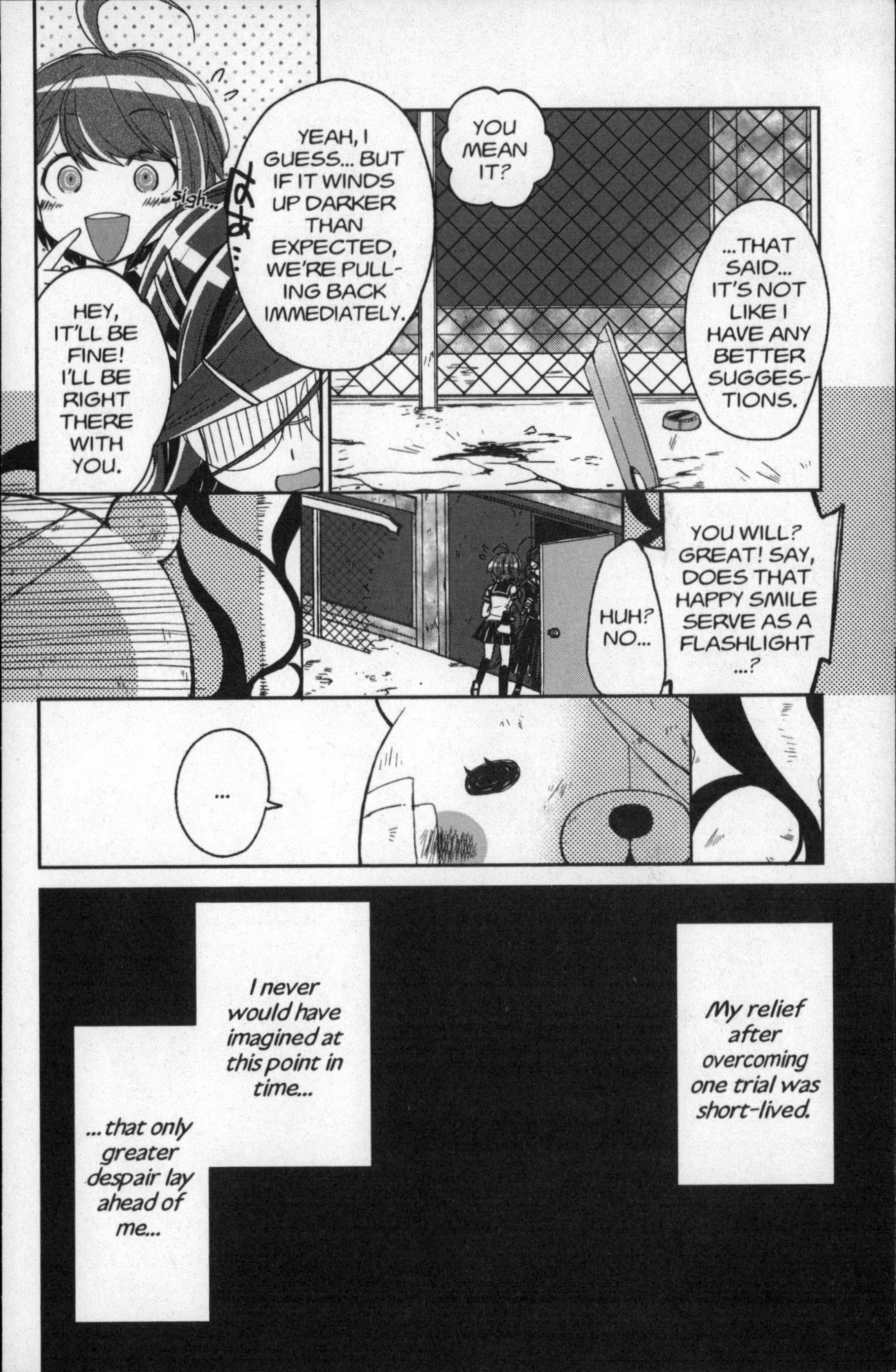
...THAT SAID... IT'S NOT LIKE I HAVE ANY BETTER SUGGESTIONS.
YOU MEAN IT?
YEAH, I GUESS... BUT IF IT WINDS UP DARKER THAN EXPECTED, WE'RE PULLING BACK IMMEDIATELY.
sigh...
HEY, IT'LL BE FINE! I'LL BE RIGHT THERE WITH YOU.
YOU WILL? GREAT! SAY, DOES THAT HAPPY SMILE SERVE AS A FLASHLIGHT ...?
HUH? NO...
...
My relief after overcoming one trial was short-lived.
I never would have imagined at this point in time...
...that only greater despair lay ahead of me...

Danganronpa Another Episode:
Ultra Despair Girls

Danganronpa Another Episode:
Ultra Despair Girls

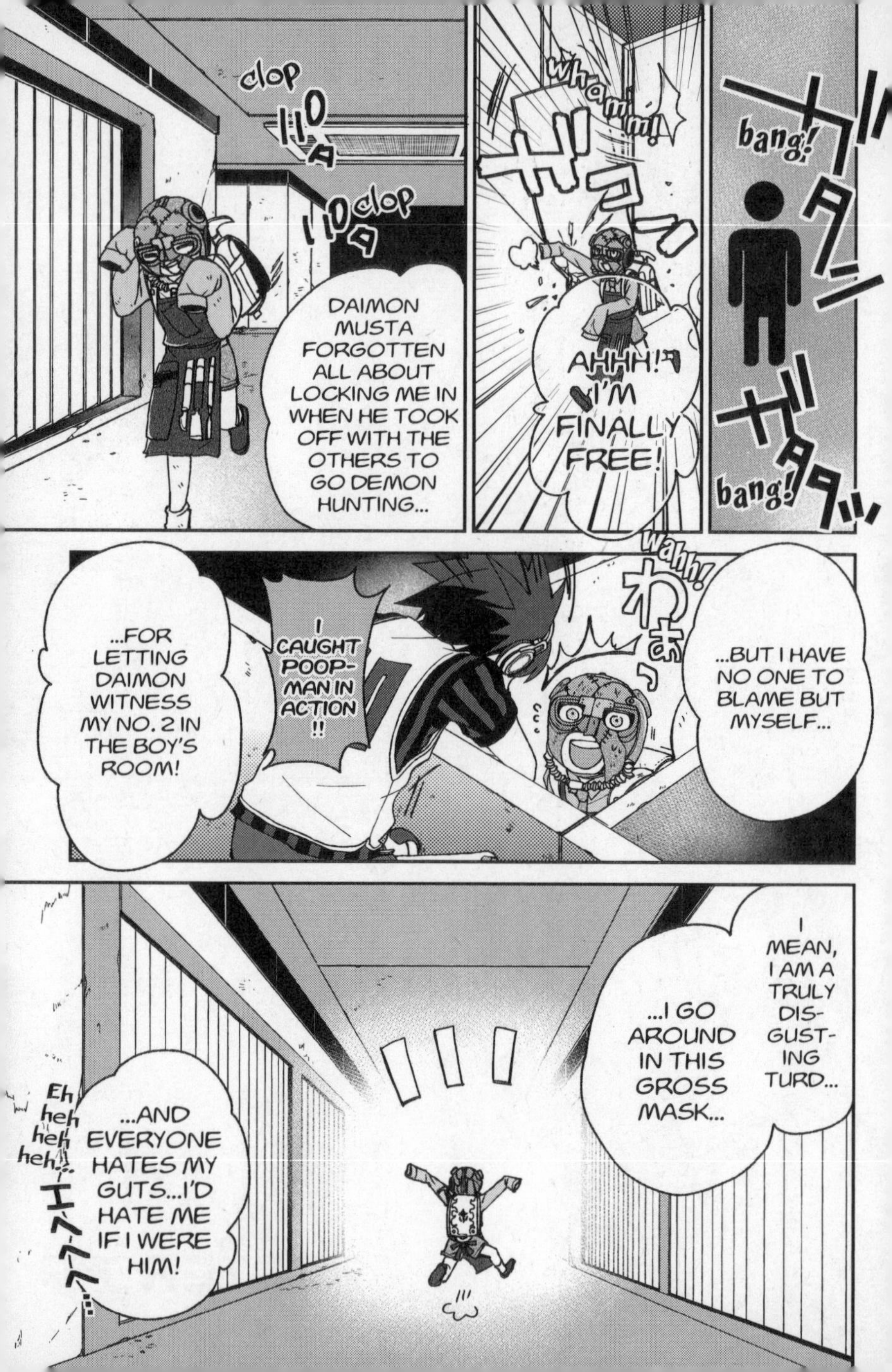
bang!
bang!
whammm!
AHHH! I'M FINALLY FREE!
clop
clop
DAIMON MUSTA FORGOTTEN ALL ABOUT LOCKING ME IN WHEN HE TOOK OFF WITH THE OTHERS TO GO DEMON HUNTING...
wahh!
...BUT I HAVE NO ONE TO BLAME BUT MYSELF...
I CAUGHT POOP-MAN IN ACTION!!
...FOR LETTING DAIMON WITNESS MY NO. 2 IN THE BOY'S ROOM!
I MEAN, I AM A TRULY DIS-GUST-ING TURD...
...I GO AROUND IN THIS GROSS MASK...
...AND EVERYONE HATES MY GUTS...I'D HATE ME IF I WERE HIM!
Eh heh heh heh...!!

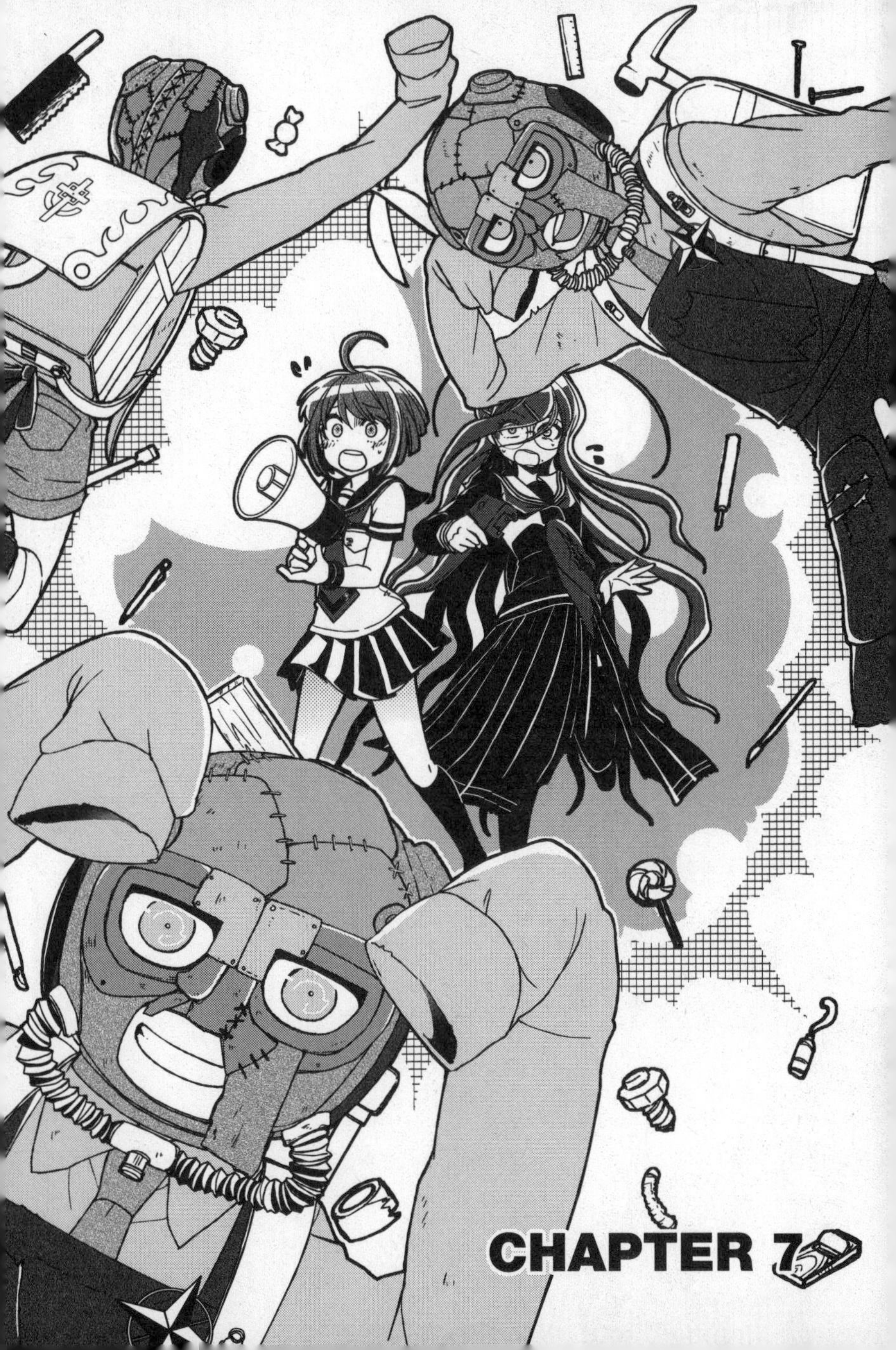
CHAPTER 7

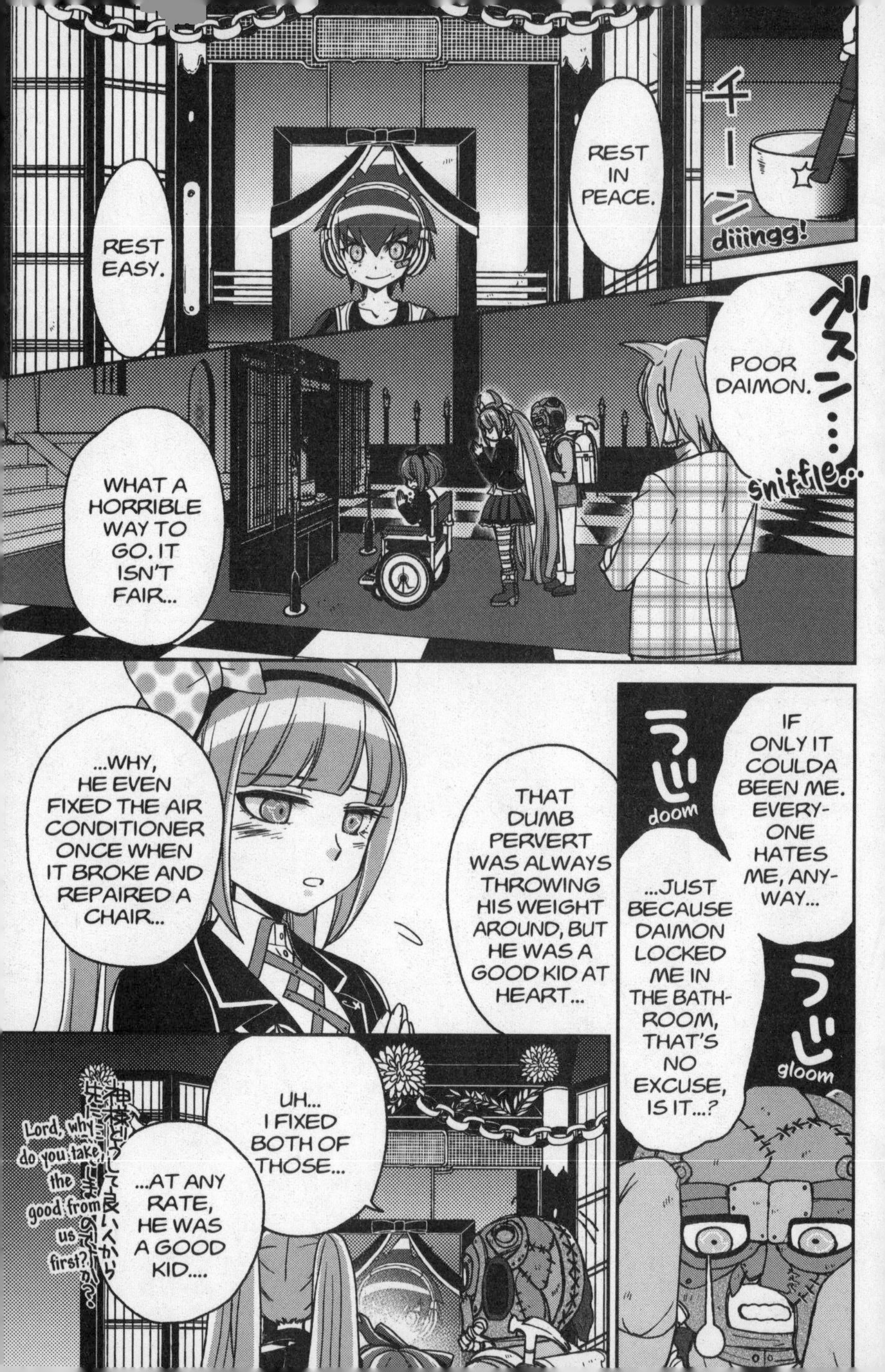
diiingg!
REST IN PEACE.
REST EASY.
POOR DAIMON.
sniffle...
WHAT A HORRIBLE WAY TO GO. IT ISN'T FAIR...
IF ONLY IT COULDA BEEN ME. EVERYONE HATES ME, ANYWAY...
doom
gloom
...JUST BECAUSE DAIMON LOCKED ME IN THE BATHROOM, THAT'S NO EXCUSE, IS IT...?
THAT DUMB PERVERT WAS ALWAYS THROWING HIS WEIGHT AROUND, BUT HE WAS A GOOD KID AT HEART...
...WHY, HE EVEN FIXED THE AIR CONDITIONER ONCE WHEN IT BROKE AND REPAIRED A CHAIR...
UH... I FIXED BOTH OF THOSE...
...AT ANY RATE, HE WAS A GOOD KID....
Lord, why do you take the good from us first?

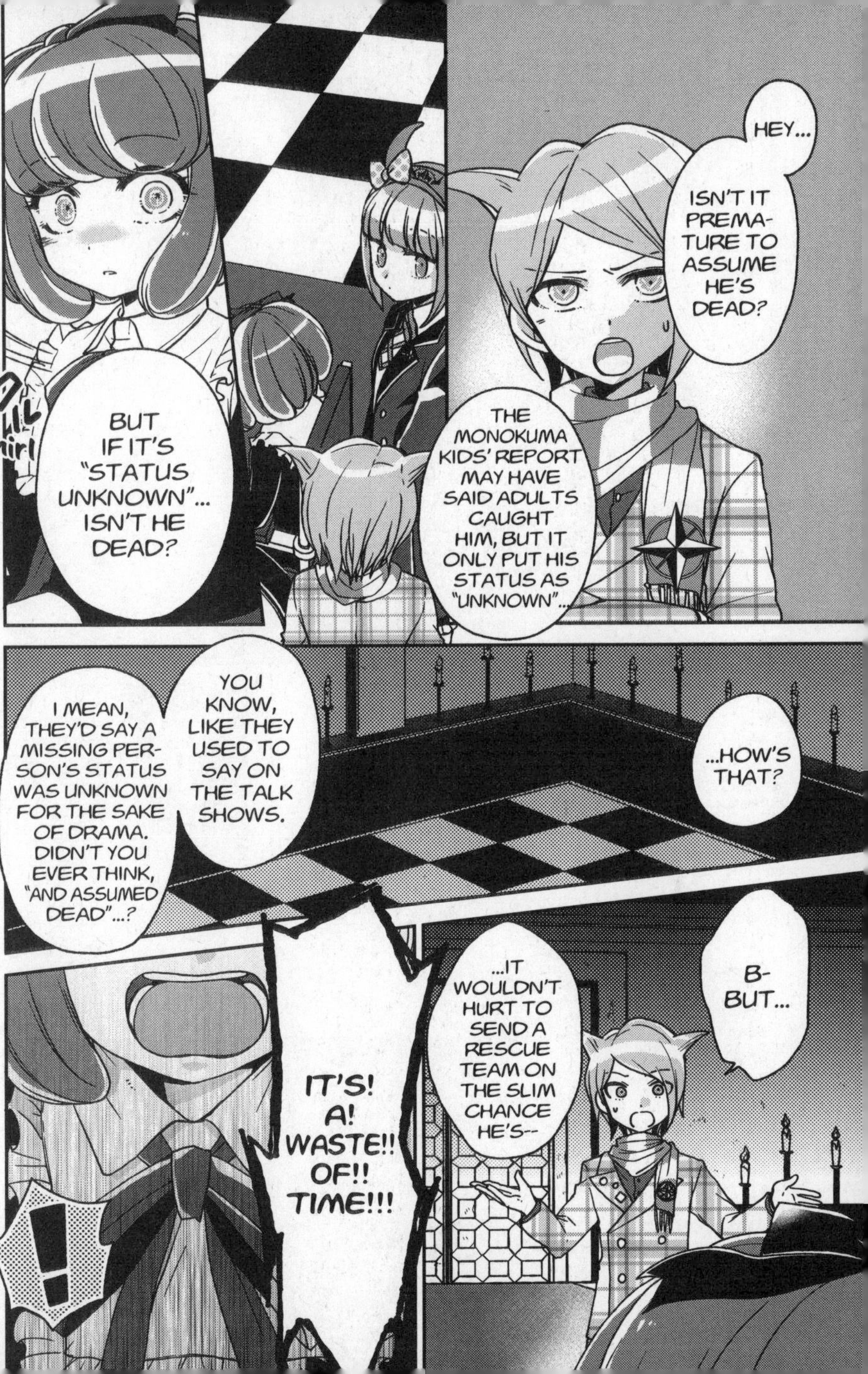
HEY...
ISN'T IT PREMATURE TO ASSUME HE'S DEAD?
THE MONOKUMA KIDS' REPORT MAY HAVE SAID ADULTS CAUGHT HIM, BUT IT ONLY PUT HIS STATUS AS "UNKNOWN"...
BUT IF IT'S "STATUS UNKNOWN"... ISN'T HE DEAD?
...HOW'S THAT?
YOU KNOW, LIKE THEY USED TO SAY ON THE TALK SHOWS.
I MEAN, THEY'D SAY A MISSING PERSON'S STATUS WAS UNKNOWN FOR THE SAKE OF DRAMA. DIDN'T YOU EVER THINK, "AND ASSUMED DEAD"...?
B-BUT...
...IT WOULDN'T HURT TO SEND A RESCUE TEAM ON THE SLIM CHANCE HE'S--
IT'S! A! WASTE!! OF!! TIME!!!
!

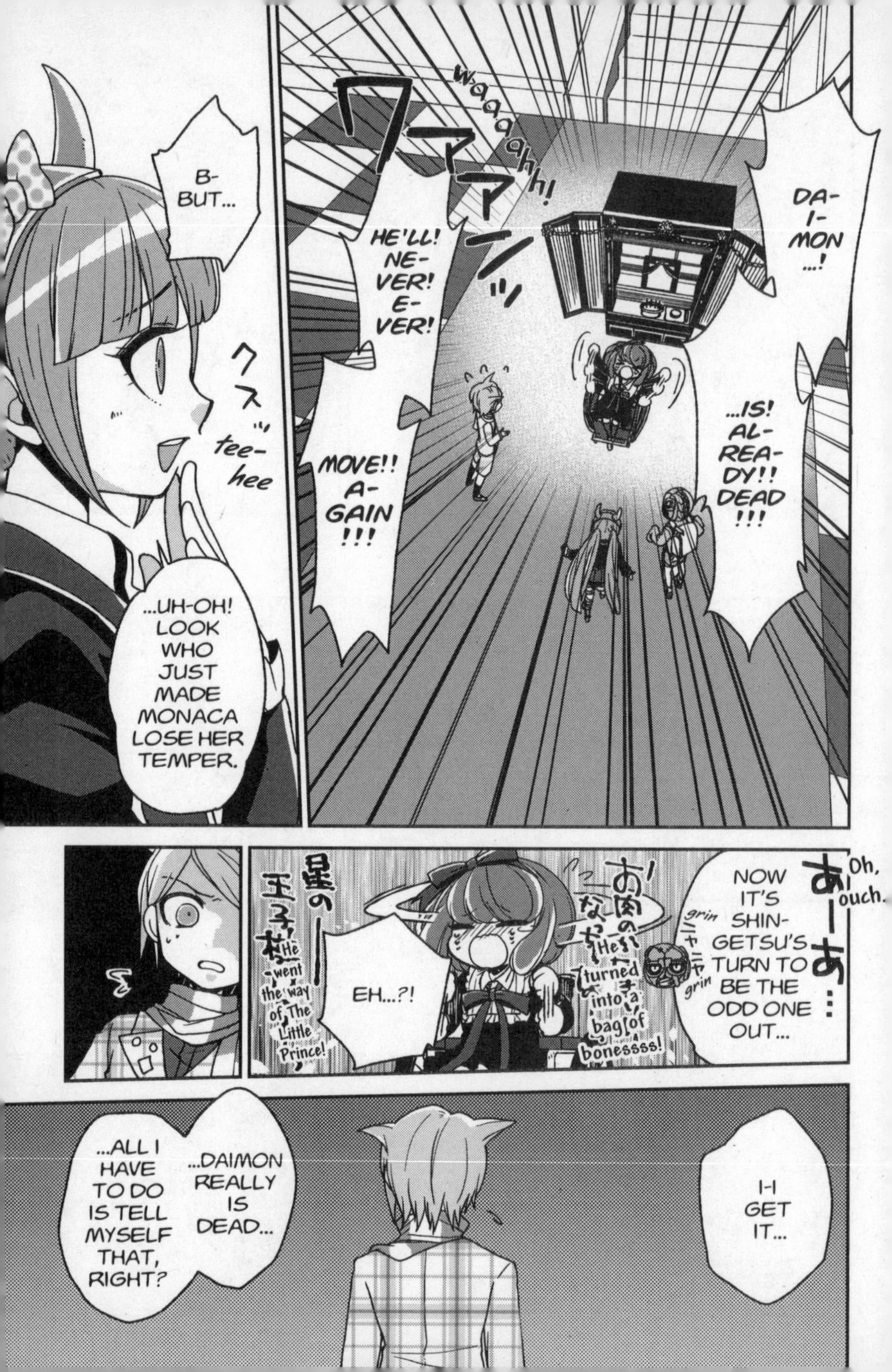

DA-I-MON...!
...IS! AL-READY!! DEAD!!!
Waaaahh!
HE'LL! NE-VER! E-VER!
MOVE!! A-GAIN!!!
B-BUT...
tee-hee
...UH-OH! LOOK WHO JUST MADE MONACA LOSE HER TEMPER.
Oh, ouch.
NOW IT'S SHIN-GETSU'S TURN TO BE THE ODD ONE OUT...
grin grin
He turned into a bag of bonessss!
He went the way of The Little Prince!
EH...?!
I-I GET IT...
...DAIMON REALLY IS DEAD...
...ALL I HAVE TO DO IS TELL MYSELF THAT, RIGHT?

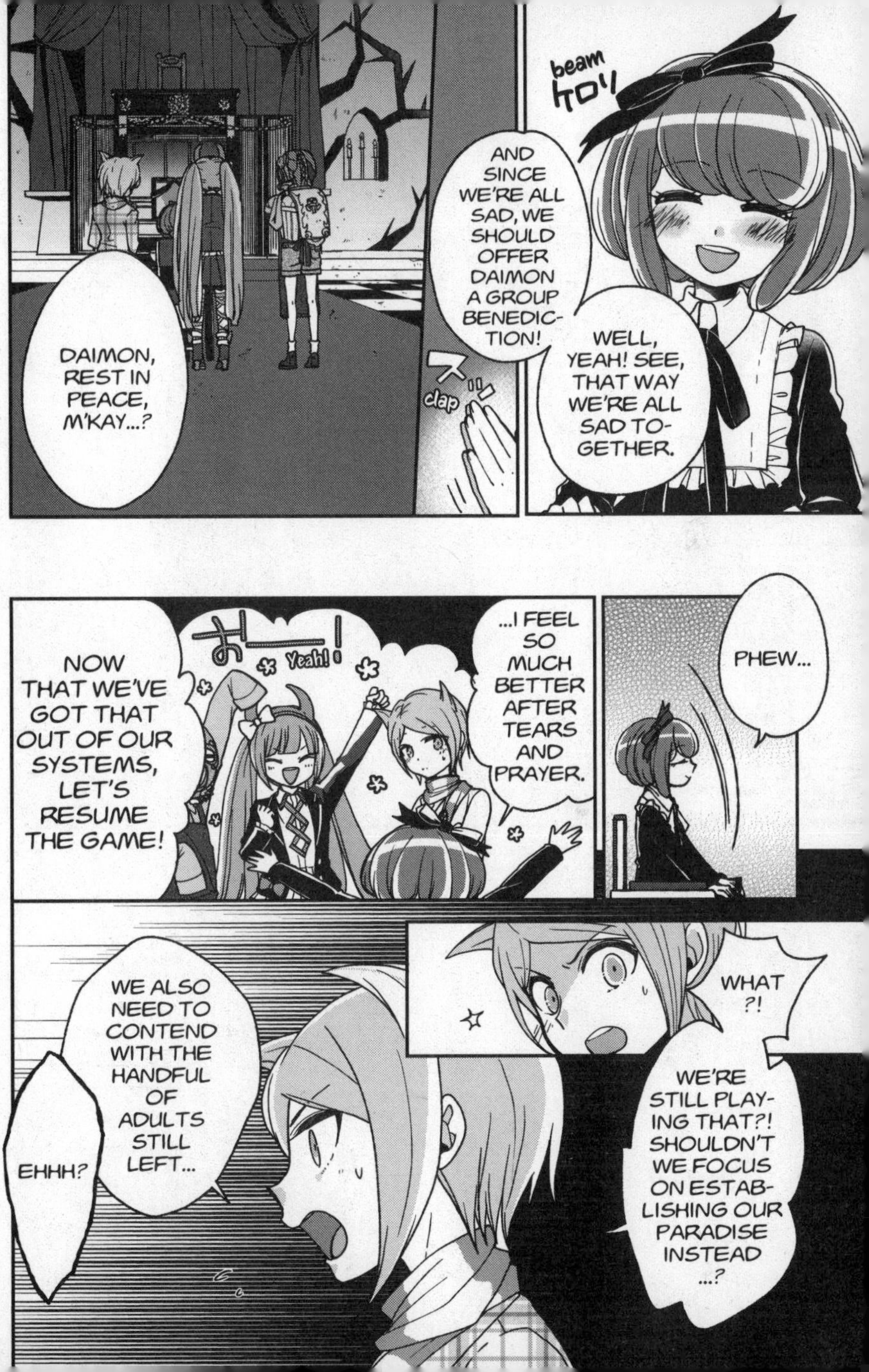
beam
AND SINCE WE'RE ALL SAD, WE SHOULD OFFER DAIMON A GROUP BENEDICTION!
WELL, YEAH! SEE, THAT WAY WE'RE ALL SAD TOGETHER.
clap
DAIMON, REST IN PEACE, M'KAY...?
PHEW...
...I FEEL SO MUCH BETTER AFTER TEARS AND PRAYER.
Yeah!
NOW THAT WE'VE GOT THAT OUT OF OUR SYSTEMS, LET'S RESUME THE GAME!
WHAT?!
WE'RE STILL PLAYING THAT?! SHOULDN'T WE FOCUS ON ESTABLISHING OUR PARADISE INSTEAD ...?
WE ALSO NEED TO CONTEND WITH THE HANDFUL OF ADULTS STILL LEFT...
EHHH?

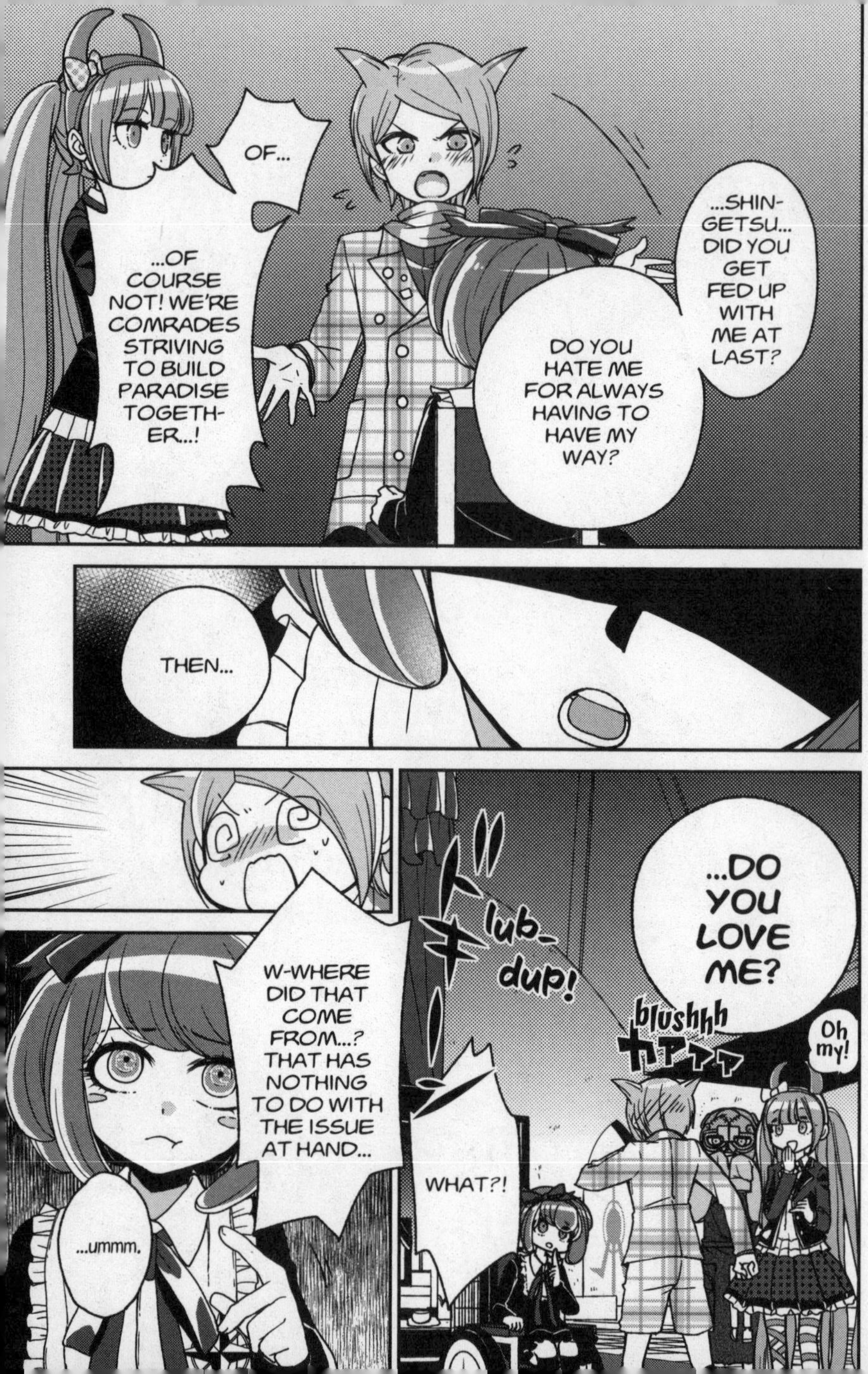
...SHIN-GETSU... DID YOU GET FED UP WITH ME AT LAST?
DO YOU HATE ME FOR ALWAYS HAVING TO HAVE MY WAY?
OF...
...OF COURSE NOT! WE'RE COMRADES STRIVING TO BUILD PARADISE TOGETH-ER...!
THEN...
...DO YOU LOVE ME?
lub-dup!
blushhh
Oh my!
WHAT?!
W-WHERE DID THAT COME FROM...? THAT HAS NOTHING TO DO WITH THE ISSUE AT HAND...
...ummm.

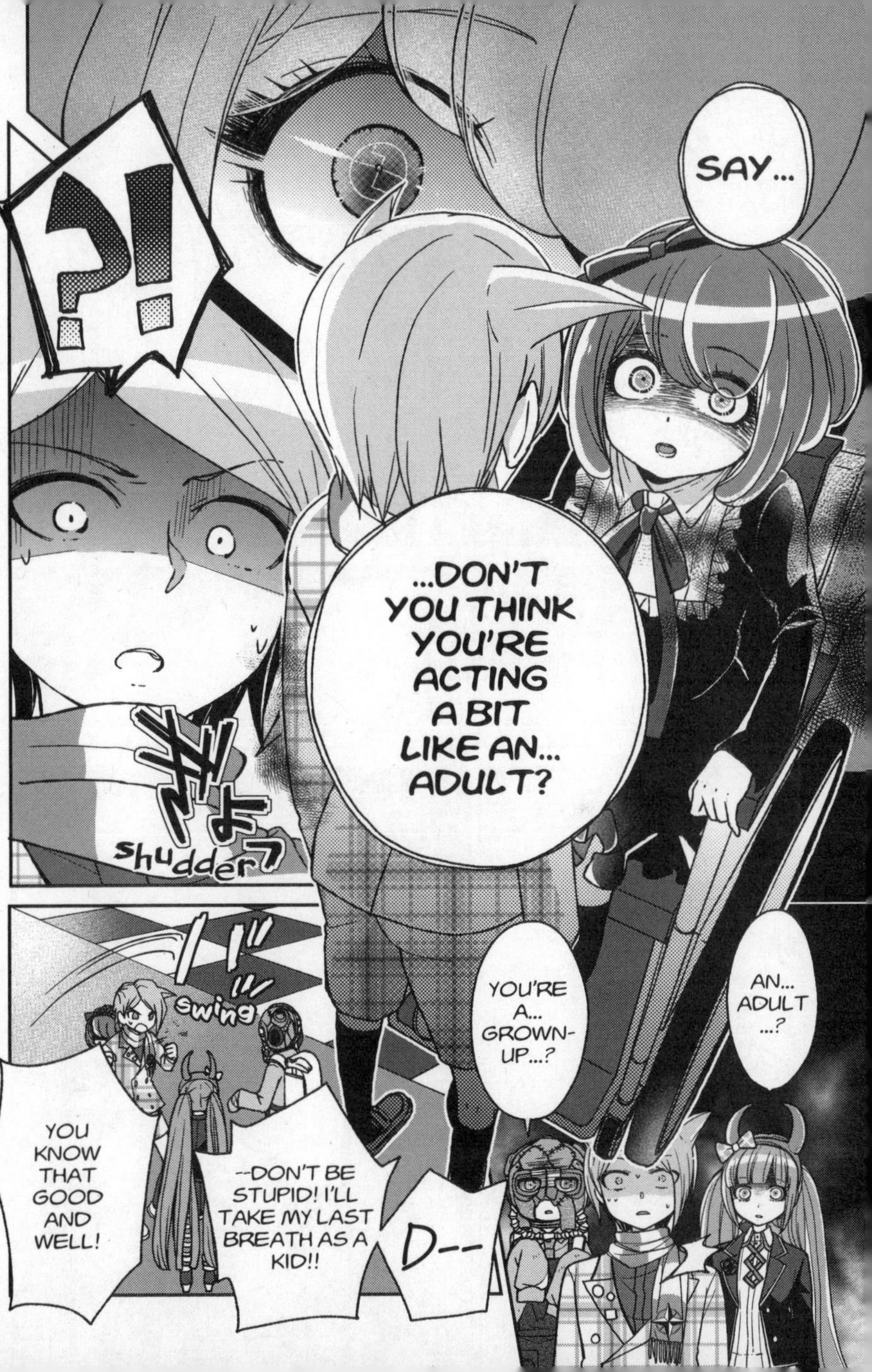
SAY...
...DON'T YOU THINK YOU'RE ACTING A BIT LIKE AN... ADULT?
?!
shudder
AN... ADULT ...?
YOU'RE A... GROWN-UP...?
D--
--DON'T BE STUPID! I'LL TAKE MY LAST BREATH AS A KID!!
YOU KNOW THAT GOOD AND WELL!
swing

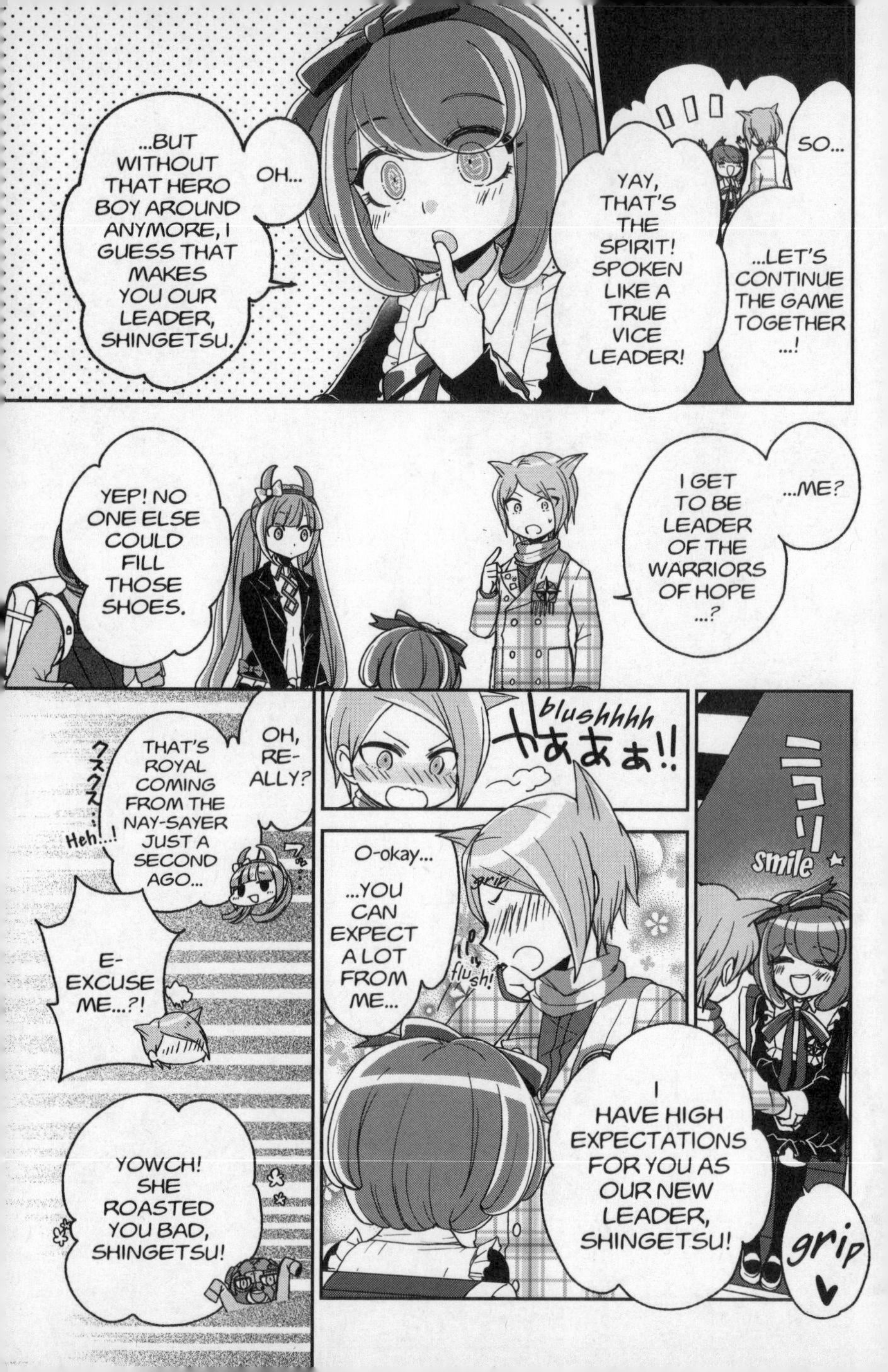
SO...
...LET'S CONTINUE THE GAME TOGETHER ...!
YAY, THAT'S THE SPIRIT! SPOKEN LIKE A TRUE VICE LEADER!
OH...
...BUT WITHOUT THAT HERO BOY AROUND ANYMORE, I GUESS THAT MAKES YOU OUR LEADER, SHINGETSU.
...ME?
I GET TO BE LEADER OF THE WARRIORS OF HOPE ...?
YEP! NO ONE ELSE COULD FILL THOSE SHOES.
ニコリ
smile
I HAVE HIGH EXPECTATIONS FOR YOU AS OUR NEW LEADER, SHINGETSU!
grip
かあぁぁ!!
blushhhh
O-okay...
...YOU CAN EXPECT A LOT FROM ME...
flush!
OH, RE-ALLY?
THAT'S ROYAL COMING FROM THE NAY-SAYER JUST A SECOND AGO...
クスクス
Heh...!
E-EXCUSE ME...?!
YOWCH! SHE ROASTED YOU BAD, SHINGETSU!

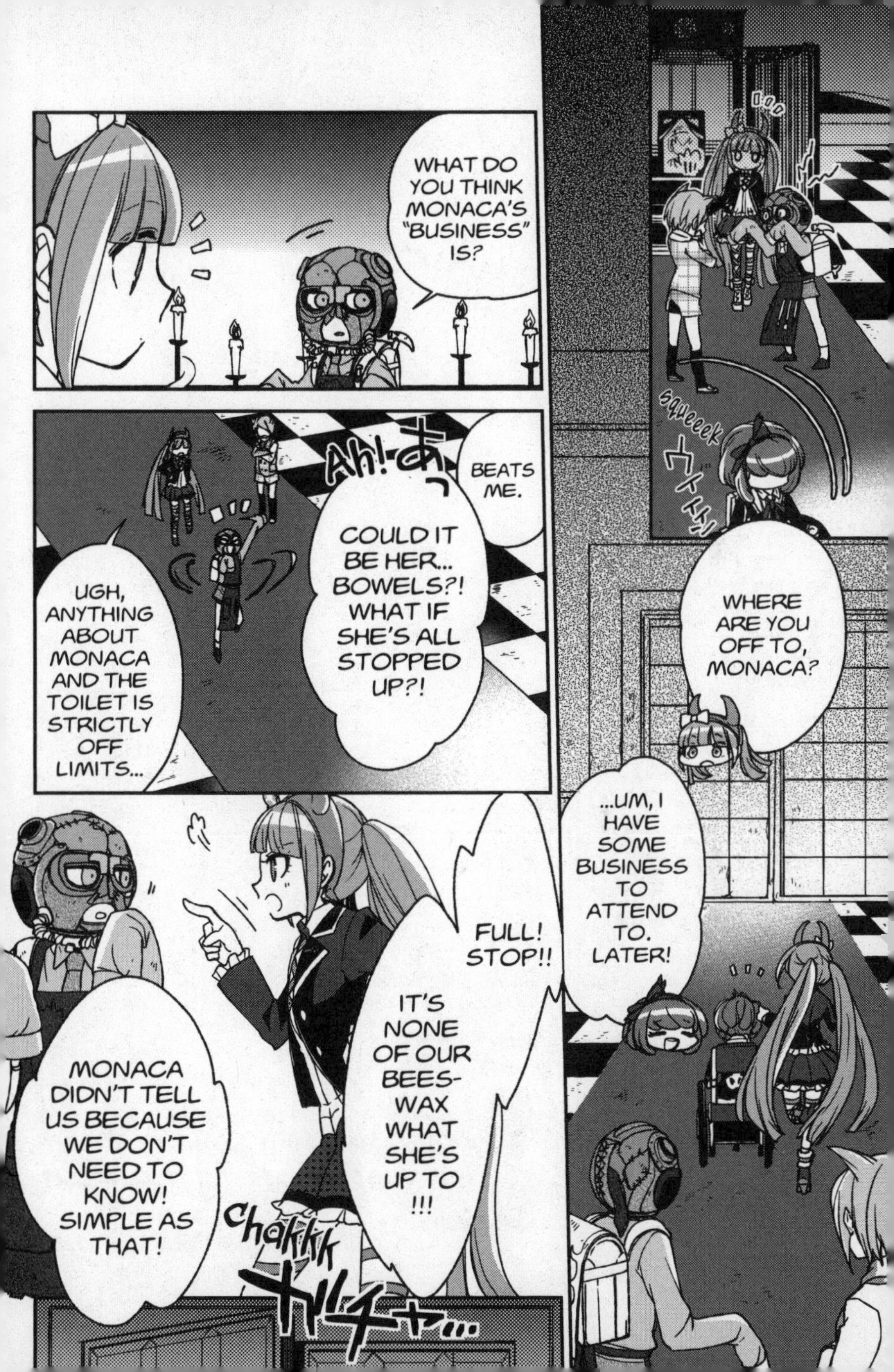
squeeeek
ウイイイン
WHERE ARE YOU OFF TO, MONACA?
...UM, I HAVE SOME BUSINESS TO ATTEND TO. LATER!
WHAT DO YOU THINK MONACA'S "BUSINESS" IS?
BEATS ME.
Ah! あっ
COULD IT BE HER... BOWELS?! WHAT IF SHE'S ALL STOPPED UP?!
UGH, ANYTHING ABOUT MONACA AND THE TOILET IS STRICTLY OFF LIMITS...
FULL! STOP!!
IT'S NONE OF OUR BEES-WAX WHAT SHE'S UP TO !!!
MONACA DIDN'T TELL US BECAUSE WE DON'T NEED TO KNOW! SIMPLE AS THAT!
Chakkk
ガチャ...

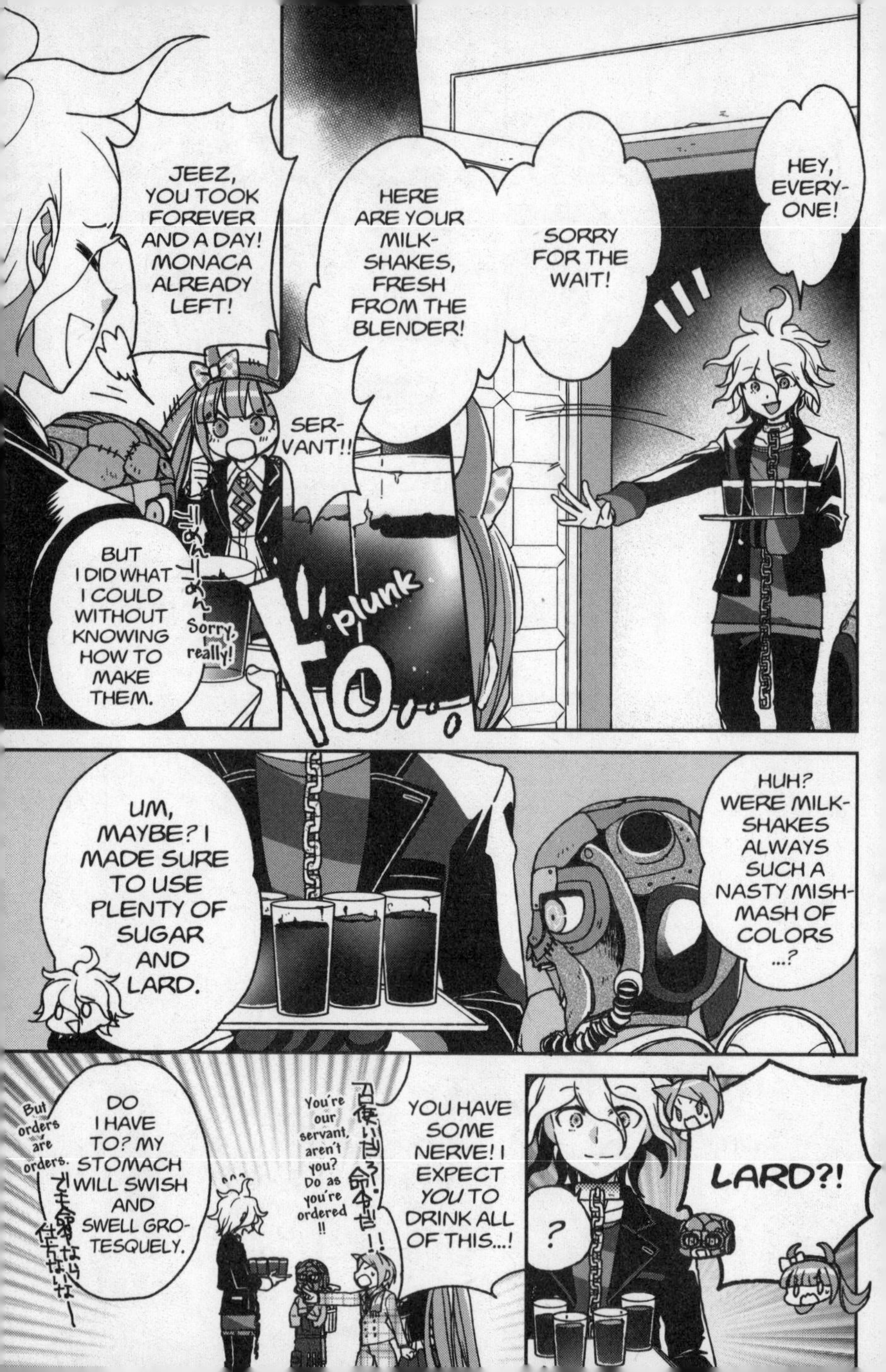
HEY, EVERY-ONE!
SORRY FOR THE WAIT!
HERE ARE YOUR MILK-SHAKES, FRESH FROM THE BLENDER!
JEEZ, YOU TOOK FOREVER AND A DAY! MONACA ALREADY LEFT!
SER-VANT!!
BUT I DID WHAT I COULD WITHOUT KNOWING HOW TO MAKE THEM.
ごめんごめん
Sorry, really!
plunk
HUH? WERE MILK-SHAKES ALWAYS SUCH A NASTY MISH-MASH OF COLORS ...?
UM, MAYBE? I MADE SURE TO USE PLENTY OF SUGAR AND LARD.
LARD?!
?
YOU HAVE SOME NERVE! I EXPECT YOU TO DRINK ALL OF THIS...!
召使いだろ、命令だ!!
You're our servant, aren't you? Do as you're ordered!!
DO I HAVE TO? MY STOMACH WILL SWISH AND SWELL GRO-TESQUELY.
でも命令なら仕方ないなー
But orders are orders.

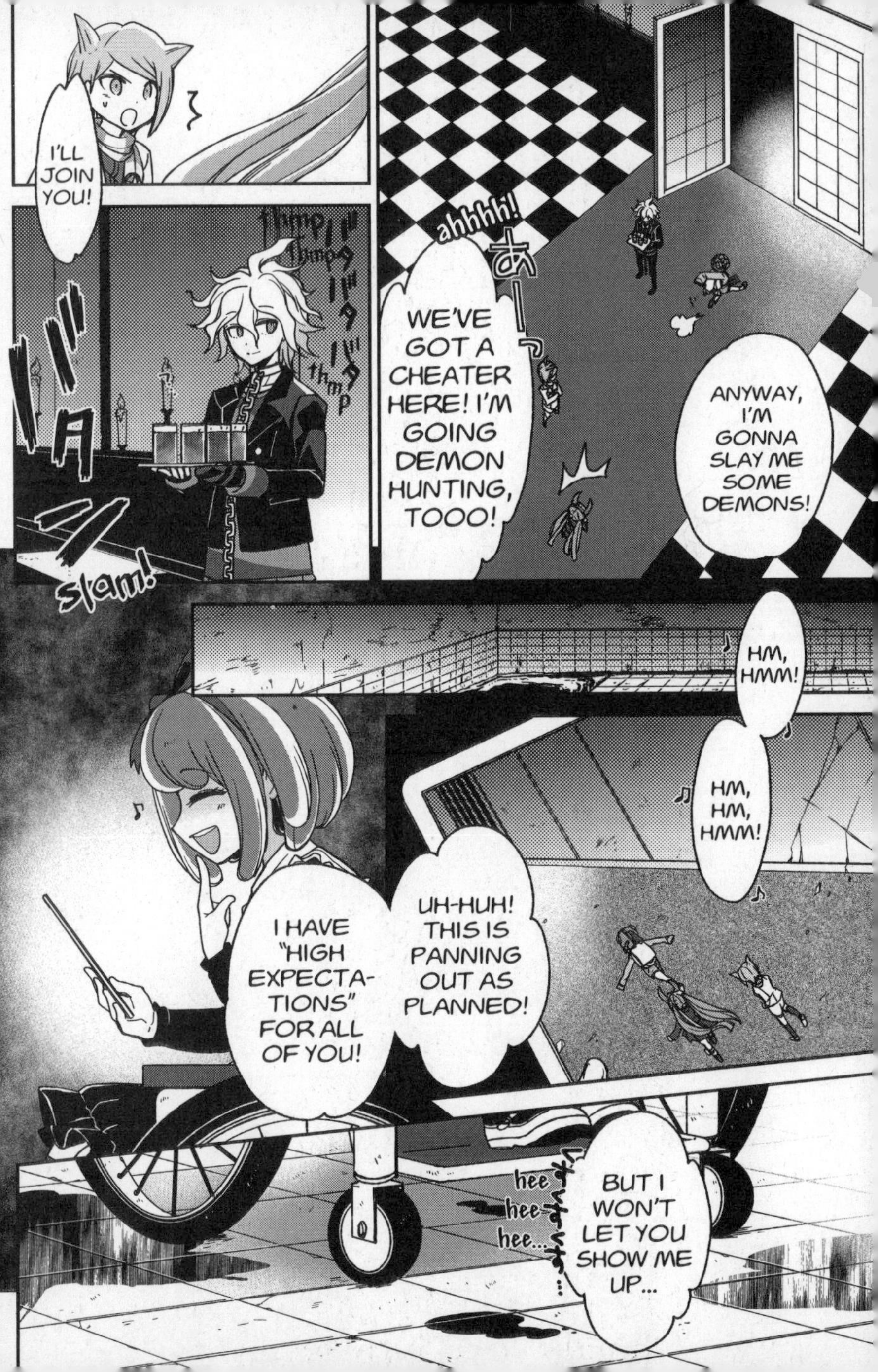
ANYWAY, I'M GONNA SLAY ME SOME DEMONS!
ahhhh!
あーっ
WE'VE GOT A CHEATER HERE! I'M GOING DEMON HUNTING, TOOO!
I'LL JOIN YOU!
thmp thmp thmp
slam!
HM, HMM!
HM, HM, HMM!
UH-HUH! THIS IS PANNING OUT AS PLANNED!
I HAVE "HIGH EXPECTATIONS" FOR ALL OF YOU!
BUT I WON'T LET YOU SHOW ME UP...
hee hee hee...

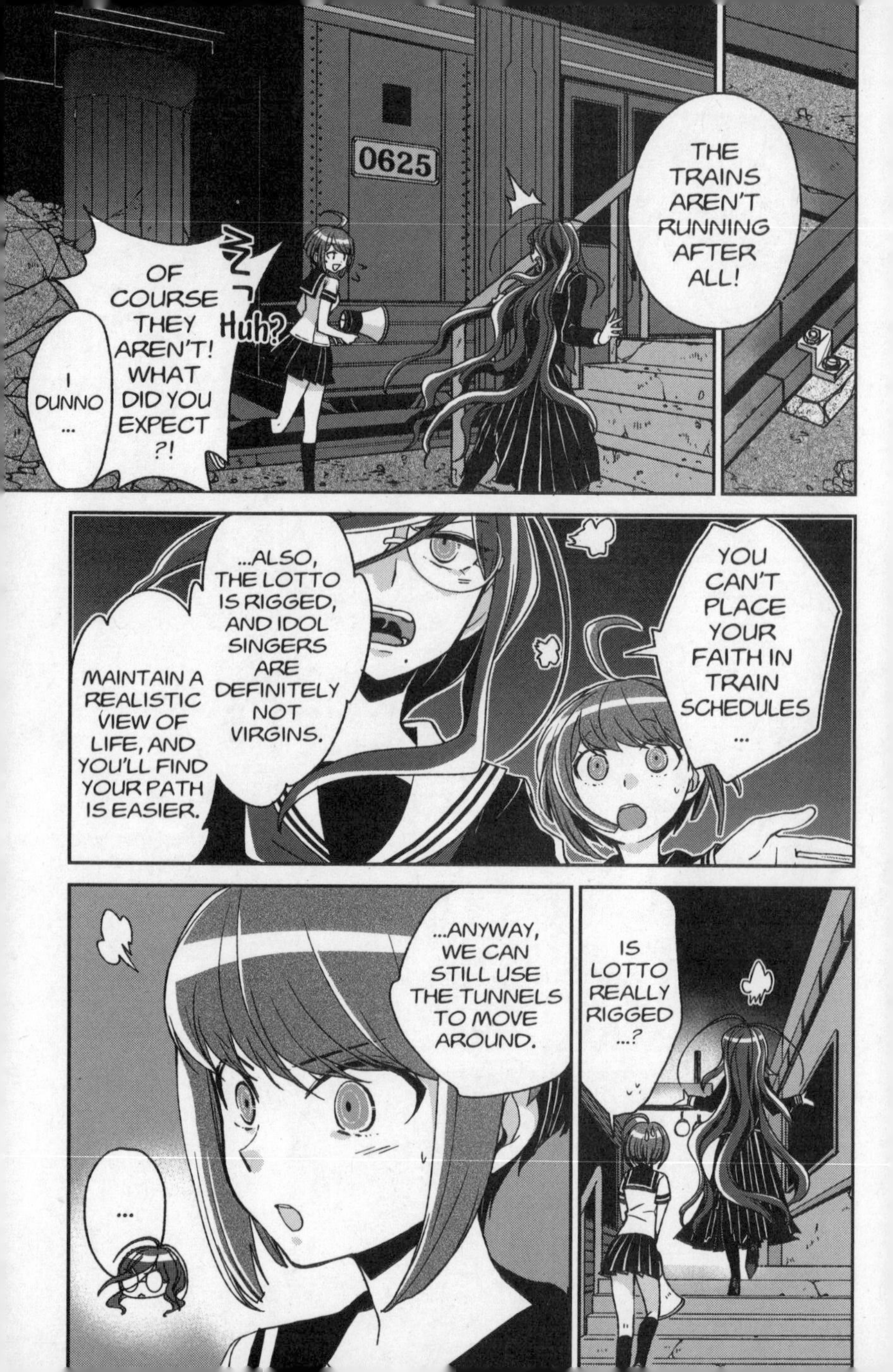
THE TRAINS AREN'T RUNNING AFTER ALL!
Huh?
OF COURSE THEY AREN'T! WHAT DID YOU EXPECT?!
I DUNNO ...
YOU CAN'T PLACE YOUR FAITH IN TRAIN SCHEDULES ...
...ALSO, THE LOTTO IS RIGGED, AND IDOL SINGERS ARE DEFINITELY NOT VIRGINS.
MAINTAIN A REALISTIC VIEW OF LIFE, AND YOU'LL FIND YOUR PATH IS EASIER.
IS LOTTO REALLY RIGGED ...?
...ANYWAY, WE CAN STILL USE THE TUNNELS TO MOVE AROUND.
...

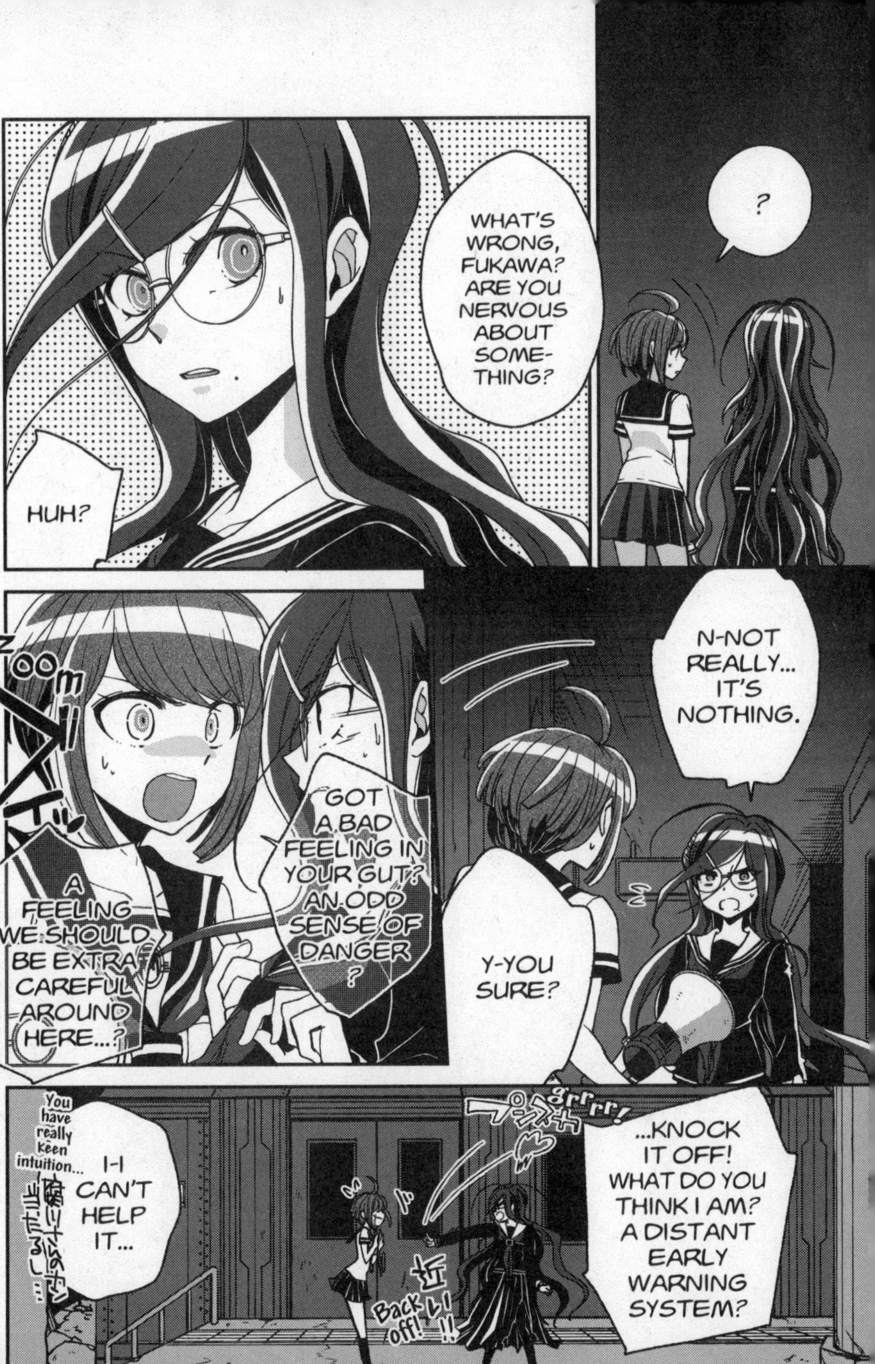
?
WHAT'S WRONG, FUKAWA? ARE YOU NERVOUS ABOUT SOME-THING?
HUH?
N-NOT REALLY... IT'S NOTHING.
Y-YOU SURE?
GOT A BAD FEELING IN YOUR GUT? AN ODD SENSE OF DANGER?
A FEELING WE SHOULD BE EXTRA CAREFUL AROUND HERE...?
ZOOM
grrrr!
...KNOCK IT OFF! WHAT DO YOU THINK I AM? A DISTANT EARLY WARNING SYSTEM?
Back off!
I-I CAN'T HELP IT...
You have really keen intuition...

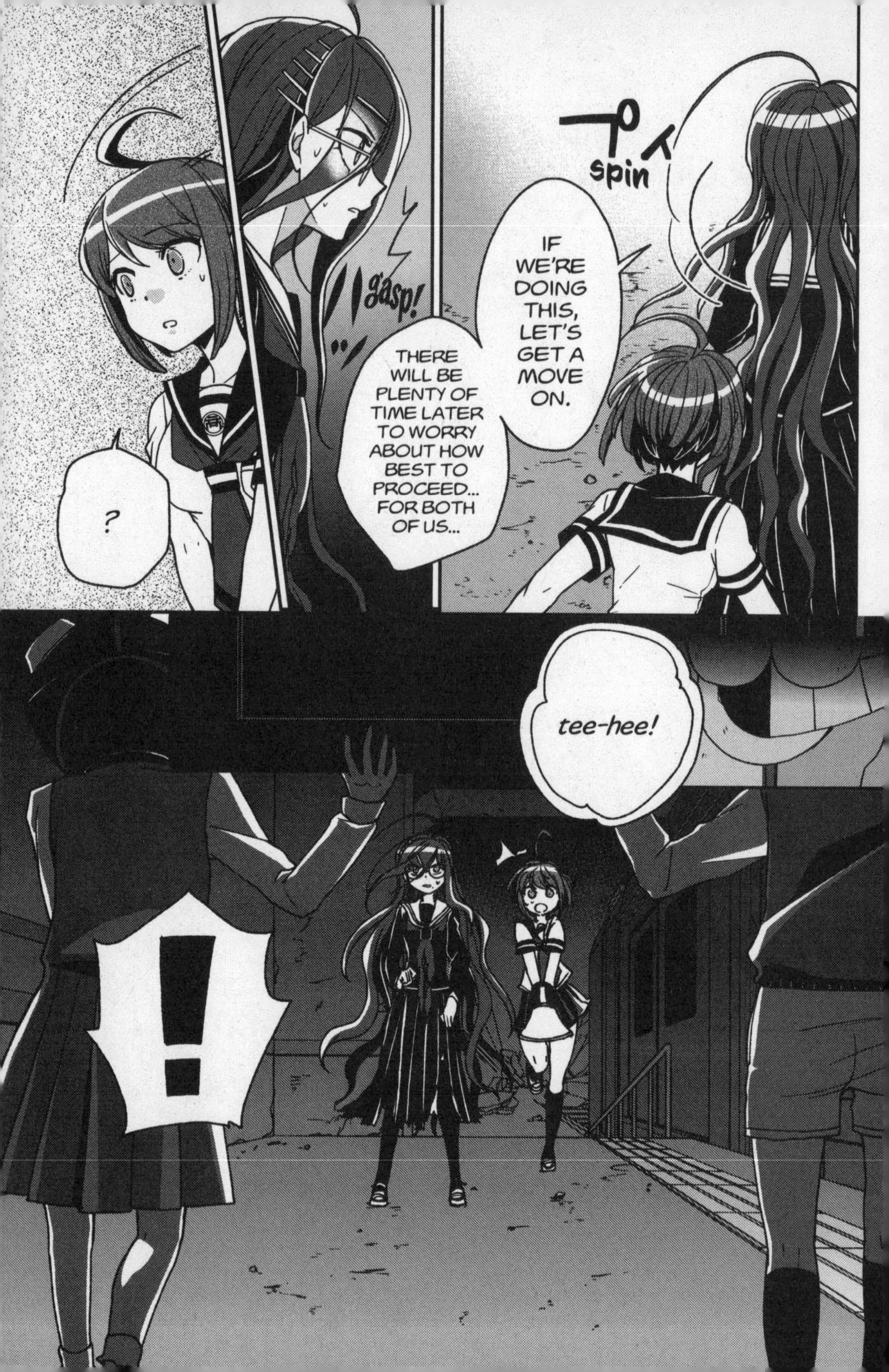
spin
IF WE'RE DOING THIS, LET'S GET A MOVE ON.
THERE WILL BE PLENTY OF TIME LATER TO WORRY ABOUT HOW BEST TO PROCEED... FOR BOTH OF US...
gasp!
?
tee-hee!
!

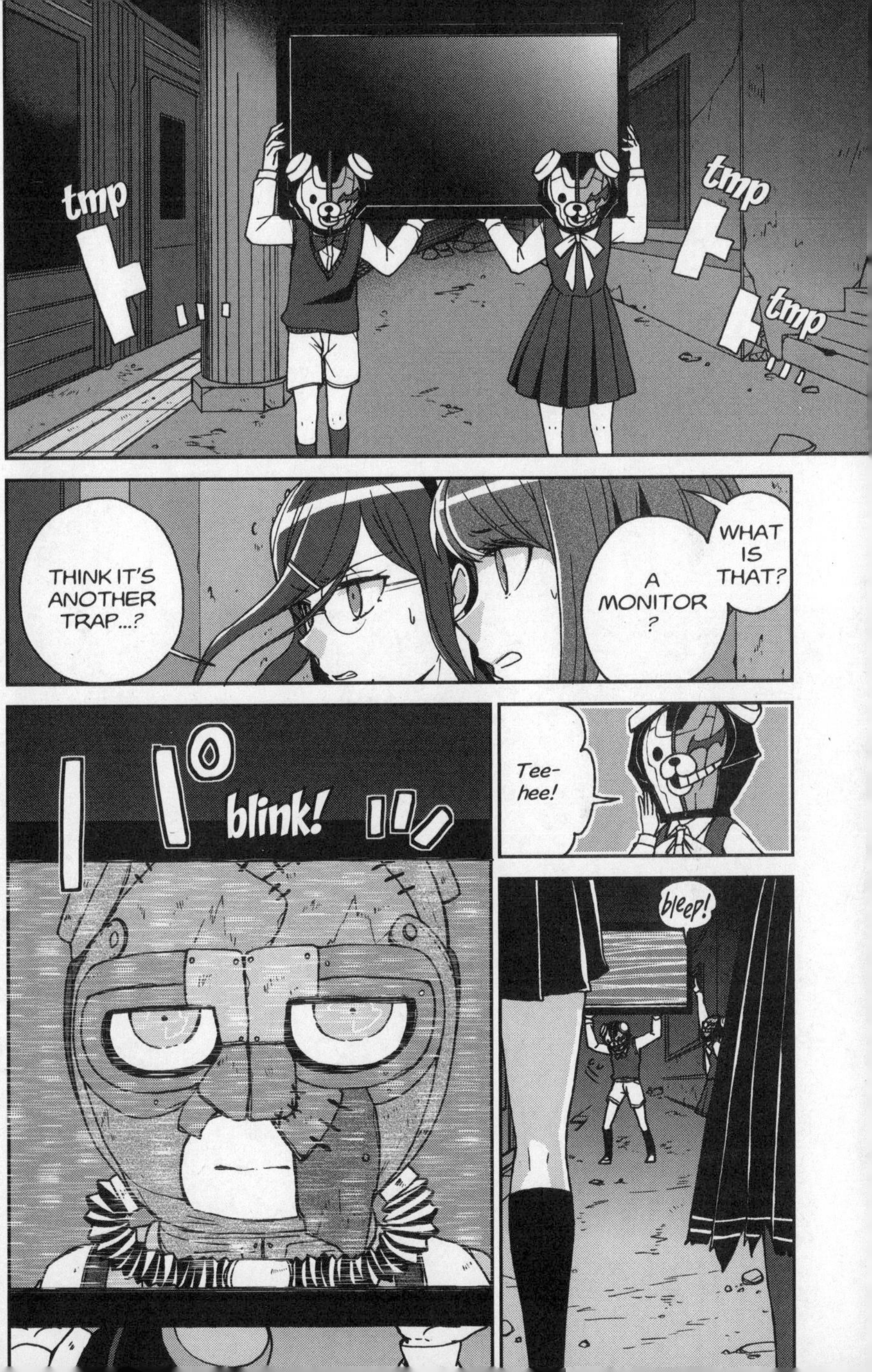
tmp
tmp
tmp
WHAT IS THAT?
A MONITOR ?
THINK IT'S ANOTHER TRAP...?
Tee-hee!
bleep!
blink!

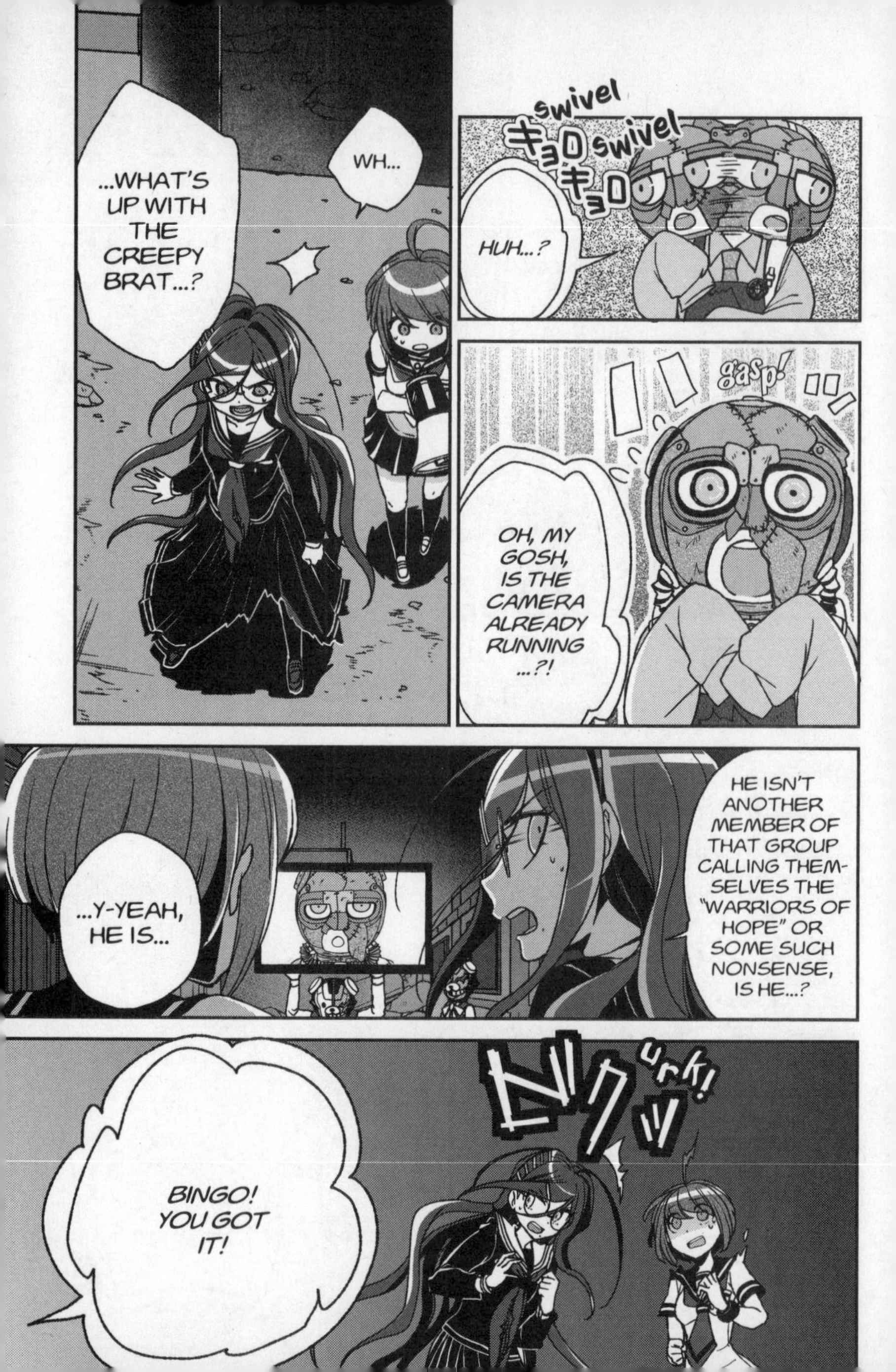
swivel swivel
キョロキョロ
HUH...?
gasp!
OH, MY GOSH, IS THE CAMERA ALREADY RUNNING ...?!
WH...
...WHAT'S UP WITH THE CREEPY BRAT...?
HE ISN'T ANOTHER MEMBER OF THAT GROUP CALLING THEM-SELVES THE "WARRIORS OF HOPE" OR SOME SUCH NONSENSE, IS HE...?
...Y-YEAH, HE IS...
BINGO! YOU GOT IT!
urk!

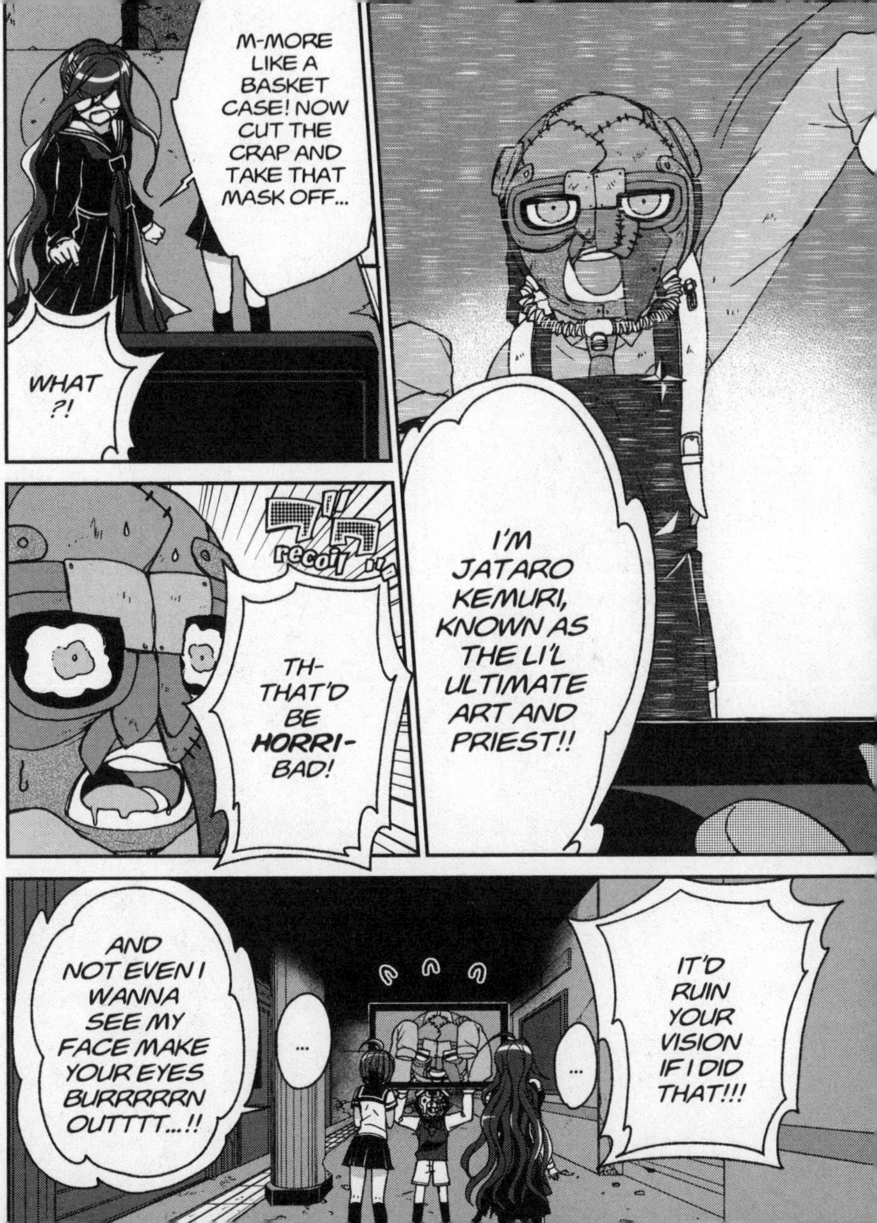
I'M JATARO KEMURI, KNOWN AS THE LI'L ULTIMATE ART AND PRIEST!!
M-MORE LIKE A BASKET CASE! NOW CUT THE CRAP AND TAKE THAT MASK OFF...
WHAT ?!
recoil
TH-THAT'D BE HORRI-BAD!
IT'D RUIN YOUR VISION IF I DID THAT!!!
...
...
AND NOT EVEN I WANNA SEE MY FACE MAKE YOUR EYES BURRRRRN OUTTTT...!!

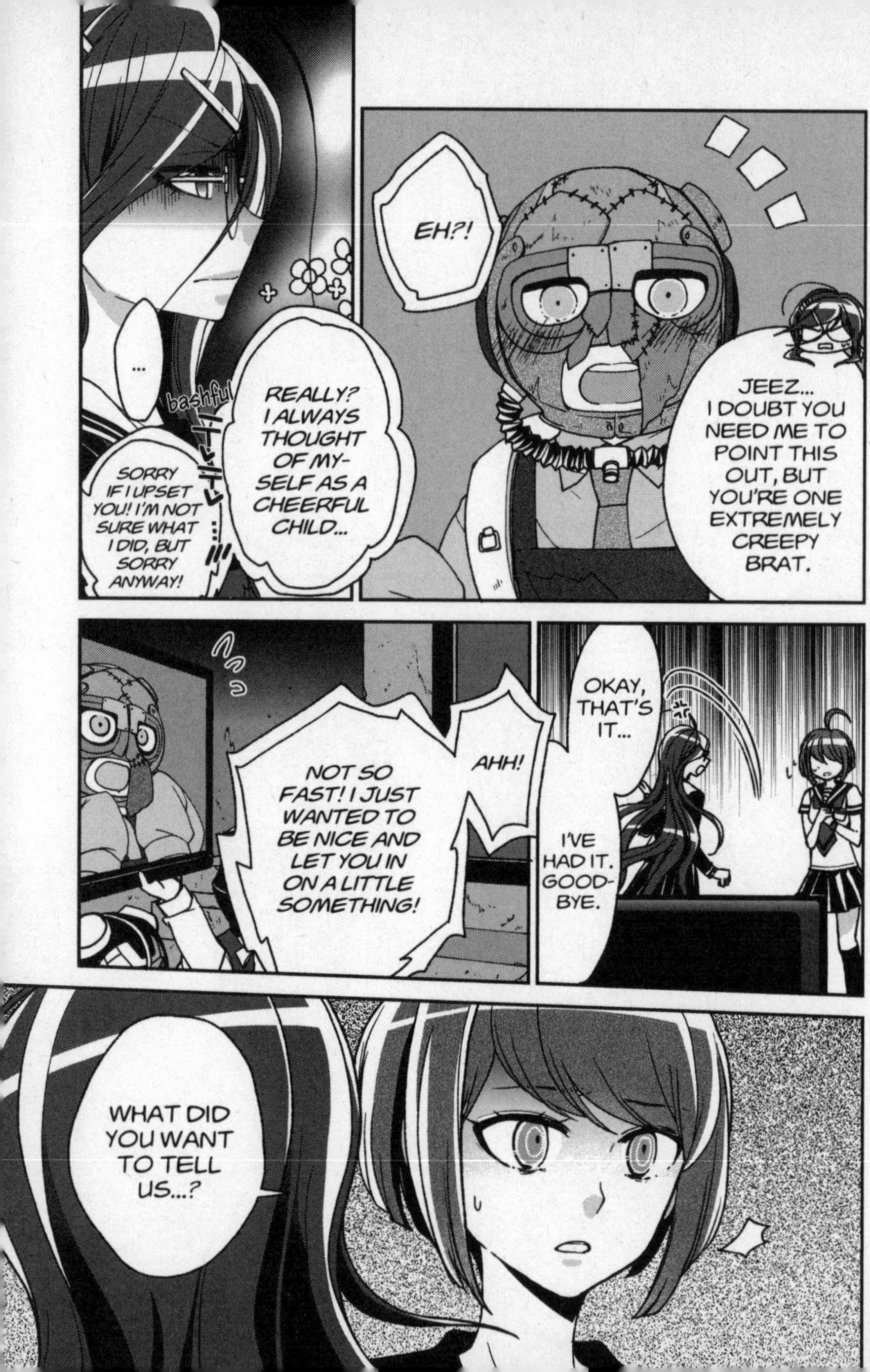
JEEZ... I DOUBT YOU NEED ME TO POINT THIS OUT, BUT YOU'RE ONE EXTREMELY CREEPY BRAT.
EH?!
REALLY? I ALWAYS THOUGHT OF MYSELF AS A CHEERFUL CHILD...
...
bashful
SORRY IF I UPSET YOU! I'M NOT SURE WHAT I DID, BUT SORRY ANYWAY!
OKAY, THAT'S IT...
I'VE HAD IT. GOODBYE.
AHH!
NOT SO FAST! I JUST WANTED TO BE NICE AND LET YOU IN ON A LITTLE SOMETHING!
WHAT DID YOU WANT TO TELL US...?

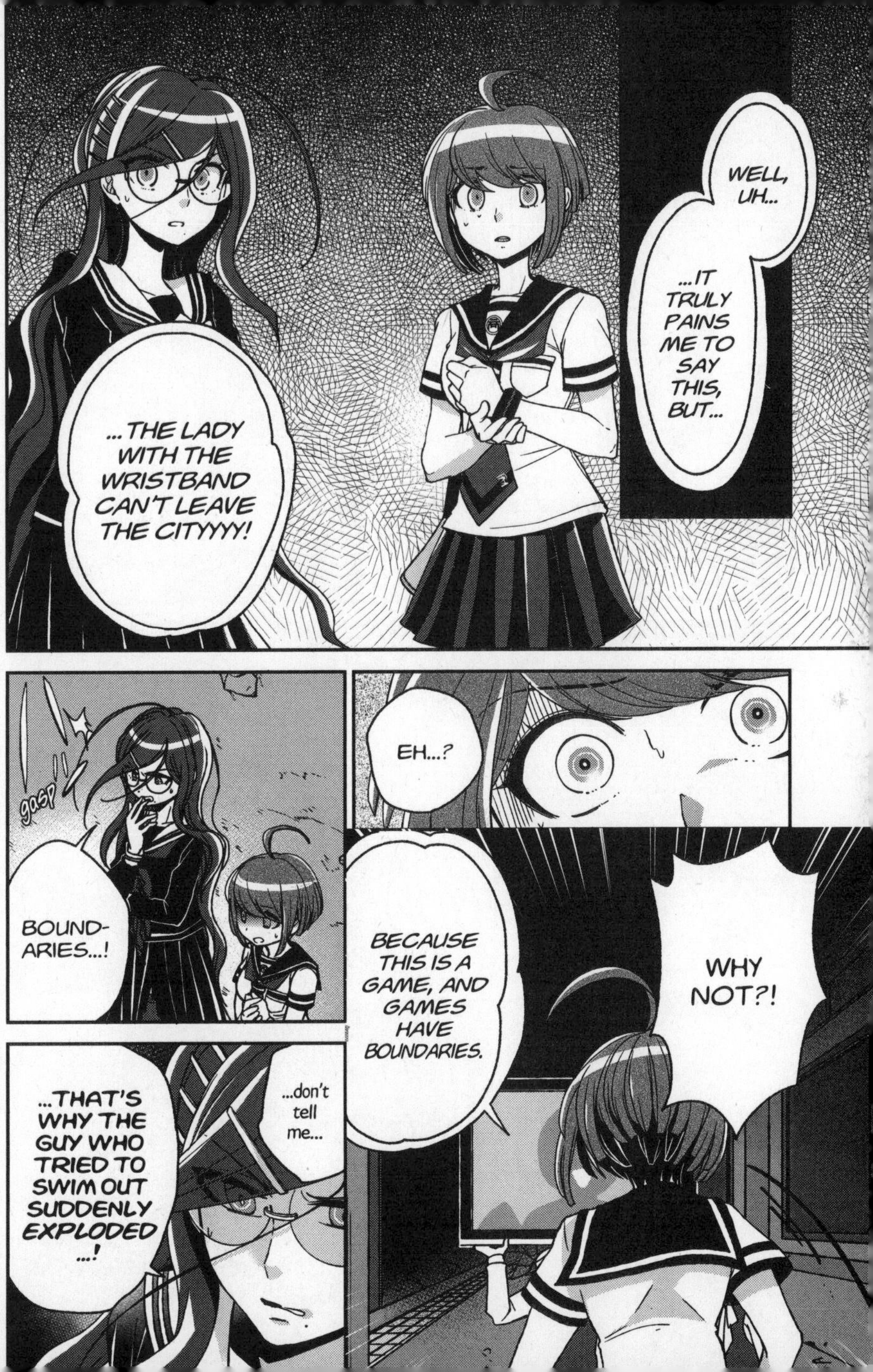

WELL, UH...
...IT TRULY PAINS ME TO SAY THIS, BUT...
...THE LADY WITH THE WRISTBAND CAN'T LEAVE THE CITYYYY!
EH...?
WHY NOT?!
BECAUSE THIS IS A GAME, AND GAMES HAVE BOUNDARIES.
gasp
BOUNDARIES...!
...don't tell me...
...THAT'S WHY THE GUY WHO TRIED TO SWIM OUT SUDDENLY EXPLODED ...!

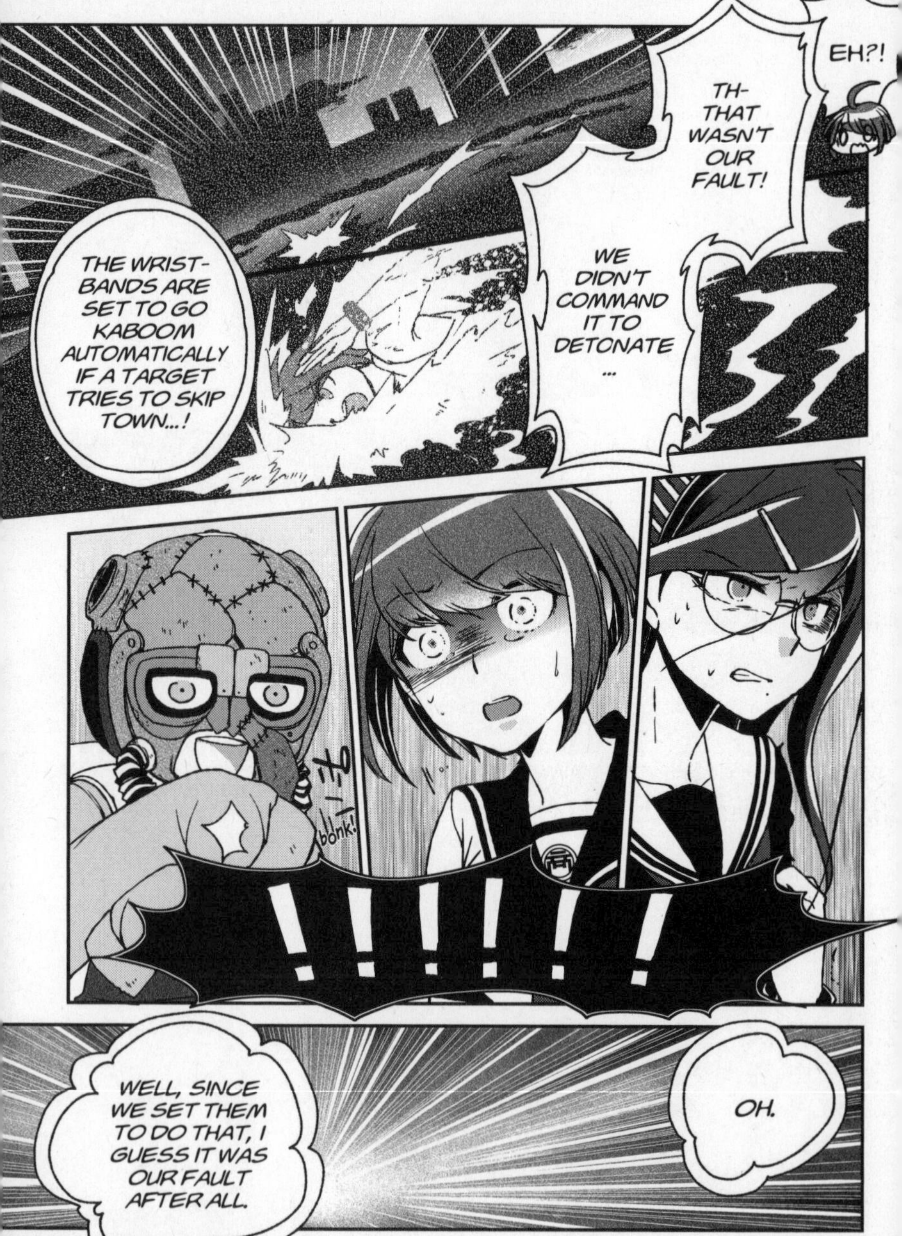
EH?!
TH- THAT WASN'T OUR FAULT!
WE DIDN'T COMMAND IT TO DETONATE ...
THE WRIST-BANDS ARE SET TO GO KABOOM AUTOMATICALLY IF A TARGET TRIES TO SKIP TOWN...!
!!!!!!
bonk!
OH.
WELL, SINCE WE SET THEM TO DO THAT, I GUESS IT WAS OUR FAULT AFTER ALL.

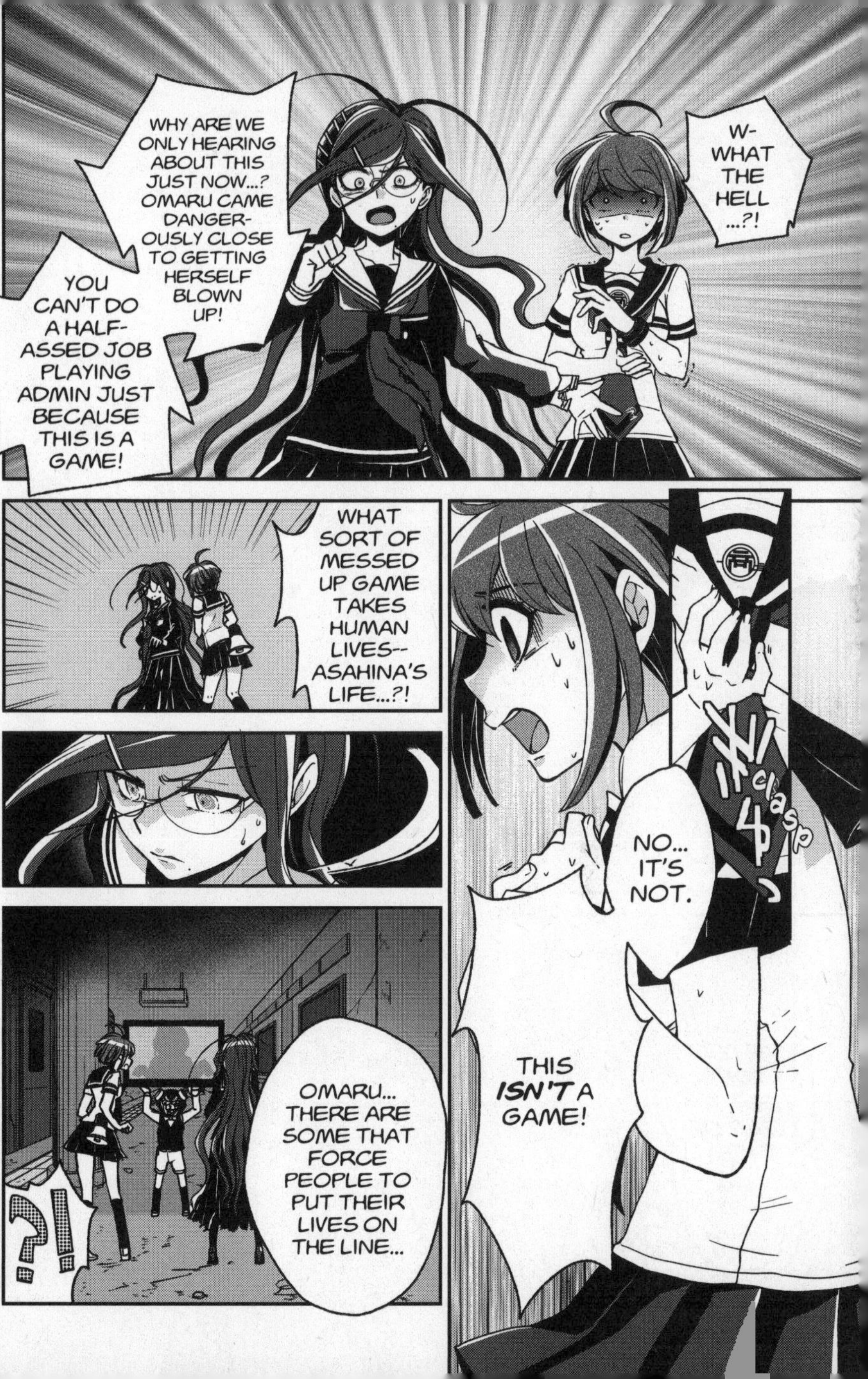
W-WHAT THE HELL ...?!
WHY ARE WE ONLY HEARING ABOUT THIS JUST NOW...? OMARU CAME DANGER-OUSLY CLOSE TO GETTING HERSELF BLOWN UP!
YOU CAN'T DO A HALF-ASSED JOB PLAYING ADMIN JUST BECAUSE THIS IS A GAME!
clasp
NO... IT'S NOT.
THIS *ISN'T* A GAME!
WHAT SORT OF MESSED UP GAME TAKES HUMAN LIVES-- ASAHINA'S LIFE...?!
OMARU... THERE ARE SOME THAT FORCE PEOPLE TO PUT THEIR LIVES ON THE LINE...
?!

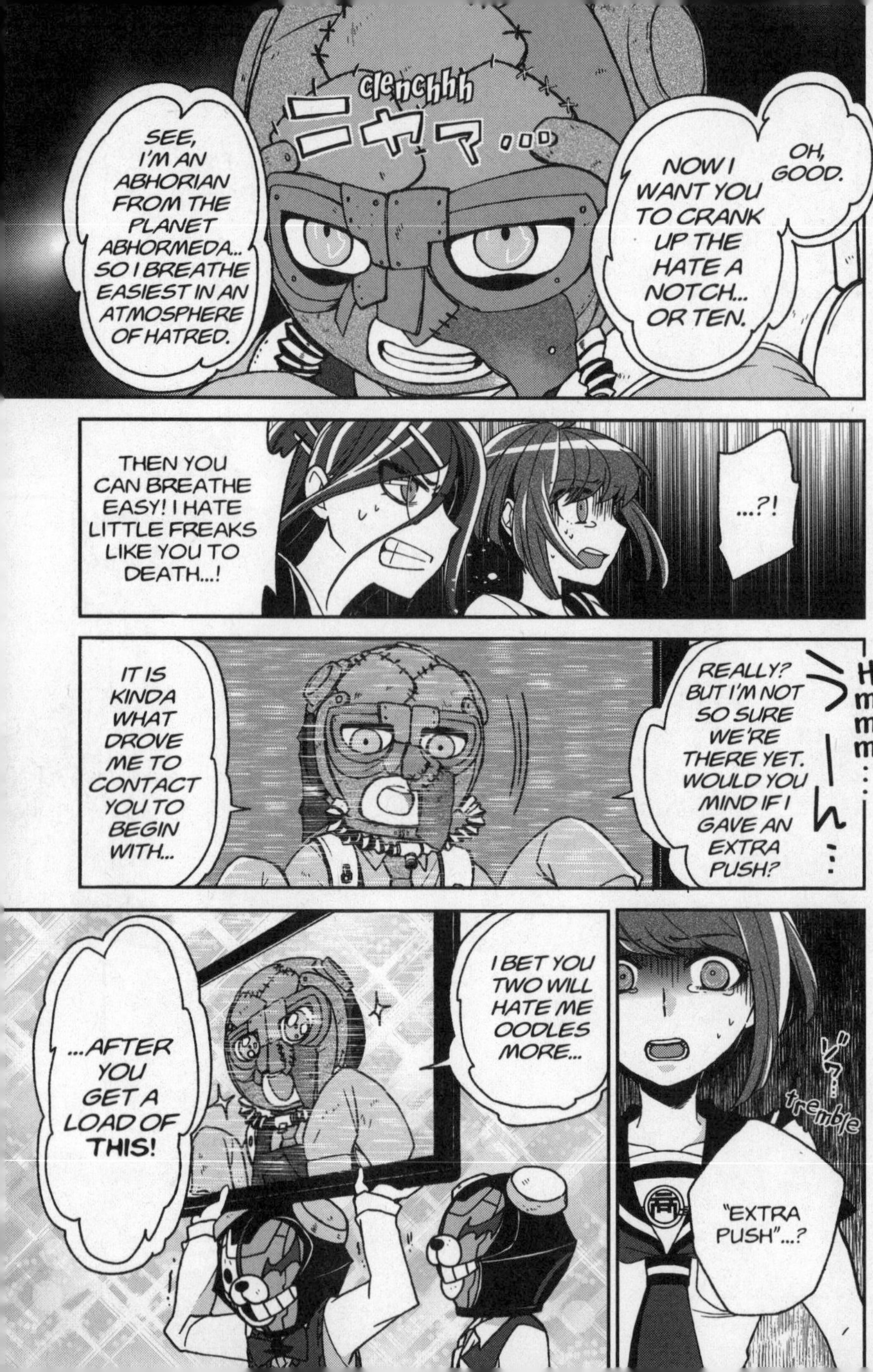
OH, GOOD. NOW I WANT YOU TO CRANK UP THE HATE A NOTCH... OR TEN.
clenchhh
SEE, I'M AN ABHORIAN FROM THE PLANET ABHORMEDA... SO I BREATHE EASIEST IN AN ATMOSPHERE OF HATRED.
...?!
THEN YOU CAN BREATHE EASY! I HATE LITTLE FREAKS LIKE YOU TO DEATH...!
Hmmm...
REALLY? BUT I'M NOT SO SURE WE'RE THERE YET. WOULD YOU MIND IF I GAVE AN EXTRA PUSH?
IT IS KINDA WHAT DROVE ME TO CONTACT YOU TO BEGIN WITH...
tremble
"EXTRA PUSH"...?
I BET YOU TWO WILL HATE ME OODLES MORE...
...AFTER YOU GET A LOAD OF **THIS!**

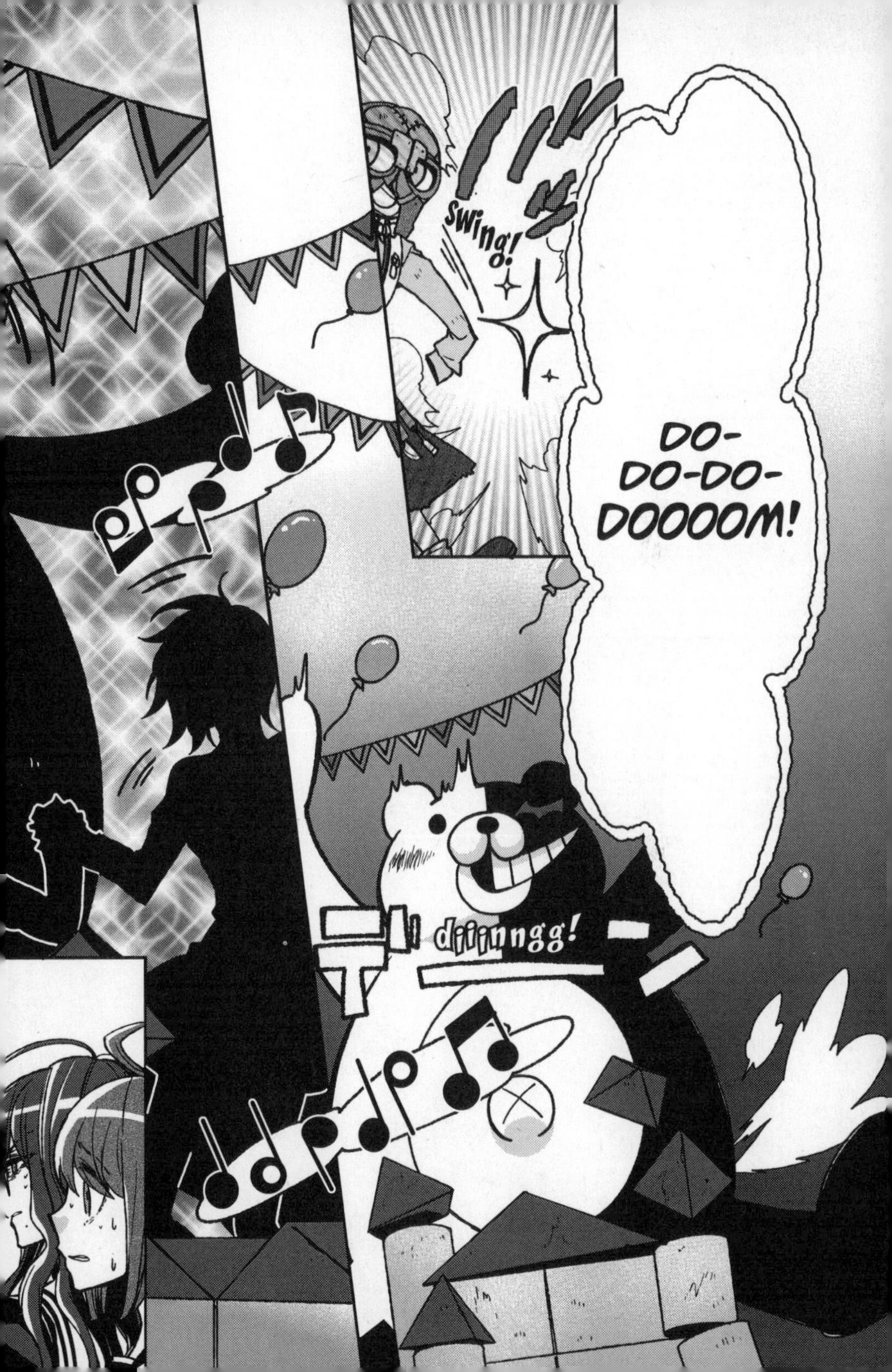
DO-
DO-DO-
DOOOOM!
SWING!
diiinngg!

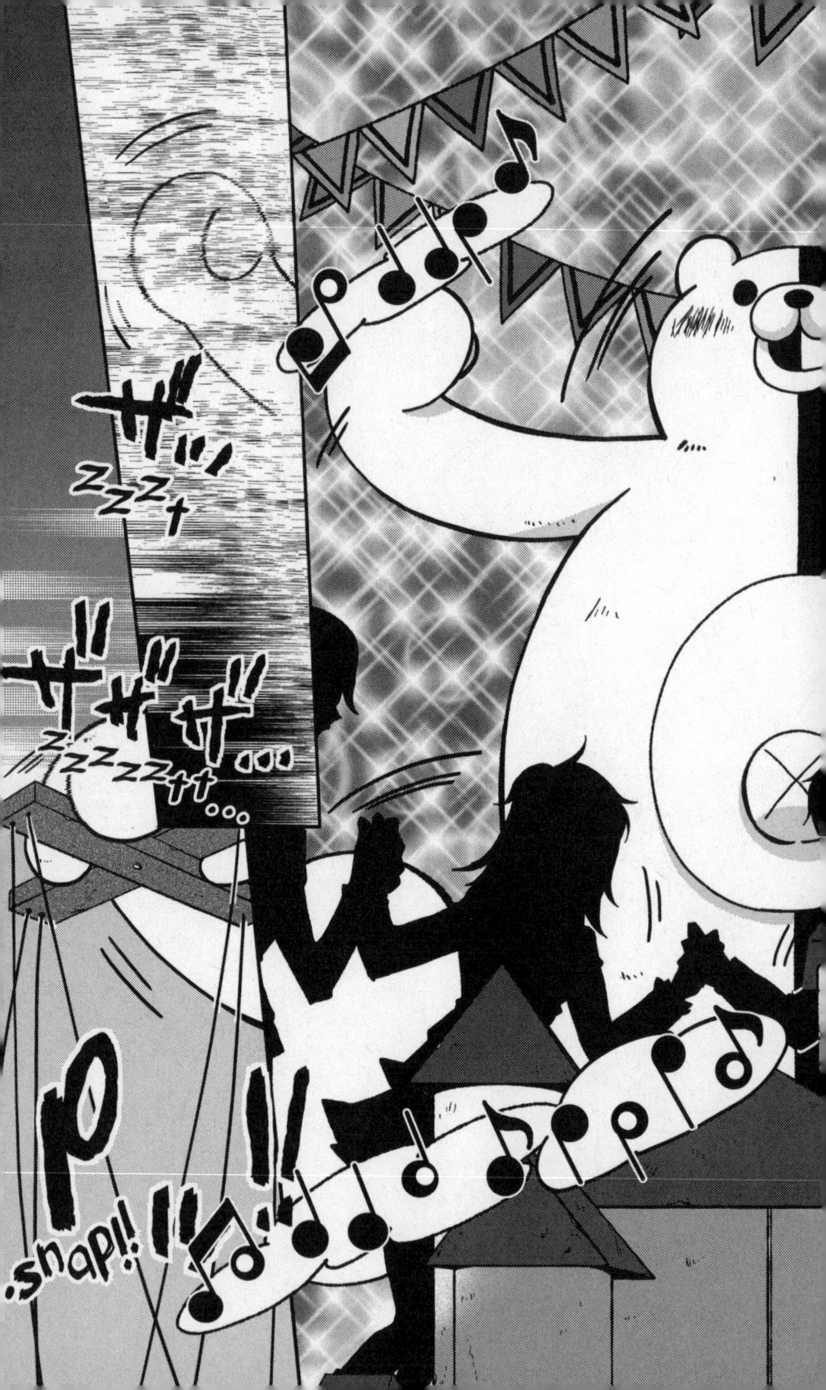
ザッ
ZZZZT
ザッザッザッ...
ZZZZZZTT...
SNAP!!

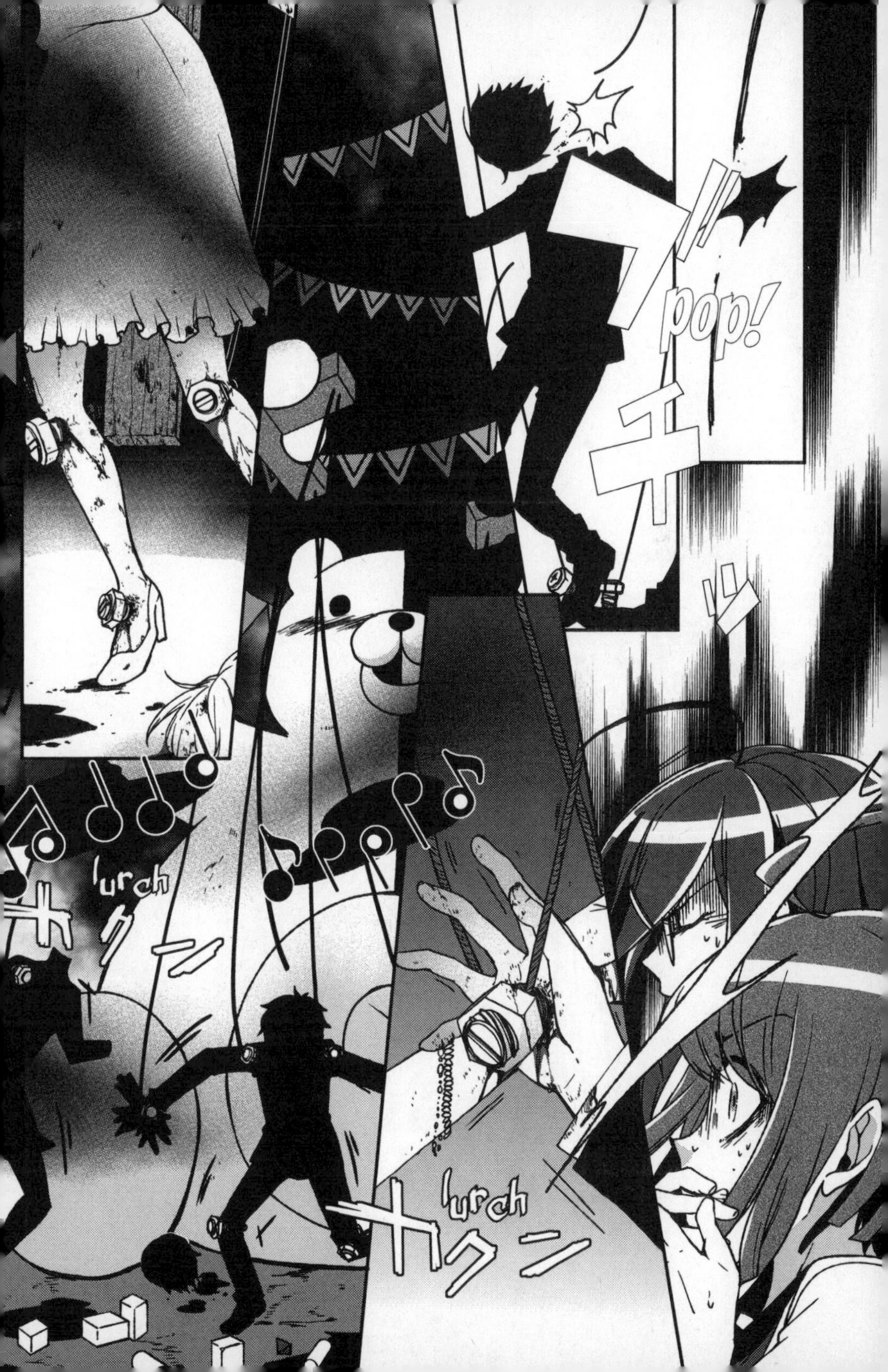
pop!
lurch
lurch

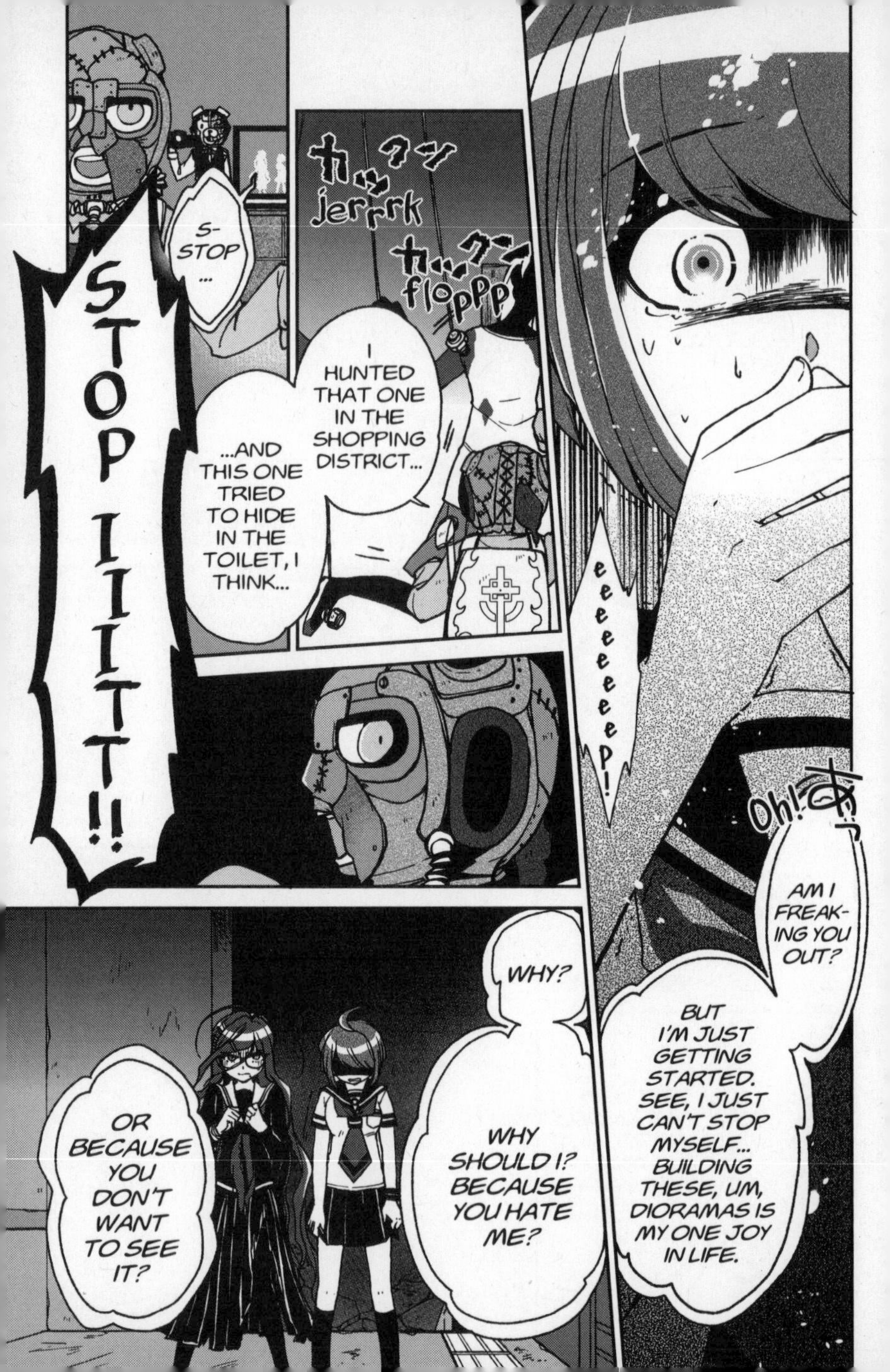
eeeeeeeep!
Oh!
AM I FREAKING YOU OUT?
BUT I'M JUST GETTING STARTED. SEE, I JUST CAN'T STOP MYSELF... BUILDING THESE, UM, DIORAMAS IS MY ONE JOY IN LIFE.
jerrrk
floppp
I HUNTED THAT ONE IN THE SHOPPING DISTRICT...
...AND THIS ONE TRIED TO HIDE IN THE TOILET, I THINK...
S-STOP...
STOP IIITT!!
WHY?
WHY SHOULD I? BECAUSE YOU HATE ME?
OR BECAUSE YOU DON'T WANT TO SEE IT?

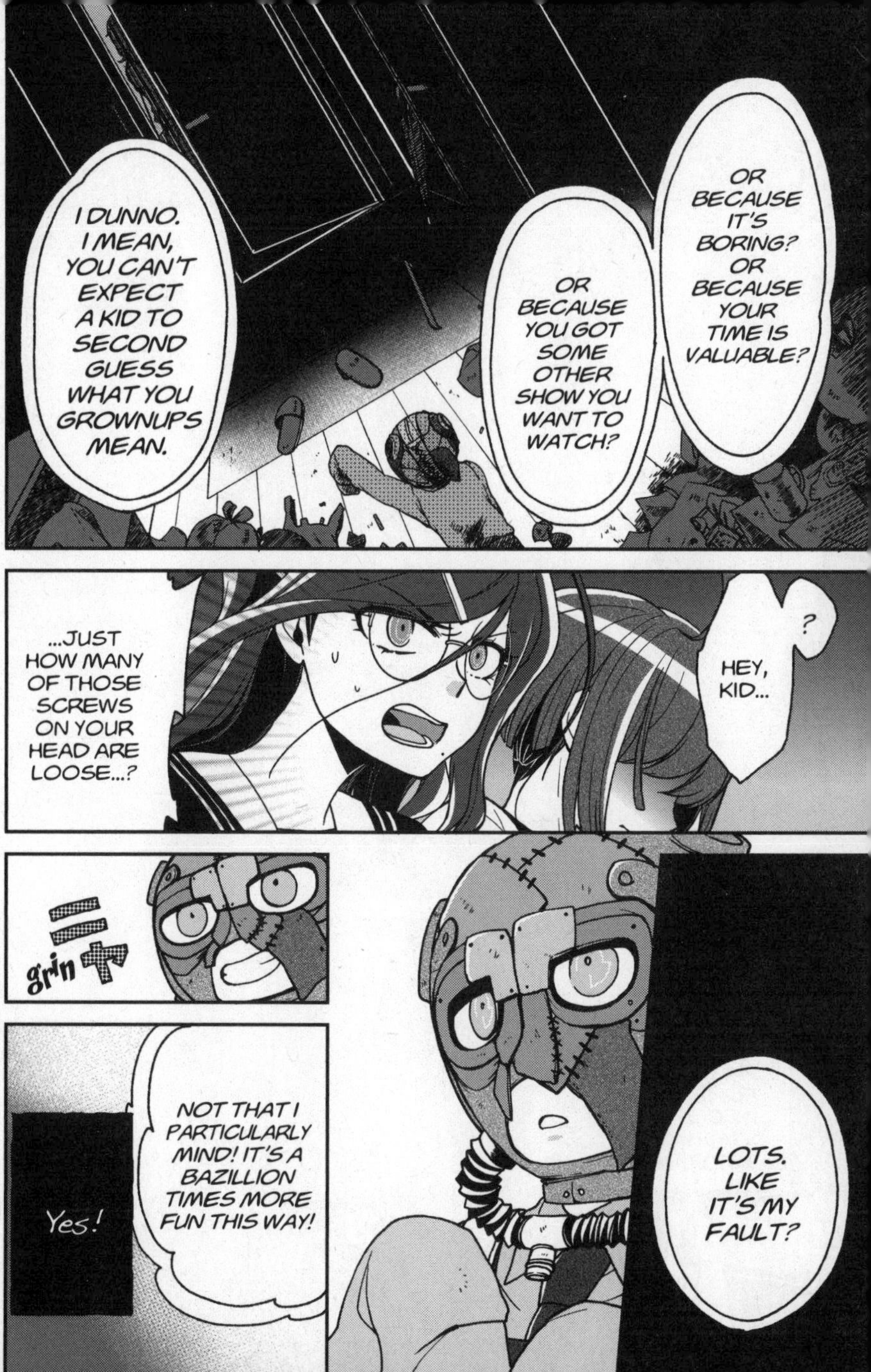
OR BECAUSE IT'S BORING? OR BECAUSE YOUR TIME IS VALUABLE?
OR BECAUSE YOU GOT SOME OTHER SHOW YOU WANT TO WATCH?
I DUNNO. I MEAN, YOU CAN'T EXPECT A KID TO SECOND GUESS WHAT YOU GROWNUPS MEAN.
?
HEY, KID...
...JUST HOW MANY OF THOSE SCREWS ON YOUR HEAD ARE LOOSE...?
LOTS. LIKE IT'S MY FAULT?
grin
NOT THAT I PARTICULARLY MIND! IT'S A BAZILLION TIMES MORE FUN THIS WAY!
Yes!

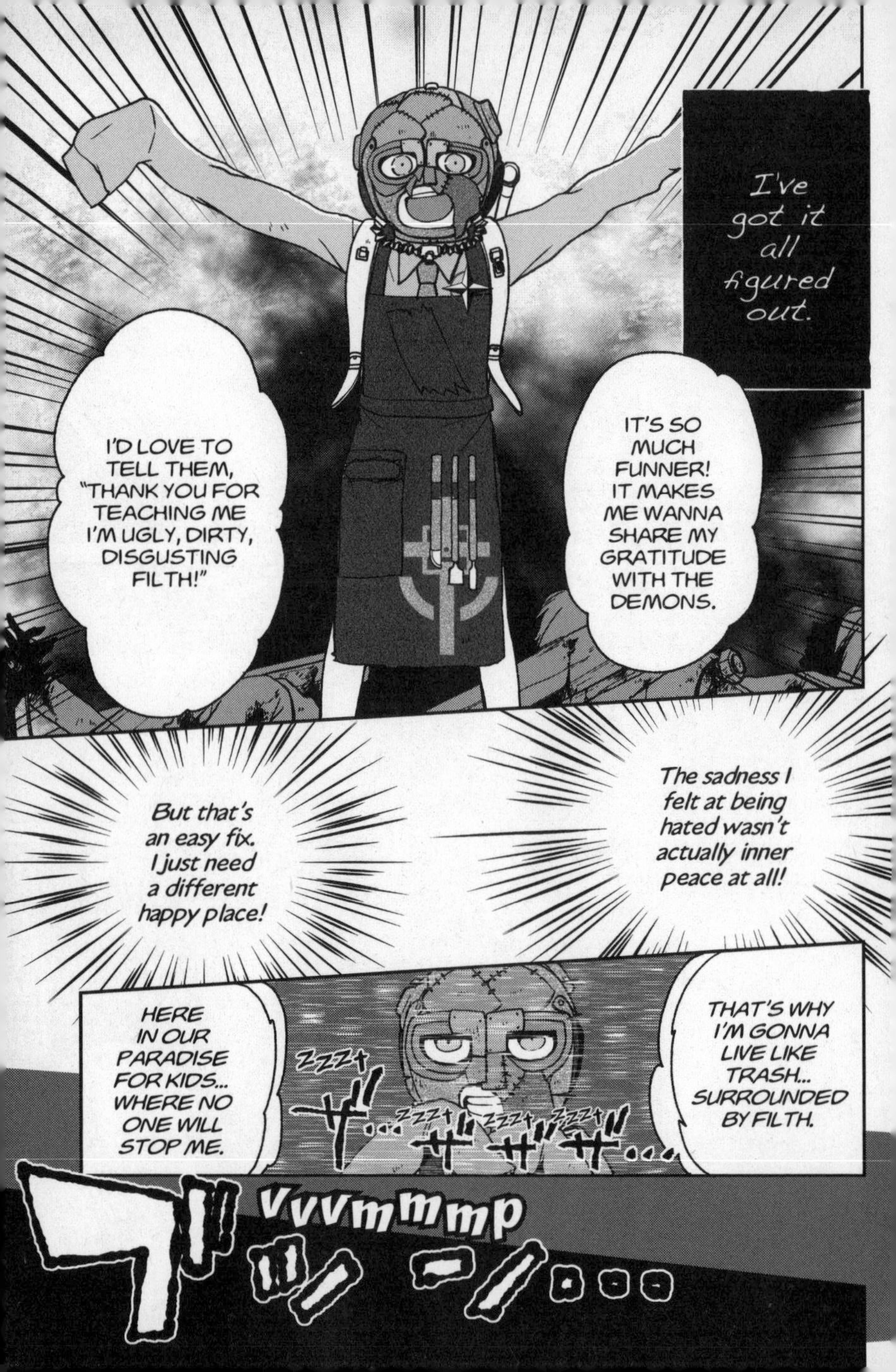
I've got it all figured out.
IT'S SO MUCH FUNNER! IT MAKES ME WANNA SHARE MY GRATITUDE WITH THE DEMONS.
I'D LOVE TO TELL THEM, "THANK YOU FOR TEACHING ME I'M UGLY, DIRTY, DISGUSTING FILTH!"
The sadness I felt at being hated wasn't actually inner peace at all!
But that's an easy fix. I just need a different happy place!
THAT'S WHY I'M GONNA LIVE LIKE TRASH... SURROUNDED BY FILTH.
ZZZT
HERE IN OUR PARADISE FOR KIDS... WHERE NO ONE WILL STOP ME.
vvvmmmp

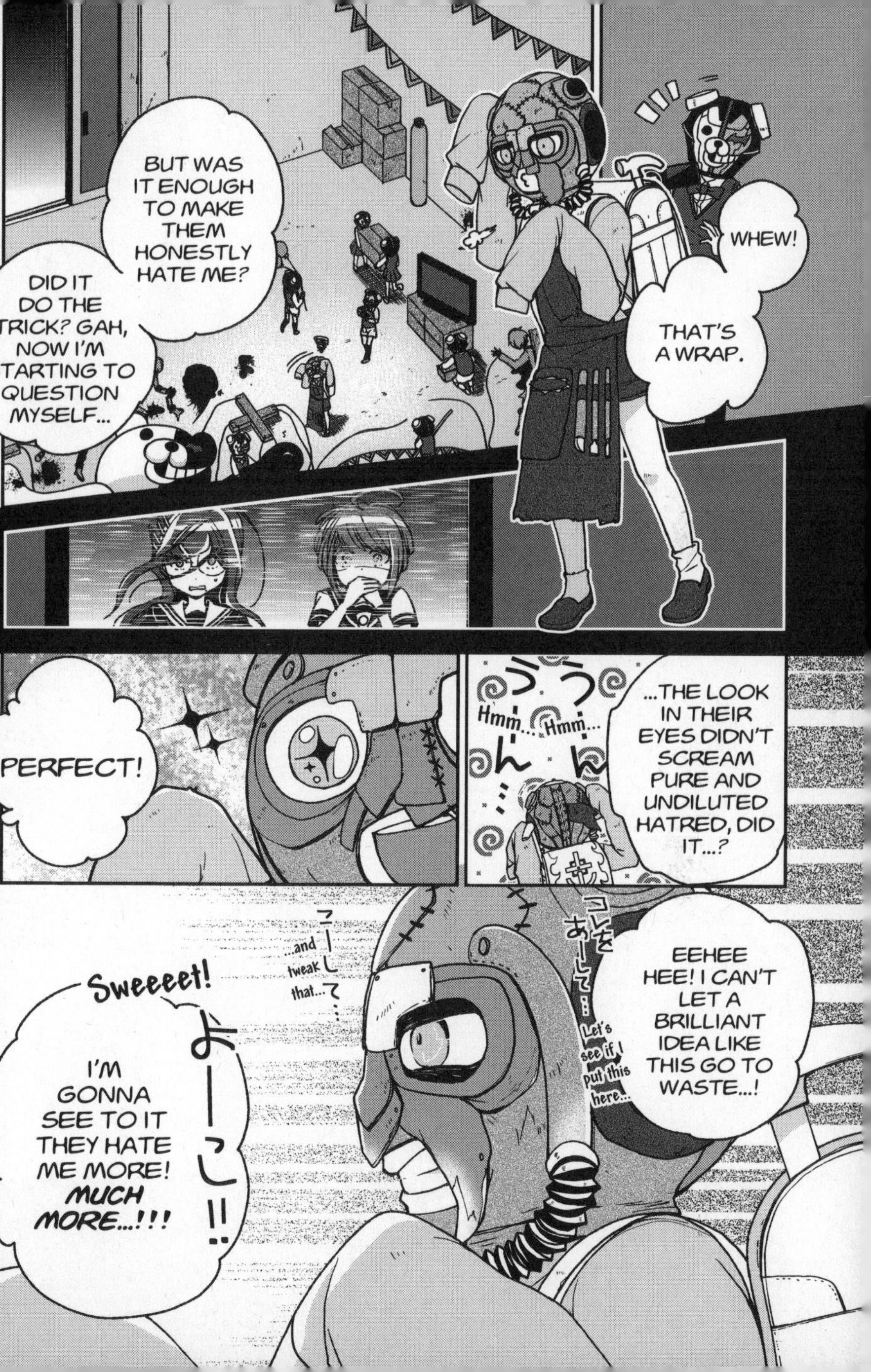
WHEW!
THAT'S A WRAP.
BUT WAS IT ENOUGH TO MAKE THEM HONESTLY HATE ME?
DID IT DO THE TRICK? GAH, NOW I'M STARTING TO QUESTION MYSELF...
...THE LOOK IN THEIR EYES DIDN'T SCREAM PURE AND UNDILUTED HATRED, DID IT...?
うーん…
Hmm...
うーん…
Hmm...
PERFECT!
EEHEE HEE! I CAN'T LET A BRILLIANT IDEA LIKE THIS GO TO WASTE...!
コレをあーして…
Let's see if I put this here...
こーして…
...and tweak that...
Sweeeet!
よーっし!!
I'M GONNA SEE TO IT THEY HATE ME MORE! *MUCH MORE...!!!*

Danganronpa Another Episode:
Ultra Despair Girls

Danganronpa Another Episode:
Ultra Despair Girls

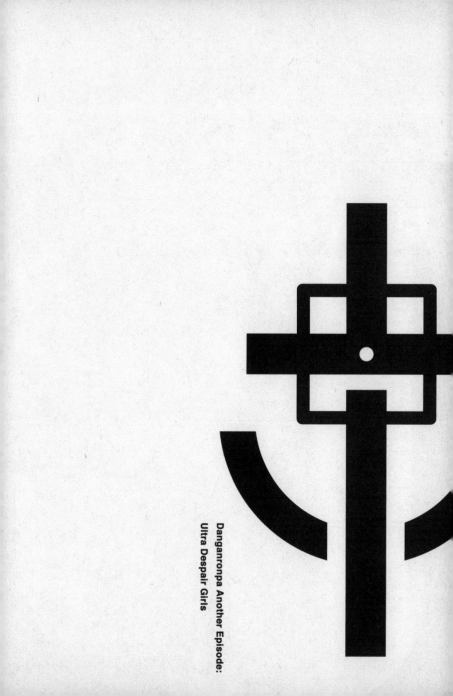

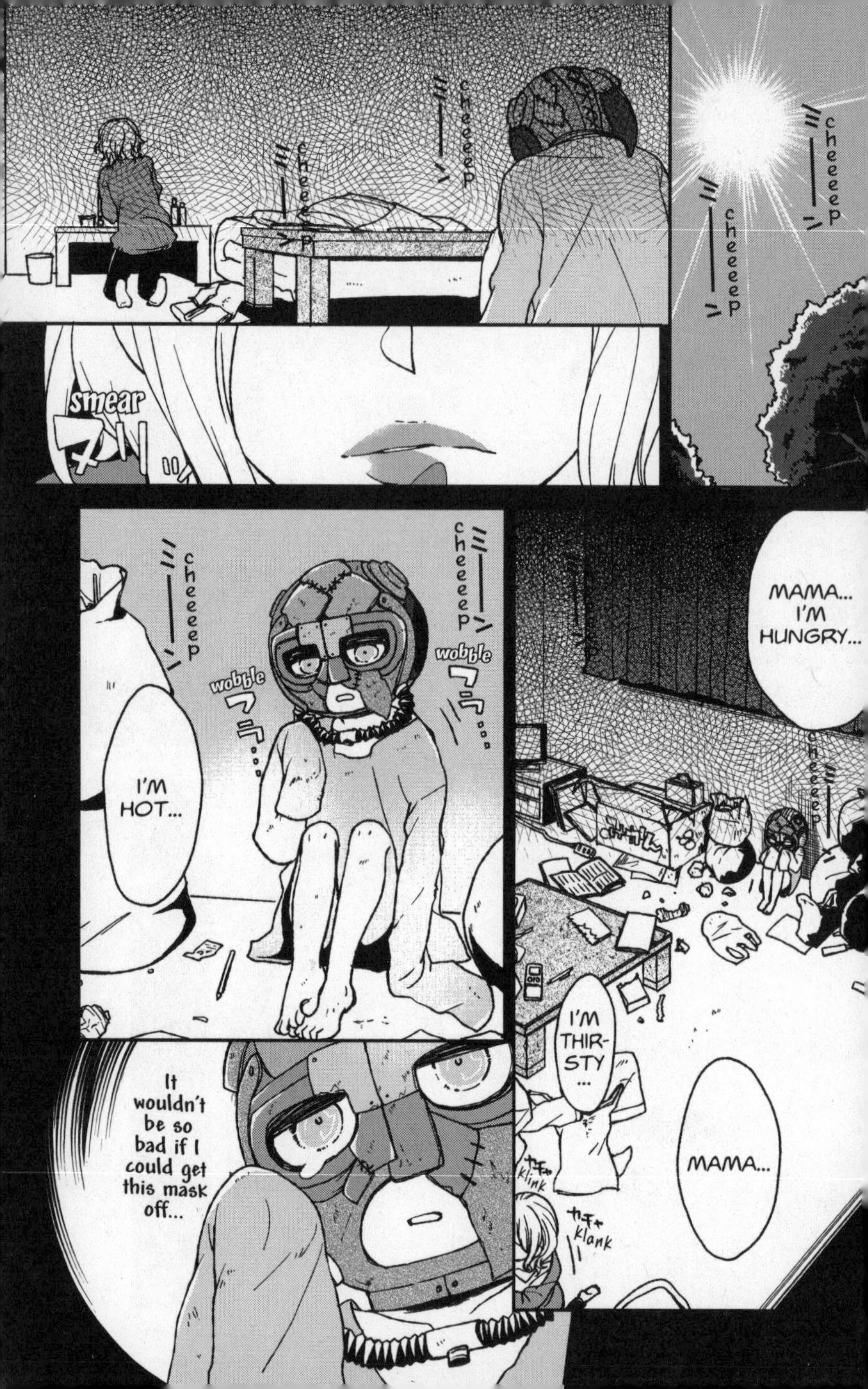
cheeeep
cheeeep
cheeeep
cheeeep
smear
MAMA... I'M HUNGRY...
cheeeep
I'M THIRSTY...
MAMA...
klink
klank
cheeeep
cheeeep
wobble
wobble
I'M HOT...
It wouldn't be so bad if I could get this mask off...

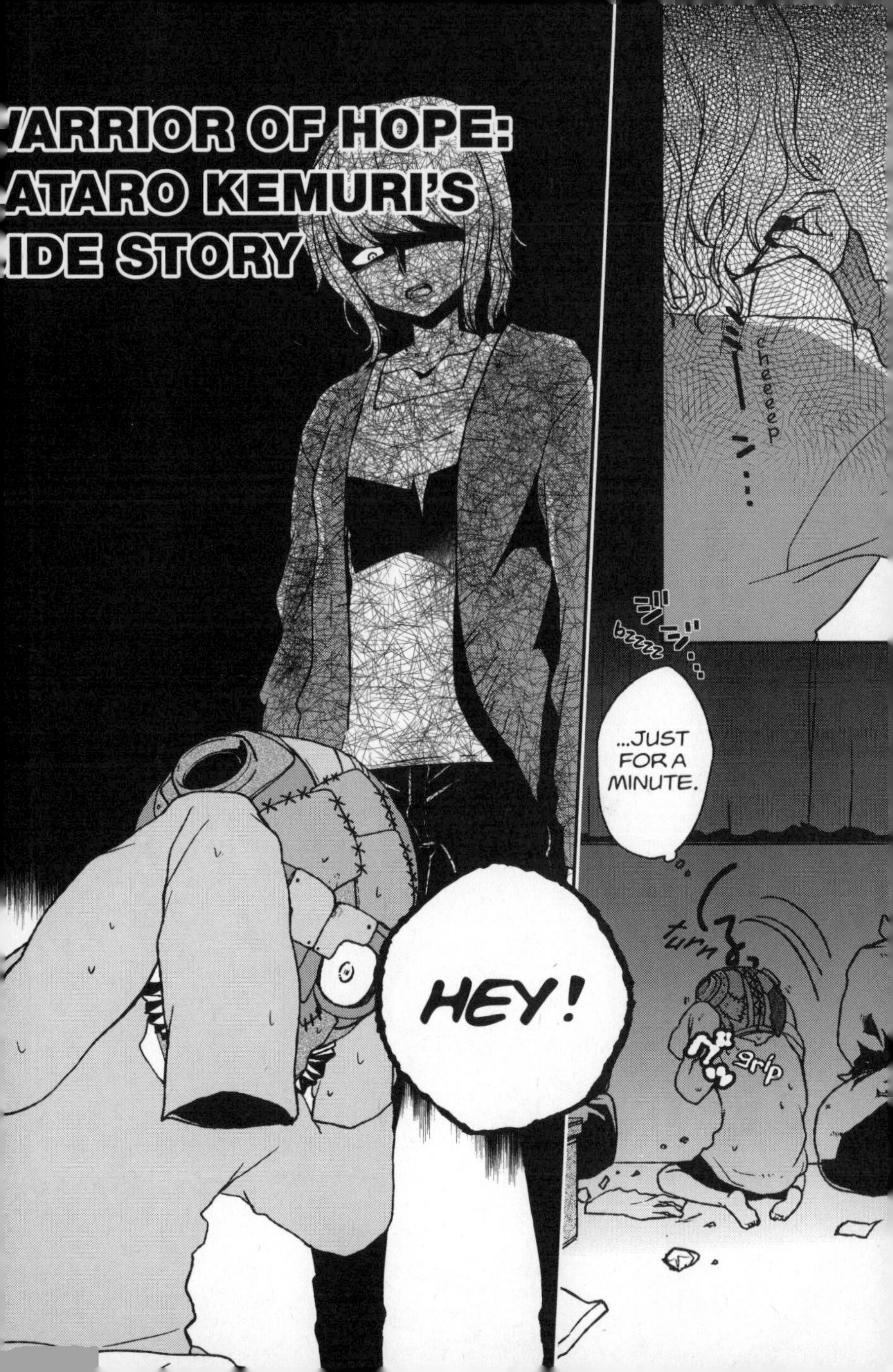
cheeeep
bzzzz
...JUST FOR A MINUTE.
turn
grip
/ARRIOR OF HOPE:
ATARO KEMURI'S
IDE STORY
HEY!

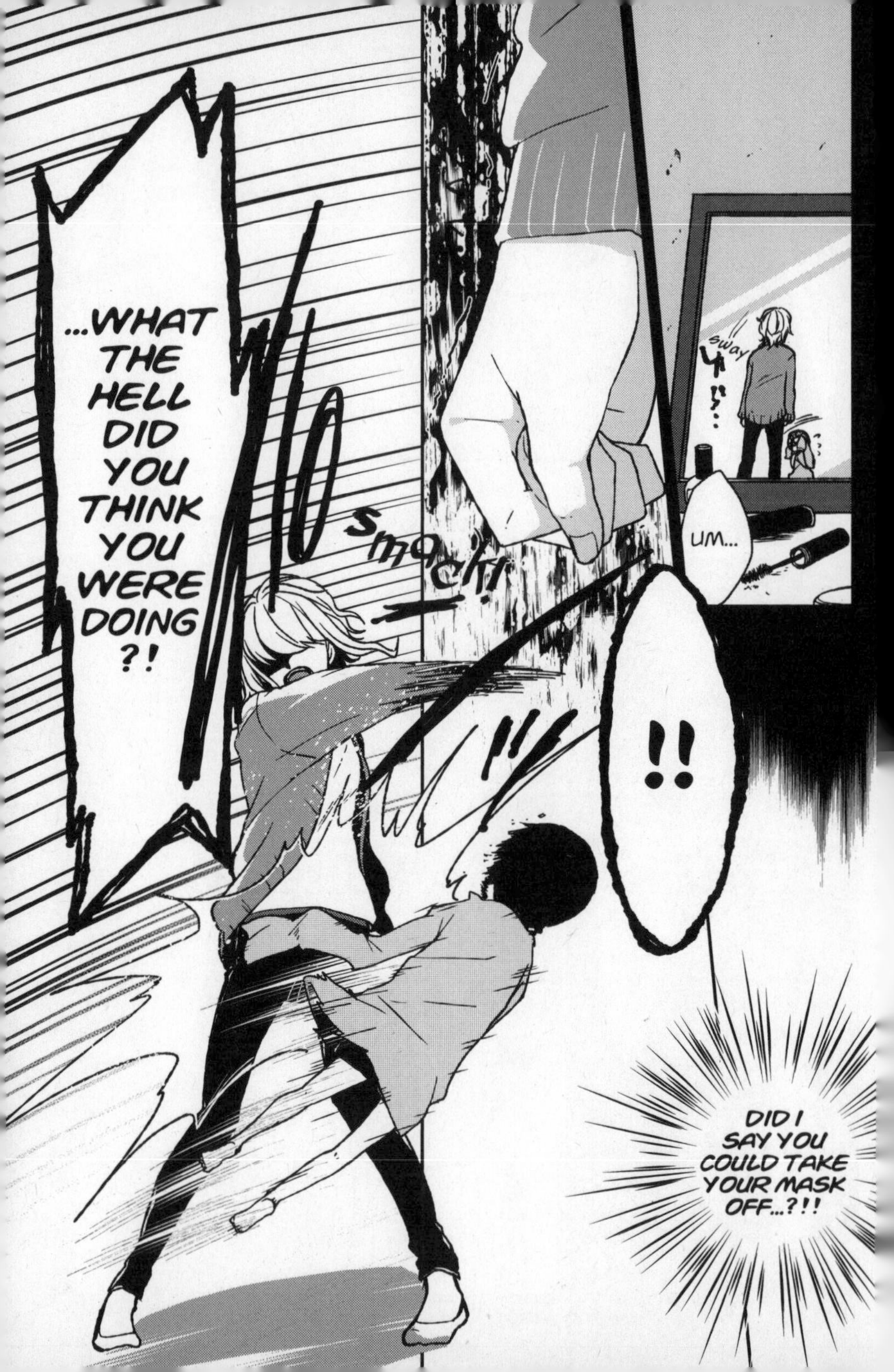
sway
UM...
!!
DID I SAY YOU COULD TAKE YOUR MASK OFF...?!!
...WHAT THE HELL DID YOU THINK YOU WERE DOING?!
smack!

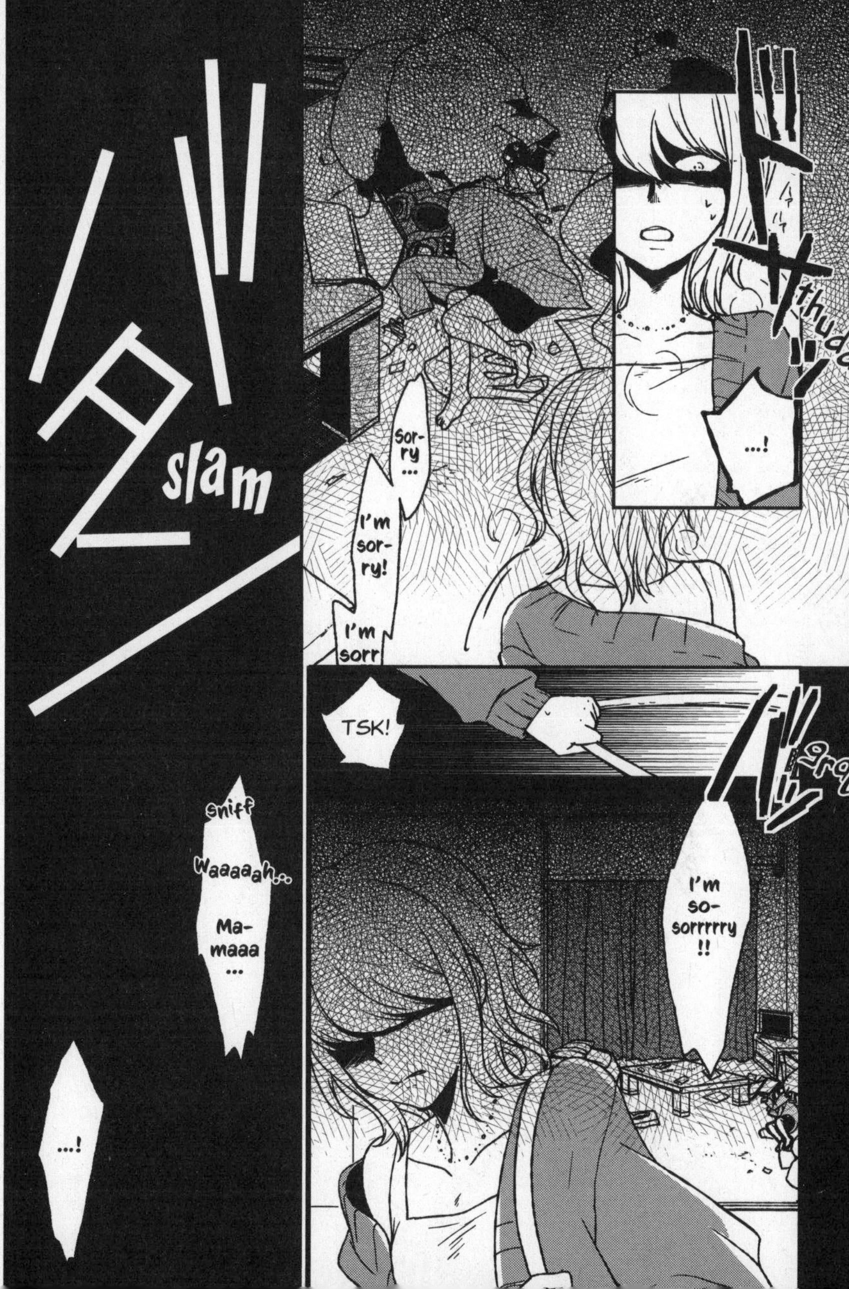
…!
thudd
Sor-ry…
I'm sor-ry!
I'm sorr
grab
TSK!
I'm so-sorrrrry!!
slam
sniff
Waaaaah…
Ma-maaa…
…!

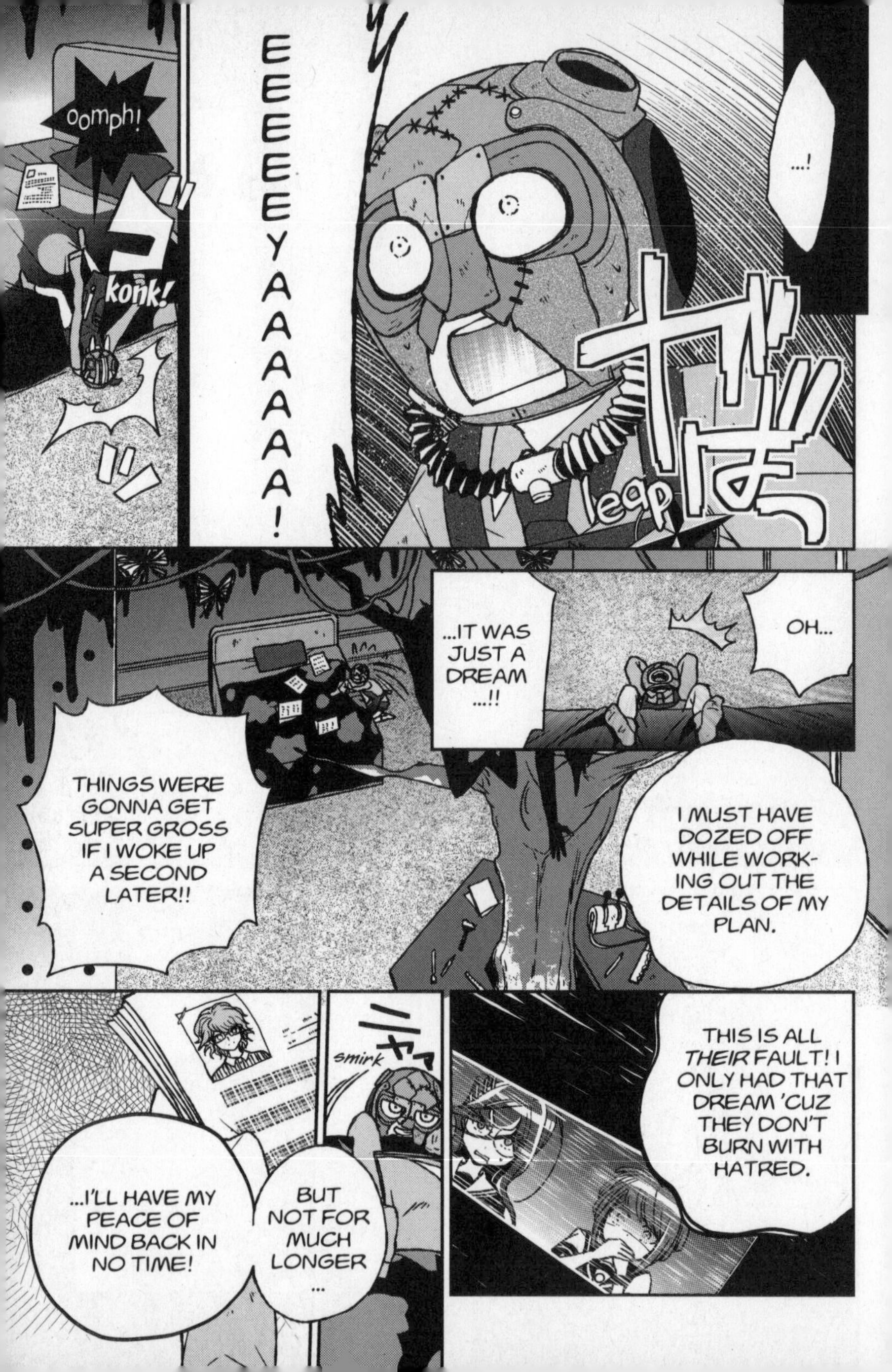
...!
EEEEEEYAAAAAAA!
leap
oomph!
konk!
OH...
...IT WAS JUST A DREAM ...!!
I MUST HAVE DOZED OFF WHILE WORKING OUT THE DETAILS OF MY PLAN.
THINGS WERE GONNA GET SUPER GROSS IF I WOKE UP A SECOND LATER!!
THIS IS ALL *THEIR* FAULT! I ONLY HAD THAT DREAM 'CUZ THEY DON'T BURN WITH HATRED.
smirk
BUT NOT FOR MUCH LONGER ...
...I'LL HAVE MY PEACE OF MIND BACK IN NO TIME!

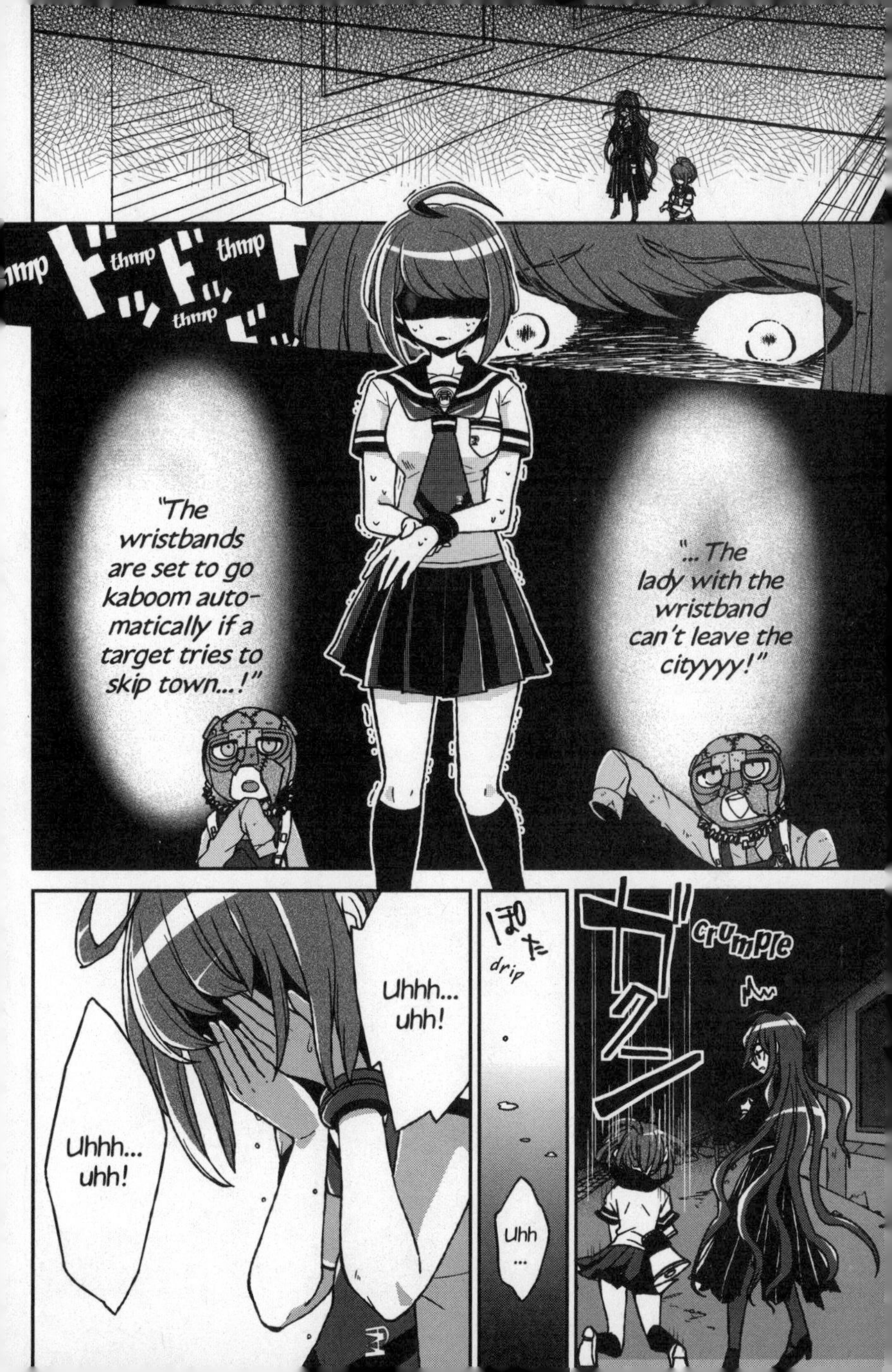
thmp
thmp
thmp
thmp
"... The lady with the wristband can't leave the cityyyy!"
"The wristbands are set to go kaboom automatically if a target tries to skip town...!"
crumple
ぽた
drip
Uhh ...
Uhhh... uhh!
Uhhh... uhh!

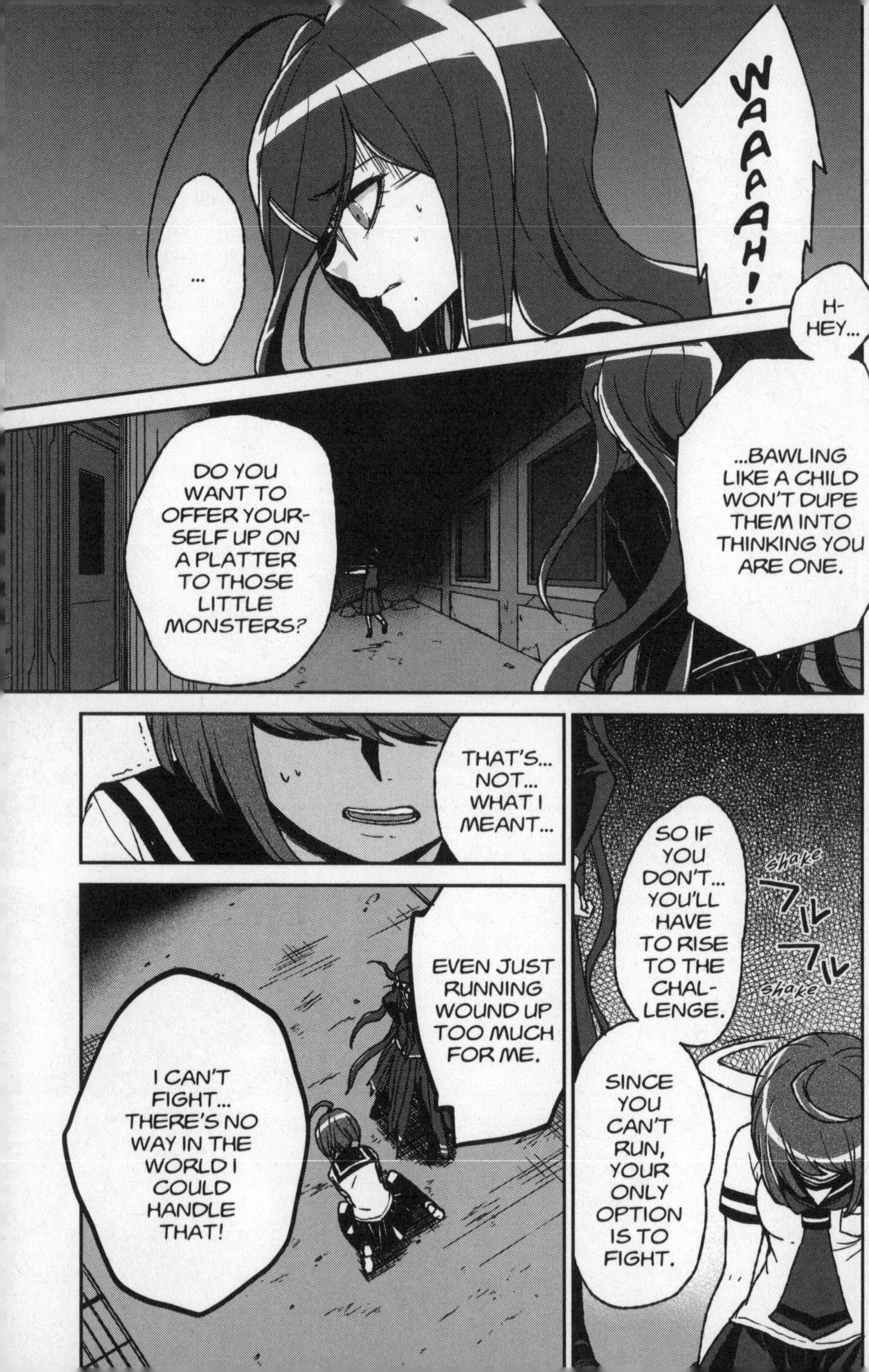
WAAAAH!
H-HEY...
...
...BAWLING LIKE A CHILD WON'T DUPE THEM INTO THINKING YOU ARE ONE.
DO YOU WANT TO OFFER YOUR-SELF UP ON A PLATTER TO THOSE LITTLE MONSTERS?
SO IF YOU DON'T... YOU'LL HAVE TO RISE TO THE CHAL-LENGE.
shake
shake
SINCE YOU CAN'T RUN, YOUR ONLY OPTION IS TO FIGHT.
THAT'S... NOT... WHAT I MEANT...
EVEN JUST RUNNING WOUND UP TOO MUCH FOR ME.
I CAN'T FIGHT... THERE'S NO WAY IN THE WORLD I COULD HANDLE THAT!

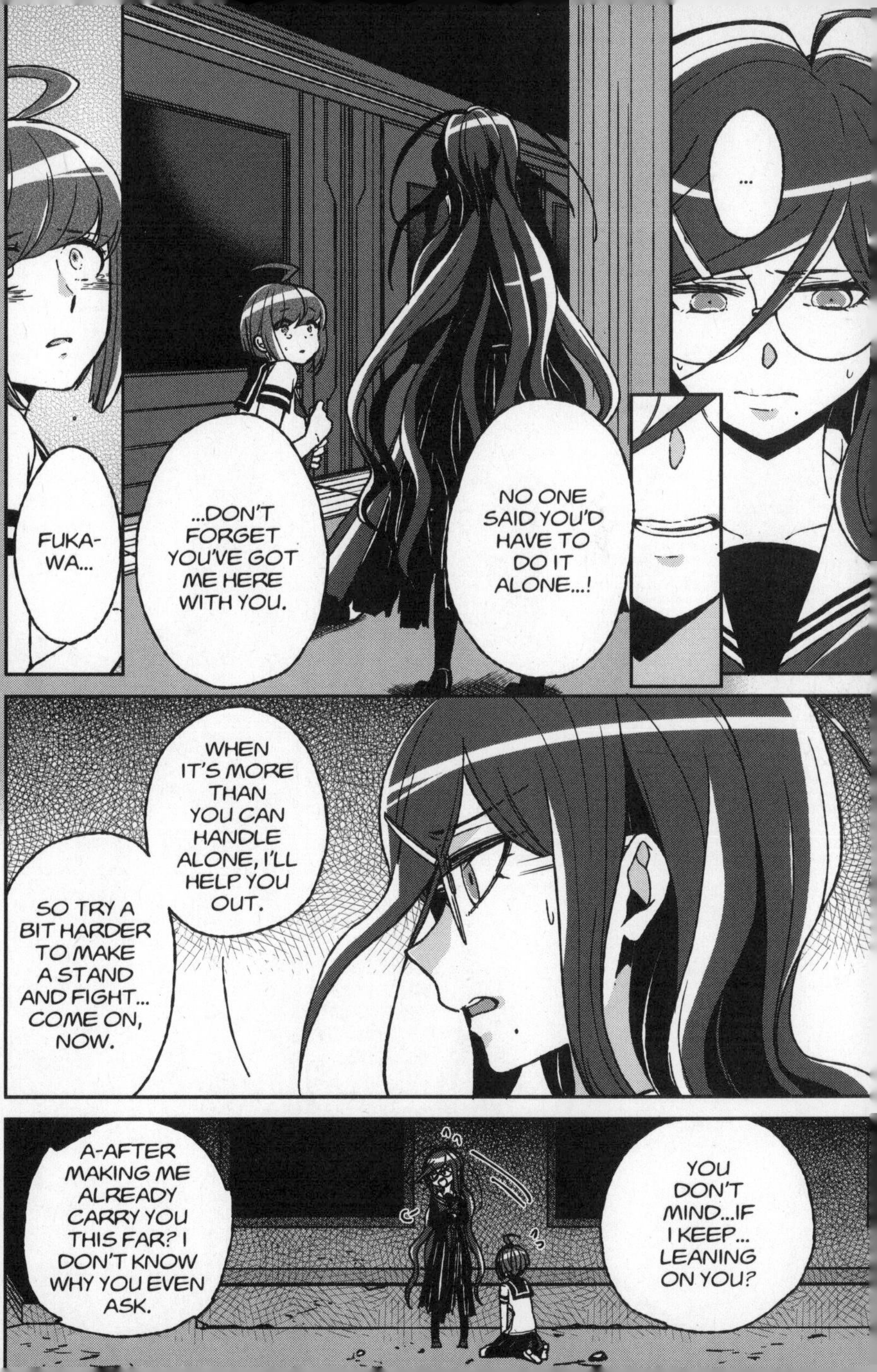
...
NO ONE SAID YOU'D HAVE TO DO IT ALONE...!
...DON'T FORGET YOU'VE GOT ME HERE WITH YOU.
FUKA-WA...
WHEN IT'S MORE THAN YOU CAN HANDLE ALONE, I'LL HELP YOU OUT.
SO TRY A BIT HARDER TO MAKE A STAND AND FIGHT... COME ON, NOW.
YOU DON'T MIND...IF I KEEP... LEANING ON YOU?
A-AFTER MAKING ME ALREADY CARRY YOU THIS FAR? I DON'T KNOW WHY YOU EVEN ASK.

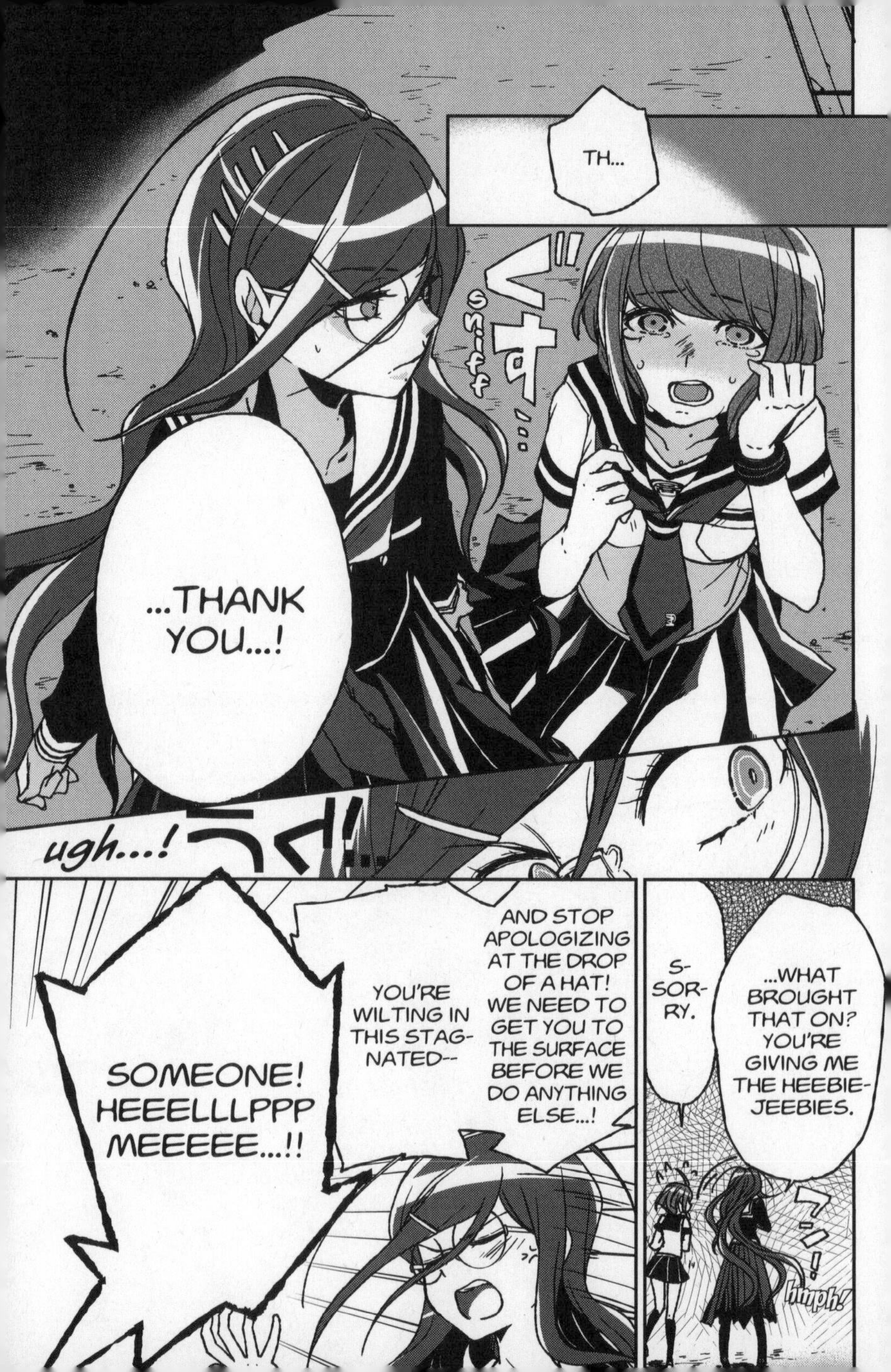
TH...
snifff...
...THANK YOU...!
ugh...!
...WHAT BROUGHT THAT ON? YOU'RE GIVING ME THE HEEBIE-JEEBIES.
S-SORRY.
hmph!
AND STOP APOLOGIZING AT THE DROP OF A HAT! WE NEED TO GET YOU TO THE SURFACE BEFORE WE DO ANYTHING ELSE...!
YOU'RE WILTING IN THIS STAGNATED--
SOMEONE! HEEELLLPPP MEEEEE...!!

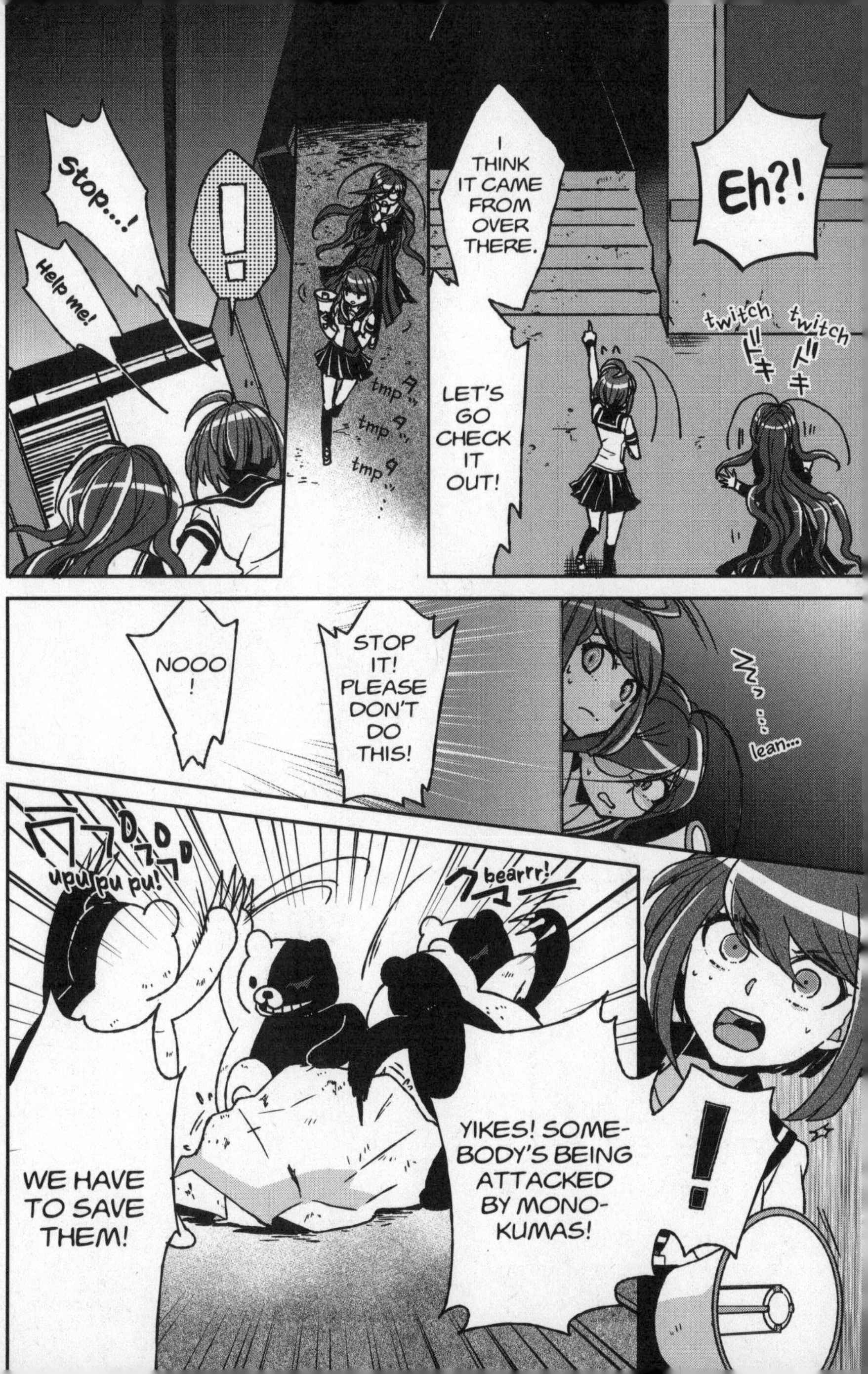
Eh?!
twitch ドキ
twitch ドキ
I THINK IT CAME FROM OVER THERE.
LET'S GO CHECK IT OUT!
tmp
tmp
tmp
!
Stop...!
Help me!
lean...
STOP IT! PLEASE DON'T DO THIS!
NOOO!
!
YIKES! SOMEBODY'S BEING ATTACKED BY MONOKUMAS!
bearrr!
upupu pu pu!
WE HAVE TO SAVE THEM!

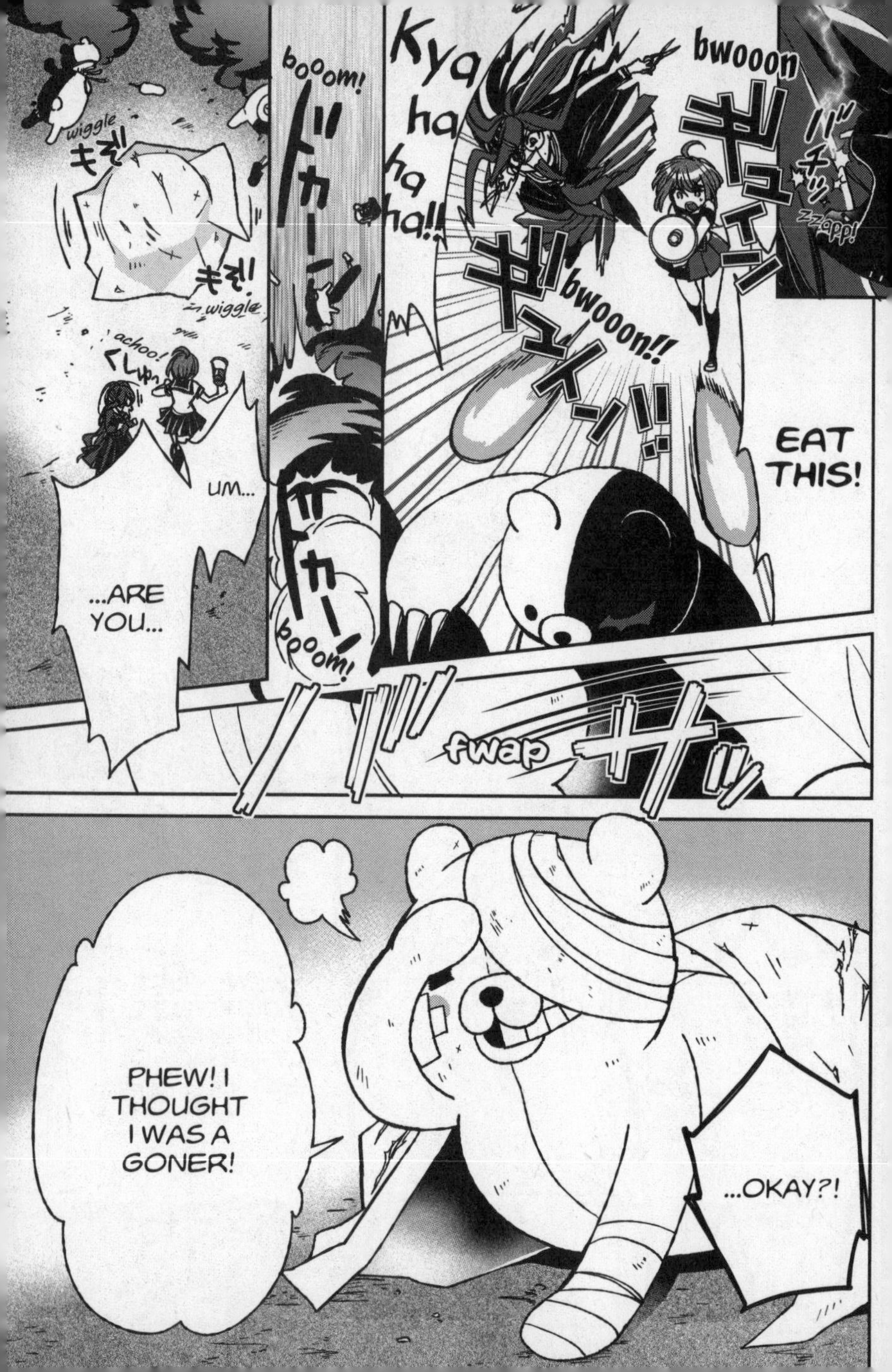

バチッ
zzapp!
bwooon
ギュイーン
Kya ha ha ha!!
bwooon!!
ギュイーン!!
EAT THIS!
booom!
ドカーン
ドカーン
booom!
wiggle
もぞ
もぞ!!
wiggle
achoo!
くしゅっ
UM...
...ARE YOU...
fwap
...OKAY?!
PHEW! I THOUGHT I WAS A GONER!

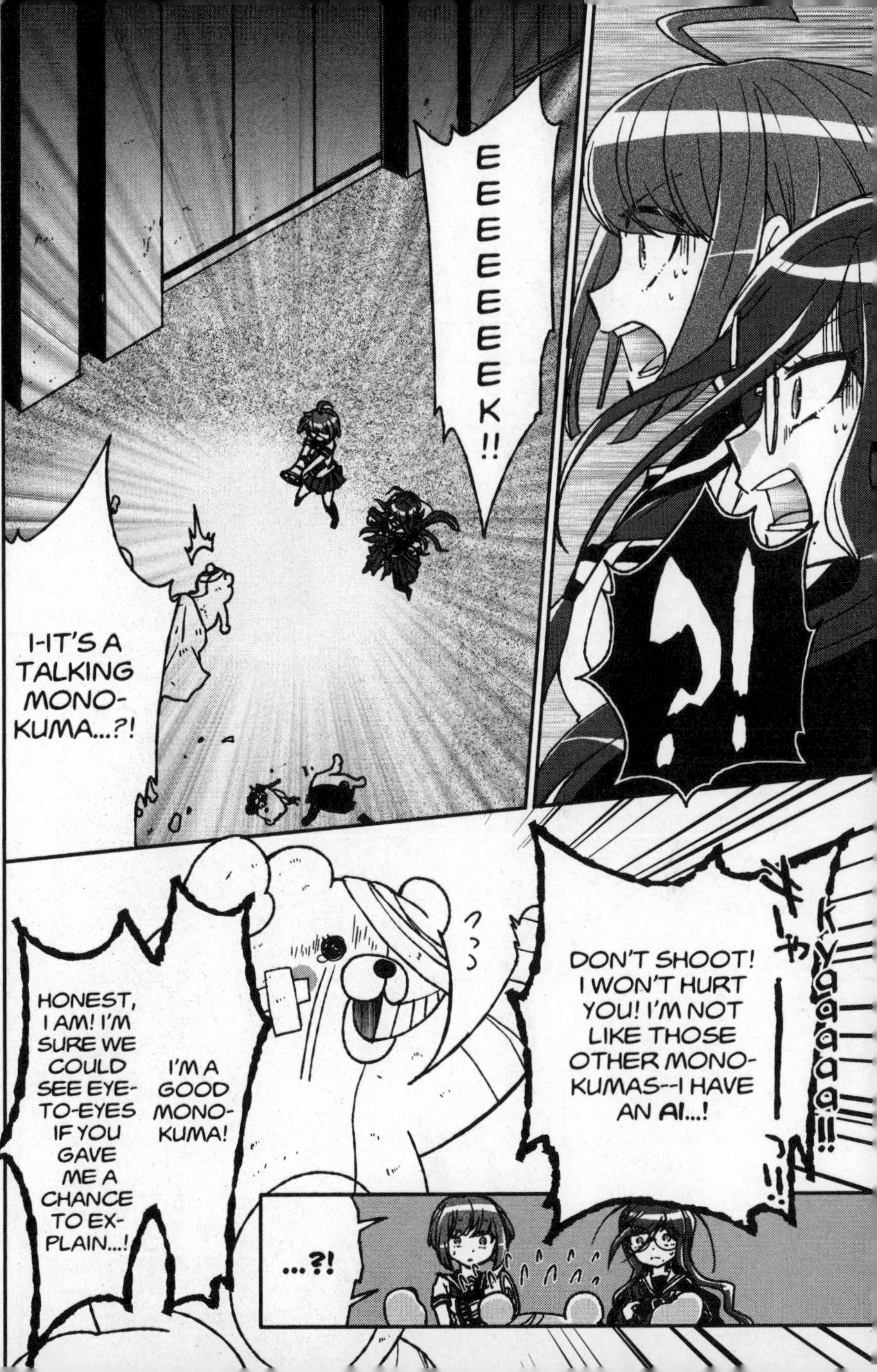
?!
EEEEEEEK!!
I-IT'S A TALKING MONO-KUMA...?!
Kyaaaaaaa!!
DON'T SHOOT! I WON'T HURT YOU! I'M NOT LIKE THOSE OTHER MONO-KUMAS--I HAVE AN AI...!
I'M A GOOD MONO-KUMA!
HONEST, I AM! I'M SURE WE COULD SEE EYE-TO-EYES IF YOU GAVE ME A CHANCE TO EX-PLAIN...!
...?!

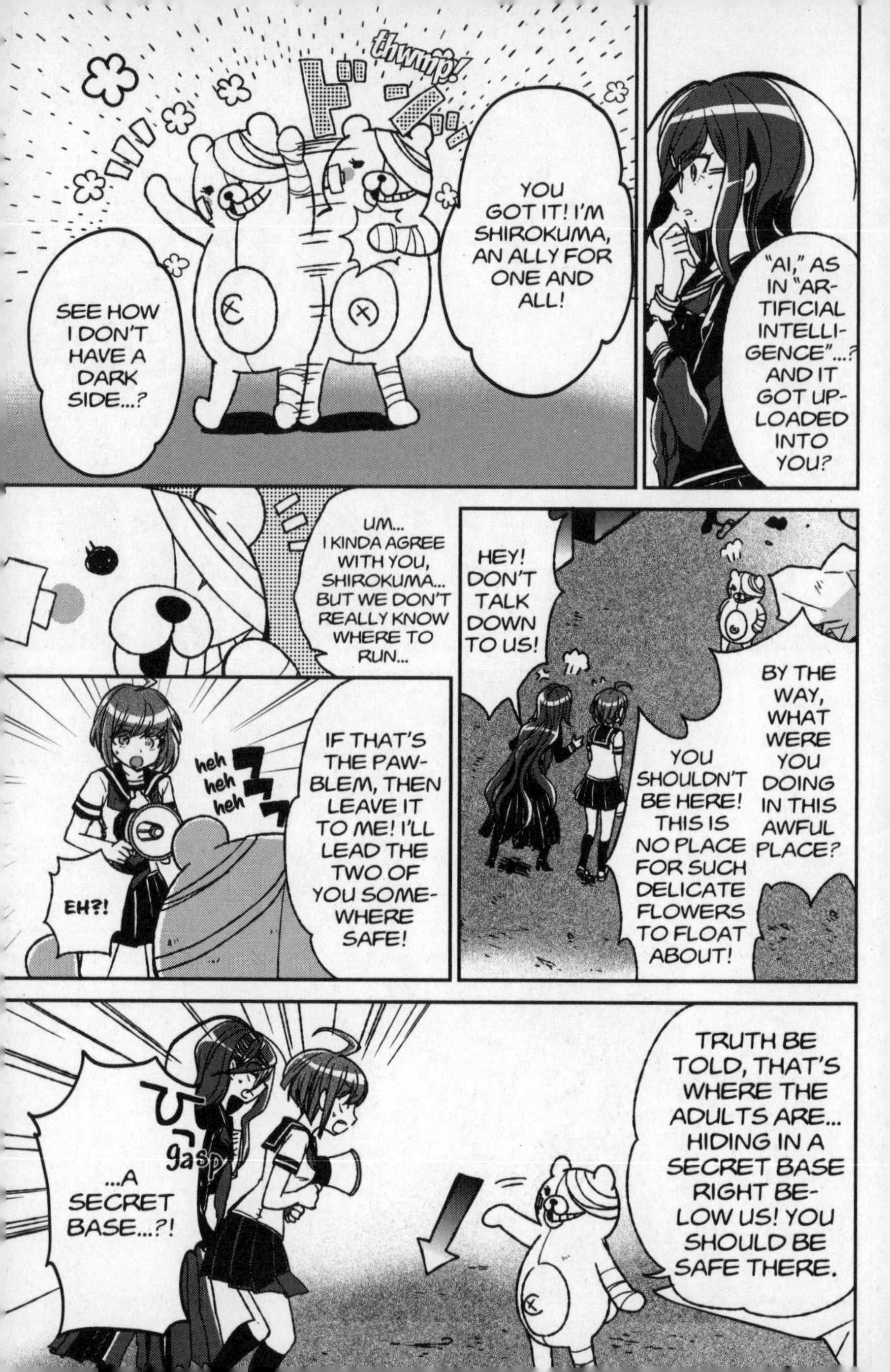
"AI," AS IN "ARTIFICIAL INTELLIGENCE"...? AND IT GOT UPLOADED INTO YOU?
thwmp!
YOU GOT IT! I'M SHIROKUMA, AN ALLY FOR ONE AND ALL!
SEE HOW I DON'T HAVE A DARK SIDE...?
BY THE WAY, WHAT WERE YOU DOING IN THIS AWFUL PLACE?
YOU SHOULDN'T BE HERE! THIS IS NO PLACE FOR SUCH DELICATE FLOWERS TO FLOAT ABOUT!
HEY! DON'T TALK DOWN TO US!
UM... I KINDA AGREE WITH YOU, SHIROKUMA... BUT WE DON'T REALLY KNOW WHERE TO RUN...
IF THAT'S THE PAWBLEM, THEN LEAVE IT TO ME! I'LL LEAD THE TWO OF YOU SOMEWHERE SAFE!
heh heh heh
EH?!
TRUTH BE TOLD, THAT'S WHERE THE ADULTS ARE... HIDING IN A SECRET BASE RIGHT BELOW US! YOU SHOULD BE SAFE THERE.
gasp
...A SECRET BASE...?!

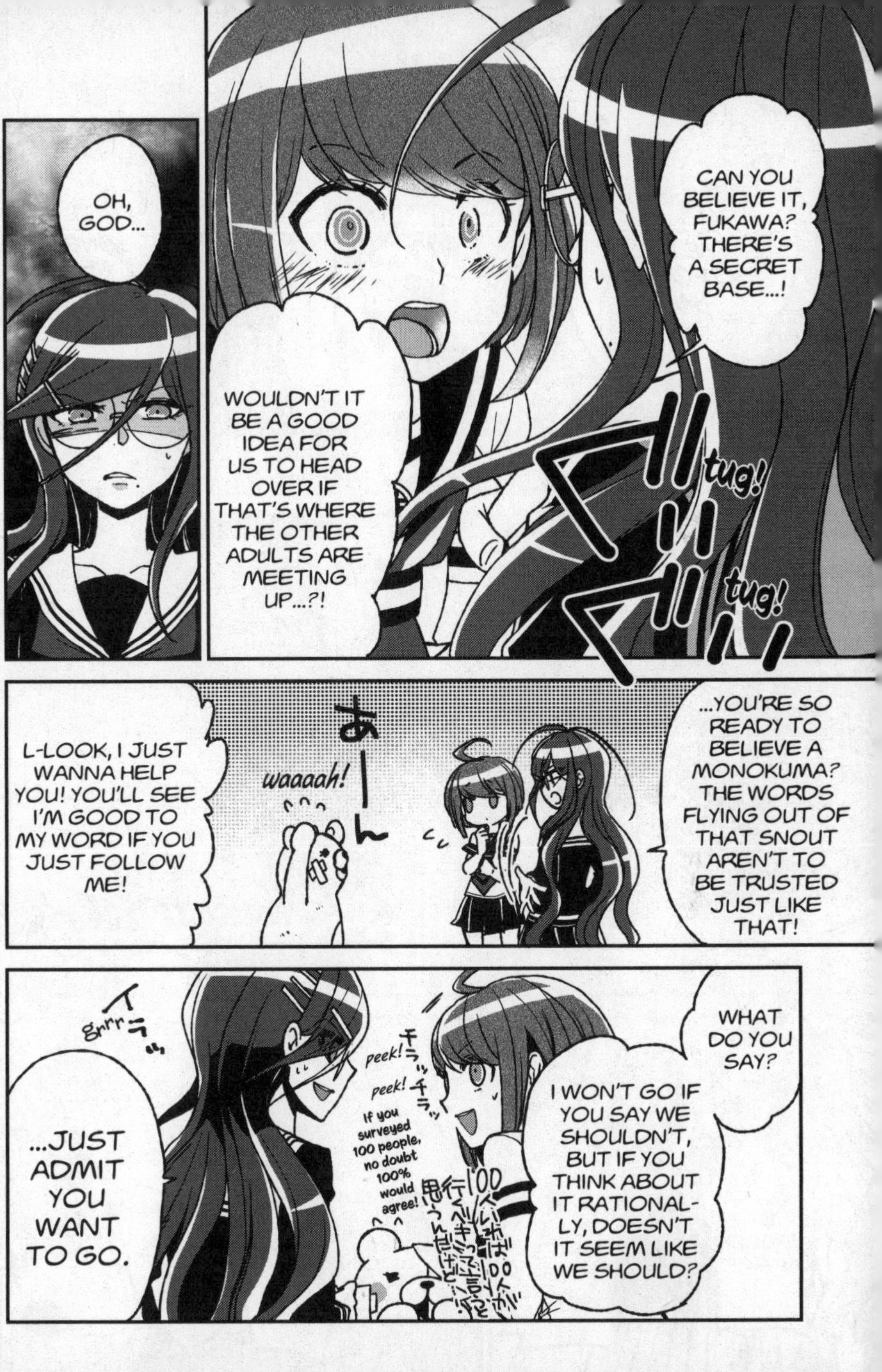
CAN YOU BELIEVE IT, FUKAWA? THERE'S A SECRET BASE...!
WOULDN'T IT BE A GOOD IDEA FOR US TO HEAD OVER IF THAT'S WHERE THE OTHER ADULTS ARE MEETING UP...?!
tug!
tug!
OH, GOD...
...YOU'RE SO READY TO BELIEVE A MONOKUMA? THE WORDS FLYING OUT OF THAT SNOUT AREN'T TO BE TRUSTED JUST LIKE THAT!
あーん
waaaah!
L-LOOK, I JUST WANNA HELP YOU! YOU'LL SEE I'M GOOD TO MY WORD IF YOU JUST FOLLOW ME!
WHAT DO YOU SAY?
I WON'T GO IF YOU SAY WE SHOULDN'T, BUT IF YOU THINK ABOUT IT RATIONALLY, DOESN'T IT SEEM LIKE WE SHOULD?
peek! チラッ
peek! チラッ
If you surveyed 100 people, no doubt 100% would agree!
イラッ
grrr
...JUST ADMIT YOU WANT TO GO.

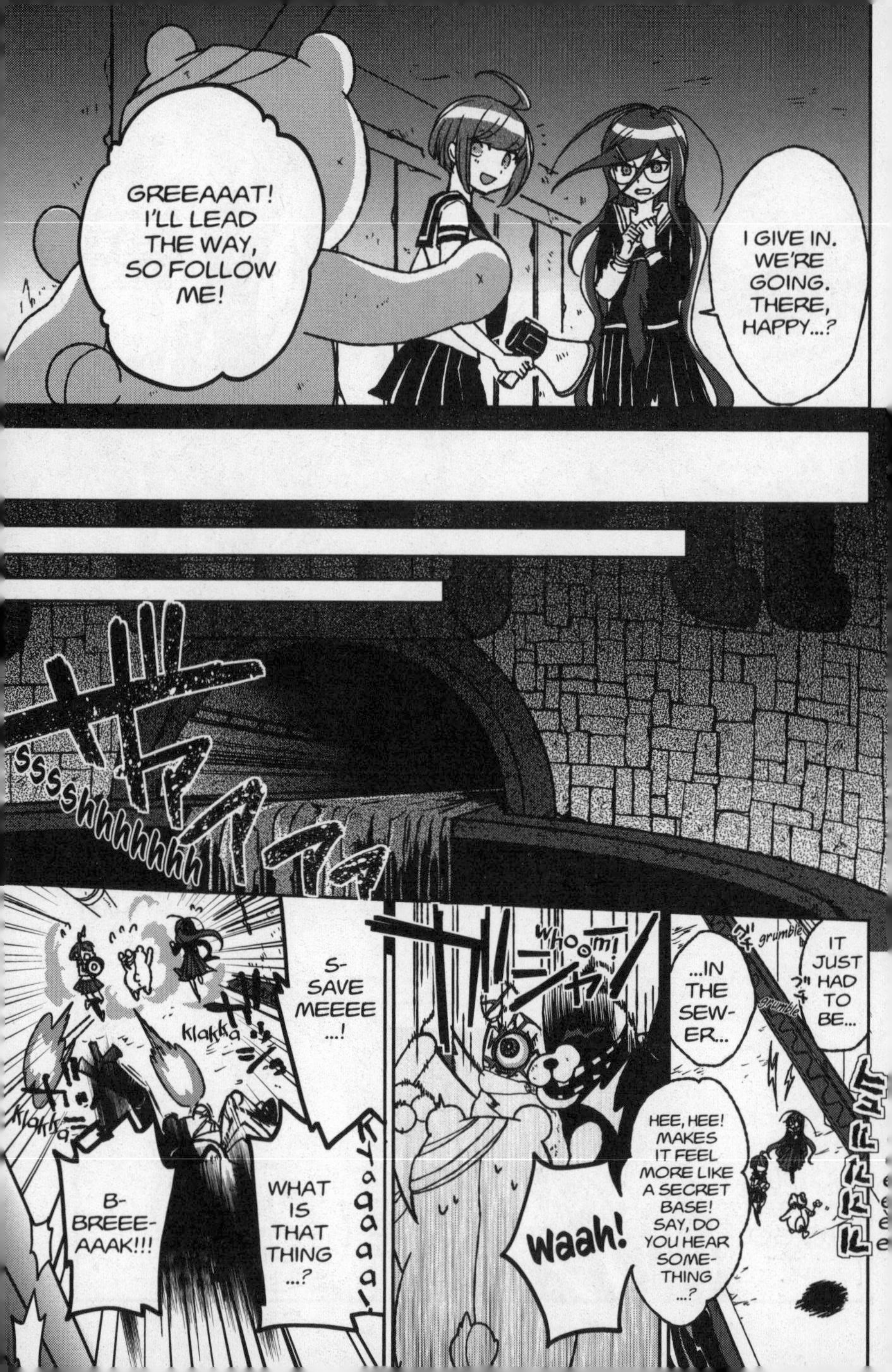
I GIVE IN. WE'RE GOING. THERE, HAPPY...?
GREEAAAT! I'LL LEAD THE WAY, SO FOLLOW ME!
Sssshhhhhhhh
IT JUST HAD TO BE...
grumble
grumble
...IN THE SEWER...
eeee
HEE, HEE! MAKES IT FEEL MORE LIKE A SECRET BASE! SAY, DO YOU HEAR SOMETHING...?
whoom!
waah!
S-SAVE MEEEE...!
klakka
klakka
Ktaaaaaa!
WHAT IS THAT THING...?
B-BREEEAAAK!!!

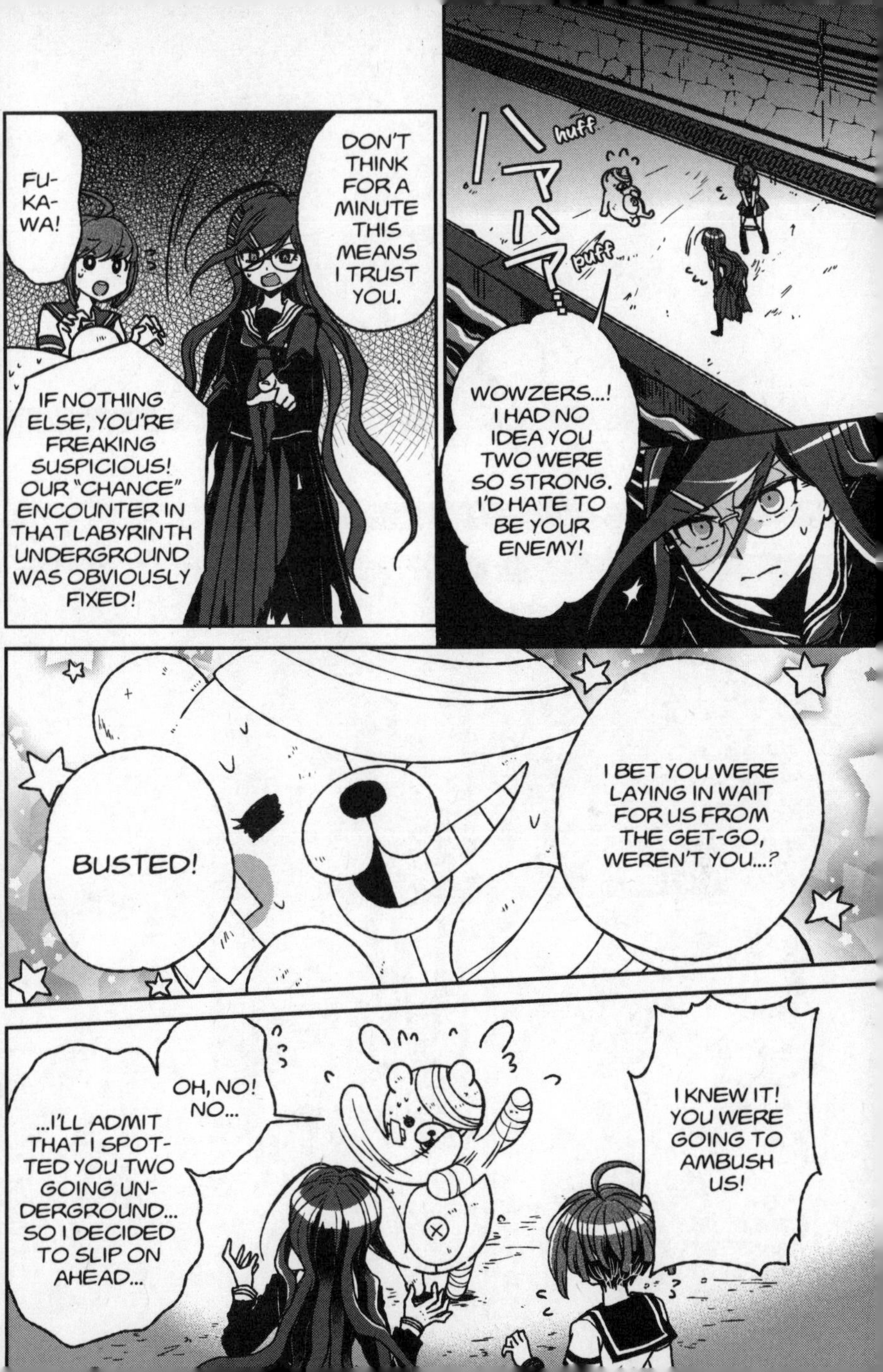
huff
puff
WOWZERS...! I HAD NO IDEA YOU TWO WERE SO STRONG. I'D HATE TO BE YOUR ENEMY!
DON'T THINK FOR A MINUTE THIS MEANS I TRUST YOU.
FU-KA-WA!
IF NOTHING ELSE, YOU'RE FREAKING SUSPICIOUS! OUR "CHANCE" ENCOUNTER IN THAT LABYRINTH UNDERGROUND WAS OBVIOUSLY FIXED!
I BET YOU WERE LAYING IN WAIT FOR US FROM THE GET-GO, WEREN'T YOU...?
BUSTED!
I KNEW IT! YOU WERE GOING TO AMBUSH US!
OH, NO! NO...
...I'LL ADMIT THAT I SPOTTED YOU TWO GOING UNDERGROUND... SO I DECIDED TO SLIP ON AHEAD...

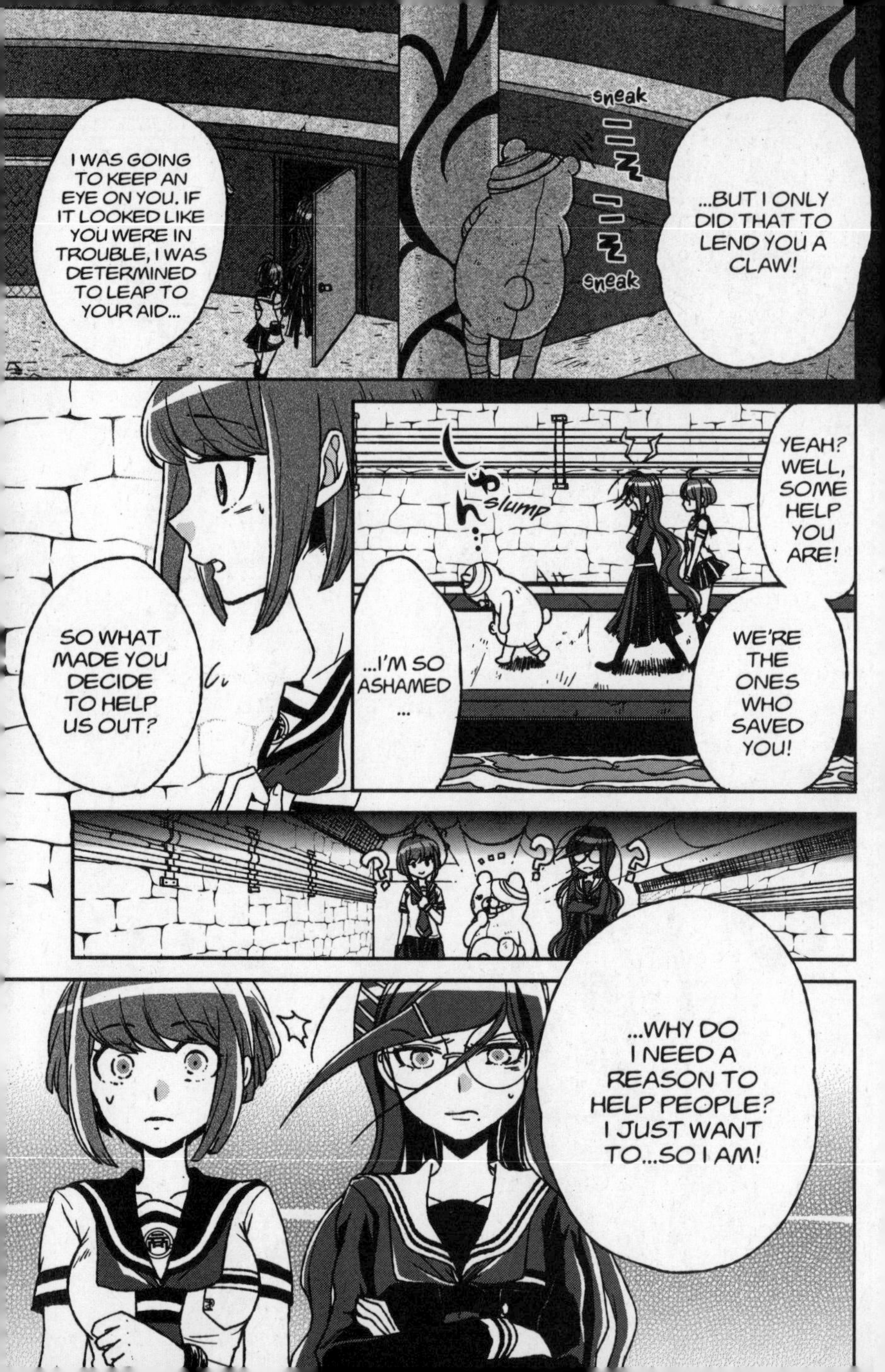
sneak
...BUT I ONLY DID THAT TO LEND YOU A CLAW!
sneak
I WAS GOING TO KEEP AN EYE ON YOU. IF IT LOOKED LIKE YOU WERE IN TROUBLE, I WAS DETERMINED TO LEAP TO YOUR AID...
YEAH? WELL, SOME HELP YOU ARE!
WE'RE THE ONES WHO SAVED YOU!
slump
...I'M SO ASHAMED...
SO WHAT MADE YOU DECIDE TO HELP US OUT?
...WHY DO I NEED A REASON TO HELP PEOPLE? I JUST WANT TO...SO I AM!

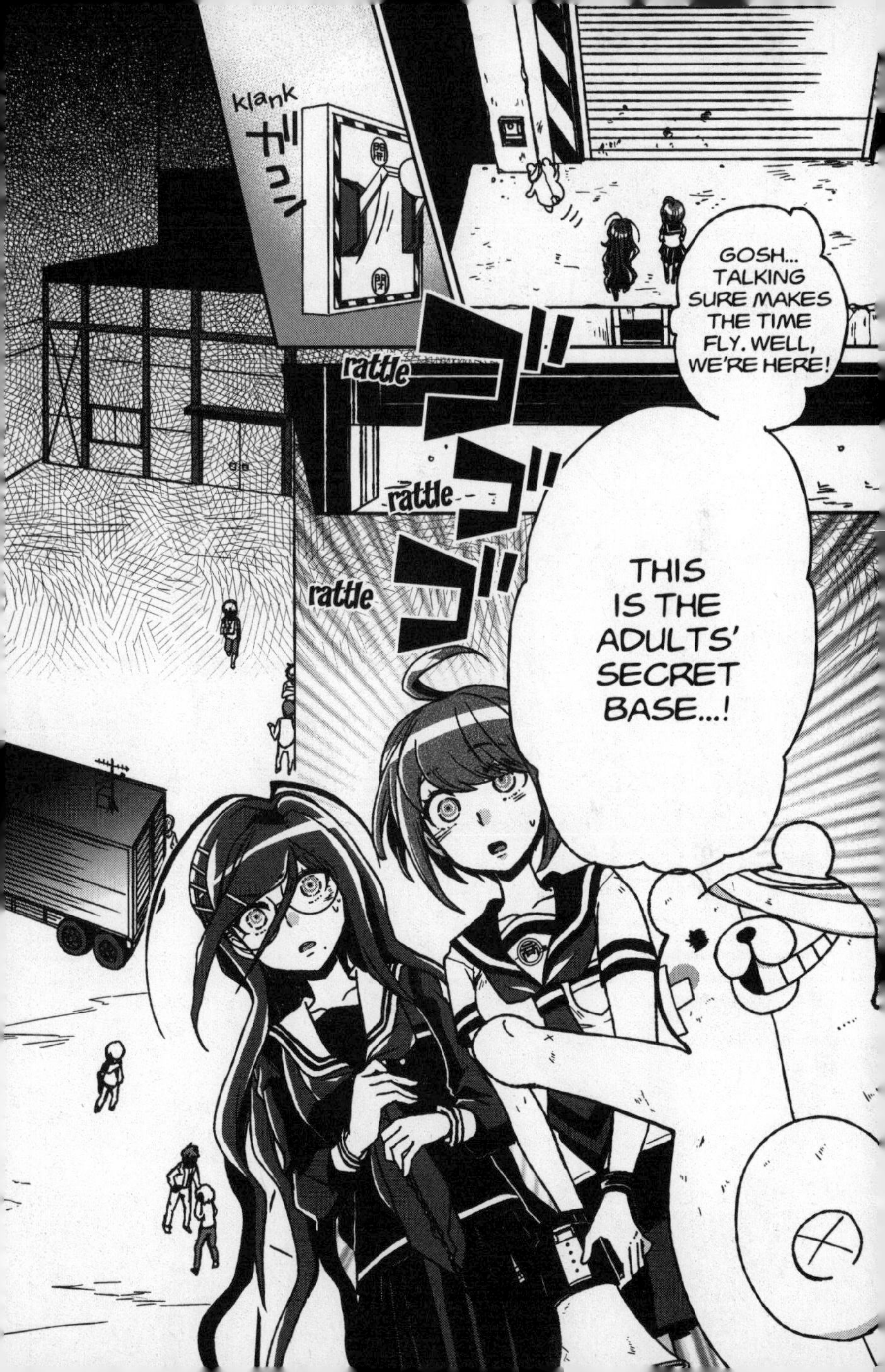
GOSH... TALKING SURE MAKES THE TIME FLY. WELL, WE'RE HERE!
klank
ガコン
rattle
rattle
rattle
ゴゴゴ
THIS IS THE ADULTS' SECRET BASE...!

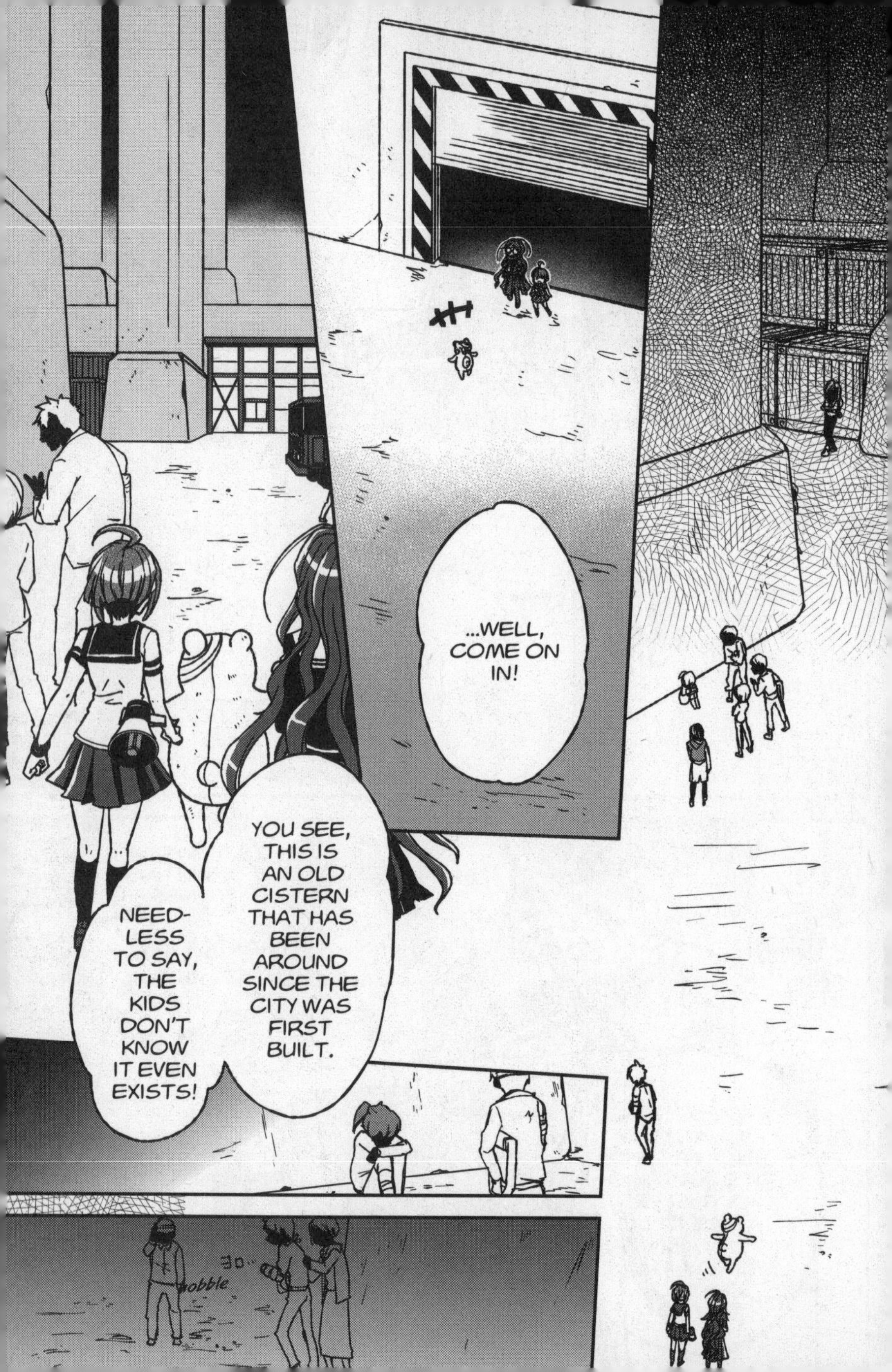
...WELL, COME ON IN!
YOU SEE, THIS IS AN OLD CISTERN THAT HAS BEEN AROUND SINCE THE CITY WAS FIRST BUILT.
NEEDLESS TO SAY, THE KIDS DON'T KNOW IT EVEN EXISTS!

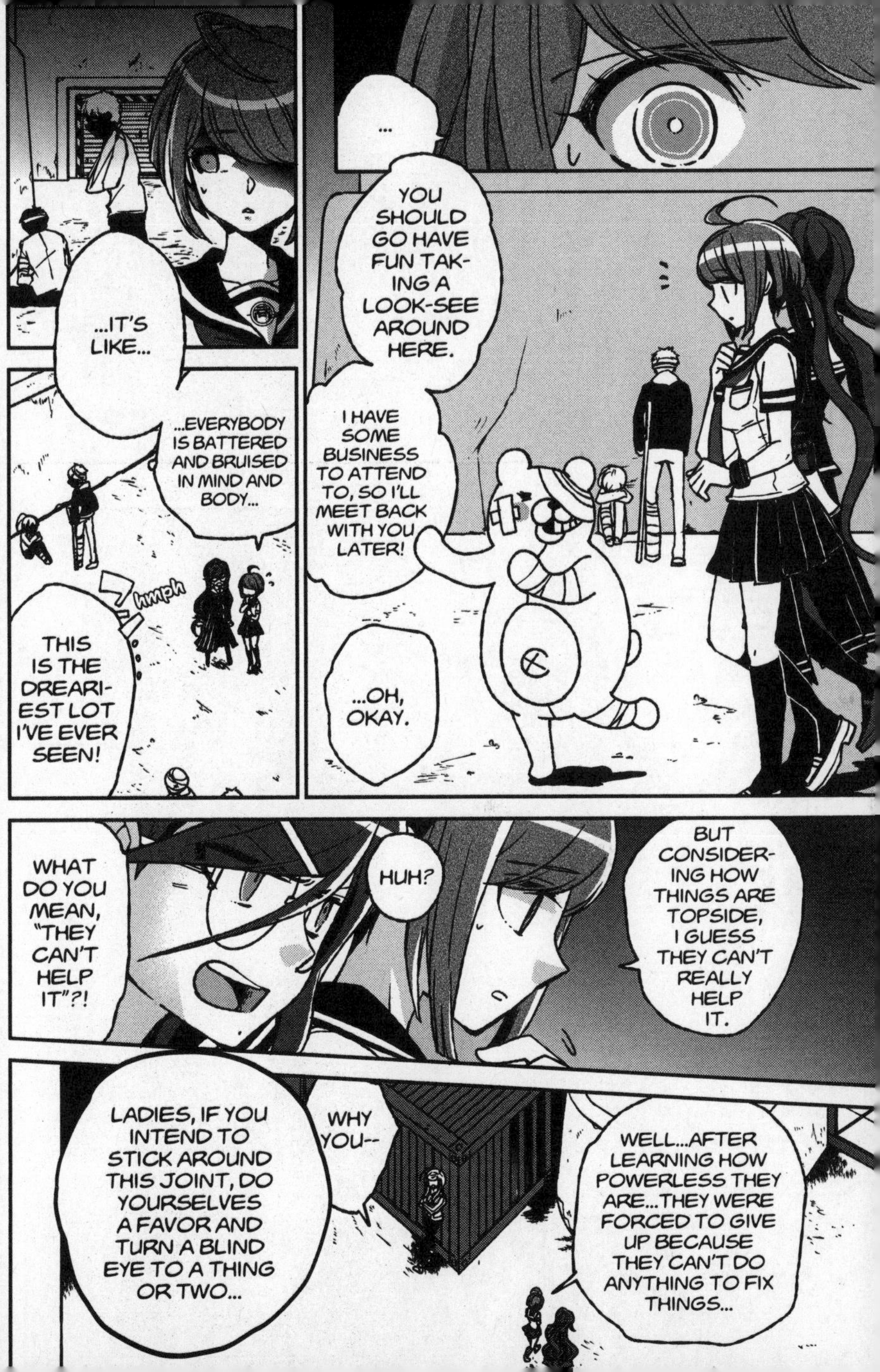
...
YOU SHOULD GO HAVE FUN TAKING A LOOK-SEE AROUND HERE.
I HAVE SOME BUSINESS TO ATTEND TO, SO I'LL MEET BACK WITH YOU LATER!
...OH, OKAY.
...IT'S LIKE...
...EVERYBODY IS BATTERED AND BRUISED IN MIND AND BODY...
hmph
THIS IS THE DREARIEST LOT I'VE EVER SEEN!
BUT CONSIDERING HOW THINGS ARE TOPSIDE, I GUESS THEY CAN'T REALLY HELP IT.
HUH?
WHAT DO YOU MEAN, "THEY CAN'T HELP IT"?!
WELL...AFTER LEARNING HOW POWERLESS THEY ARE...THEY WERE FORCED TO GIVE UP BECAUSE THEY CAN'T DO ANYTHING TO FIX THINGS...
WHY YOU--
LADIES, IF YOU INTEND TO STICK AROUND THIS JOINT, DO YOURSELVES A FAVOR AND TURN A BLIND EYE TO A THING OR TWO...

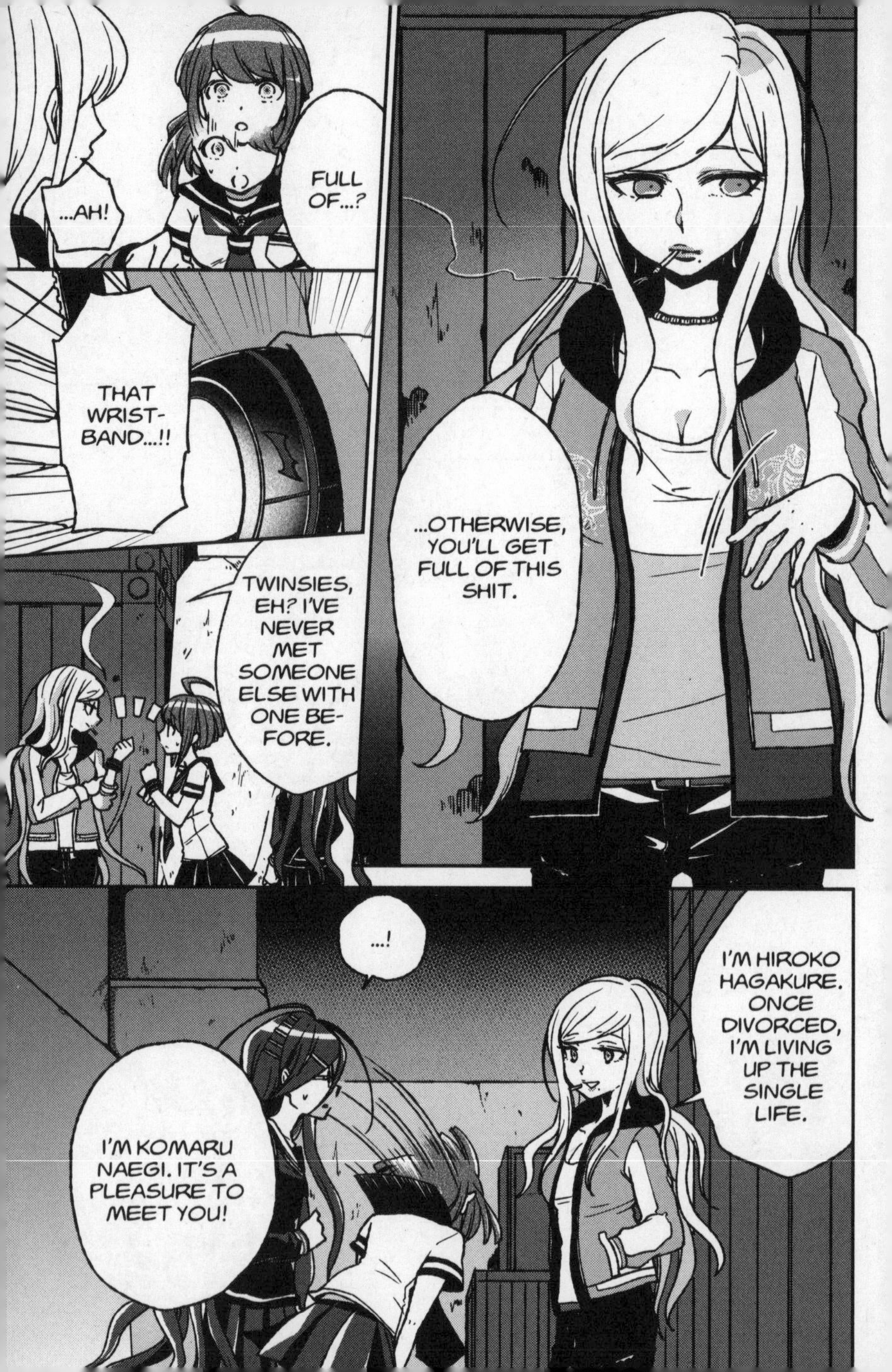
...OTHERWISE, YOU'LL GET FULL OF THIS SHIT.
FULL OF...?
...AH!
THAT WRIST-BAND...!!
TWINSIES, EH? I'VE NEVER MET SOMEONE ELSE WITH ONE BE-FORE.
I'M HIROKO HAGAKURE. ONCE DIVORCED, I'M LIVING UP THE SINGLE LIFE.
...!
I'M KOMARU NAEGI. IT'S A PLEASURE TO MEET YOU!

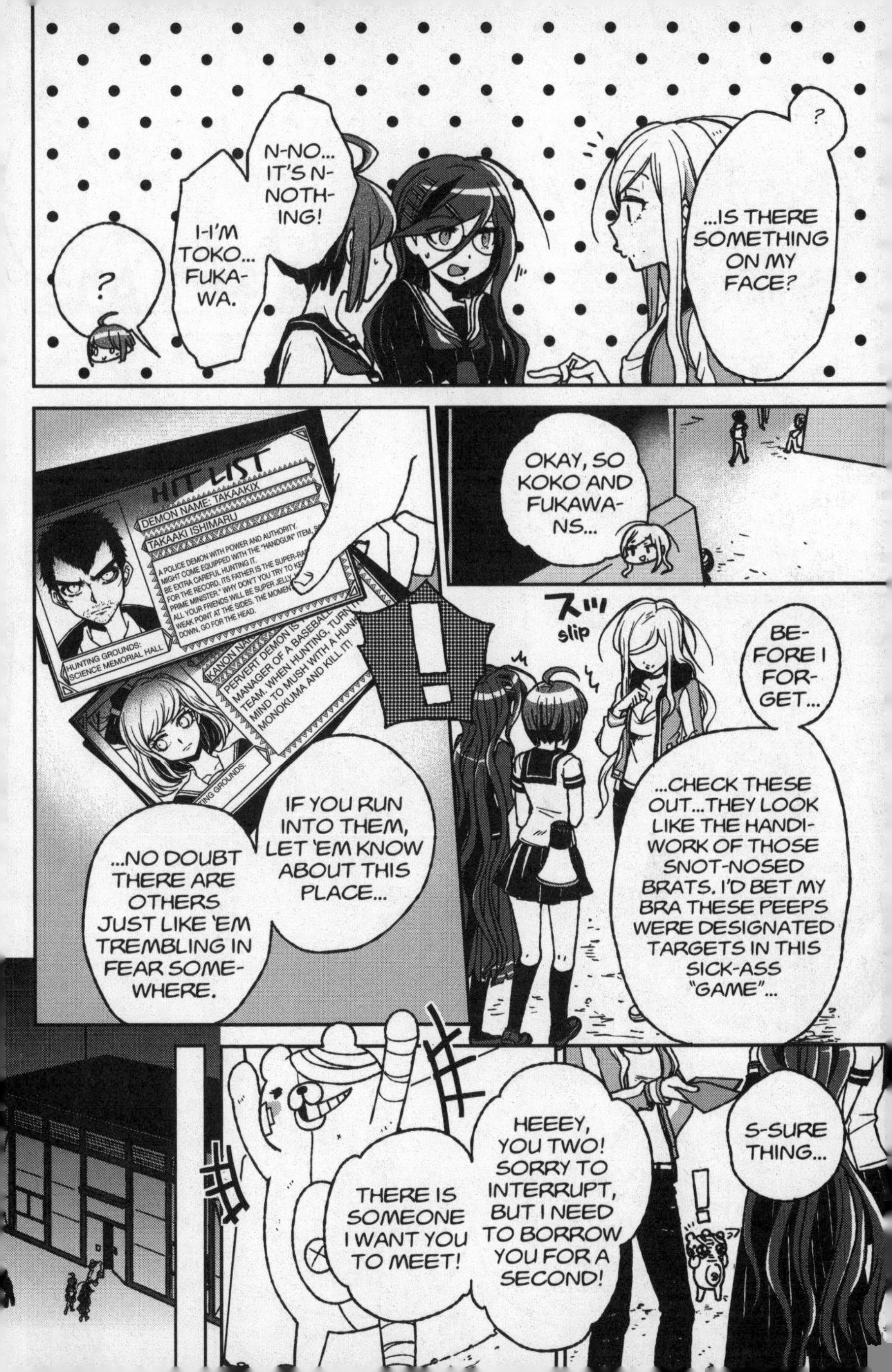
?
...IS THERE SOMETHING ON MY FACE?
N-NO... IT'S N-NOTHING!
I-I'M TOKO... FUKAWA.
?
OKAY, SO KOKO AND FUKAWANS...
スッ
slip
BEFORE I FORGET...
...CHECK THESE OUT...THEY LOOK LIKE THE HANDIWORK OF THOSE SNOT-NOSED BRATS. I'D BET MY BRA THESE PEEPS WERE DESIGNATED TARGETS IN THIS SICK-ASS "GAME"...
!
HIT LIST
DEMON NAME: TAKAAKIX
TAKAAKI ISHIMARU
A POLICE DEMON WITH POWER AND AUTHORITY.
MIGHT COME EQUIPPED WITH THE "HANDGUN" ITEM,
BE EXTRA CAREFUL HUNTING IT.
FOR THE RECORD, ITS FATHER IS THE
PRIME MINISTER." WHY DON'T YOU TRY TO
ALL YOUR FRIENDS WILL BE SUPER JELLY.
WEAK POINT AT THE SIDES. THE
DOWN, GO FOR THE HEAD.
HUNTING GROUNDS:
SCIENCE MEMORIAL HALL
PERVERT DEMON IS
MANAGER OF A
TEAM. WHEN HUNTING,
MIND TO MUSH WITH A
MONOKUMA AND KILL IT!
IF YOU RUN INTO THEM, LET 'EM KNOW ABOUT THIS PLACE...
...NO DOUBT THERE ARE OTHERS JUST LIKE 'EM TREMBLING IN FEAR SOMEWHERE.
S-SURE THING...
!
HEEEY, YOU TWO! SORRY TO INTERRUPT, BUT I NEED TO BORROW YOU FOR A SECOND!
THERE IS SOMEONE I WANT YOU TO MEET!

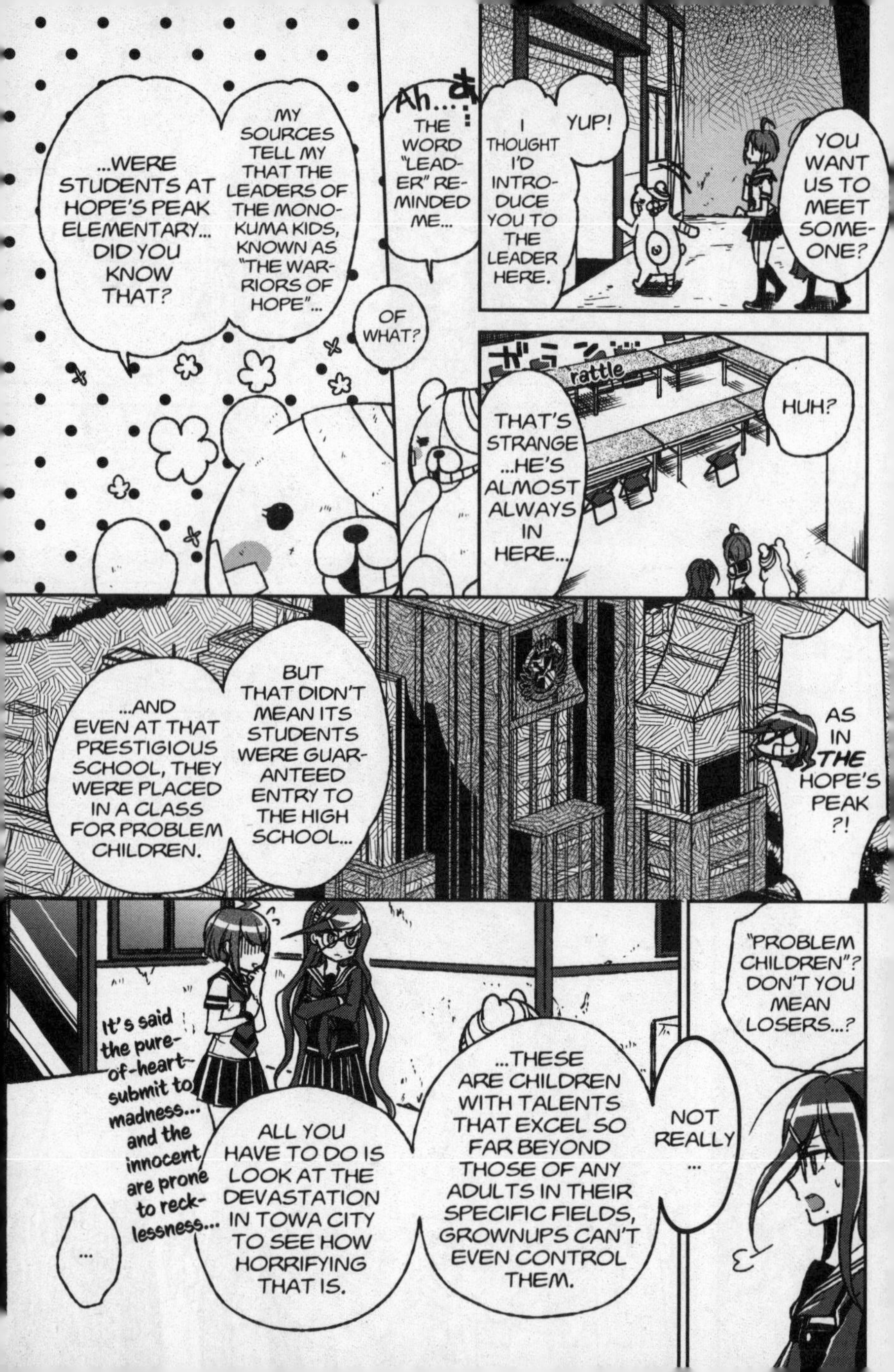
YOU WANT US TO MEET SOME-ONE?
YUP!
I THOUGHT I'D INTRO-DUCE YOU TO THE LEADER HERE.
HUH?
rattle
THAT'S STRANGE ...HE'S ALMOST ALWAYS IN HERE...
Ah...
THE WORD "LEAD-ER" RE-MINDED ME...
OF WHAT?
MY SOURCES TELL MY THAT THE LEADERS OF THE MONO-KUMA KIDS, KNOWN AS "THE WAR-RIORS OF HOPE"...
...WERE STUDENTS AT HOPE'S PEAK ELEMENTARY... DID YOU KNOW THAT?
AS IN THE HOPE'S PEAK ?!
BUT THAT DIDN'T MEAN ITS STUDENTS WERE GUAR-ANTEED ENTRY TO THE HIGH SCHOOL...
...AND EVEN AT THAT PRESTIGIOUS SCHOOL, THEY WERE PLACED IN A CLASS FOR PROBLEM CHILDREN.
"PROBLEM CHILDREN"? DON'T YOU MEAN LOSERS...?
NOT REALLY ...
...THESE ARE CHILDREN WITH TALENTS THAT EXCEL SO FAR BEYOND THOSE OF ANY ADULTS IN THEIR SPECIFIC FIELDS, GROWNUPS CAN'T EVEN CONTROL THEM.
ALL YOU HAVE TO DO IS LOOK AT THE DEVASTATION IN TOWA CITY TO SEE HOW HORRIFYING THAT IS.
It's said the pure-of-heart submit to madness... and the innocent are prone to reck-lessness...
...

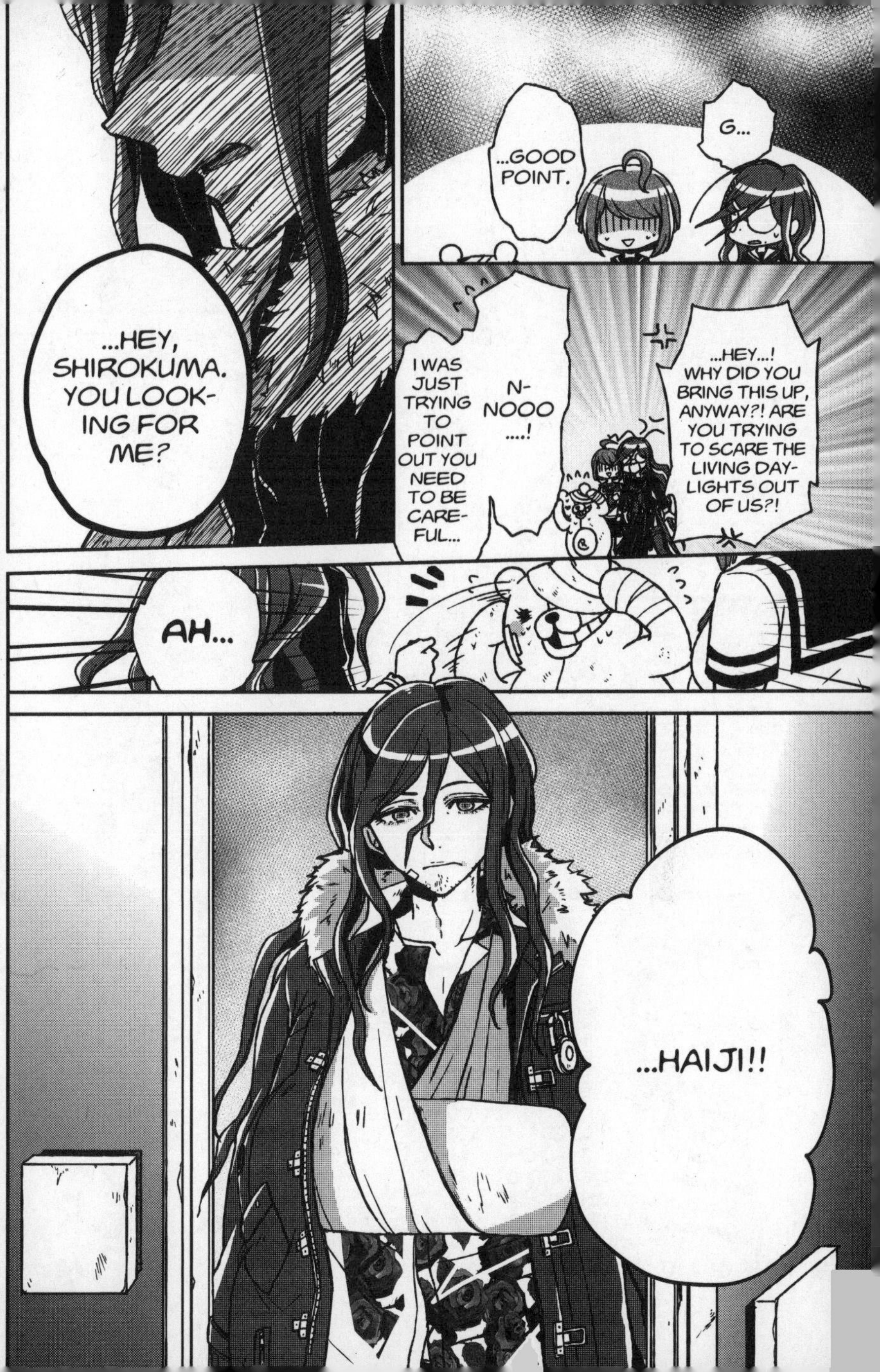
G...
...GOOD POINT.
...HEY...! WHY DID YOU BRING THIS UP, ANYWAY?! ARE YOU TRYING TO SCARE THE LIVING DAY-LIGHTS OUT OF US?!
N-NOOO ....!
I WAS JUST TRYING TO POINT OUT YOU NEED TO BE CARE-FUL...
...HEY, SHIROKUMA. YOU LOOK-ING FOR ME?
AH...
...HAIJI!!

Danganronpa Another Episode:
Ultra Despair Girls

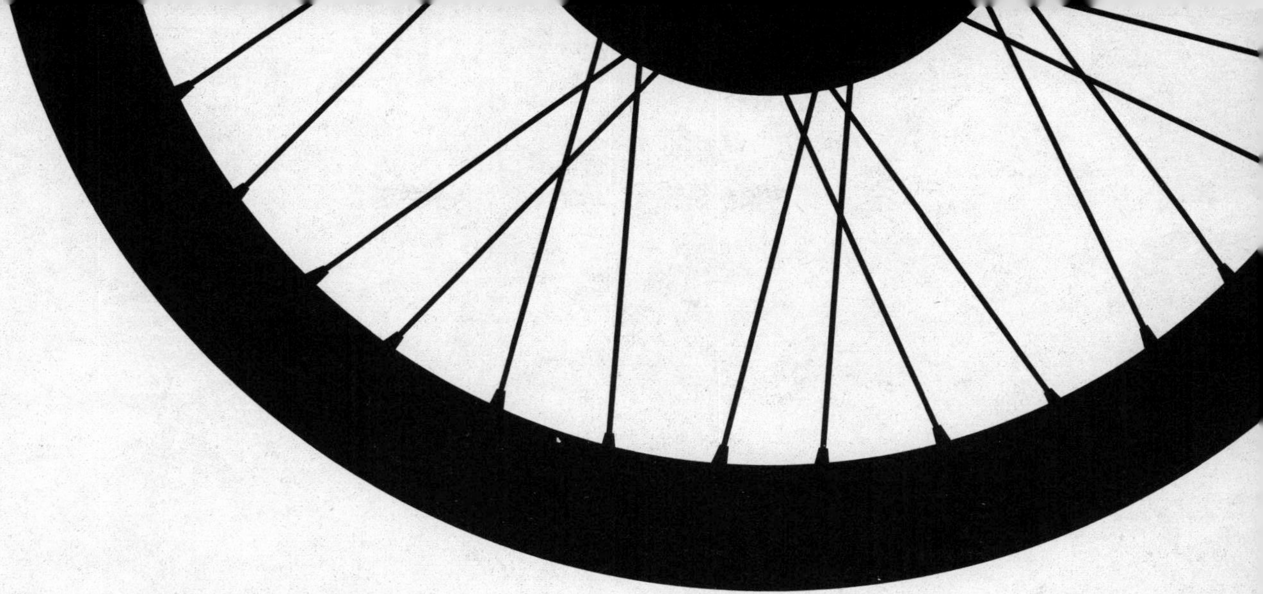

Danganronpa Another Episode:
Ultra Despair Girls

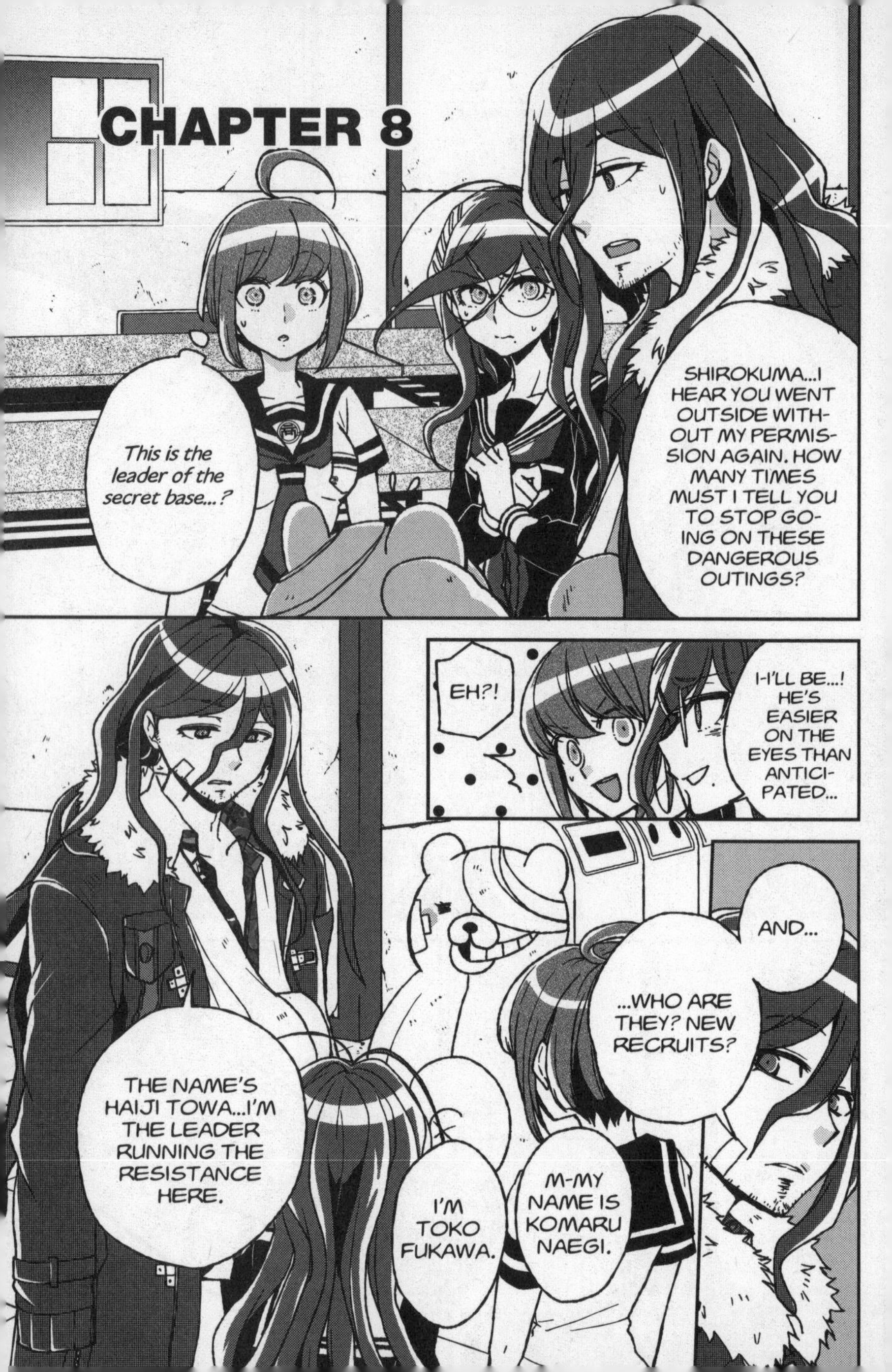
CHAPTER 8
SHIROKUMA...I HEAR YOU WENT OUTSIDE WITH-OUT MY PERMIS-SION AGAIN. HOW MANY TIMES MUST I TELL YOU TO STOP GO-ING ON THESE DANGEROUS OUTINGS?
This is the leader of the secret base...?
I-I'LL BE...! HE'S EASIER ON THE EYES THAN ANTICI-PATED...
EH?!
AND...
...WHO ARE THEY? NEW RECRUITS?
M-MY NAME IS KOMARU NAEGI.
I'M TOKO FUKAWA.
THE NAME'S HAIJI TOWA...I'M THE LEADER RUNNING THE RESISTANCE HERE.

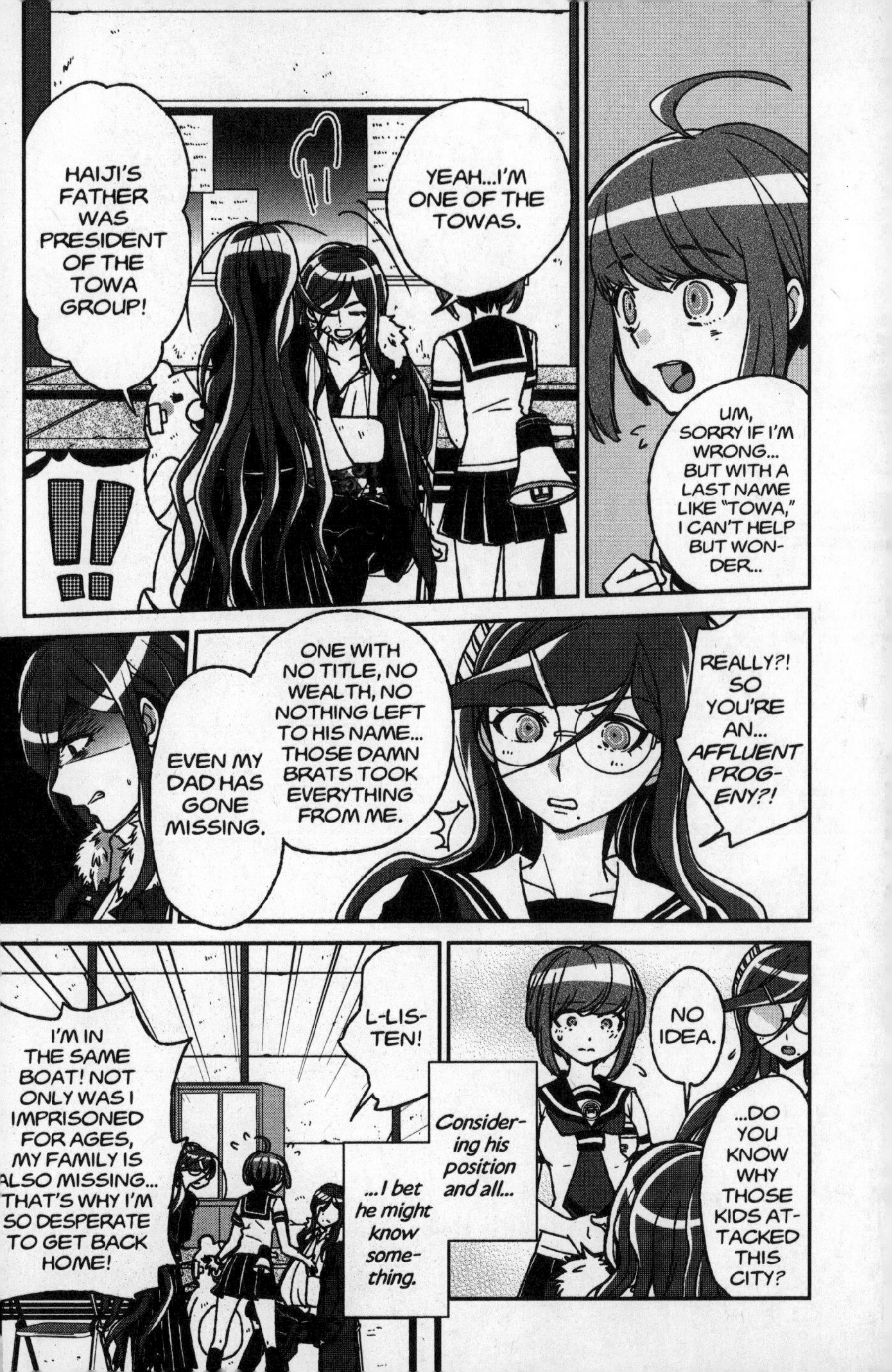
UM, SORRY IF I'M WRONG... BUT WITH A LAST NAME LIKE "TOWA," I CAN'T HELP BUT WONDER...
YEAH...I'M ONE OF THE TOWAS.
HAIJI'S FATHER WAS PRESIDENT OF THE TOWA GROUP!
!!
REALLY?! SO YOU'RE AN... *AFFLUENT PROGENY*?!
ONE WITH NO TITLE, NO WEALTH, NO NOTHING LEFT TO HIS NAME... THOSE DAMN BRATS TOOK EVERYTHING FROM ME.
EVEN MY DAD HAS GONE MISSING.
...DO YOU KNOW WHY THOSE KIDS ATTACKED THIS CITY?
NO IDEA.
Considering his position and all...
...I bet he might know something.
L-LISTEN!
I'M IN THE SAME BOAT! NOT ONLY WAS I IMPRISONED FOR AGES, MY FAMILY IS ALSO MISSING... THAT'S WHY I'M SO DESPERATE TO GET BACK HOME!

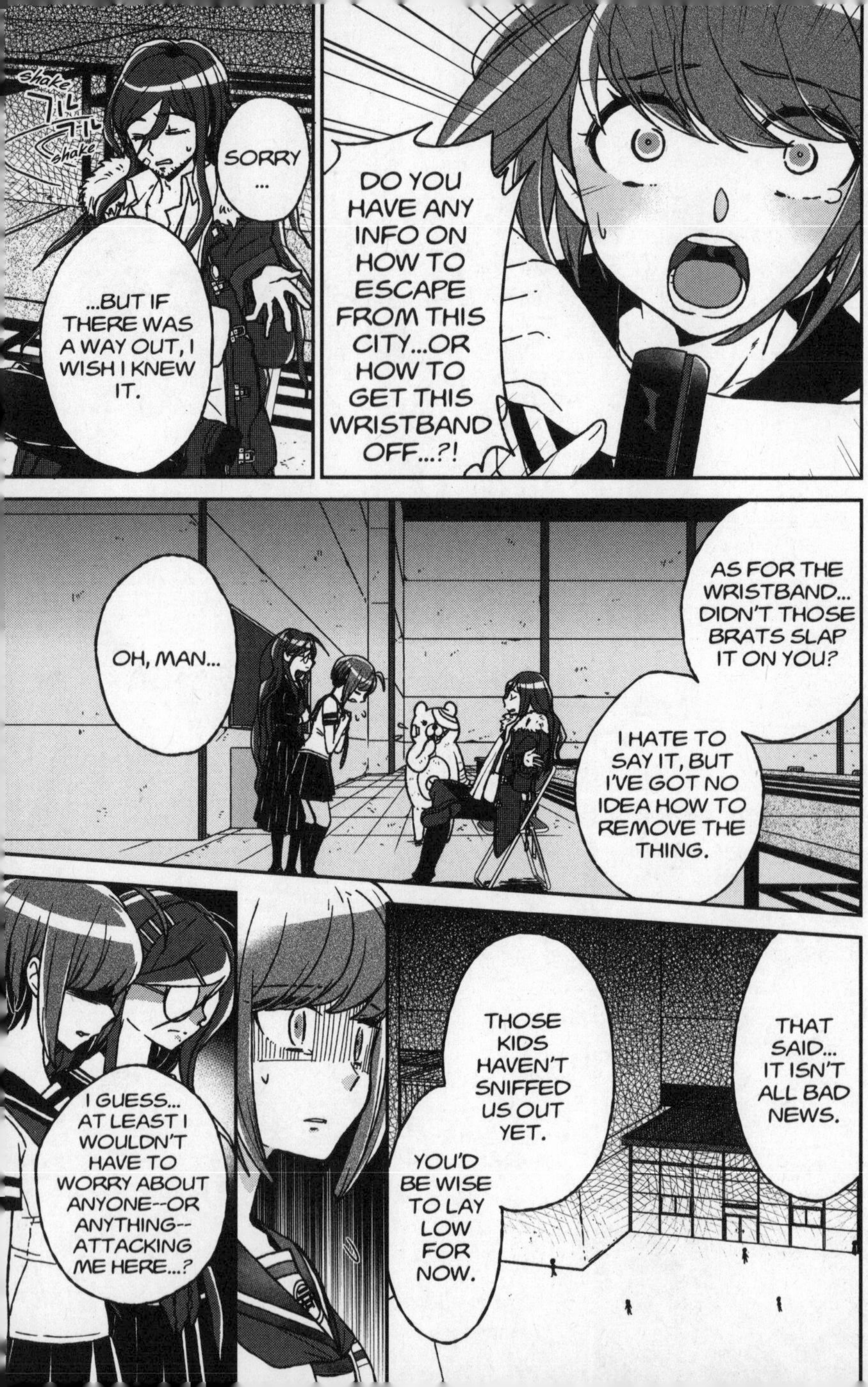
DO YOU HAVE ANY INFO ON HOW TO ESCAPE FROM THIS CITY...OR HOW TO GET THIS WRISTBAND OFF...?!
shake
フル
フル
shake
SORRY ...
...BUT IF THERE WAS A WAY OUT, I WISH I KNEW IT.
AS FOR THE WRISTBAND... DIDN'T THOSE BRATS SLAP IT ON YOU?
I HATE TO SAY IT, BUT I'VE GOT NO IDEA HOW TO REMOVE THE THING.
OH, MAN...
THAT SAID... IT ISN'T ALL BAD NEWS.
THOSE KIDS HAVEN'T SNIFFED US OUT YET.
YOU'D BE WISE TO LAY LOW FOR NOW.
I GUESS... AT LEAST I WOULDN'T HAVE TO WORRY ABOUT ANYONE--OR ANYTHING--ATTACKING ME HERE...?

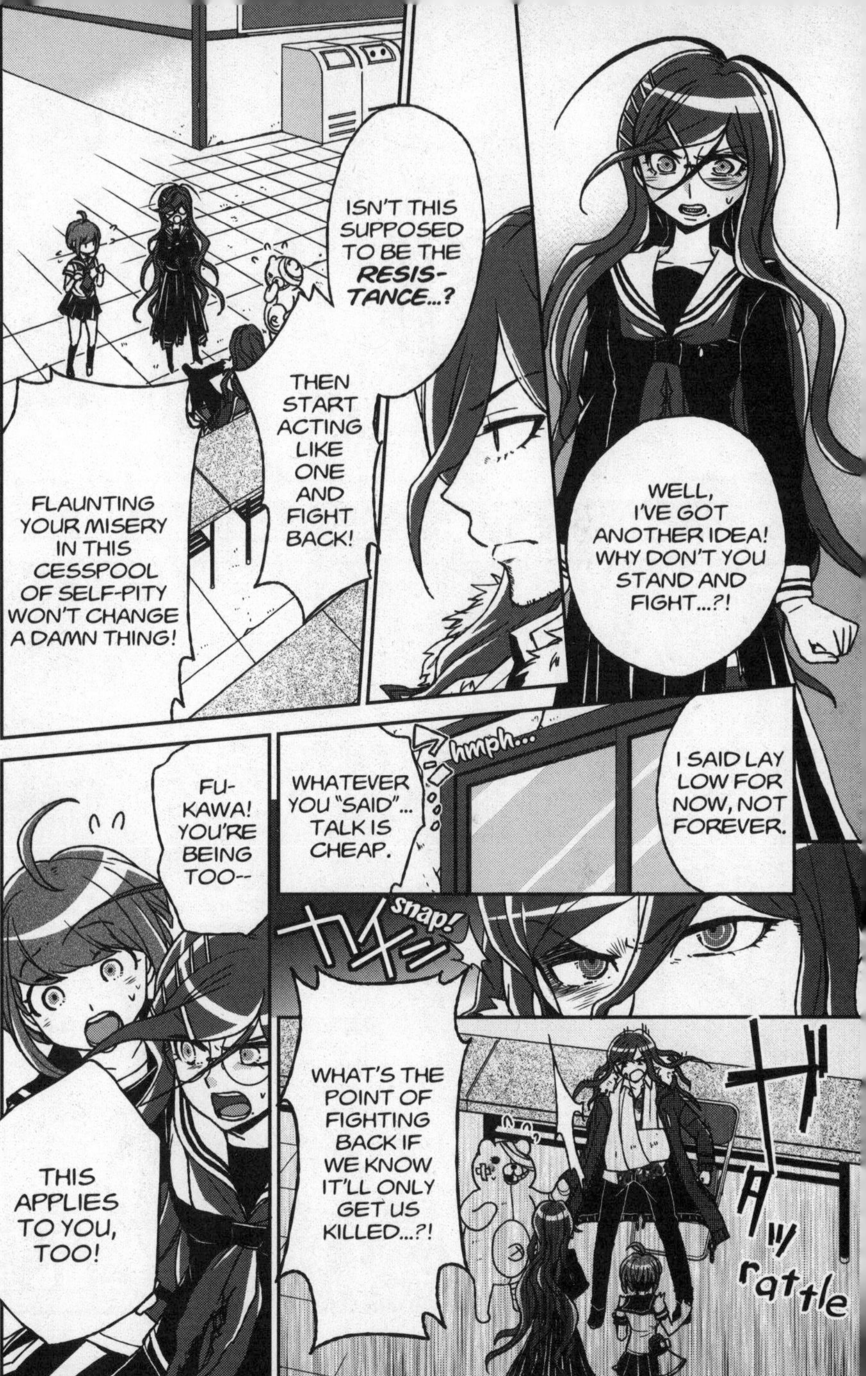
FLAUNTING YOUR MISERY IN THIS CESSPOOL OF SELF-PITY WON'T CHANGE A DAMN THING!
ISN'T THIS SUPPOSED TO BE THE *RESISTANCE*...?
THEN START ACTING LIKE ONE AND FIGHT BACK!
WELL, I'VE GOT ANOTHER IDEA! WHY DON'T YOU STAND AND FIGHT...?!
I SAID LAY LOW FOR NOW, NOT FOREVER.
hmph...
WHATEVER YOU "SAID"... TALK IS CHEAP.
snap!
WHAT'S THE POINT OF FIGHTING BACK IF WE KNOW IT'LL ONLY GET US KILLED...?!
rattle
FU-KAWA! YOU'RE BEING TOO--
THIS APPLIES TO YOU, TOO!

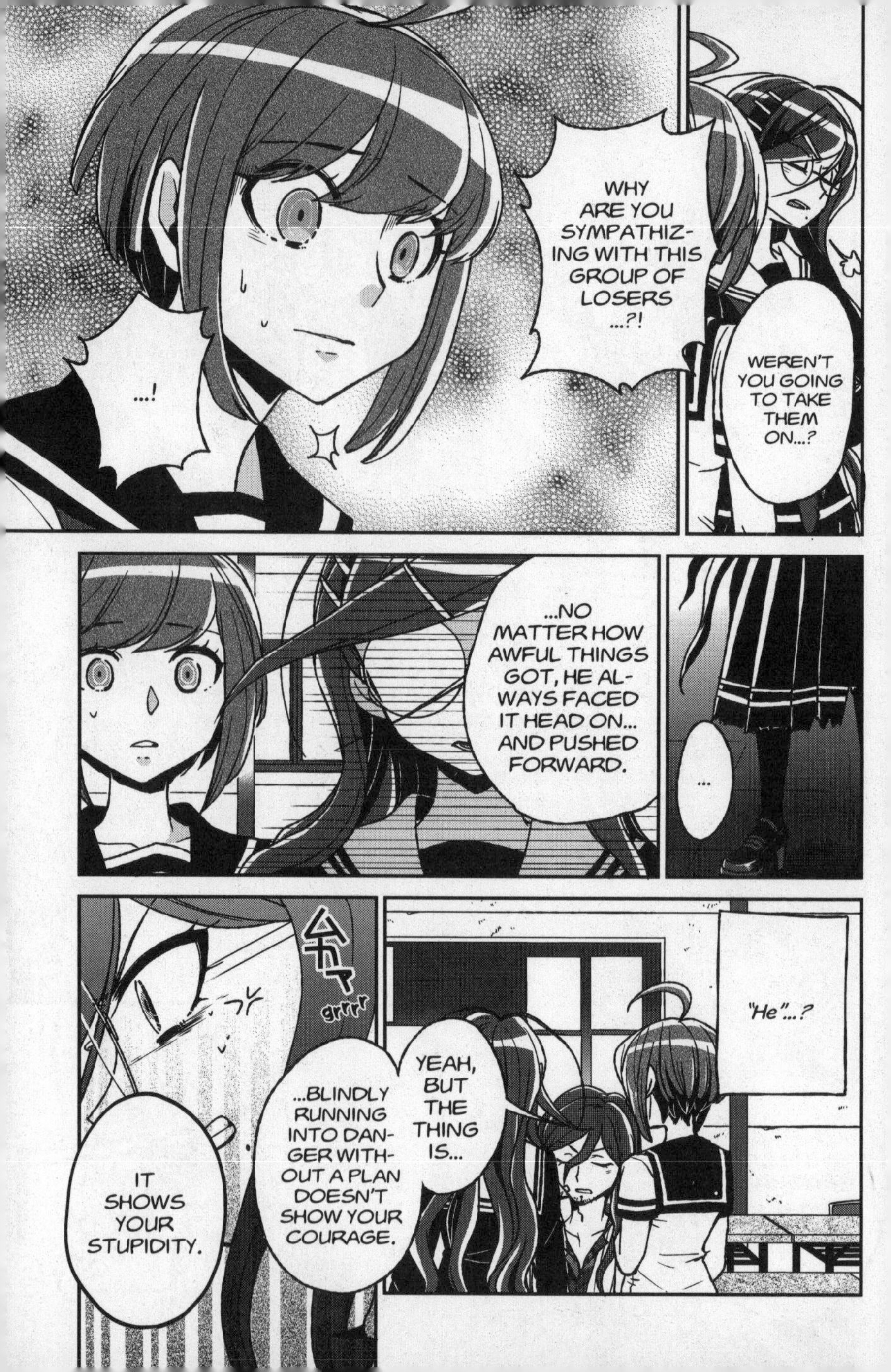
WHY ARE YOU SYMPATHIZING WITH THIS GROUP OF LOSERS ...?!
WEREN'T YOU GOING TO TAKE THEM ON...?
...!
...
...NO MATTER HOW AWFUL THINGS GOT, HE ALWAYS FACED IT HEAD ON... AND PUSHED FORWARD.
"He"...?
YEAH, BUT THE THING IS...
...BLINDLY RUNNING INTO DANGER WITHOUT A PLAN DOESN'T SHOW YOUR COURAGE.
ムカァ
grrr
IT SHOWS YOUR STUPIDITY.

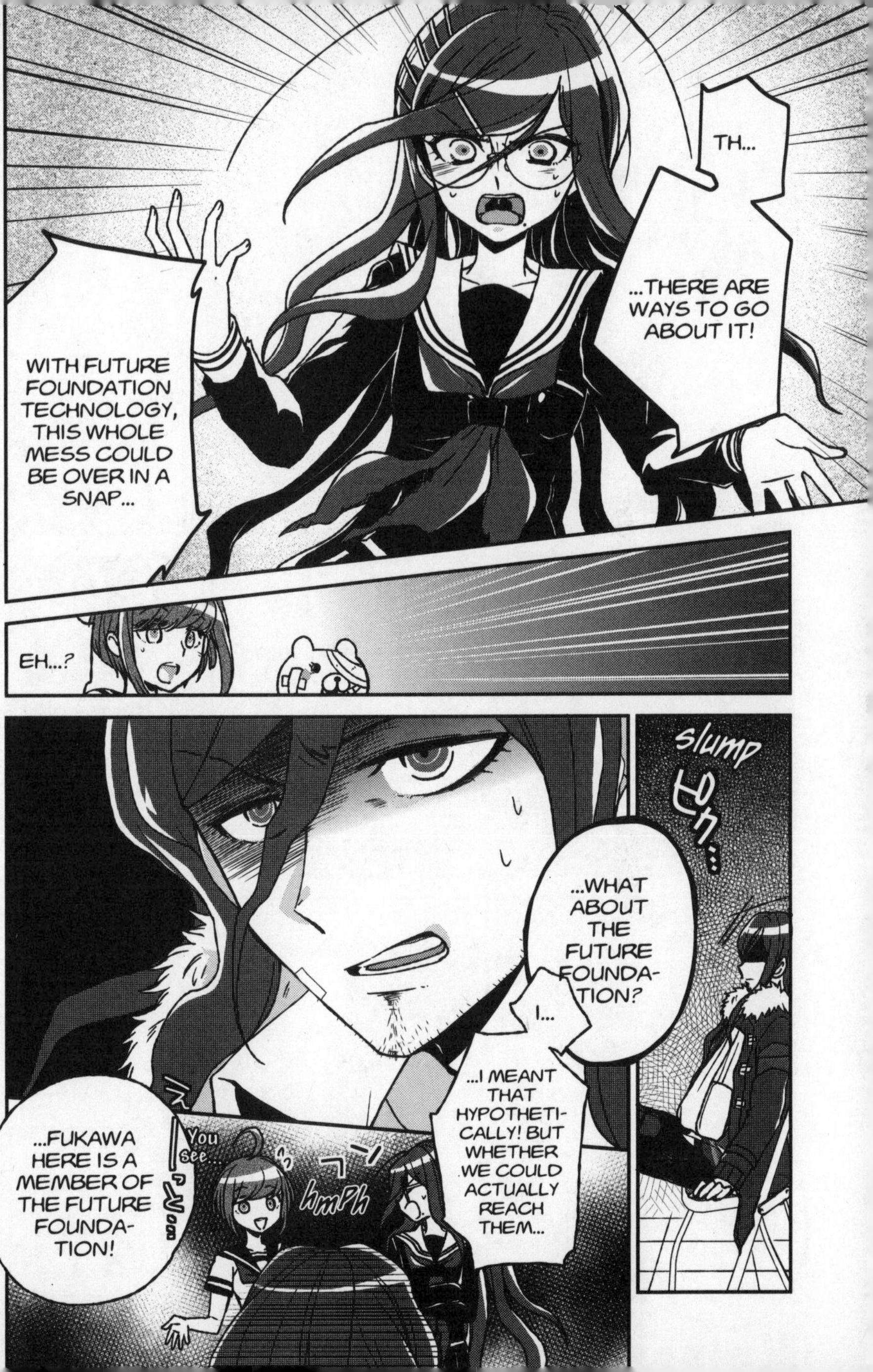
TH...
...THERE ARE WAYS TO GO ABOUT IT!
WITH FUTURE FOUNDATION TECHNOLOGY, THIS WHOLE MESS COULD BE OVER IN A SNAP...
EH...?
slump
...WHAT ABOUT THE FUTURE FOUNDATION?
I...
...I MEANT THAT HYPOTHETICALLY! BUT WHETHER WE COULD ACTUALLY REACH THEM...
hmph
You see...
...FUKAWA HERE IS A MEMBER OF THE FUTURE FOUNDATION!

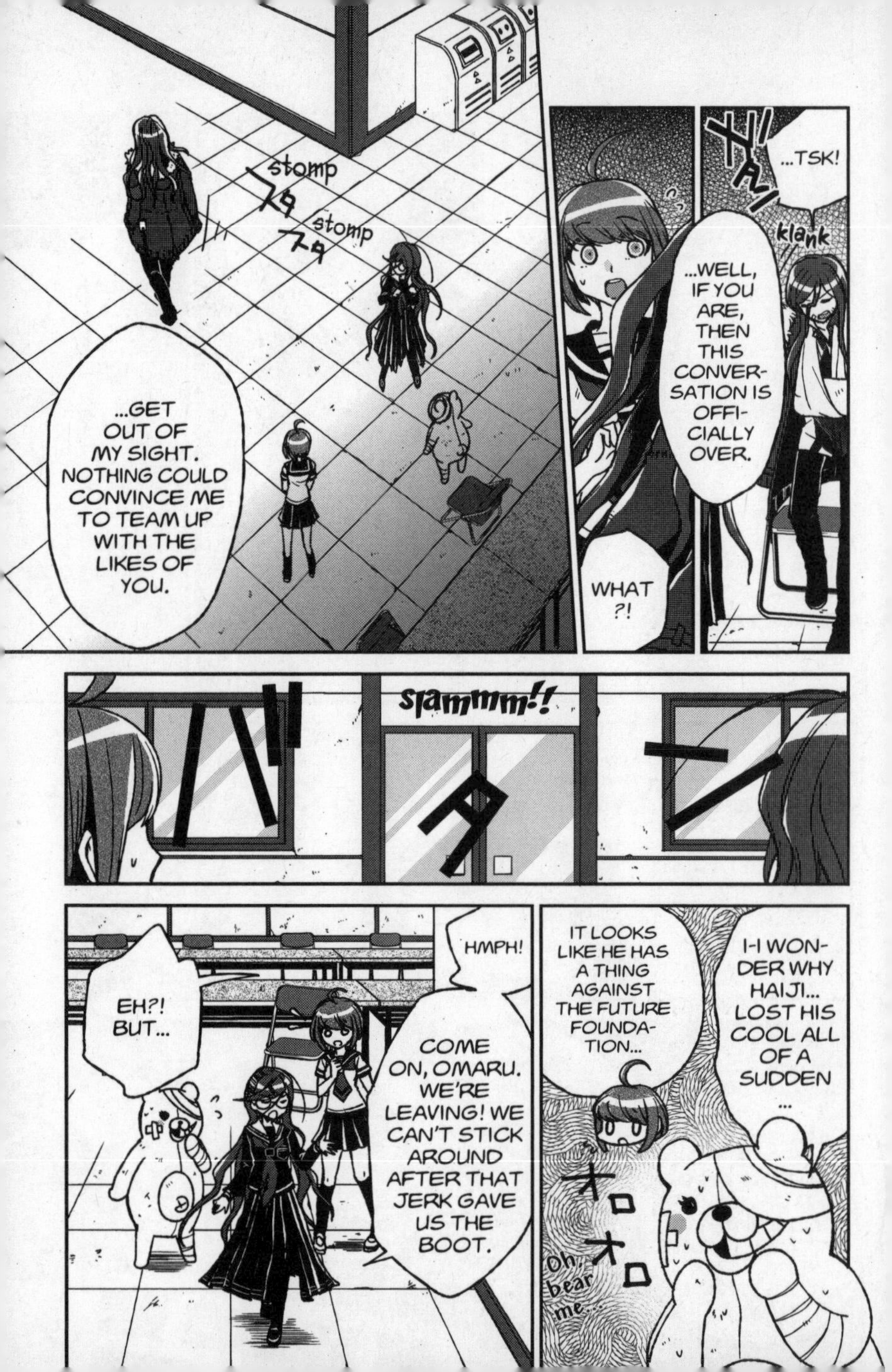
...TSK!
klank
...WELL, IF YOU ARE, THEN THIS CONVERSATION IS OFFICIALLY OVER.
WHAT?!
stomp
stomp
...GET OUT OF MY SIGHT. NOTHING COULD CONVINCE ME TO TEAM UP WITH THE LIKES OF YOU.
slammm!!
I-I WONDER WHY HAIJI... LOST HIS COOL ALL OF A SUDDEN...
IT LOOKS LIKE HE HAS A THING AGAINST THE FUTURE FOUNDATION...
Oh, bear me...
HMPH!
COME ON, OMARU. WE'RE LEAVING! WE CAN'T STICK AROUND AFTER THAT JERK GAVE US THE BOOT.
EH?! BUT...

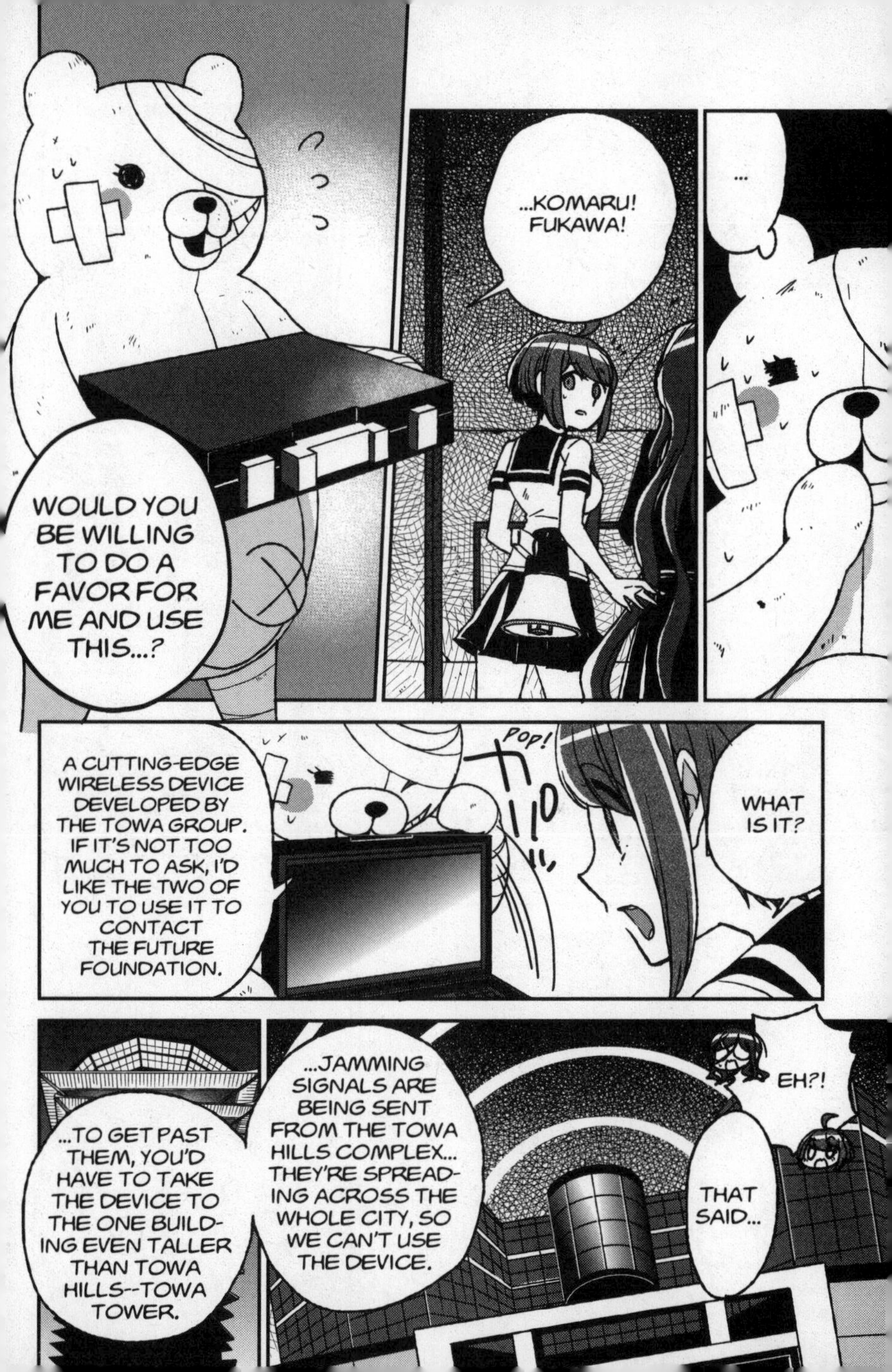
...
...KOMARU! FUKAWA!
WOULD YOU BE WILLING TO DO A FAVOR FOR ME AND USE THIS...?
WHAT IS IT?
Pop!
A CUTTING-EDGE WIRELESS DEVICE DEVELOPED BY THE TOWA GROUP. IF IT'S NOT TOO MUCH TO ASK, I'D LIKE THE TWO OF YOU TO USE IT TO CONTACT THE FUTURE FOUNDATION.
EH?!
THAT SAID...
...JAMMING SIGNALS ARE BEING SENT FROM THE TOWA HILLS COMPLEX... THEY'RE SPREADING ACROSS THE WHOLE CITY, SO WE CAN'T USE THE DEVICE.
...TO GET PAST THEM, YOU'D HAVE TO TAKE THE DEVICE TO THE ONE BUILDING EVEN TALLER THAN TOWA HILLS--TOWA TOWER.

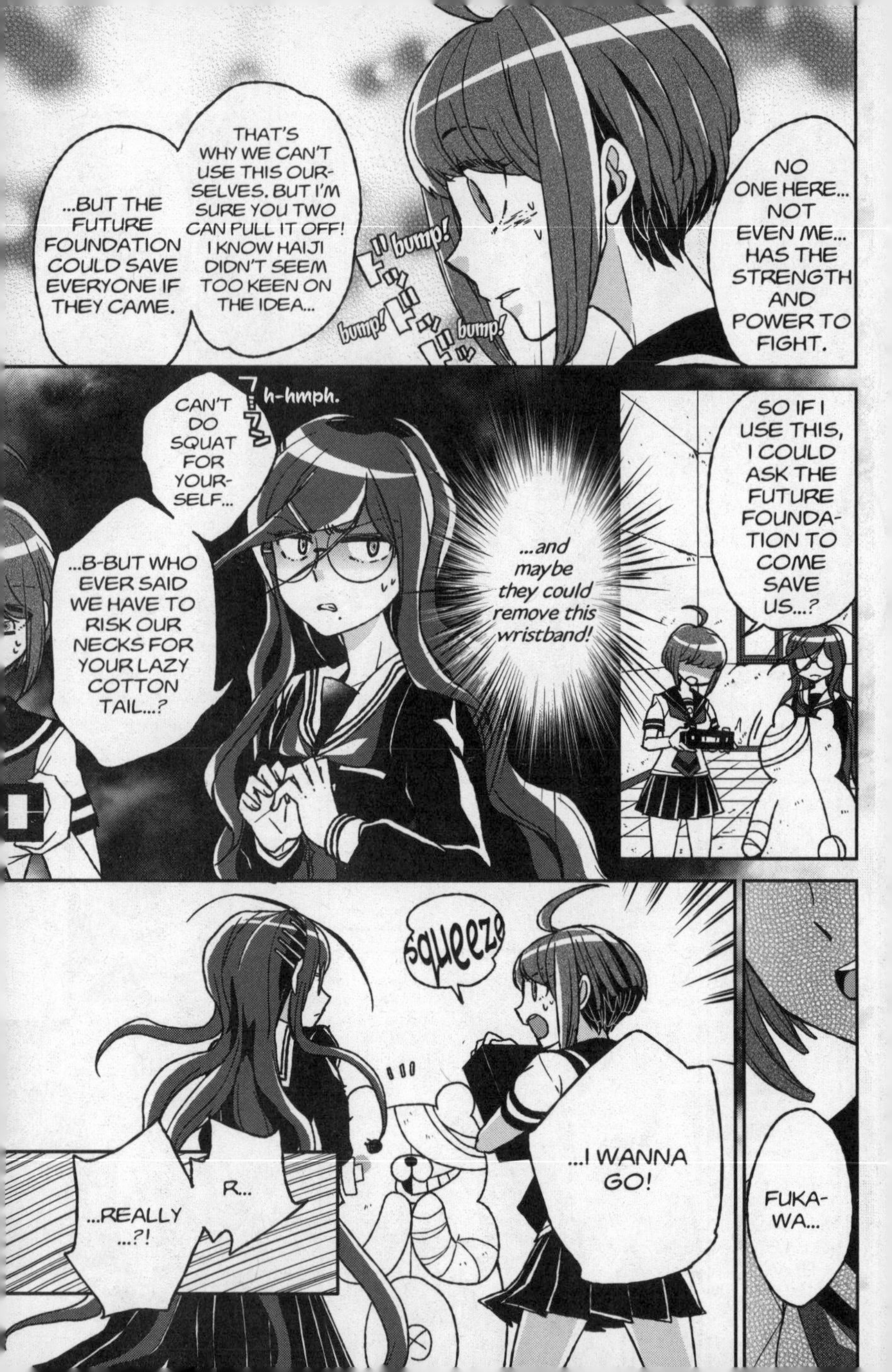
NO ONE HERE... NOT EVEN ME... HAS THE STRENGTH AND POWER TO FIGHT.
bump! bump! bump!
THAT'S WHY WE CAN'T USE THIS OURSELVES. BUT I'M SURE YOU TWO CAN PULL IT OFF! I KNOW HAIJI DIDN'T SEEM TOO KEEN ON THE IDEA...
...BUT THE FUTURE FOUNDATION COULD SAVE EVERYONE IF THEY CAME.
SO IF I USE THIS, I COULD ASK THE FUTURE FOUNDATION TO COME SAVE US...?
...and maybe they could remove this wristband!
h-hmph.
CAN'T DO SQUAT FOR YOURSELF...
...B-BUT WHO EVER SAID WE HAVE TO RISK OUR NECKS FOR YOUR LAZY COTTON TAIL...?
FUKAWA...
squeeze
...I WANNA GO!
R... ...REALLY ...?!

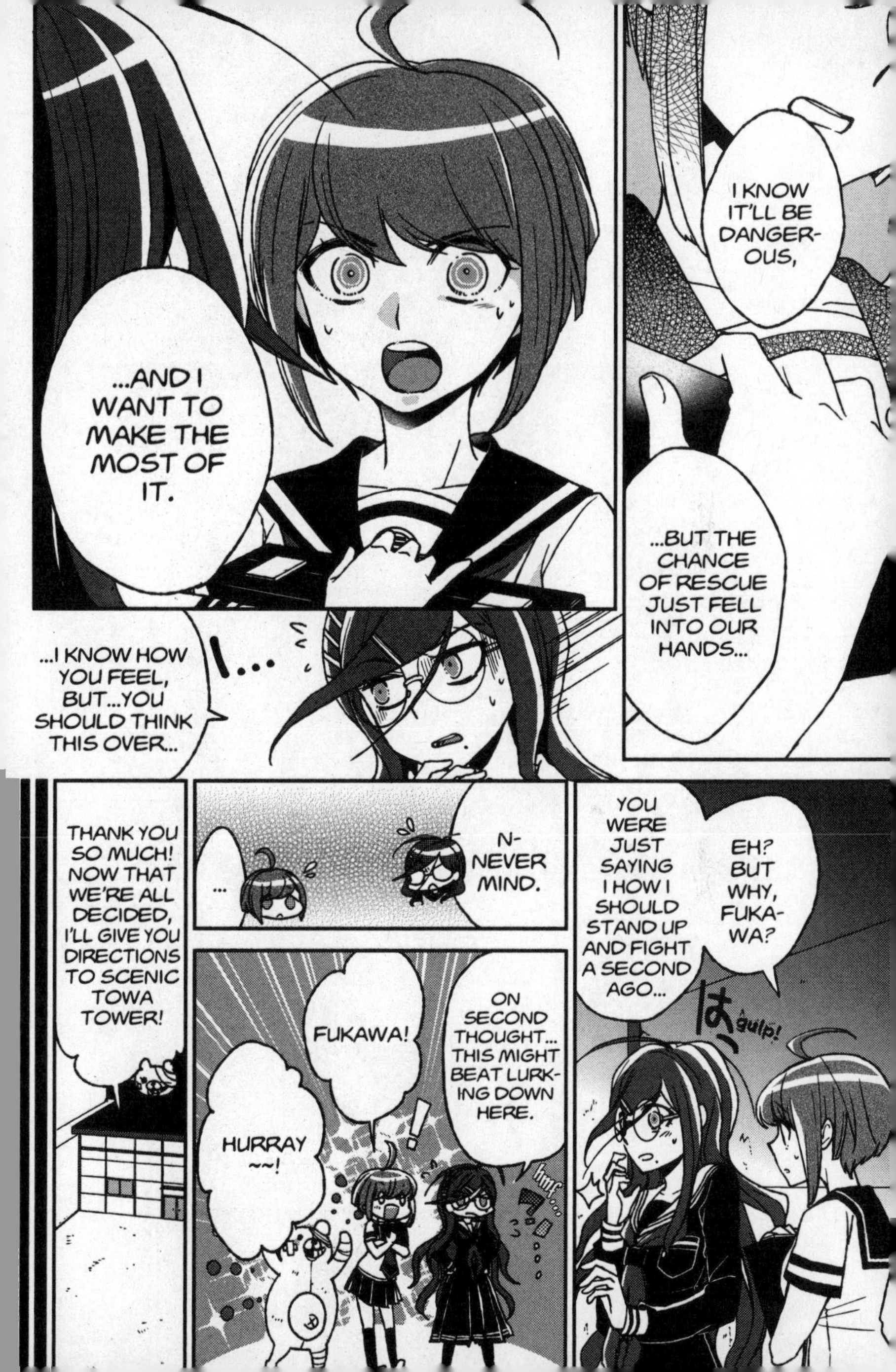
I KNOW IT'LL BE DANGER-OUS,
...BUT THE CHANCE OF RESCUE JUST FELL INTO OUR HANDS...
...AND I WANT TO MAKE THE MOST OF IT.
I...
...I KNOW HOW YOU FEEL, BUT...YOU SHOULD THINK THIS OVER...
EH? BUT WHY, FUKA-WA?
YOU WERE JUST SAYING I HOW I SHOULD STAND UP AND FIGHT A SECOND AGO...
は
gulp!
N-NEVER MIND.
...
ON SECOND THOUGHT... THIS MIGHT BEAT LURK-ING DOWN HERE.
FUKAWA!
!
HURRAY ~~!
hmf...
THANK YOU SO MUCH! NOW THAT WE'RE ALL DECIDED, I'LL GIVE YOU DIRECTIONS TO SCENIC TOWA TOWER!

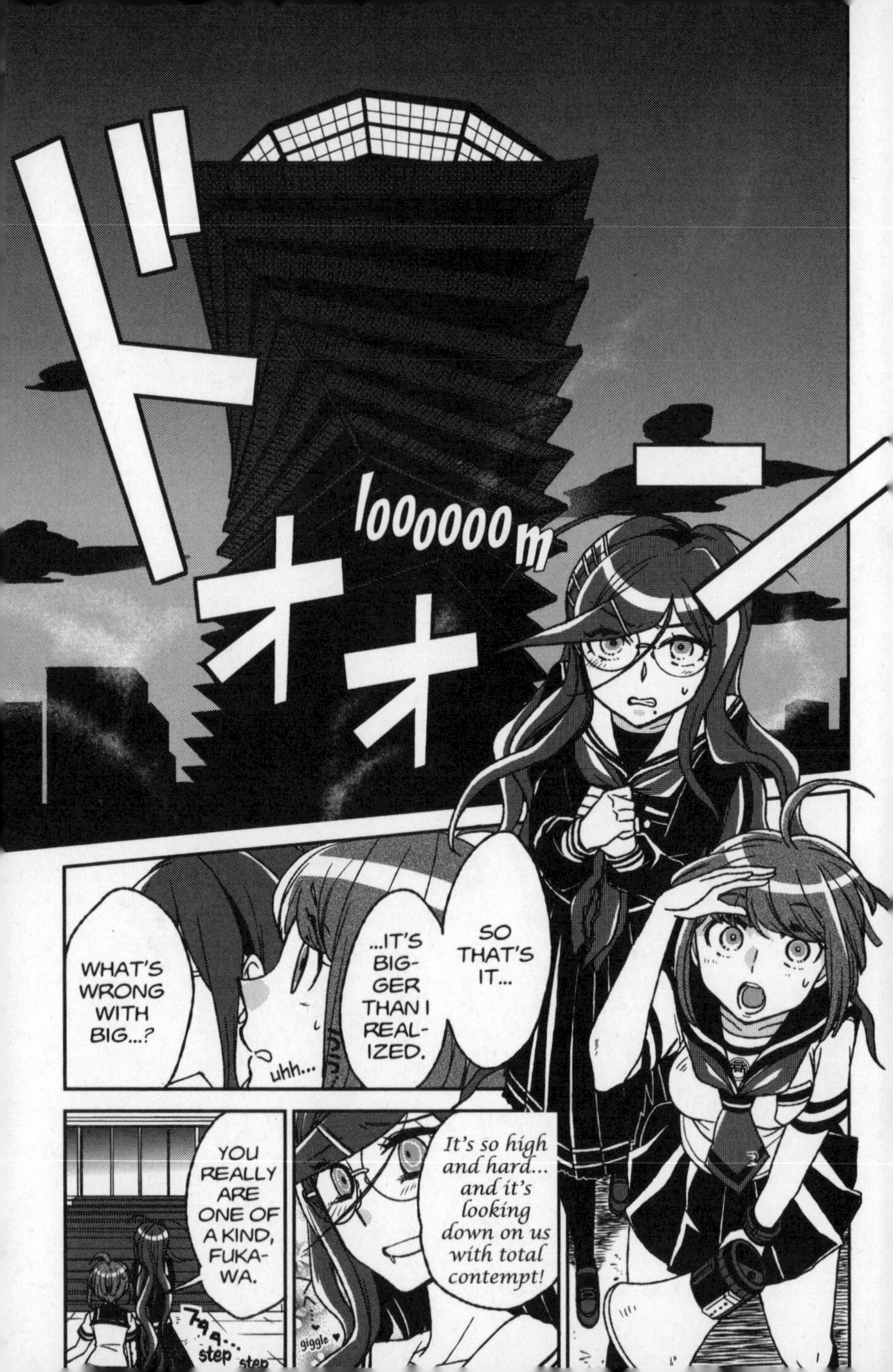

ドオオー
looooooom
SO THAT'S IT...
...IT'S BIGGER THAN I REALIZED.
WHAT'S WRONG WITH BIG...?
uhh...
It's so high and hard... and it's looking down on us with total contempt!
giggle ♥
YOU REALLY ARE ONE OF A KIND, FUKAWA.
step step

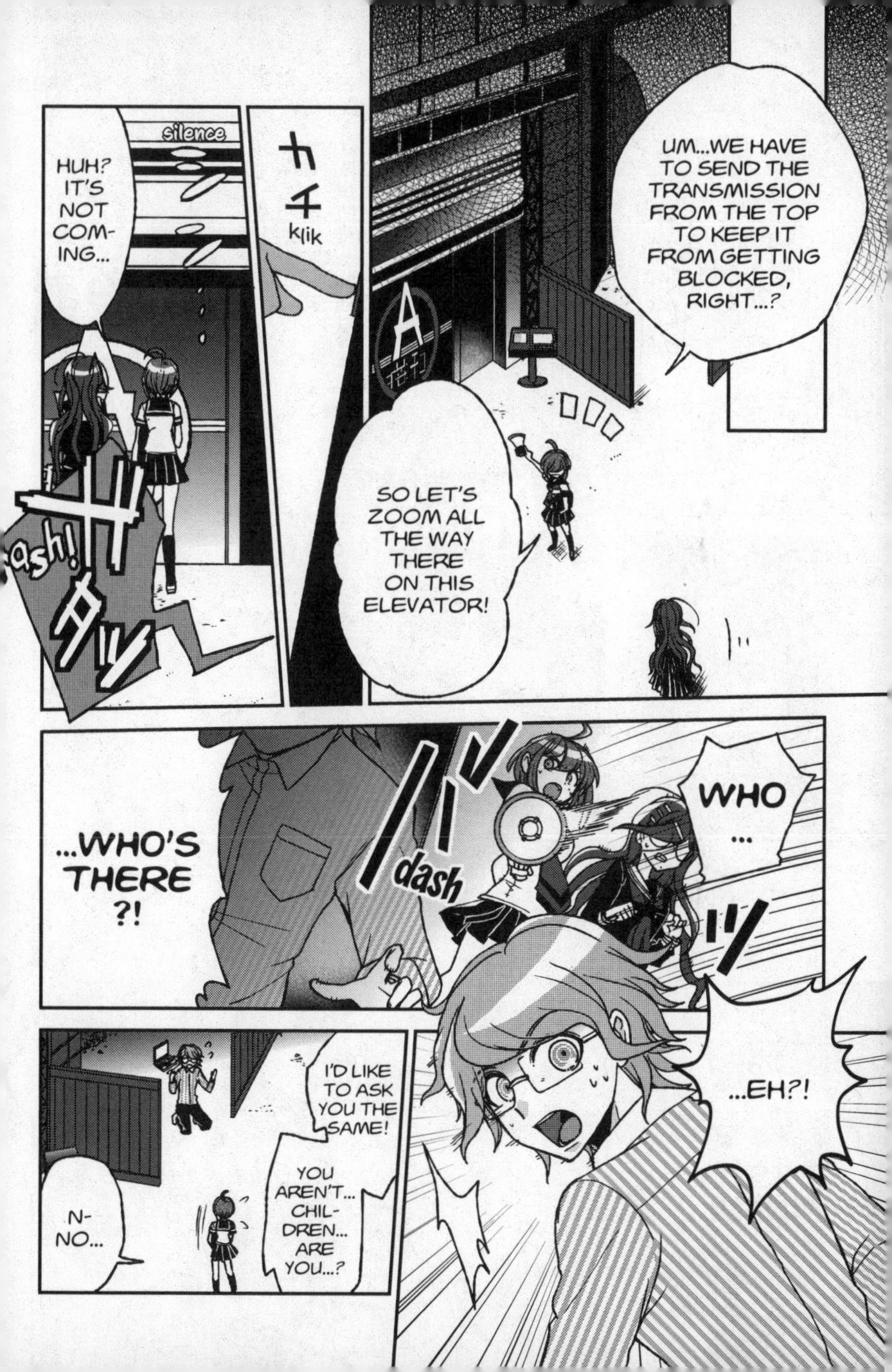
UM...WE HAVE TO SEND THE TRANSMISSION FROM THE TOP TO KEEP IT FROM GETTING BLOCKED, RIGHT...?
SO LET'S ZOOM ALL THE WAY THERE ON THIS ELEVATOR!
カチ
klik
silence
HUH? IT'S NOT COM-ING...
タッ
ash!
WHO ...
dash
...WHO'S THERE ?!
...EH?!
I'D LIKE TO ASK YOU THE SAME!
YOU AREN'T... CHIL-DREN... ARE YOU...?
N-NO...

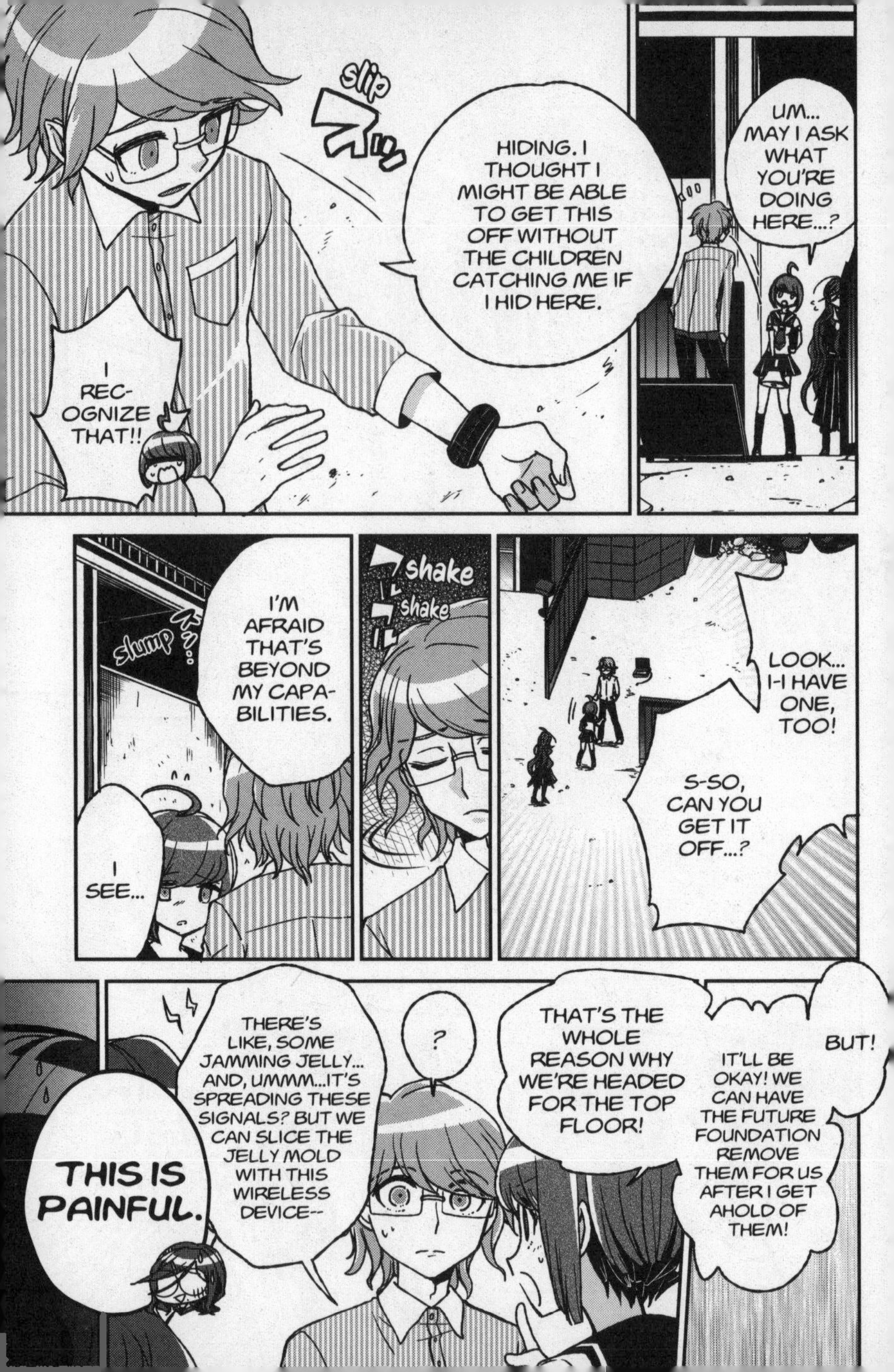
UM... MAY I ASK WHAT YOU'RE DOING HERE...?
slip
HIDING. I THOUGHT I MIGHT BE ABLE TO GET THIS OFF WITHOUT THE CHILDREN CATCHING ME IF I HID HERE.
I RECOGNIZE THAT!!
LOOK... I-I HAVE ONE, TOO!
S-SO, CAN YOU GET IT OFF...?
shake
shake
I'M AFRAID THAT'S BEYOND MY CAPABILITIES.
slump
I SEE...
BUT!
IT'LL BE OKAY! WE CAN HAVE THE FUTURE FOUNDATION REMOVE THEM FOR US AFTER I GET AHOLD OF THEM!
THAT'S THE WHOLE REASON WHY WE'RE HEADED FOR THE TOP FLOOR!
?
THERE'S LIKE, SOME JAMMING JELLY... AND, UMMM...IT'S SPREADING THESE SIGNALS? BUT WE CAN SLICE THE JELLY MOLD WITH THIS WIRELESS DEVICE--
THIS IS PAINFUL.

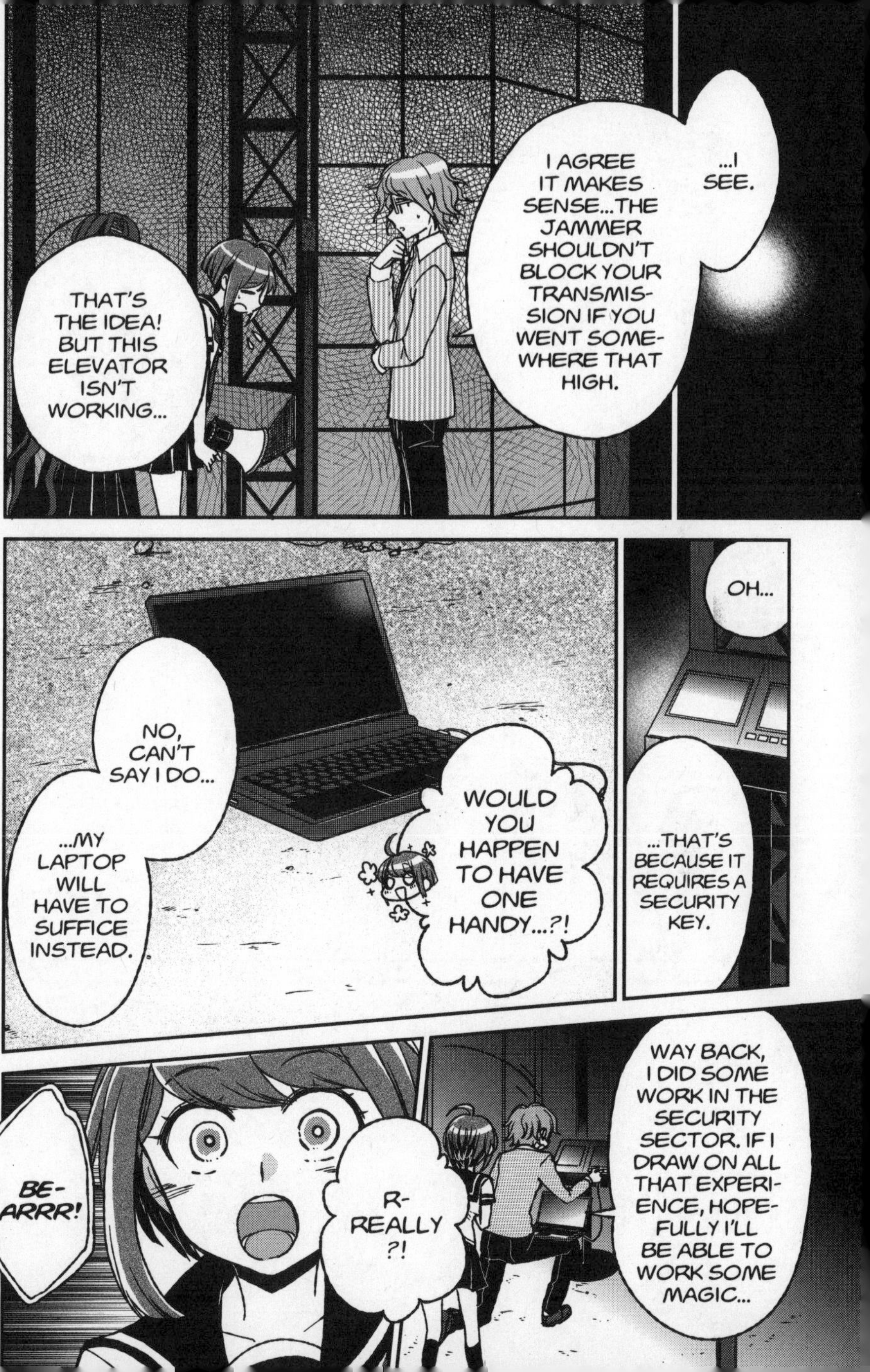
...I SEE.
I AGREE IT MAKES SENSE...THE JAMMER SHOULDN'T BLOCK YOUR TRANSMISSION IF YOU WENT SOMEWHERE THAT HIGH.
THAT'S THE IDEA! BUT THIS ELEVATOR ISN'T WORKING...
OH...
...THAT'S BECAUSE IT REQUIRES A SECURITY KEY.
WOULD YOU HAPPEN TO HAVE ONE HANDY...?!
NO, CAN'T SAY I DO...
...MY LAPTOP WILL HAVE TO SUFFICE INSTEAD.
WAY BACK, I DID SOME WORK IN THE SECURITY SECTOR. IF I DRAW ON ALL THAT EXPERIENCE, HOPEFULLY I'LL BE ABLE TO WORK SOME MAGIC...
R-REALLY?!
BE-ARRR!

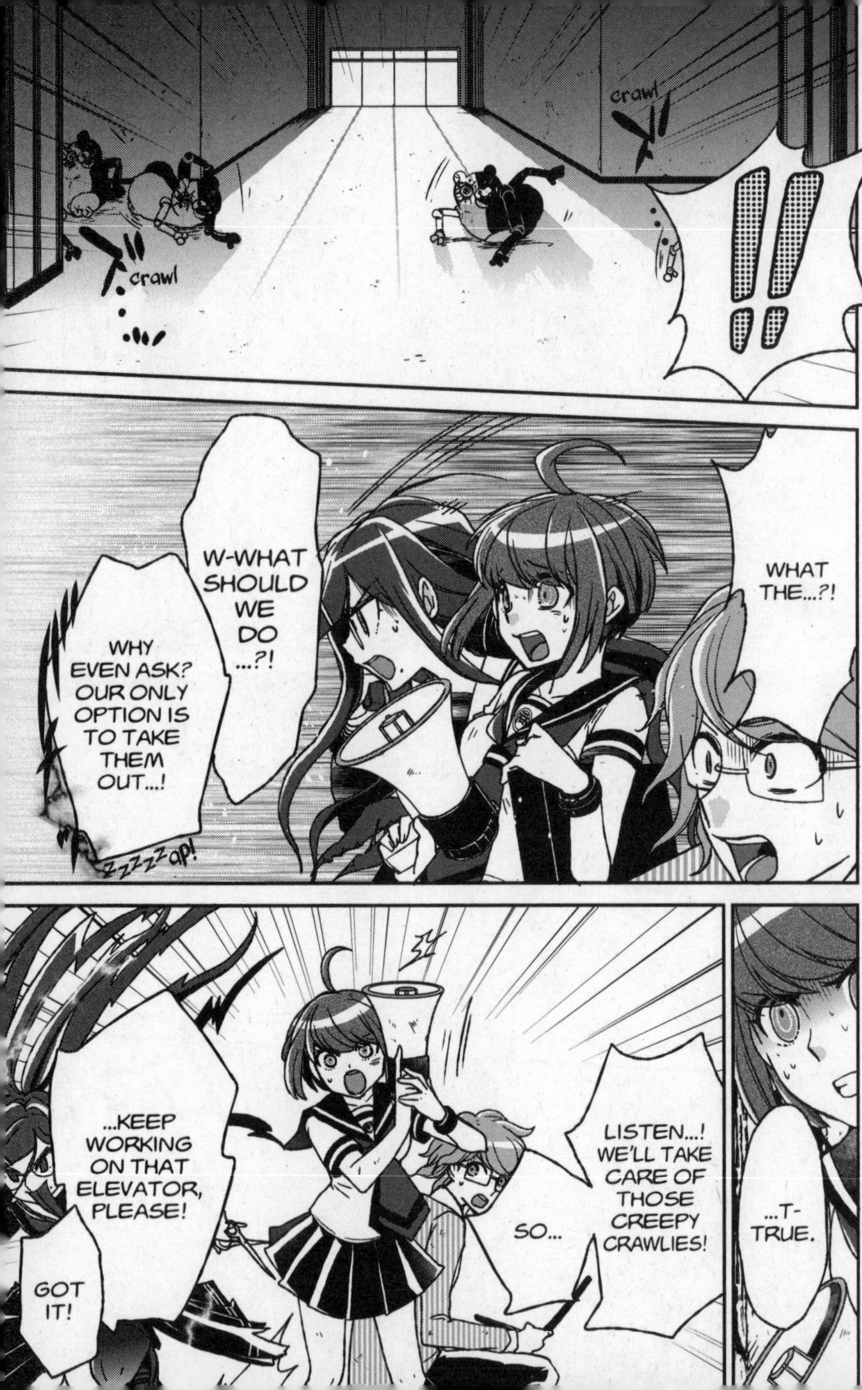
!!
crawl
crawl
WHAT THE...?!
W-WHAT SHOULD WE DO ...?!
WHY EVEN ASK? OUR ONLY OPTION IS TO TAKE THEM OUT...!
ZZZZZap!
...T-TRUE.
LISTEN...! WE'LL TAKE CARE OF THOSE CREEPY CRAWLIES!
SO...
...KEEP WORKING ON THAT ELEVATOR, PLEASE!
GOT IT!

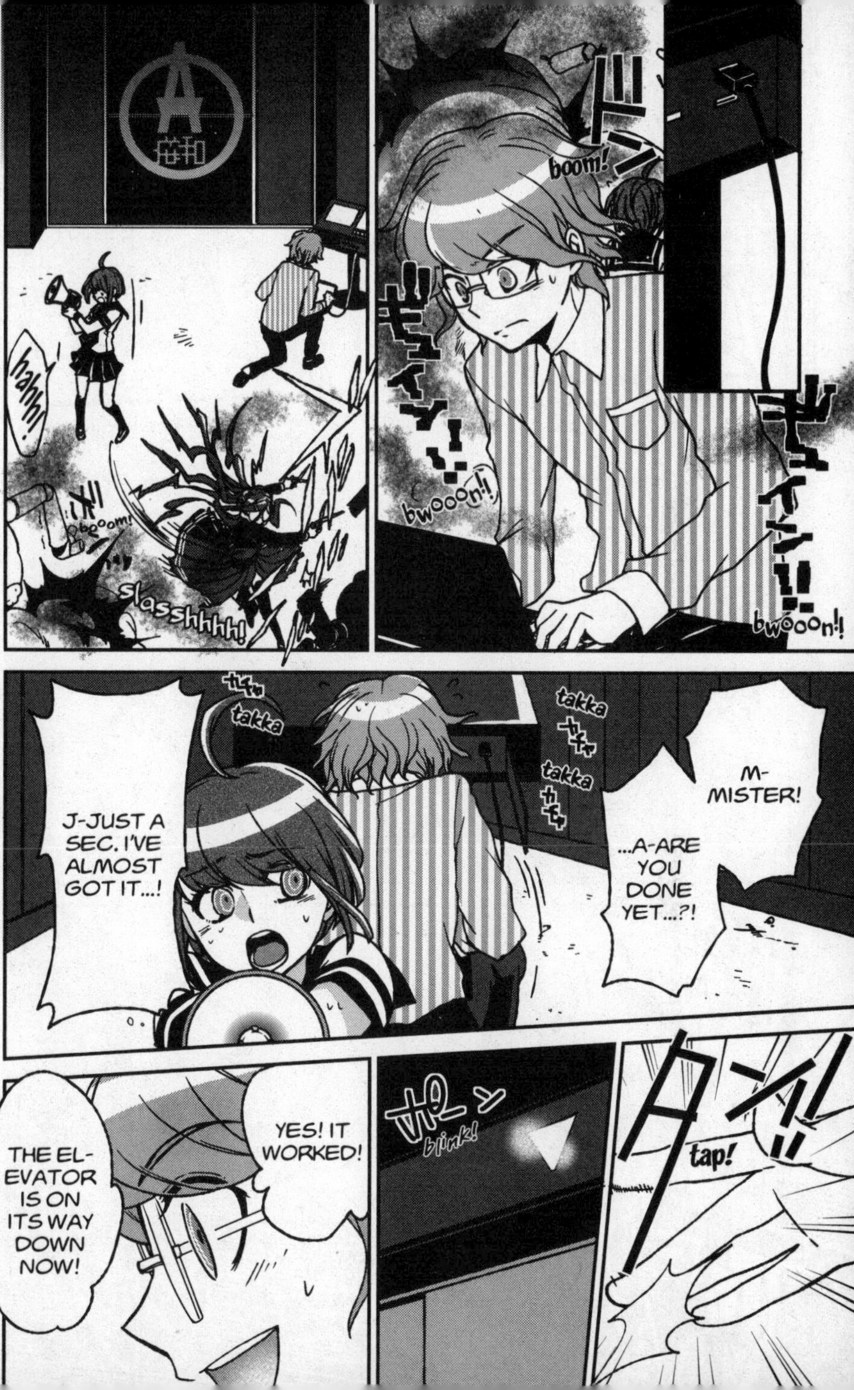
boom!
bwooon!!
bwooon!!
hahh!
boom!
slasshhhh!
takka
takka
takka
M- MISTER!
...A-ARE YOU DONE YET...?!
J-JUST A SEC. I'VE ALMOST GOT IT...!
tap!
blink!
YES! IT WORKED!
THE EL- EVATOR IS ON ITS WAY DOWN NOW!

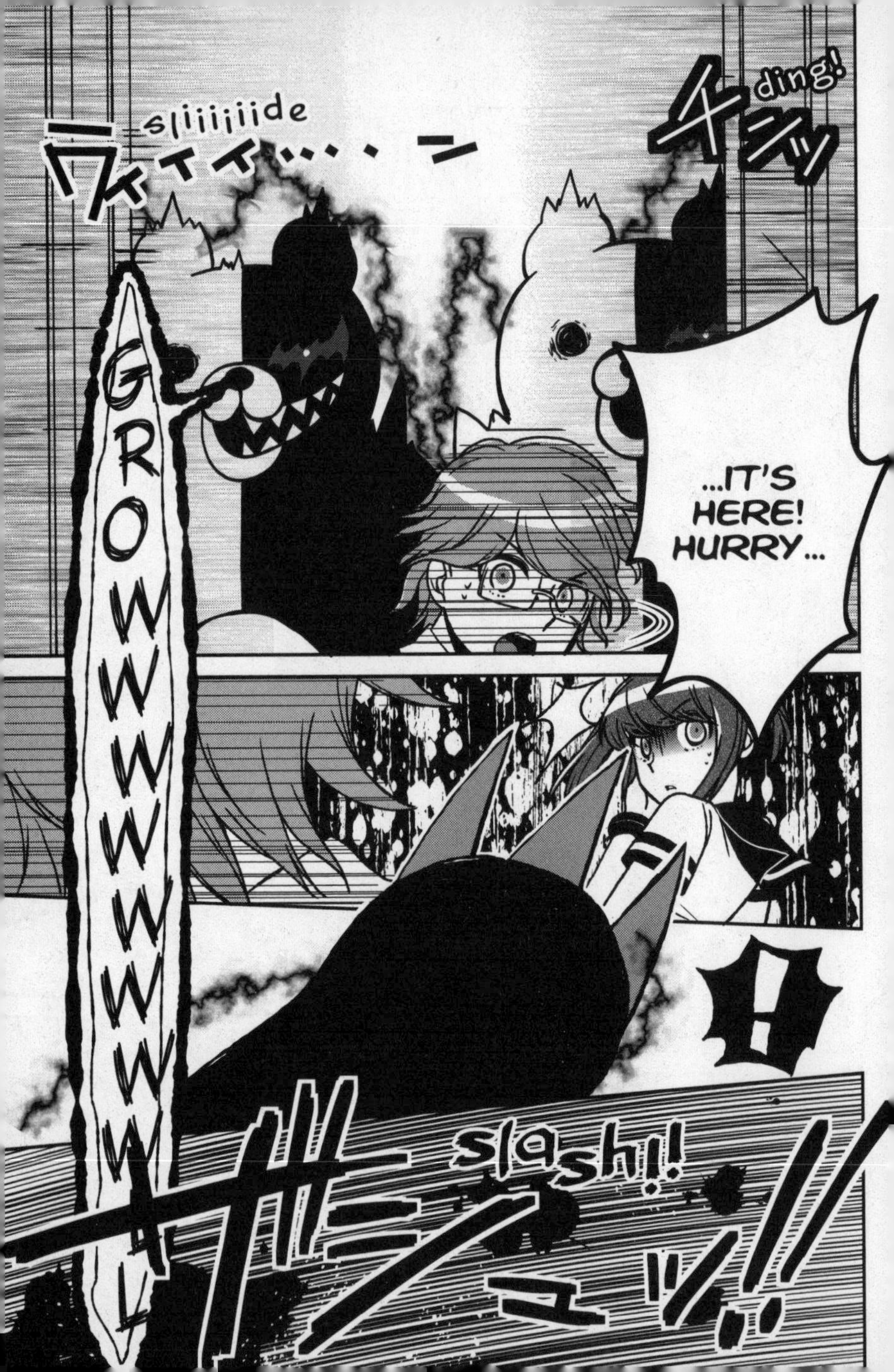
ding!
...IT'S HERE! HURRY...
sliiiiiide
GROWWWWWWWWWWWL
!
slash!!

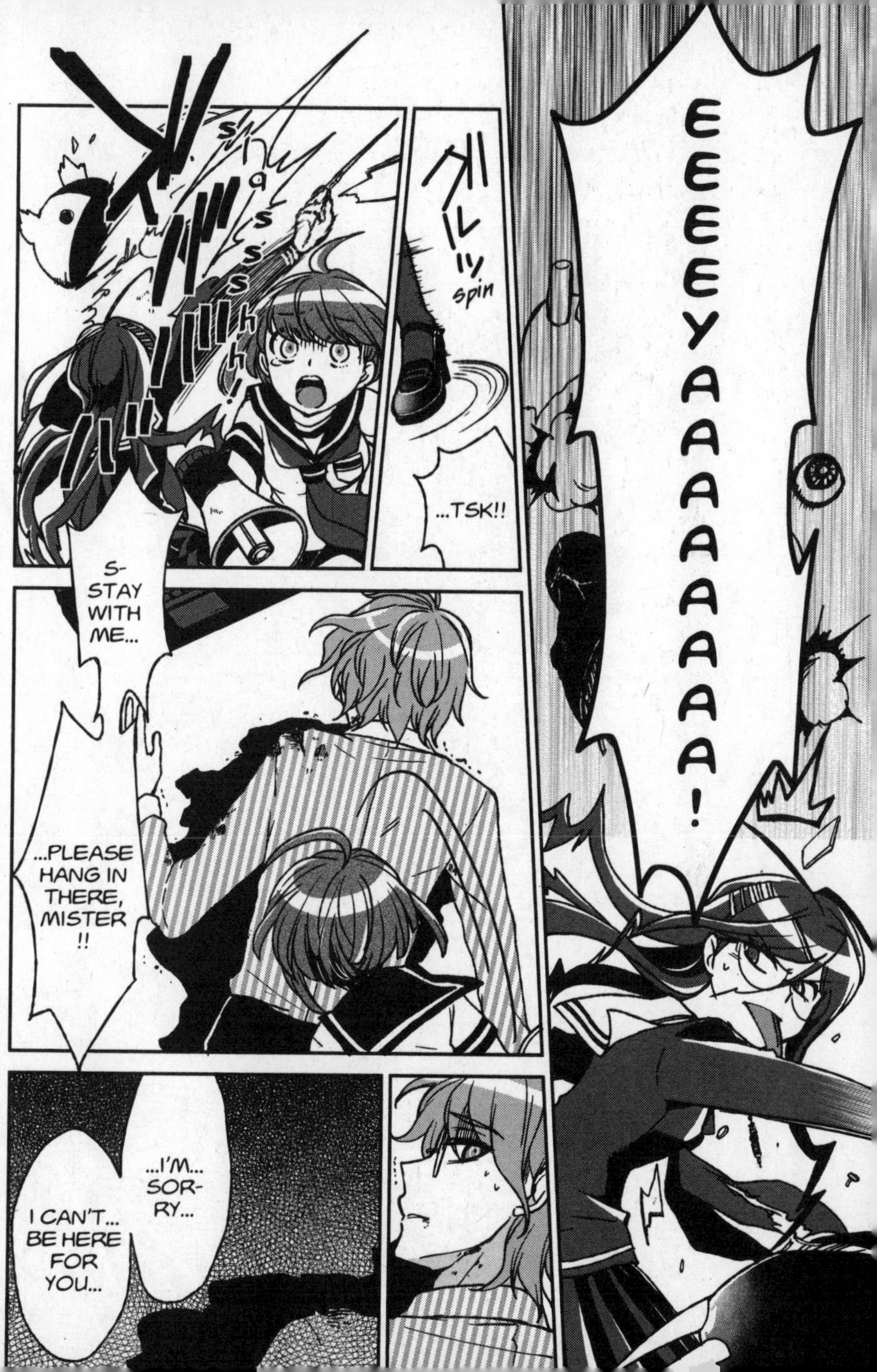
EEEEYAAAAAAAAA!
spin
...TSK!!
S-
STAY
WITH
ME...
...PLEASE
HANG IN
THERE,
MISTER
!!
...I'M...
SOR-
RY...
I CAN'T...
BE HERE
FOR
YOU...

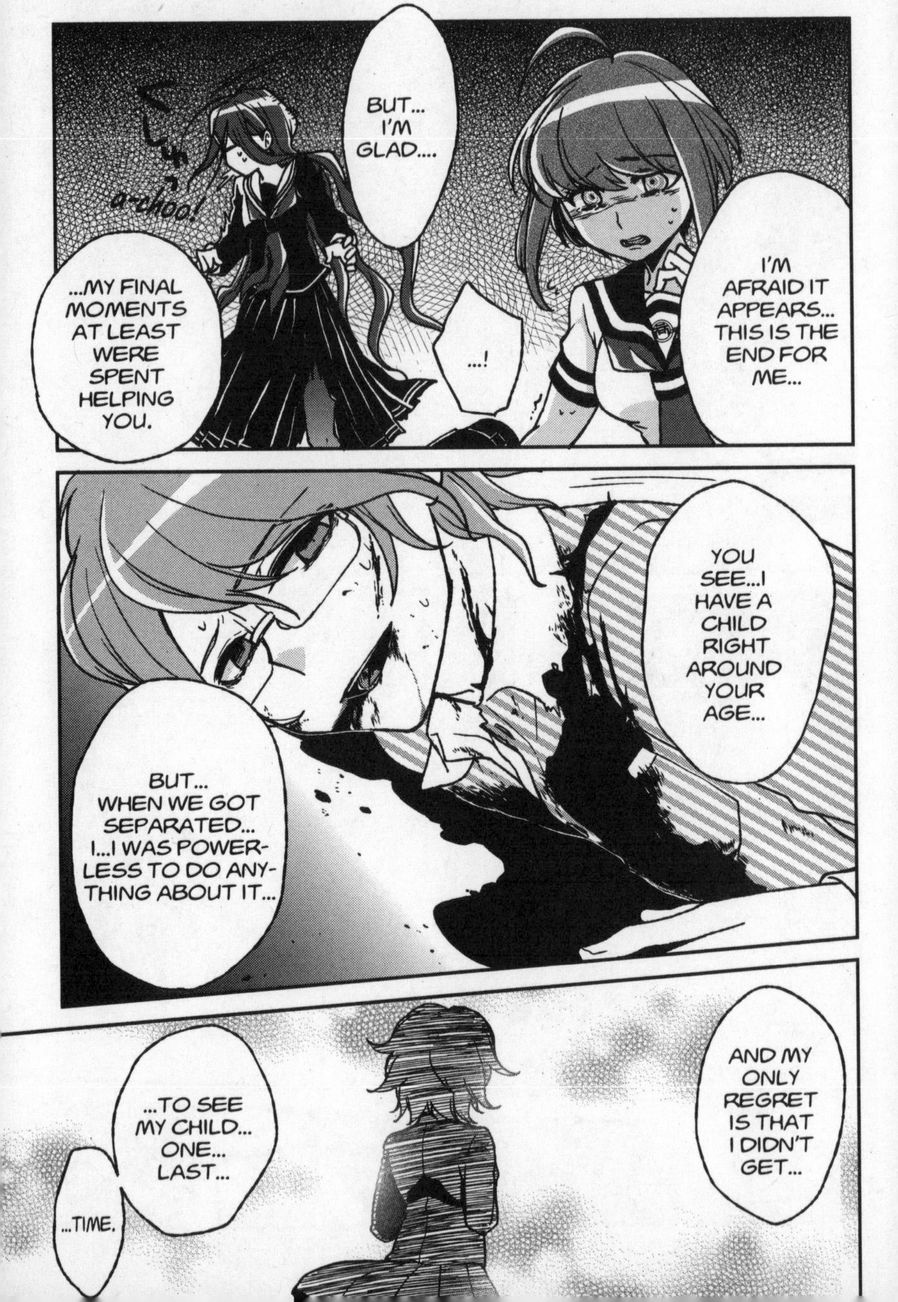
I'M AFRAID IT APPEARS... THIS IS THE END FOR ME...
...!
BUT... I'M GLAD....
...MY FINAL MOMENTS AT LEAST WERE SPENT HELPING YOU.
a-choo!
YOU SEE...I HAVE A CHILD RIGHT AROUND YOUR AGE...
BUT... WHEN WE GOT SEPARATED... I...I WAS POWER-LESS TO DO ANY-THING ABOUT IT...
AND MY ONLY REGRET IS THAT I DIDN'T GET...
...TO SEE MY CHILD... ONE... LAST...
...TIME.

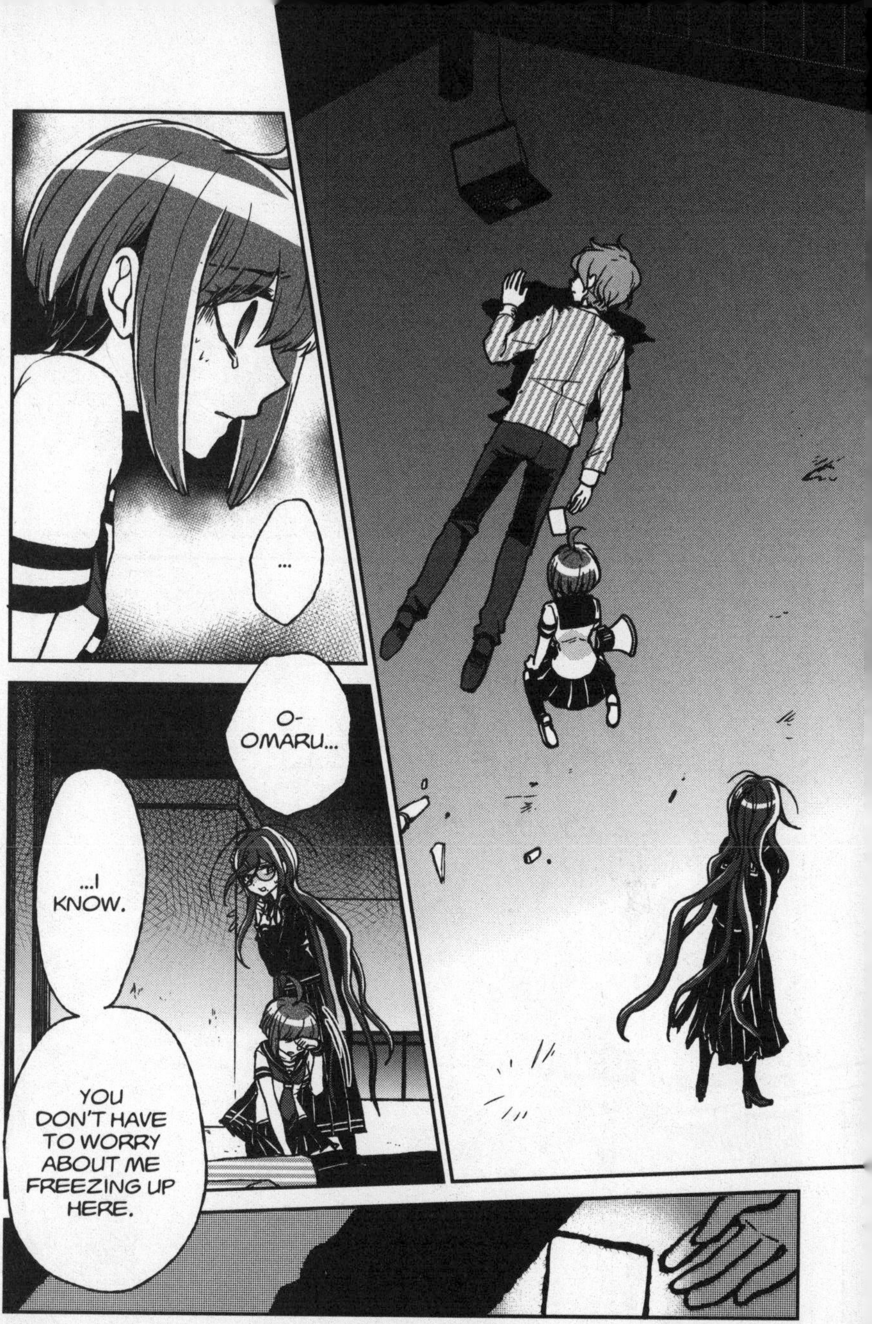
...
O-OMARU...
...I KNOW.
YOU DON'T HAVE TO WORRY ABOUT ME FREEZING UP HERE.

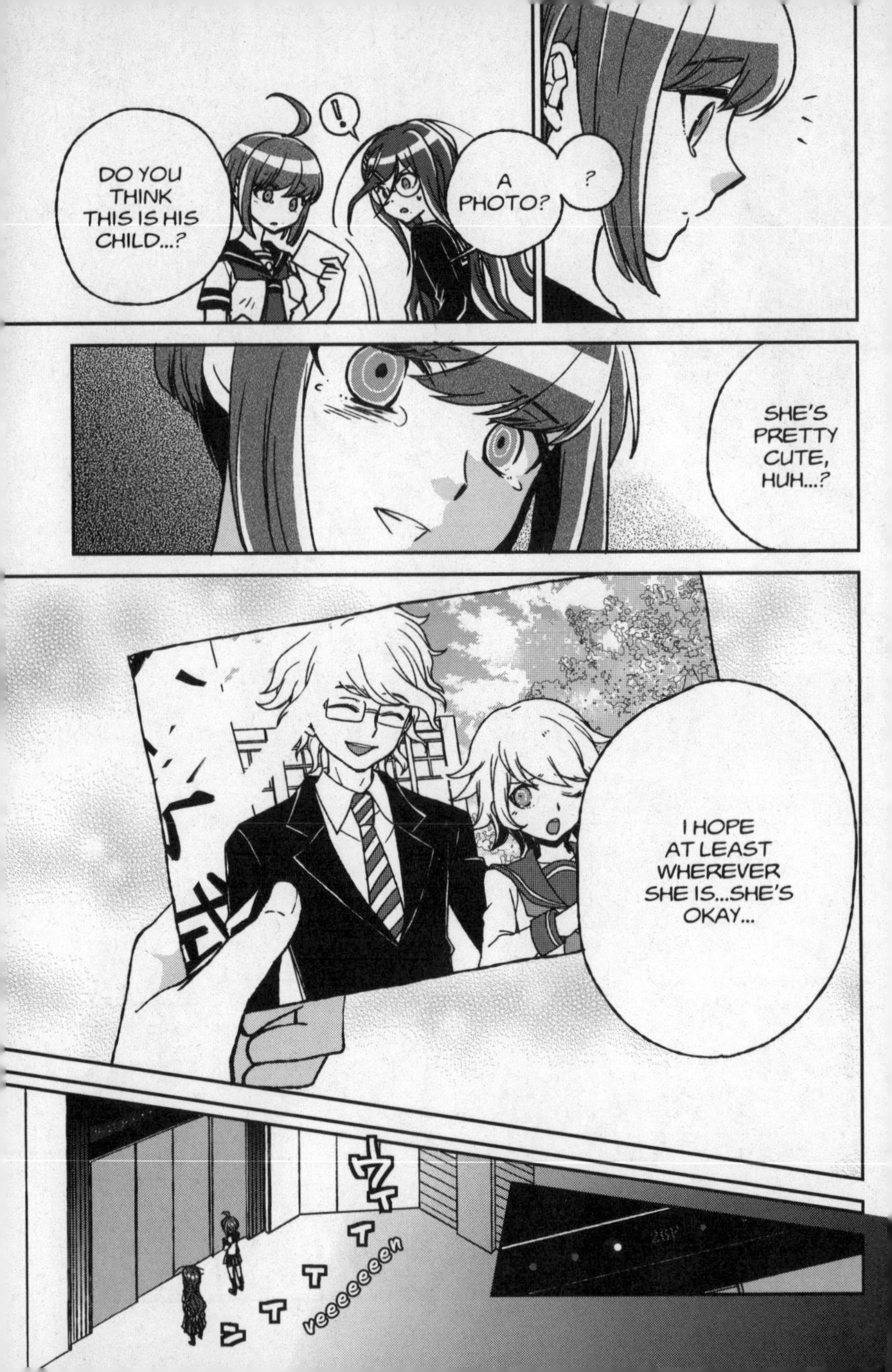
A PHOTO?
?
DO YOU THINK THIS IS HIS CHILD...?
!
SHE'S PRETTY CUTE, HUH...?
I HOPE AT LEAST WHEREVER SHE IS...SHE'S OKAY...
veeeeeeen

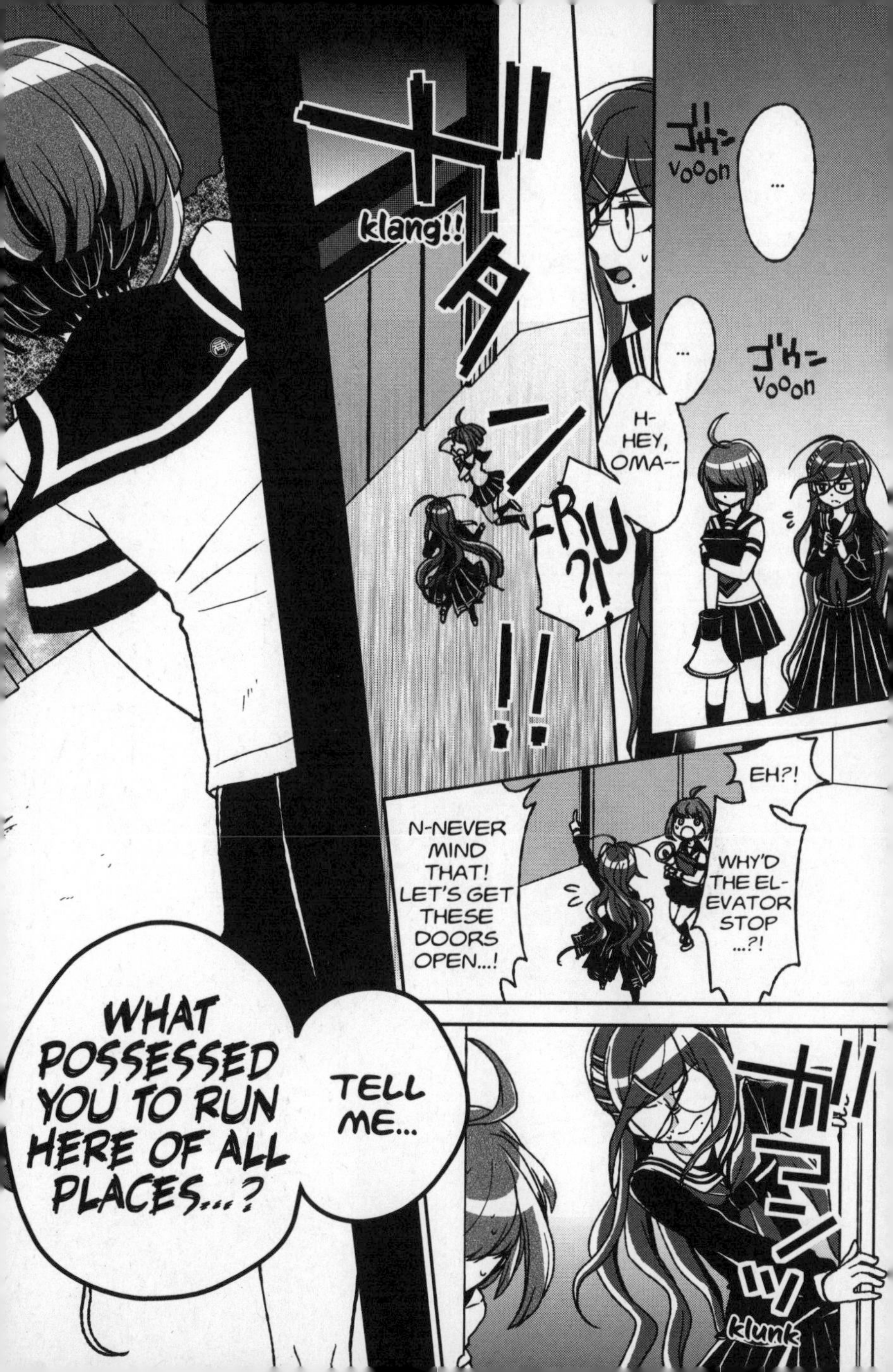
ゴゥン
vooon
...
ゴゥン
vooon
...
H-HEY, OMA--
RU?!
klang!!
!!
EH?!
WHY'D THE EL-EVATOR STOP ...?!
N-NEVER MIND THAT! LET'S GET THESE DOORS OPEN...!
klunk
TELL ME...
WHAT POSSESSED YOU TO RUN HERE OF ALL PLACES...?

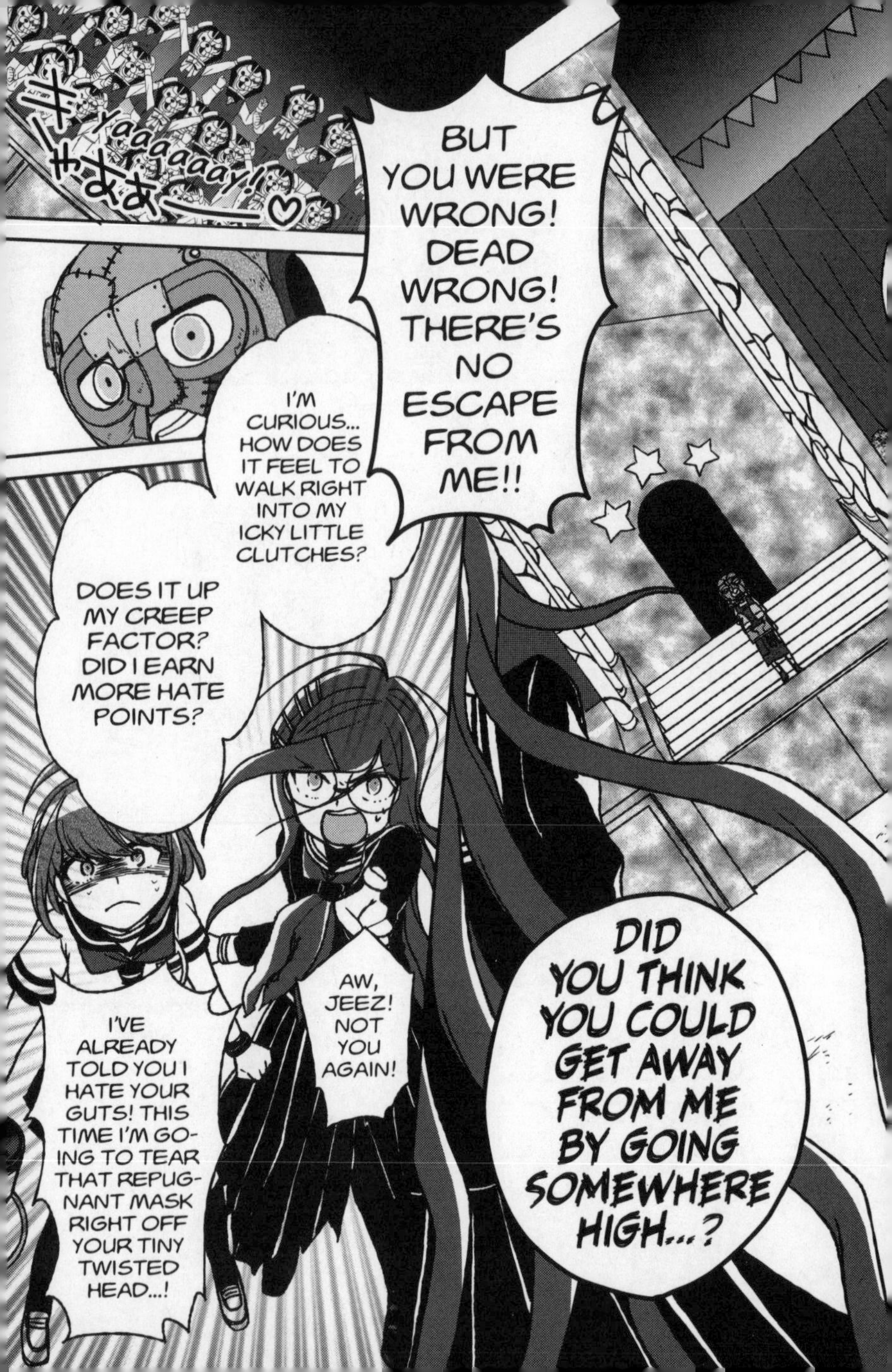
BUT YOU WERE WRONG! DEAD WRONG! THERE'S NO ESCAPE FROM ME!!
Yaaaaaaay!!
I'M CURIOUS... HOW DOES IT FEEL TO WALK RIGHT INTO MY ICKY LITTLE CLUTCHES?
DOES IT UP MY CREEP FACTOR? DID I EARN MORE HATE POINTS?
DID YOU THINK YOU COULD GET AWAY FROM ME BY GOING SOMEWHERE HIGH...?
AW, JEEZ! NOT YOU AGAIN!
I'VE ALREADY TOLD YOU I HATE YOUR GUTS! THIS TIME I'M GO-ING TO TEAR THAT REPUG-NANT MASK RIGHT OFF YOUR TINY TWISTED HEAD...!

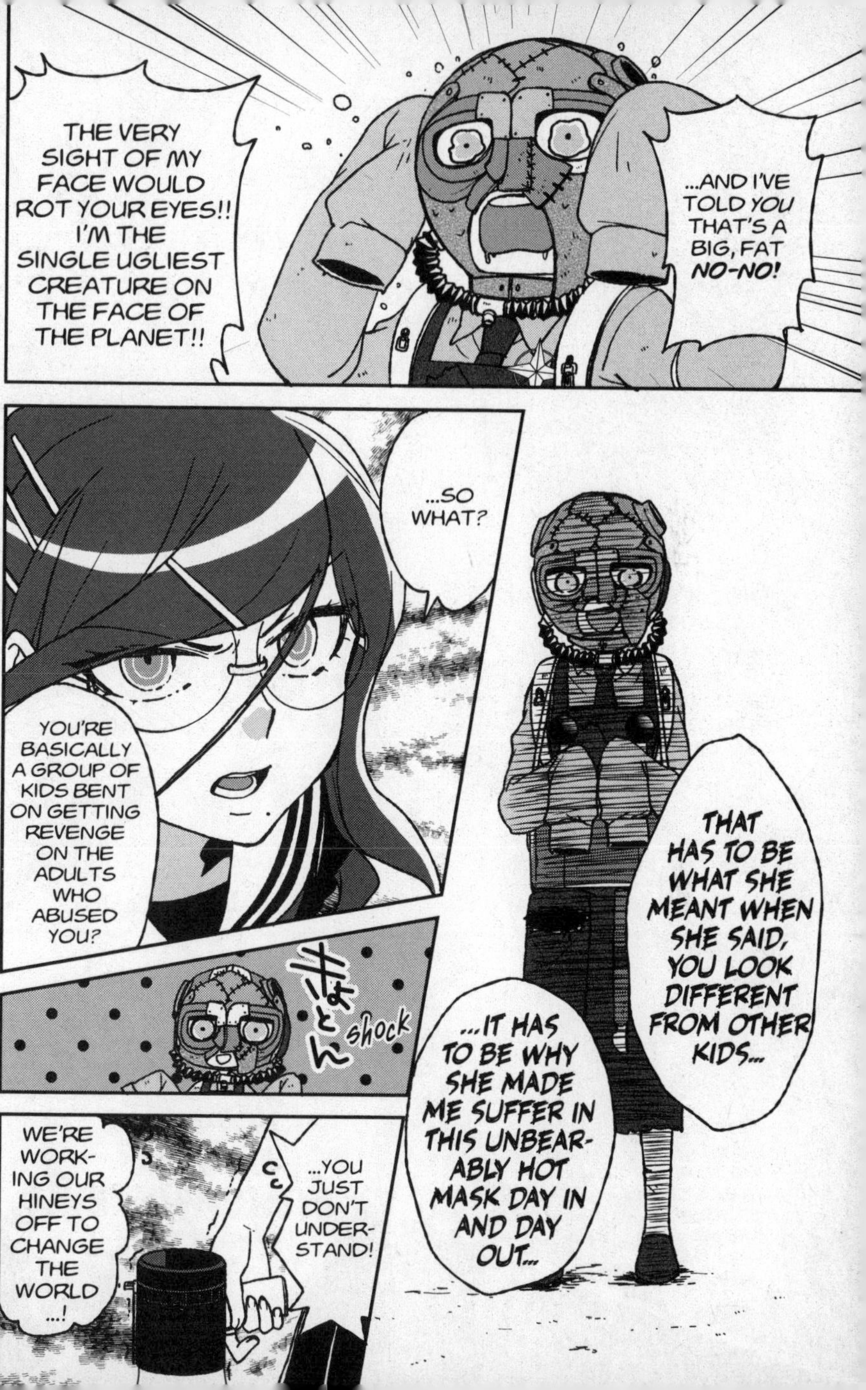
...AND I'VE TOLD YOU THAT'S A BIG, FAT NO-NO!
THE VERY SIGHT OF MY FACE WOULD ROT YOUR EYES!! I'M THE SINGLE UGLIEST CREATURE ON THE FACE OF THE PLANET!!
THAT HAS TO BE WHAT SHE MEANT WHEN SHE SAID, YOU LOOK DIFFERENT FROM OTHER KIDS...
...IT HAS TO BE WHY SHE MADE ME SUFFER IN THIS UNBEARABLY HOT MASK DAY IN AND DAY OUT...
...SO WHAT?
YOU'RE BASICALLY A GROUP OF KIDS BENT ON GETTING REVENGE ON THE ADULTS WHO ABUSED YOU?
ぎょとん shock
...YOU JUST DON'T UNDERSTAND!
WE'RE WORKING OUR HINEYS OFF TO CHANGE THE WORLD ...!

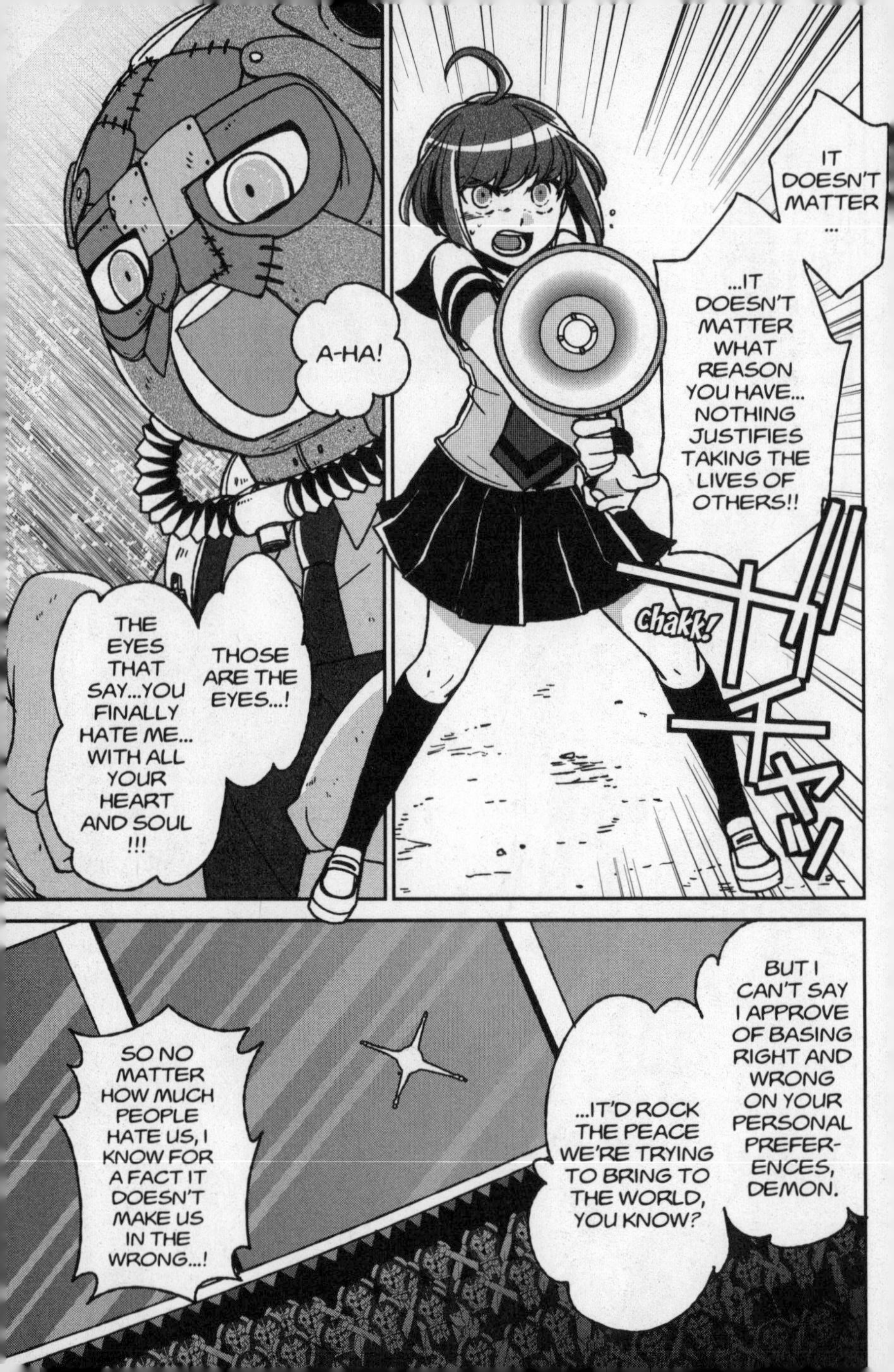
IT DOESN'T MATTER ...
...IT DOESN'T MATTER WHAT REASON YOU HAVE... NOTHING JUSTIFIES TAKING THE LIVES OF OTHERS!!
chakk!
A-HA!
THOSE ARE THE EYES...!
THE EYES THAT SAY...YOU FINALLY HATE ME... WITH ALL YOUR HEART AND SOUL !!!
BUT I CAN'T SAY I APPROVE OF BASING RIGHT AND WRONG ON YOUR PERSONAL PREFER-ENCES, DEMON.
...IT'D ROCK THE PEACE WE'RE TRYING TO BRING TO THE WORLD, YOU KNOW?
SO NO MATTER HOW MUCH PEOPLE HATE US, I KNOW FOR A FACT IT DOESN'T MAKE US IN THE WRONG...!

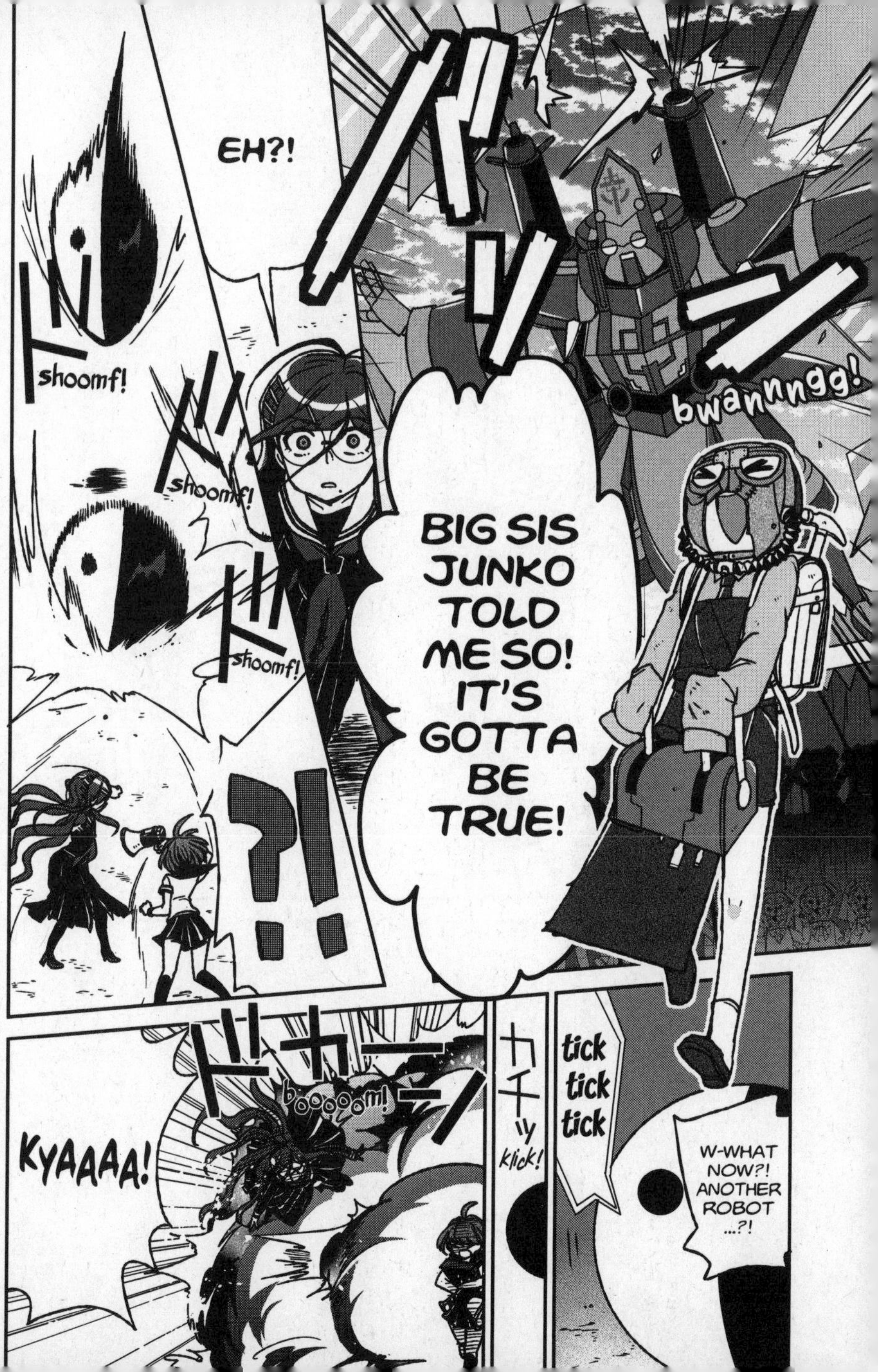
bwannngg!
BIG SIS JUNKO TOLD ME SO! IT'S GOTTA BE TRUE!
EH?!
shoomf!
shoomf!
shoomf!
?!!
W-WHAT NOW?! ANOTHER ROBOT ...?!
tick tick tick
klick!
booooom!
KYAAAA!

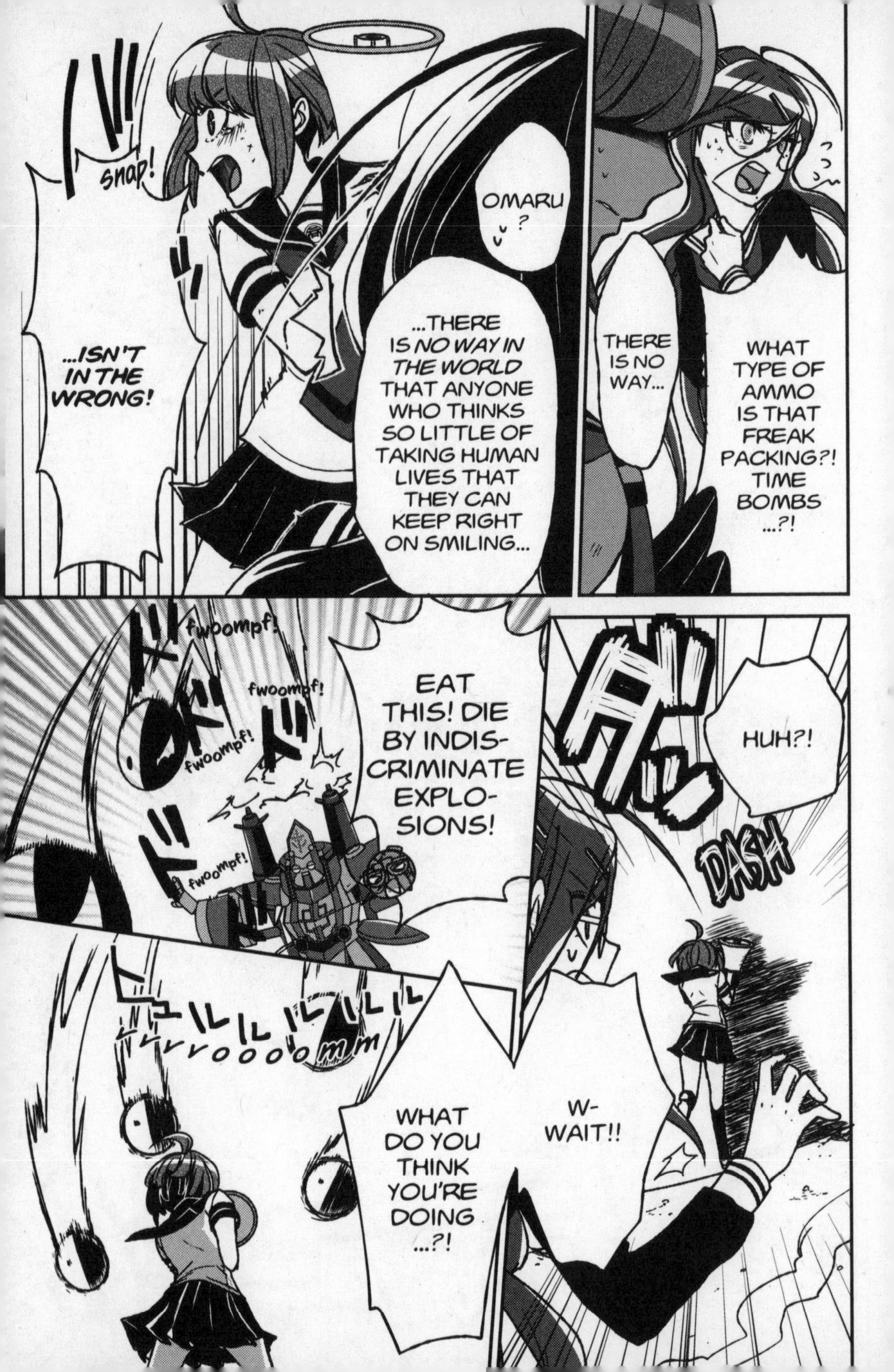
WHAT TYPE OF AMMO IS THAT FREAK PACKING?! TIME BOMBS ...?!
OMARU ?
THERE IS NO WAY...
...THERE IS NO WAY IN THE WORLD THAT ANYONE WHO THINKS SO LITTLE OF TAKING HUMAN LIVES THAT THEY CAN KEEP RIGHT ON SMILING...
snap!
...ISN'T IN THE WRONG!
HUH?!
DASH
EAT THIS! DIE BY INDIS-CRIMINATE EXPLO-SIONS!
fwoompf!
fwoompf!
fwoompf!
fwoompf!
W-WAIT!!
WHAT DO YOU THINK YOU'RE DOING ...?!
vrroooomm

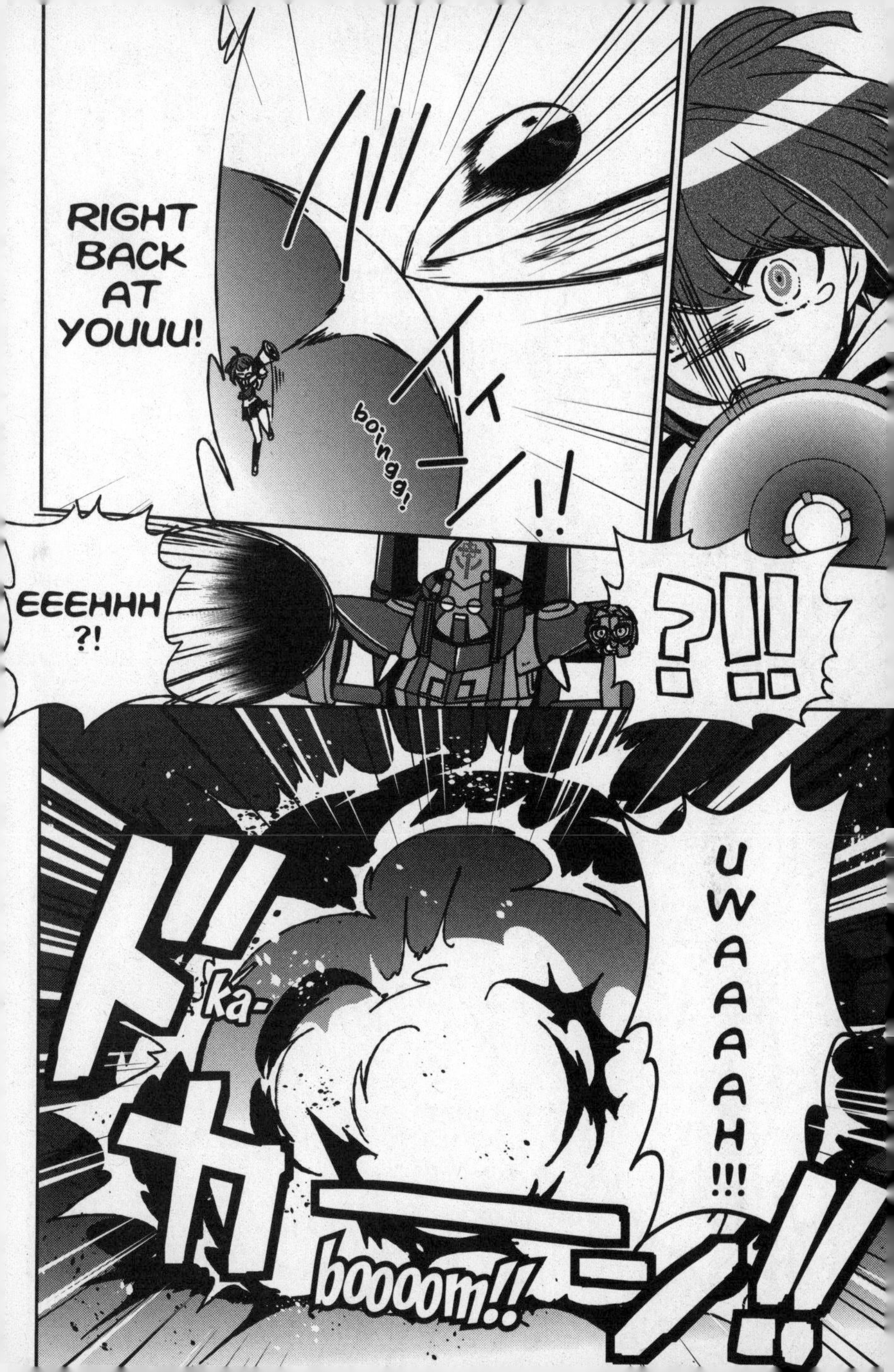
RIGHT BACK AT YOUUU!
boingg!
!!
?!!
EEEHHH ?!
UWAAAAAH!!!
ka-
boooom!!

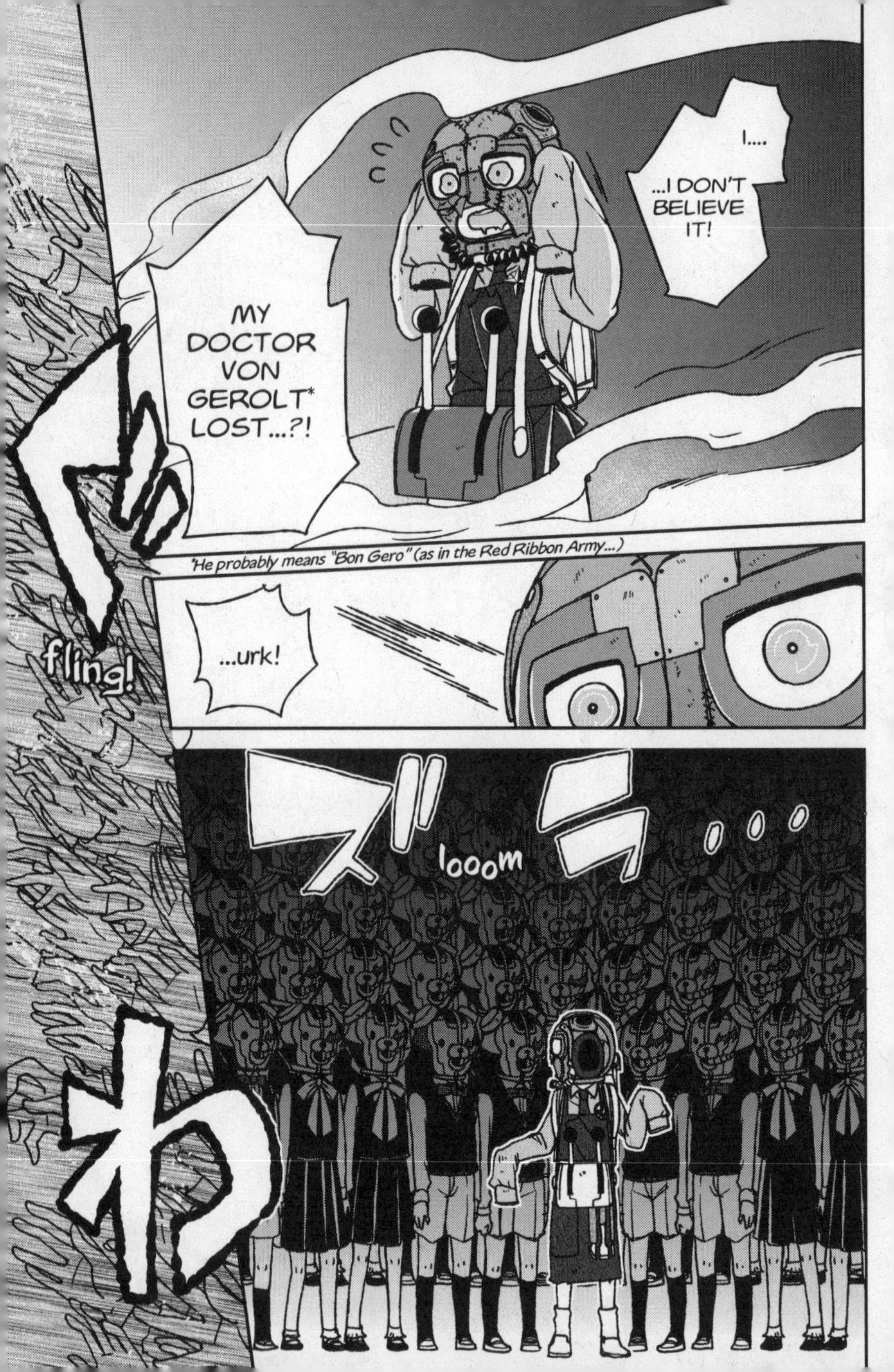
I....
...I DON'T BELIEVE IT!
MY DOCTOR VON GEROLT* LOST...?!
...urk!
looom
fling!

*He probably means "Bon Gero" (as in the Red Ribbon Army...)

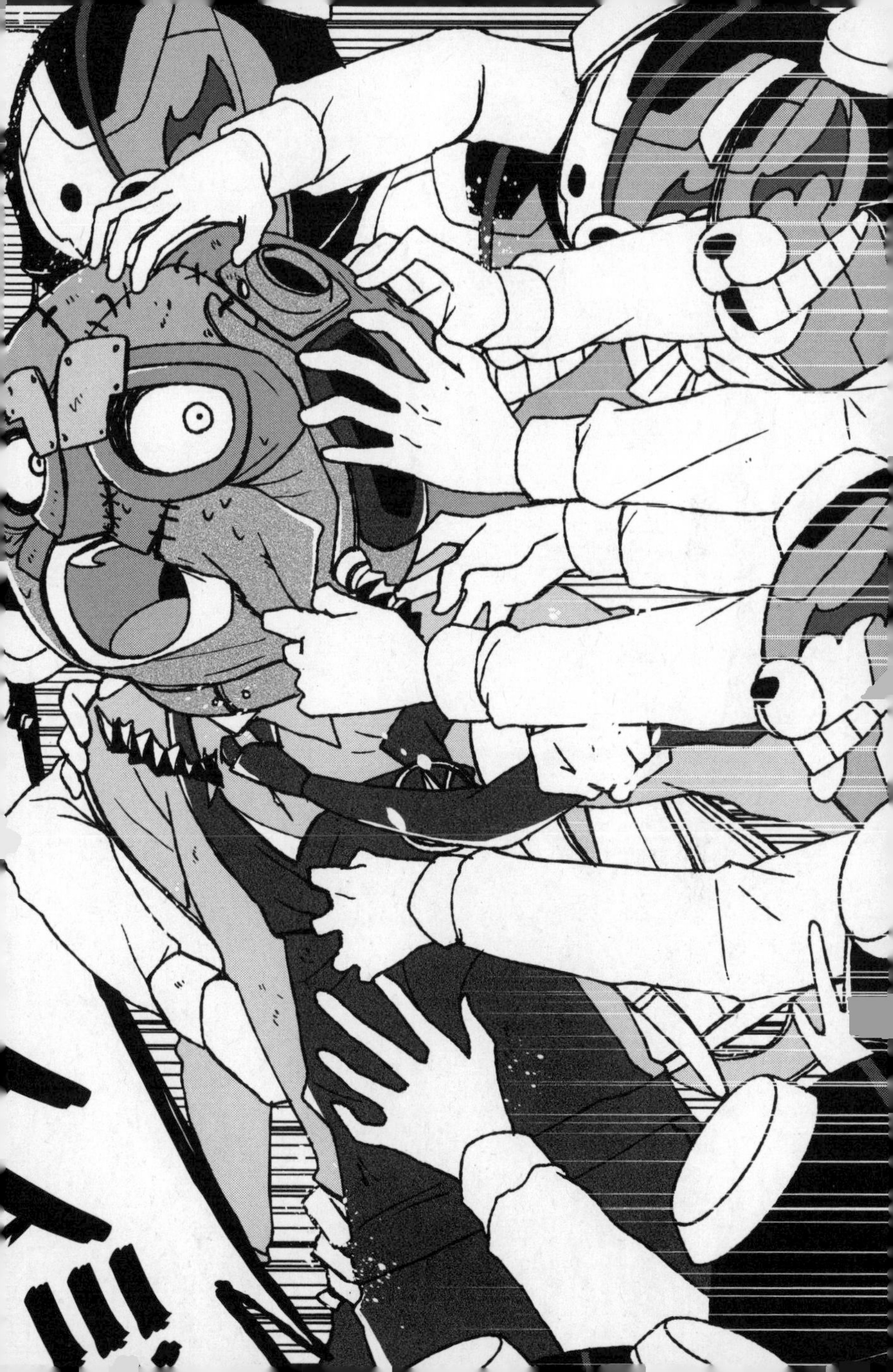

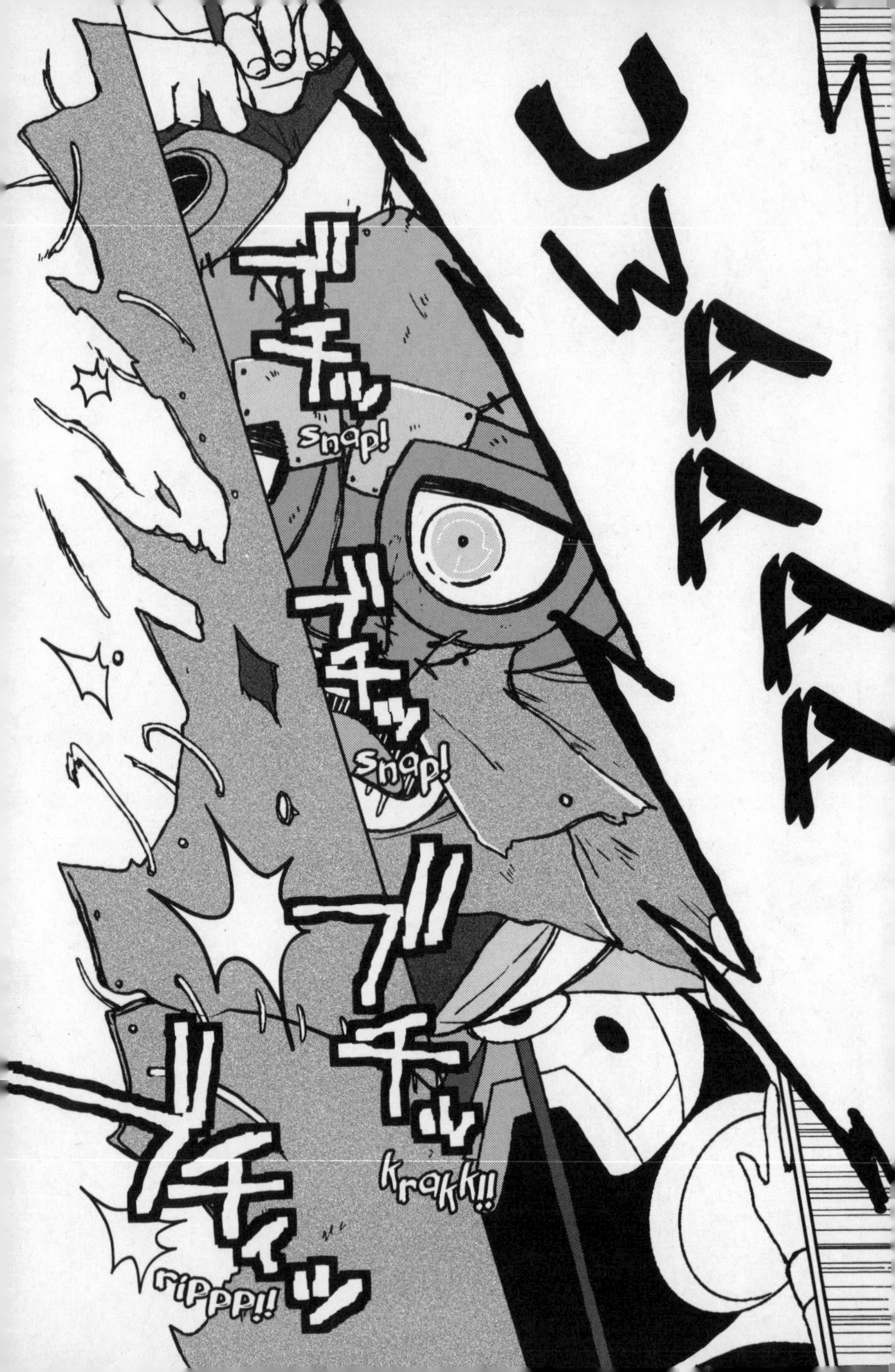
UWAAAA
ブチッ
snap!
ブチチッ
snap!
ブチッ
krakk!!
ブチィッ
rippp!!

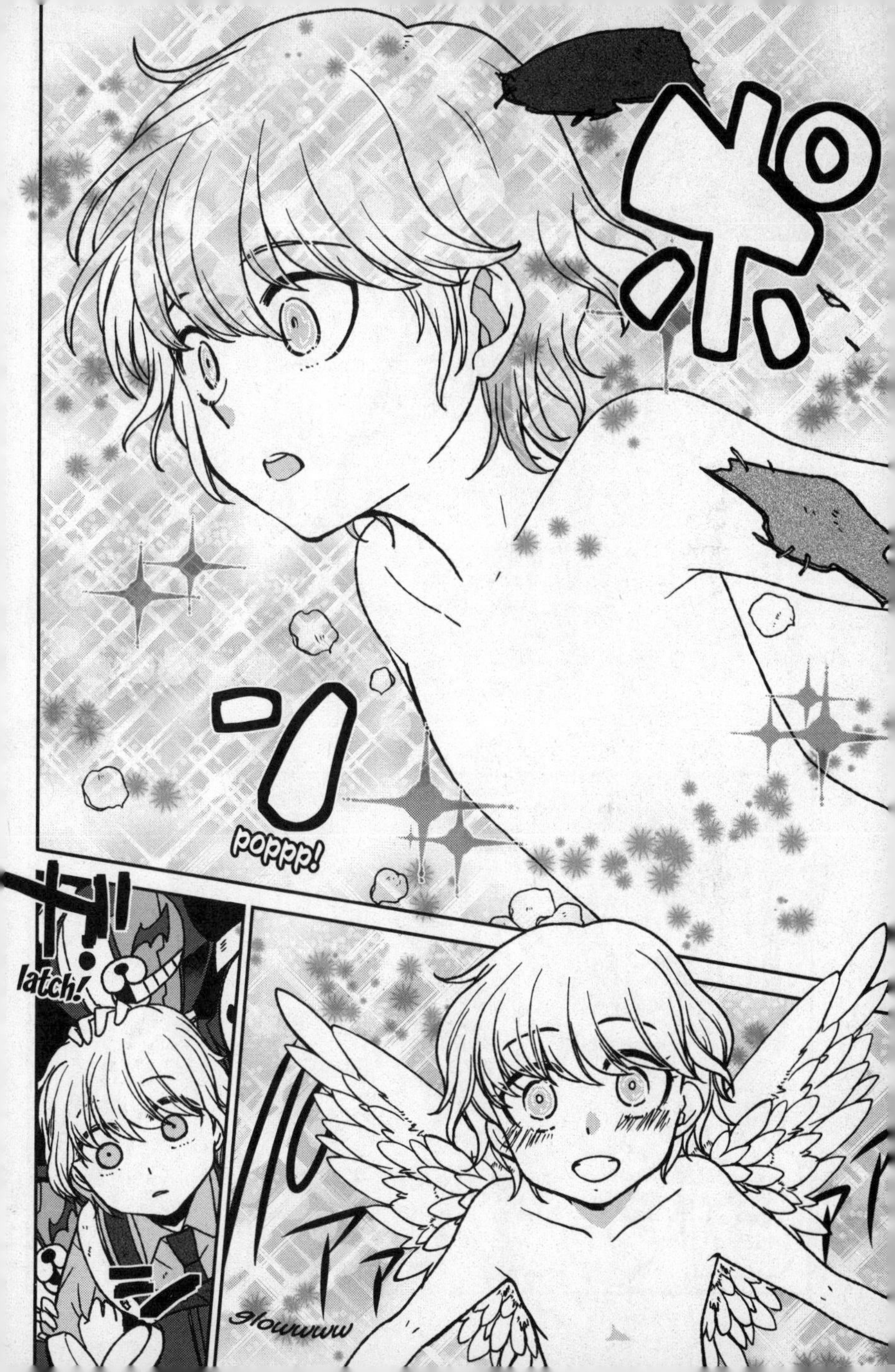
poppp!
latch!
glowwww

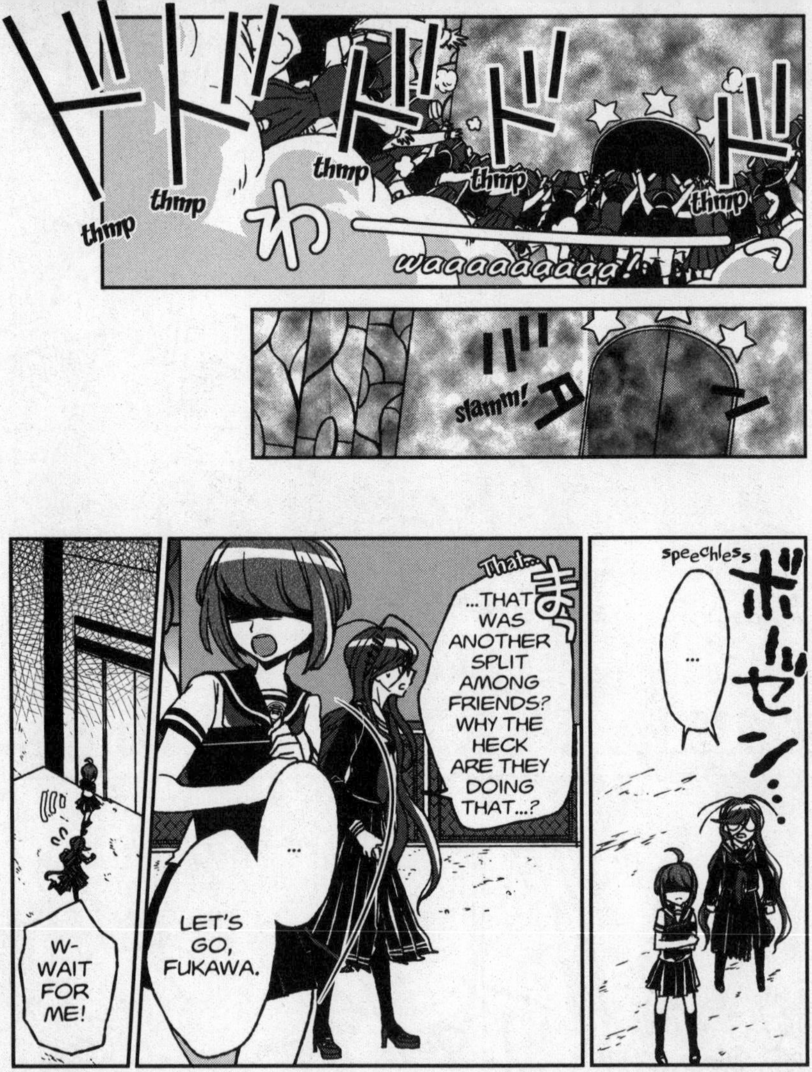
thmp
thmp
thmp
thmp
thmp
waaaaaaaaaa!
slamm!
speechless
...
That...
...THAT WAS ANOTHER SPLIT AMONG FRIENDS? WHY THE HECK ARE THEY DOING THAT...?
...
LET'S GO, FUKAWA.
W- WAIT FOR ME!

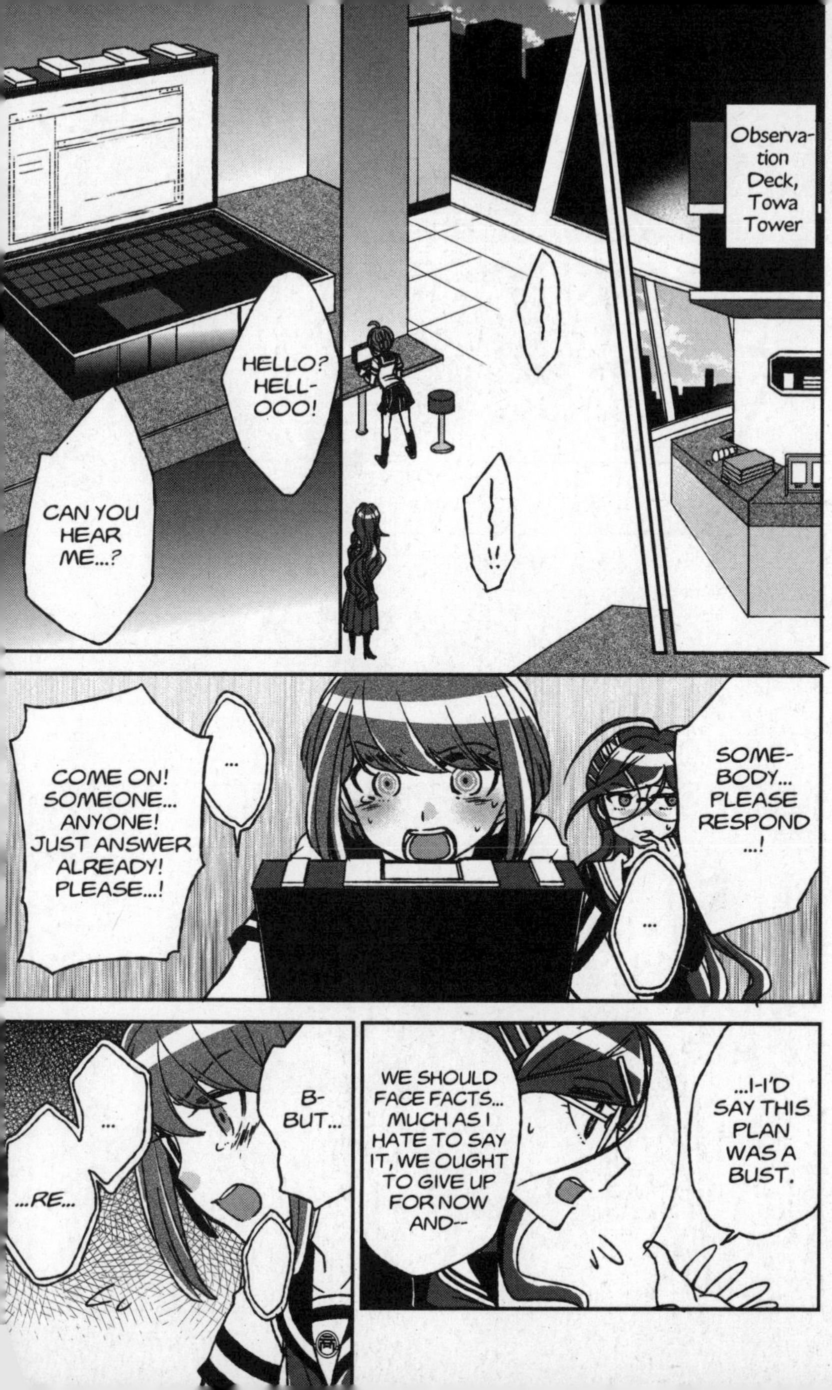

Observation Deck, Towa Tower
HELLO? HELL-OOO!
!!
CAN YOU HEAR ME...?
SOME-BODY... PLEASE RESPOND ...!
...
...
COME ON! SOMEONE... ANYONE! JUST ANSWER ALREADY! PLEASE...!
...I-I'D SAY THIS PLAN WAS A BUST.
WE SHOULD FACE FACTS... MUCH AS I HATE TO SAY IT, WE OUGHT TO GIVE UP FOR NOW AND--
B-BUT...
...
...RE...

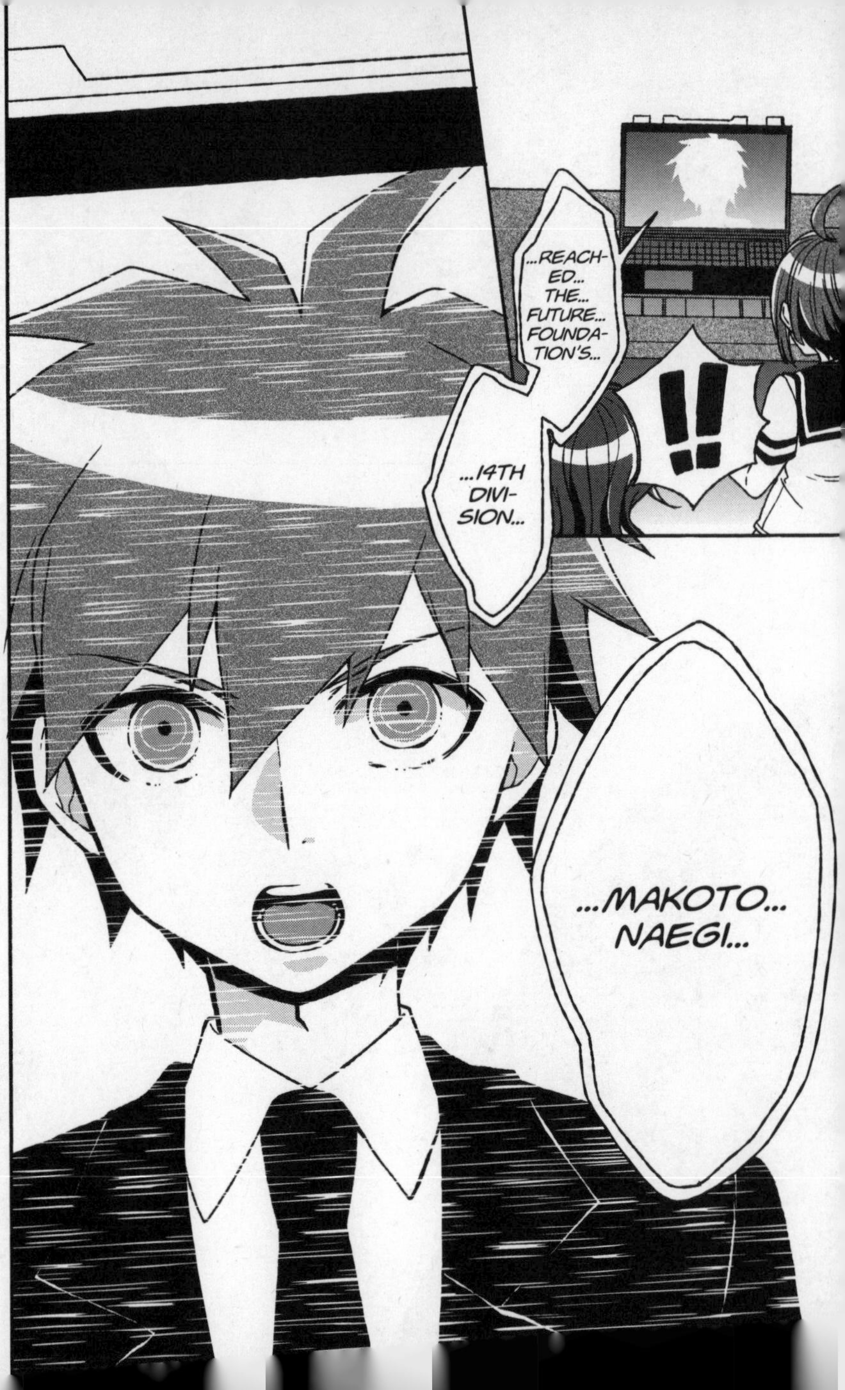
...REACHED... THE... FUTURE... FOUNDATION'S...
...14TH DIVISION...
!!
...MAKOTO... NAEGI...

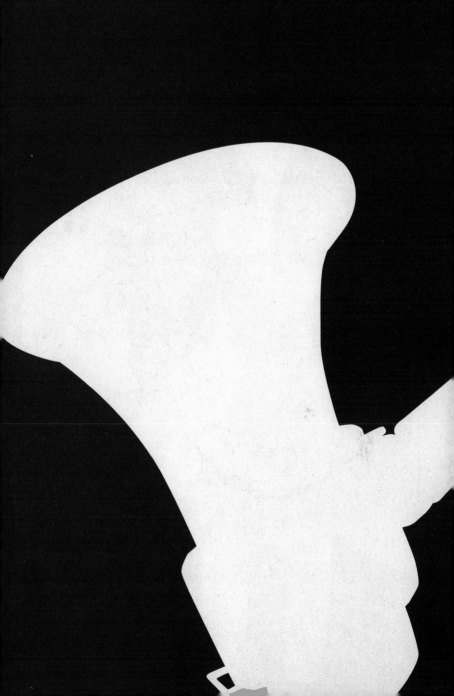

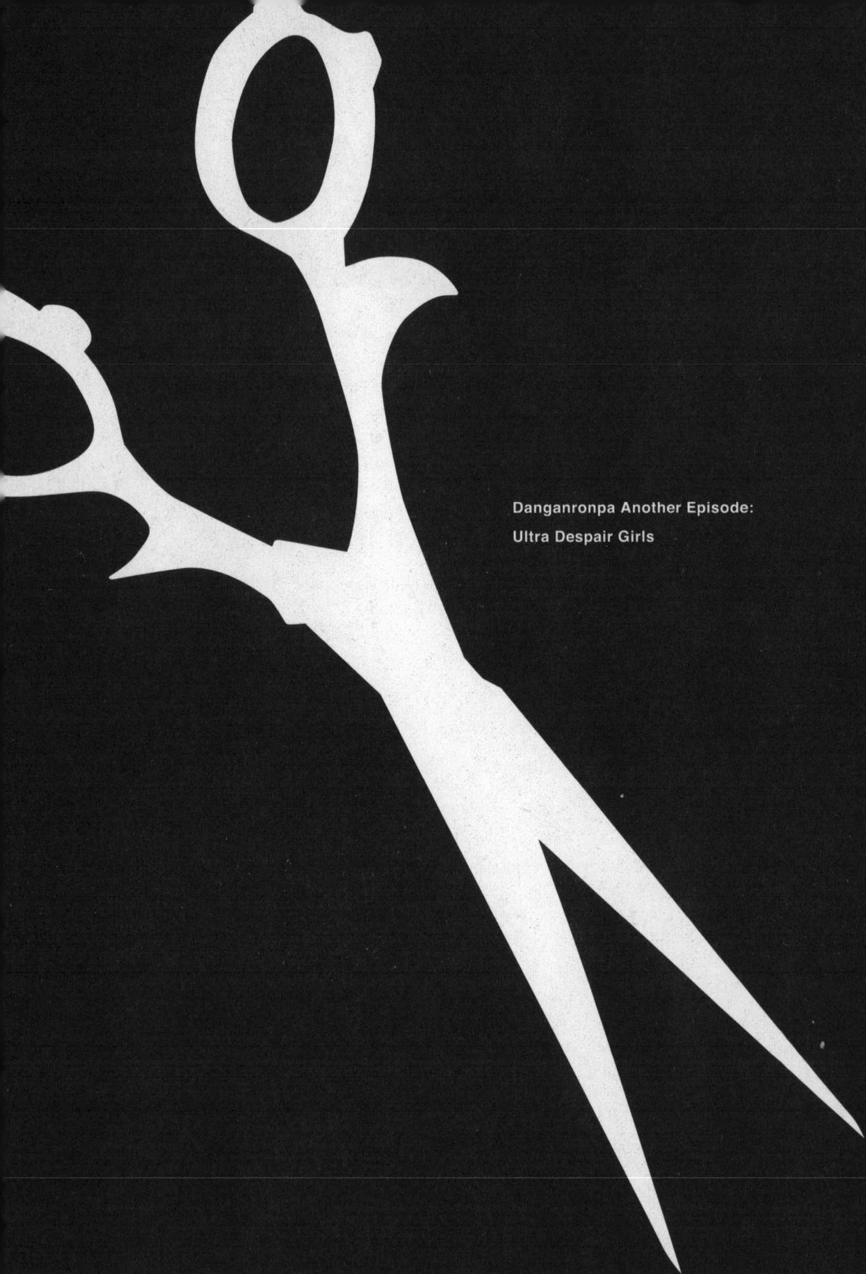

Danganronpa Another Episode:
Ultra Despair Girls

CONTINUED IN VOL. 3 . . .

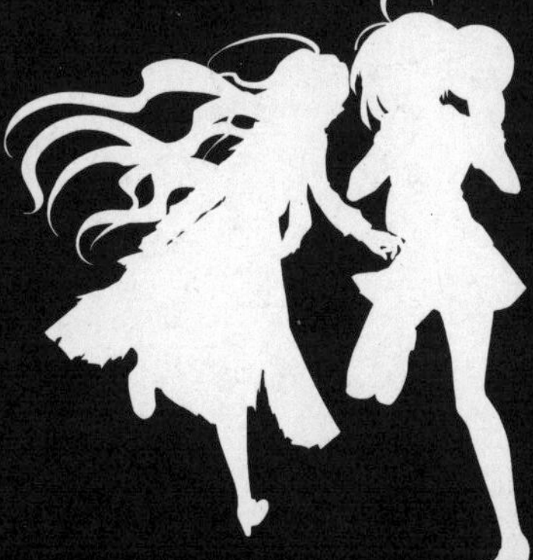

Danganronpa Another Episode:
Ultra Despair Girls

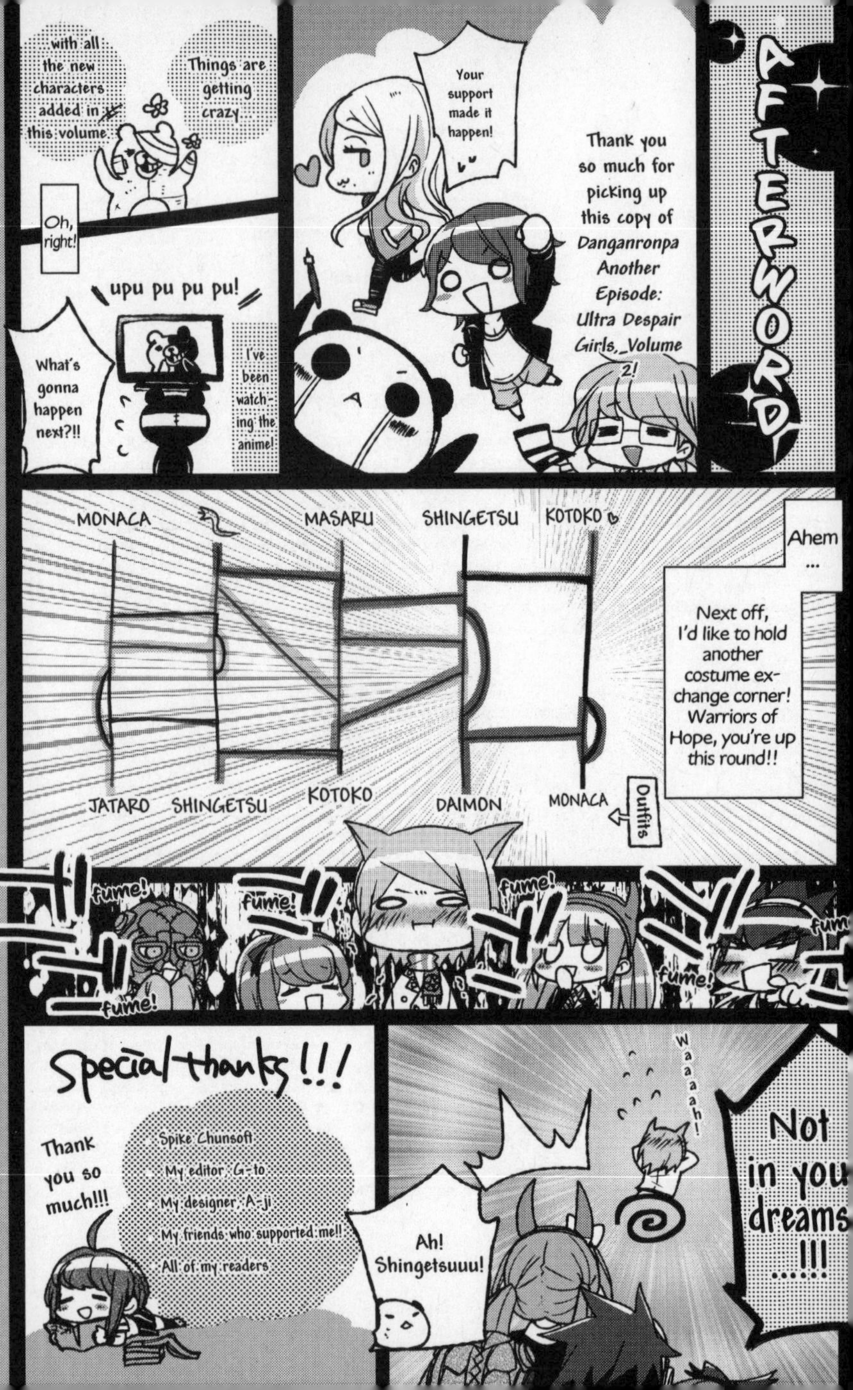
AFTERWORD
Thank you so much for picking up this copy of Danganronpa Another Episode: Ultra Despair Girls, Volume 2!
Your support made it happen!
Things are getting crazy
with all the new characters added in this volume.
upu pu pu pu!
I've been watching the anime!
Oh, right!
What's gonna happen next?!!
Ahem...
Next off, I'd like to hold another costume exchange corner! Warriors of Hope, you're up this round!!
KOTOKO
SHINGETSU
MASARU
MONACA
Outfits
MONACA
DAIMON
KOTOKO
SHINGETSU
JATARO
fume!
fume!
fume!
fume!
fume!
Not in you dreams ...!!!
Waaaah!
Ah! Shingetsuuu!
Special thanks!!!
Spike Chunsoft
My editor, G-to
My designer, A-ji
My friends who supported me!!
All of my readers
Thank you so much!!!

President and Publisher // **Mike Richardson**

Designer // **Skyler Weissenfluh**

Ultimate Digital Art Technician // **Samantha Hummer**

English-language version produced by Dark Horse Comics

DANGANRONPA ANOTHER EPISODE: ULTRA DESPAIR GIRLS VOLUME 2

Published by
Dark Horse Manga
A division of Dark Horse Comics LLC.
10956 SE Main Street
Milwaukie, OR 97222

DarkHorse.com

To find a comics shop in your area, visit comicshoplocator.com

First edition: September 2020
ISBN 978-1-50671-363-2

1 3 5 7 9 10 8 6 4 2

Printed in the United States of America

DESPAIR MAIL

c/o Dark Horse Comics | 10956 SE Main St. | Milwaukie, OR 97222 | danganronpa@darkhorse.com

Don't despair! Even if that's the name of this column. Perhaps in the spirit of certain socially distancing global circumstances you may have heard about lately, it's been requested by our Japanese liaison that we move Despair Mail out of the Danganronpa books and put it online instead, where the whole world can see it, and we can all enjoy our island life together.

Because people have been previously sending in contributions with the expectation of appearing in the books, I will be getting in contact with contributors first and asking them if they're okay with their fan art, cosplay, etc. going up on Dark Horse's social media instead, and hopefully by the time you read this, it will have already happened.

And either way, thank you all so much once again for the support you have given the Danganronpa manga thus far! Things have been a little delayed by events, but don't worry—we plan to keep publishing both Goodbye Despair and Ultra Despair Girls…and maybe other Danganronpa titles as well in the future…

—CGH

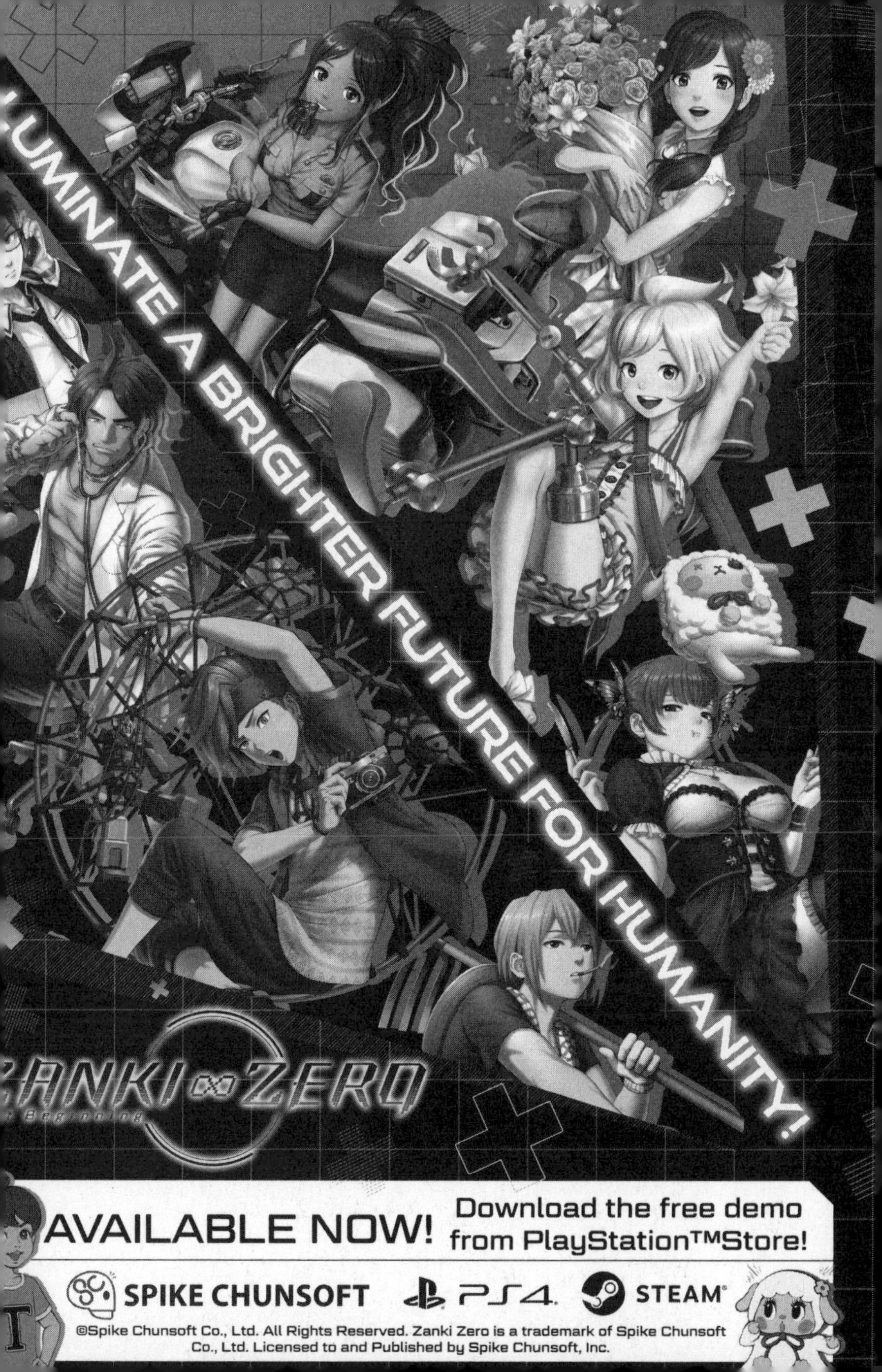

UMINATE A BRIGHTER FUTURE FOR HUMANITY!
ZANKI ZERO
AVAILABLE NOW!
Download the free demo from PlayStation™Store!
SPIKE CHUNSOFT
PS4
STEAM
©Spike Chunsoft Co., Ltd. All Rights Reserved. Zanki Zero is a trademark of Spike Chunsoft Co., Ltd. Licensed to and Published by Spike Chunsoft, Inc.